Hana-Kimi
For You in Full Blossom

8

story and art by
HISAYA NAKAJO

HANA-KIMI
For You in Full Blossom
VOLUME 8

STORY & ART BY HISAYA NAKAJO

Translation/David Ury
English Adaptation/Gerard Jones
Touch-Up Art & Lettering/Gabe Crate
Design/Izumi Evers
Editor/Jason Thompson

Managing Editor/Annette Roman
Director of Production/Noboru Watanabe
Vice President of Publishing/Alvin Lu
Sr. Director of Acquisitions/Rika Inouye
Vice President of Sales & Marketing/Liza Coppola
Publisher/Hyoe Narita

Printed in Canada

Published by VIZ Media, LLC, P.O. Box 77010, San Francisco, CA 94107

Shôjo Edition
10 9 8 7 6 5 4 3 2 1

First printing, September 2005

www.viz.com
store.viz.com

CONTENTS

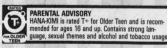

PARENTAL ADVISORY
HANA-KIMI is rated T+ for Older Teen and is recom-
mended for ages 16 and up. Contains strong lan-
guage, sexual themes and alcohol and tobacco usage.

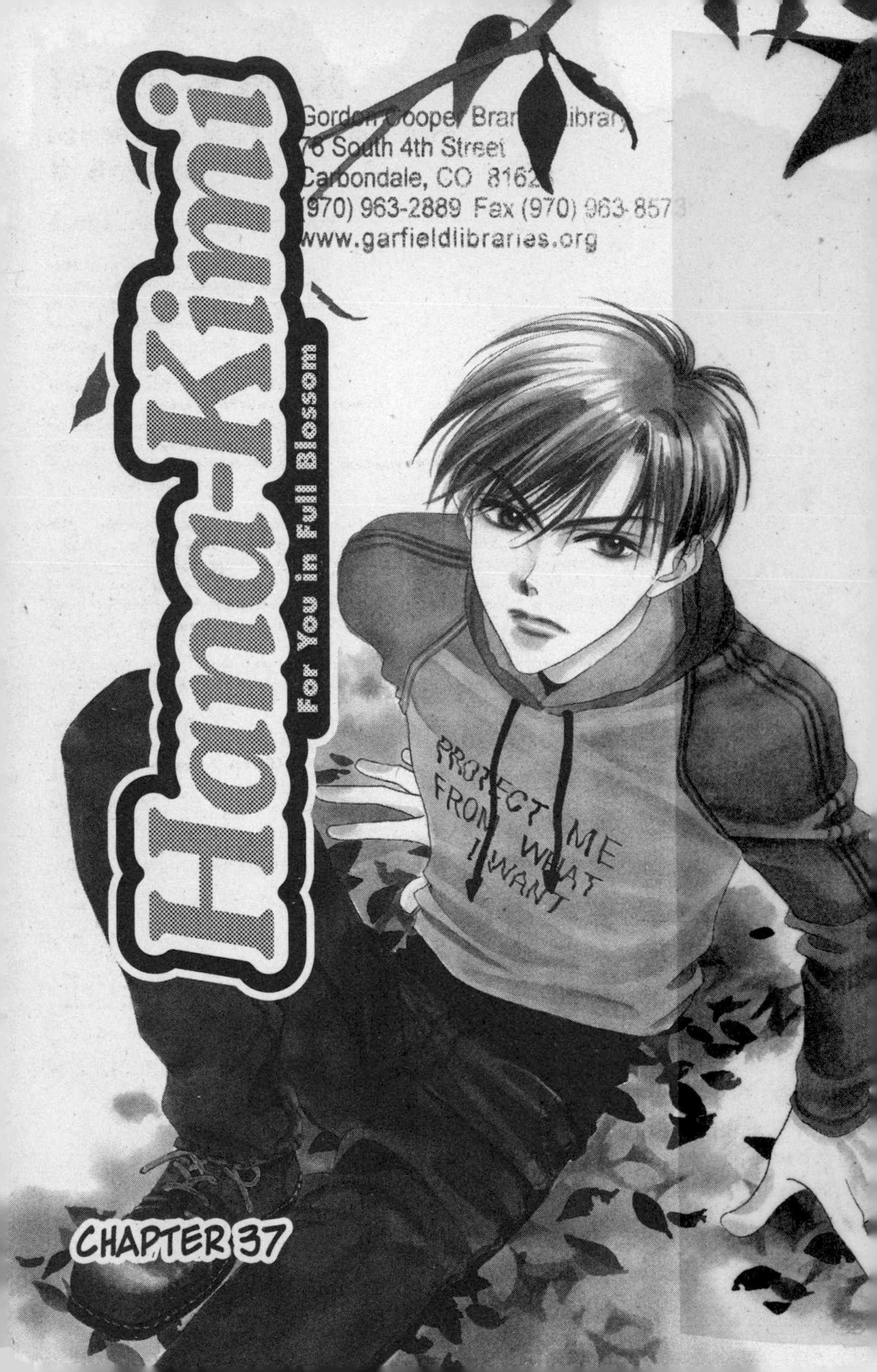
Hana-Kimi
For You in Full Blossom
PROTECT ME FROM WHAT I WANT
CHAPTER 37

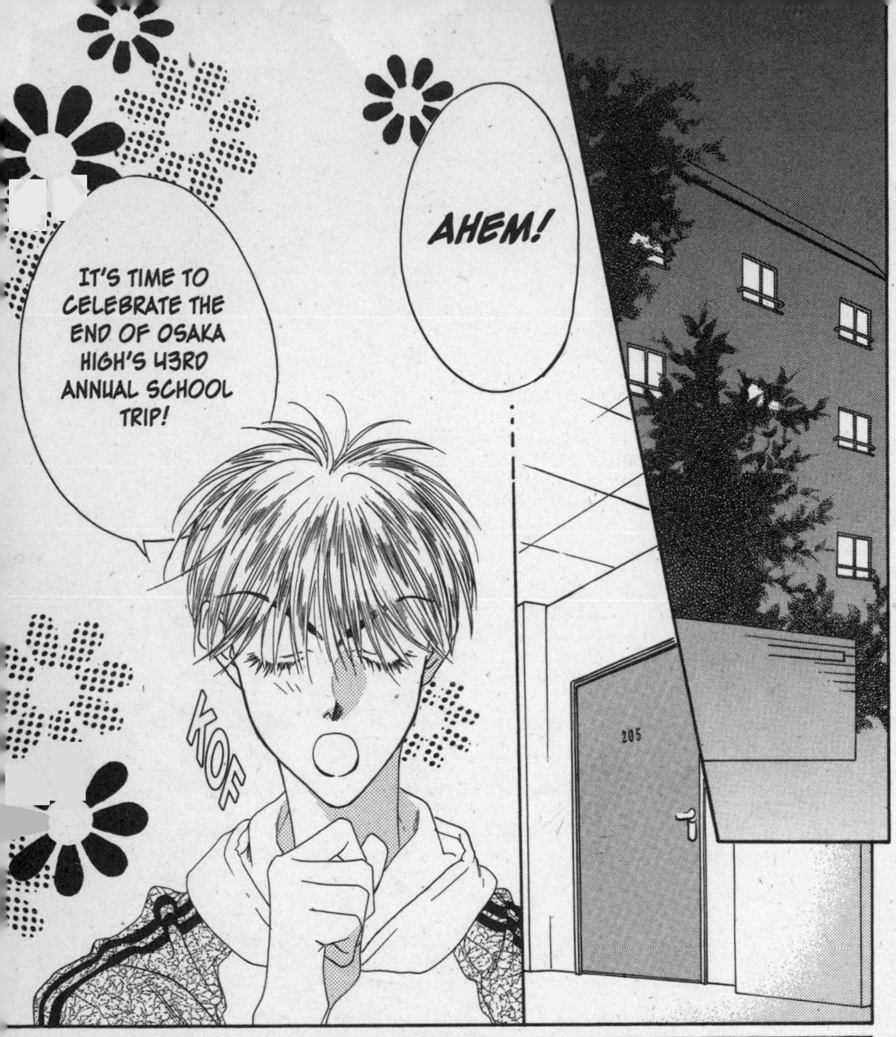
AHEM!
IT'S TIME TO CELEBRATE THE END OF OSAKA HIGH'S 43RD ANNUAL SCHOOL TRIP!
KOF

CHANGE OF IMAGE

IN THE FIRST HALF OF THIS YEAR, I CHANGED MY HAIR A LOT. FIRST IT WAS BLONDE, THEN I DYED IT BRIGHT RED, THEN I CHANGED TO ORANGE. MY HAIR WAS DOWN TO MY BACK, THEN I CUT IT TO SHOULDER LENGTH, THEN I HAD MY MOM GIVE ME A TRIM, BUT SHE CUT TOO MUCH AND I ENDED UP WITH A SHORT BOB. AGGGGH! I LOOKED LIKE A LITTLE KID!. I HADN'T CUT MY HAIR SHORT SINCE I WAS IN MY FIRST YEAR OF JUNIOR HIGH.

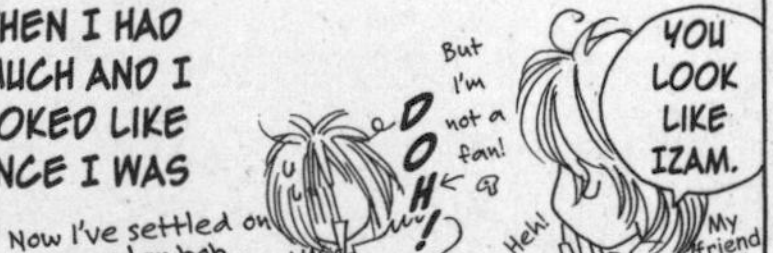
YOU LOOK LIKE IZAM.
Heh!
My friend "S"
But I'm not a fan!
DOH!
Now I've settled on a regular bob... and regular color.

(NOTE: "IZAM" IS A POP SINGER.)

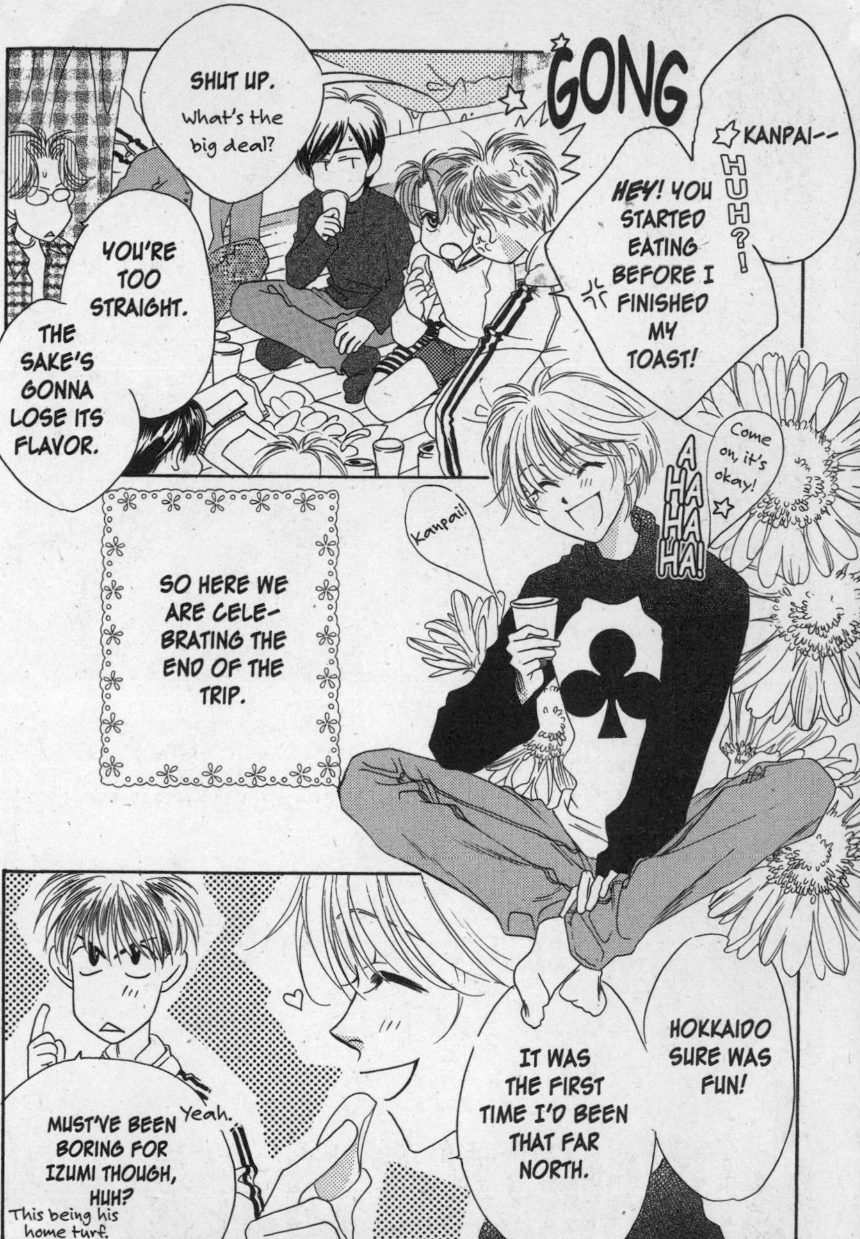
KANPAI--
GONG
HEY! YOU STARTED EATING BEFORE I FINISHED MY TOAST!
HUH?!
SHUT UP. What's the big deal?
YOU'RE TOO STRAIGHT.
THE SAKE'S GONNA LOSE ITS FLAVOR.
Come on, it's okay!
AHAHAHAHA!
Kanpai!
SO HERE WE ARE CELE-BRATING THE END OF THE TRIP.
HOKKAIDO SURE WAS FUN!
IT WAS THE FIRST TIME I'D BEEN THAT FAR NORTH.
Yeah.
MUST'VE BEEN BORING FOR IZUMI THOUGH, HUH?
This being his home turf.

"KANPAI" IS THE STANDARD JAPANESE TOAST, LIKE "CHEERS" IN ENGLISH.

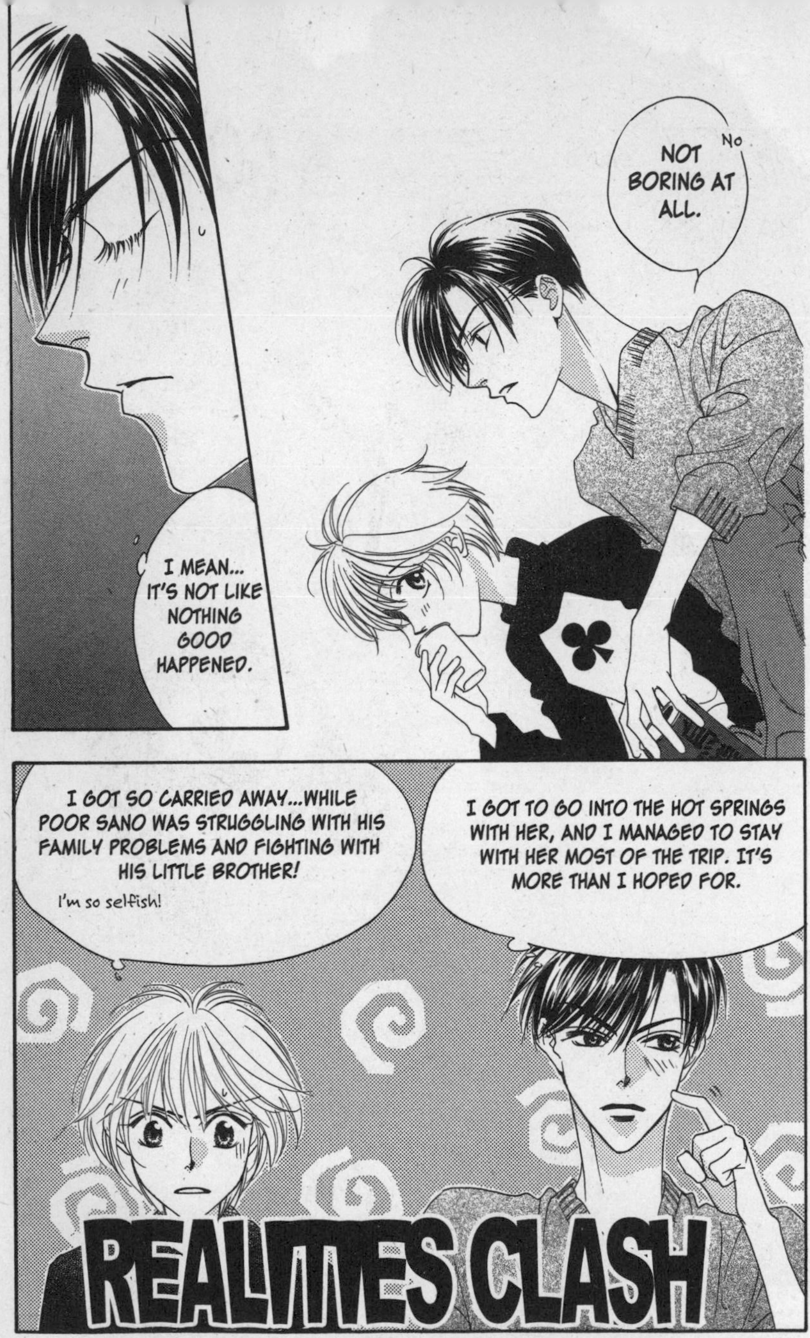
No
NOT BORING AT ALL.
I MEAN... IT'S NOT LIKE NOTHING GOOD HAPPENED.
I GOT TO GO INTO THE HOT SPRINGS WITH HER, AND I MANAGED TO STAY WITH HER MOST OF THE TRIP. IT'S MORE THAN I HOPED FOR.
I GOT SO CARRIED AWAY...WHILE POOR SANO WAS STRUGGLING WITH HIS FAMILY PROBLEMS AND FIGHTING WITH HIS LITTLE BROTHER!
I'm so selfish!
REALITIES CLASH

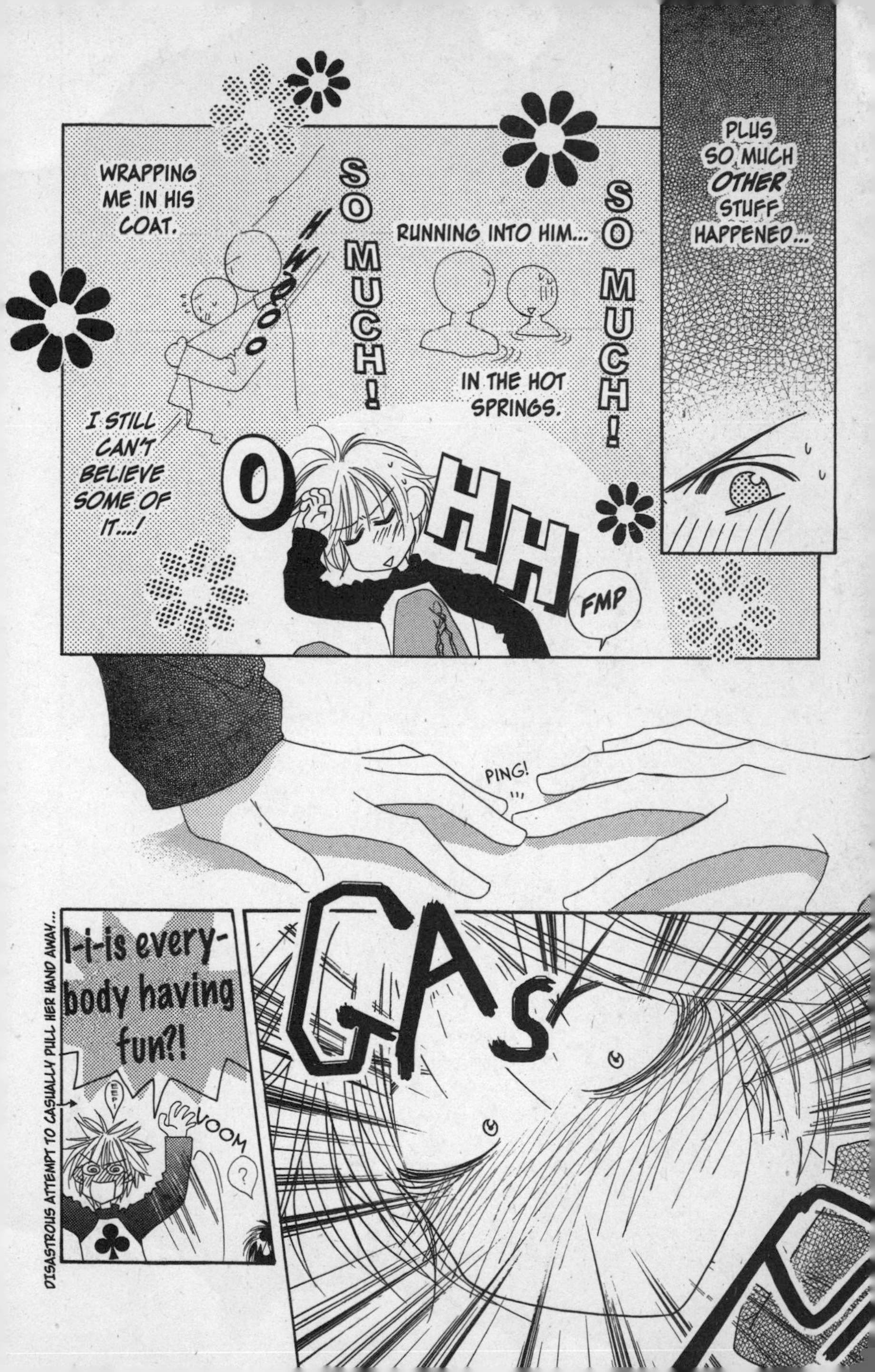
PLUS SO MUCH OTHER STUFF HAPPENED...
SO MUCH!
RUNNING INTO HIM...
IN THE HOT SPRINGS.
SO MUCH!
WRAPPING ME IN HIS COAT.
HWOOOO
I STILL CAN'T BELIEVE SOME OF IT...!
OHHH
FMP
PING!
GAS
I-i-is every-body having fun?!
VOOM
?
DISASTROUS ATTEMPT TO CASUALLY PULL HER HAND AWAY...

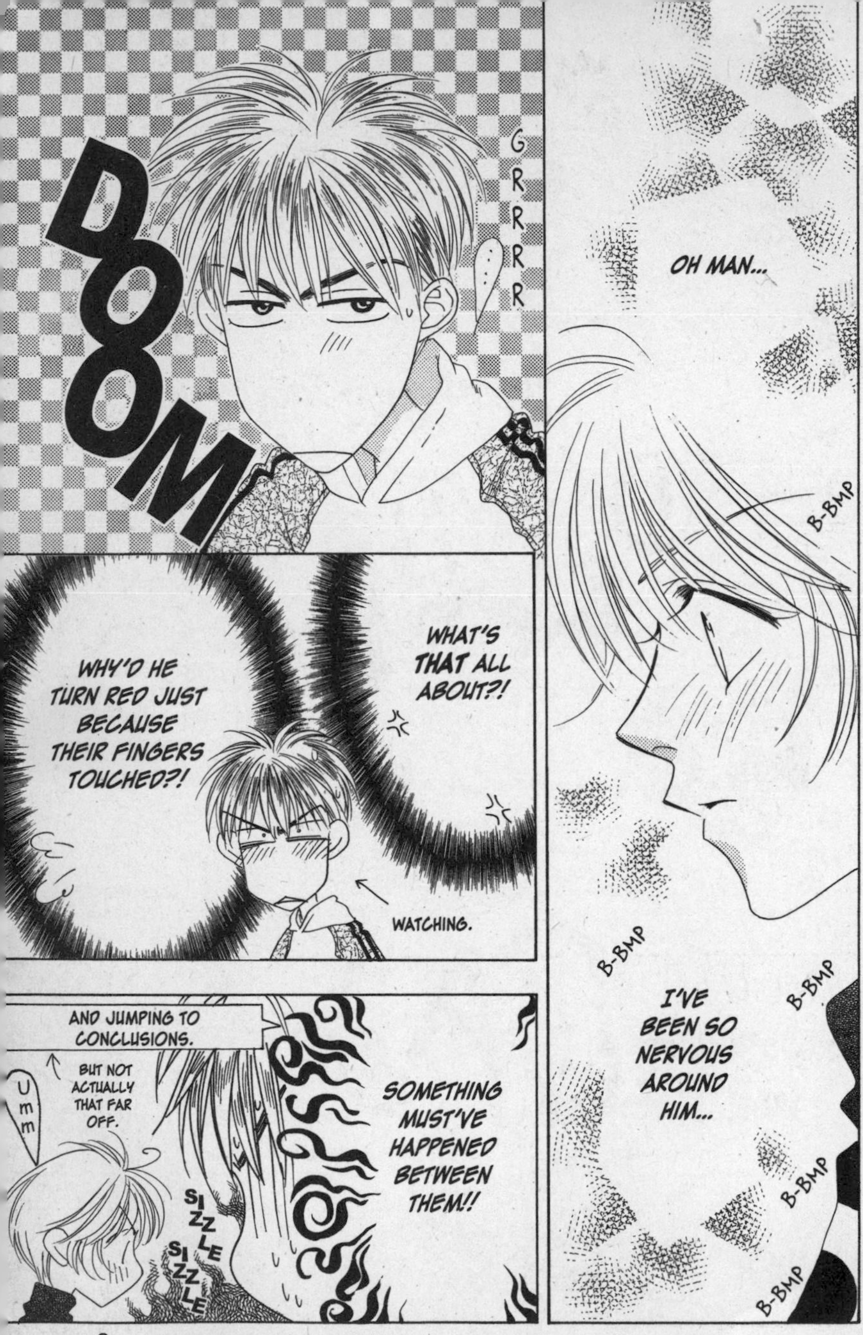
OH MAN...
B-BMP
B-BMP
I'VE BEEN SO NERVOUS AROUND HIM...
B-BMP
B-BMP
B-BMP
GRRRR
DOOM
WHAT'S THAT ALL ABOUT?!
WHY'D HE TURN RED JUST BECAUSE THEIR FINGERS TOUCHED?!
WATCHING.
SOMETHING MUST'VE HAPPENED BETWEEN THEM!!
SIZZLE
SIZZLE
AND JUMPING TO CONCLUSIONS.
BUT NOT ACTUALLY THAT FAR OFF.
Umm

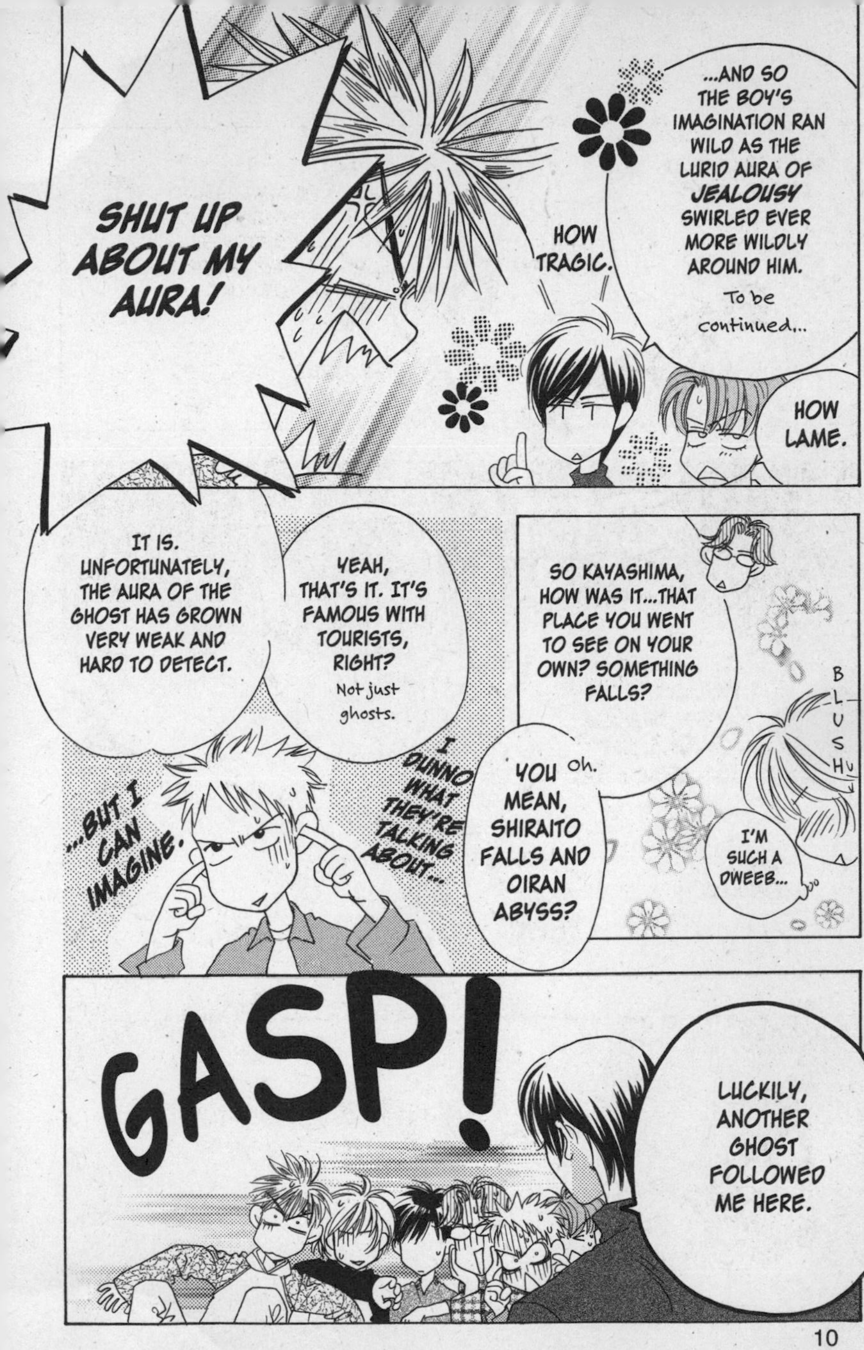
...AND SO THE BOY'S IMAGINATION RAN WILD AS THE LURID AURA OF JEALOUSY SWIRLED EVER MORE WILDLY AROUND HIM.
To be continued...
HOW TRAGIC.
HOW LAME.
SHUT UP ABOUT MY AURA!
SO KAYASHIMA, HOW WAS IT...THAT PLACE YOU WENT TO SEE ON YOUR OWN? SOMETHING FALLS?
BLUSH
I'M SUCH A DWEEB...
Oh.
YOU MEAN, SHIRAITO FALLS AND OIRAN ABYSS?
YEAH, THAT'S IT. IT'S FAMOUS WITH TOURISTS, RIGHT?
Not just ghosts.
IT IS. UNFORTUNATELY, THE AURA OF THE GHOST HAS GROWN VERY WEAK AND HARD TO DETECT.
I DUNNO WHAT THEY'RE TALKING ABOUT...
...BUT I CAN IMAGINE.
LUCKILY, ANOTHER GHOST FOLLOWED ME HERE.
GASP!

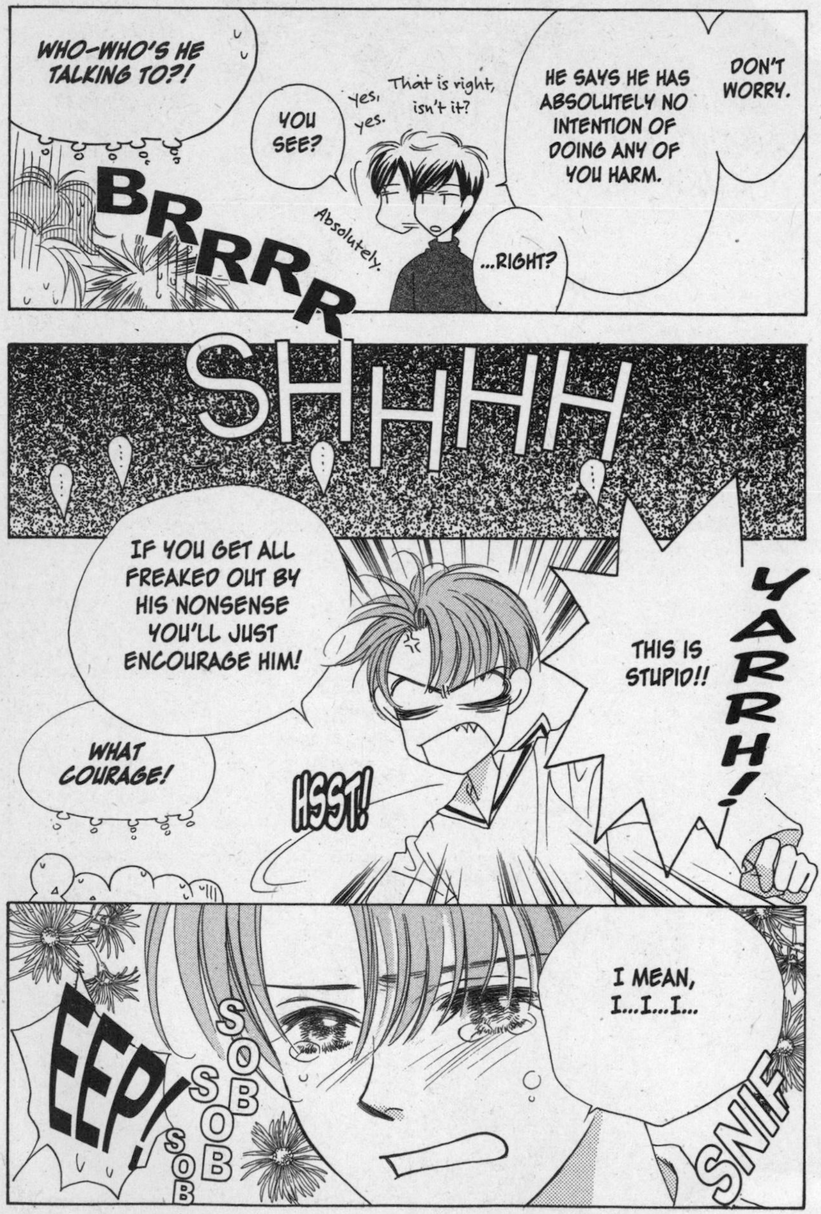
DON'T WORRY.
HE SAYS HE HAS ABSOLUTELY NO INTENTION OF DOING ANY OF YOU HARM.
...RIGHT?
That is right, isn't it?
Yes, yes.
Absolutely.
YOU SEE?
BRRRRR
WHO-WHO'S HE TALKING TO?!
SHHHH
YARRH!
THIS IS STUPID!!
IF YOU GET ALL FREAKED OUT BY HIS NONSENSE YOU'LL JUST ENCOURAGE HIM!
HSST!
WHAT COURAGE!
SNIF
I MEAN, I...I...I...
SOB
SOB
SOB
SOB
EEP!

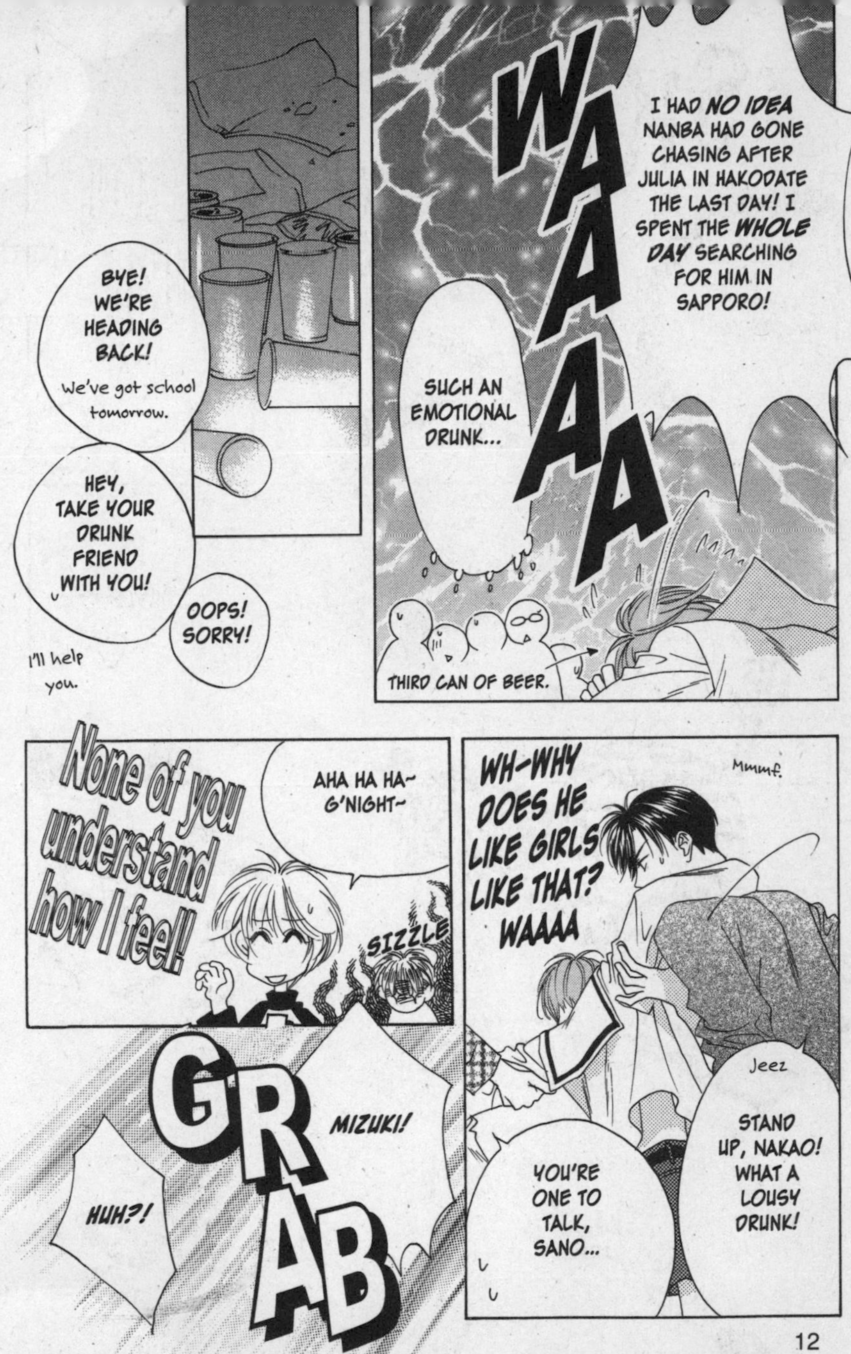
I HAD NO IDEA NANBA HAD GONE CHASING AFTER JULIA IN HAKODATE THE LAST DAY! I SPENT THE WHOLE DAY SEARCHING FOR HIM IN SAPPORO!
WAAAA
SUCH AN EMOTIONAL DRUNK...
THIRD CAN OF BEER.
BYE! WE'RE HEADING BACK!
We've got school tomorrow.
HEY, TAKE YOUR DRUNK FRIEND WITH YOU!
OOPS! SORRY!
I'll help you.
Mmmf.
WH-WHY DOES HE LIKE GIRLS LIKE THAT? WAAAA
Jeez
STAND UP, NAKAO! WHAT A LOUSY DRUNK!
YOU'RE ONE TO TALK, SANO...
AHA HA HA~ G'NIGHT~
None of you understand how I feel!
SIZZLE
MIZUKI!
GRAB
HUH?!

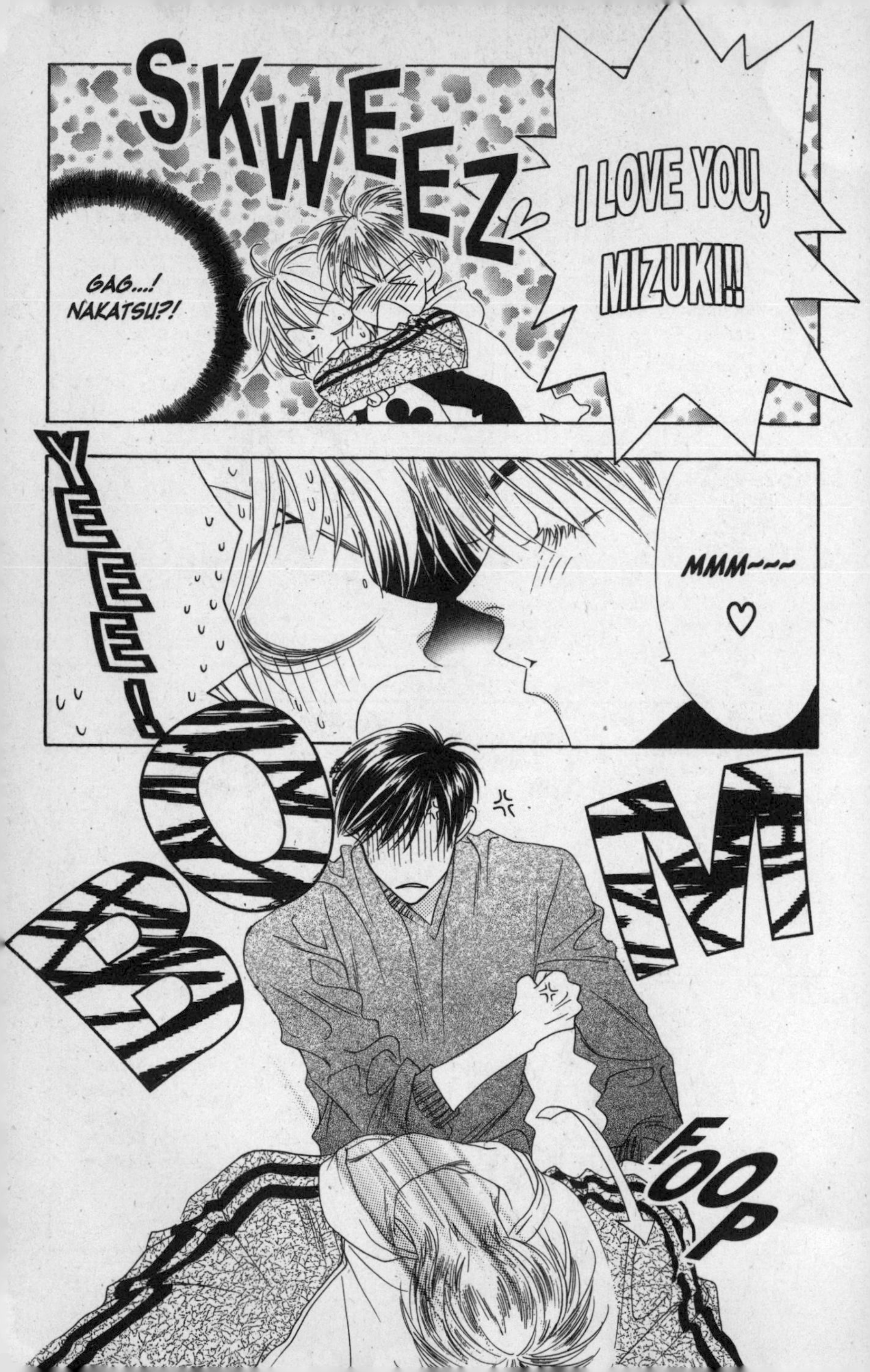
I LOVE YOU, MIZUKI!!
SKWEEZ
GAG...! NAKATSU?!
MMM~~~ ♡
YEEEE!
BOOM
FOOP

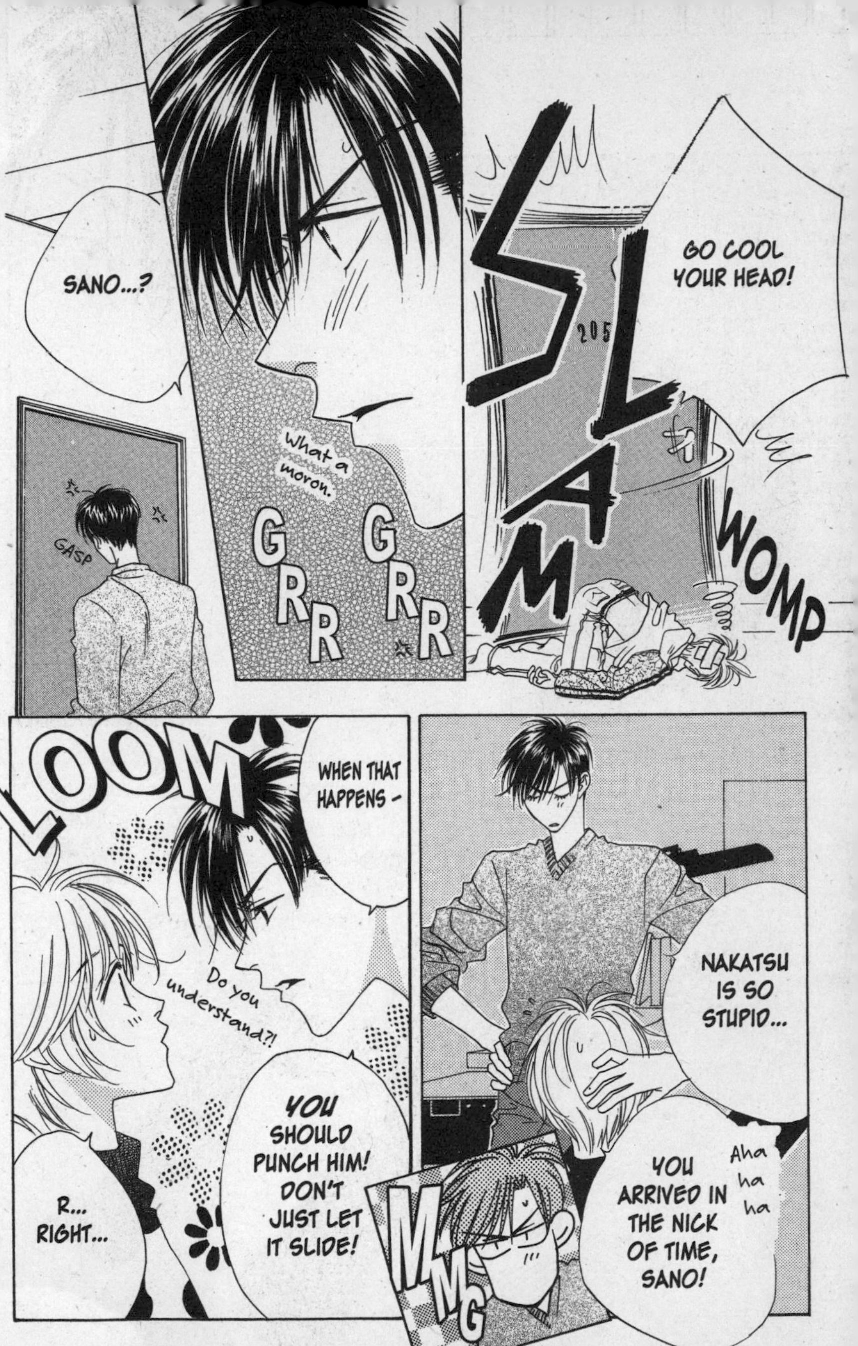
GO COOL YOUR HEAD!
SLAM
205
WOMP
What a moron.
GRR
GRR
SANO...?
GASP
NAKATSU IS SO STUPID...
YOU ARRIVED IN THE NICK OF TIME, SANO!
Aha ha ha
MMG
LOOM
WHEN THAT HAPPENS -
Do you understand?!
YOU SHOULD PUNCH HIM! DON'T JUST LET IT SLIDE!
R... RIGHT...

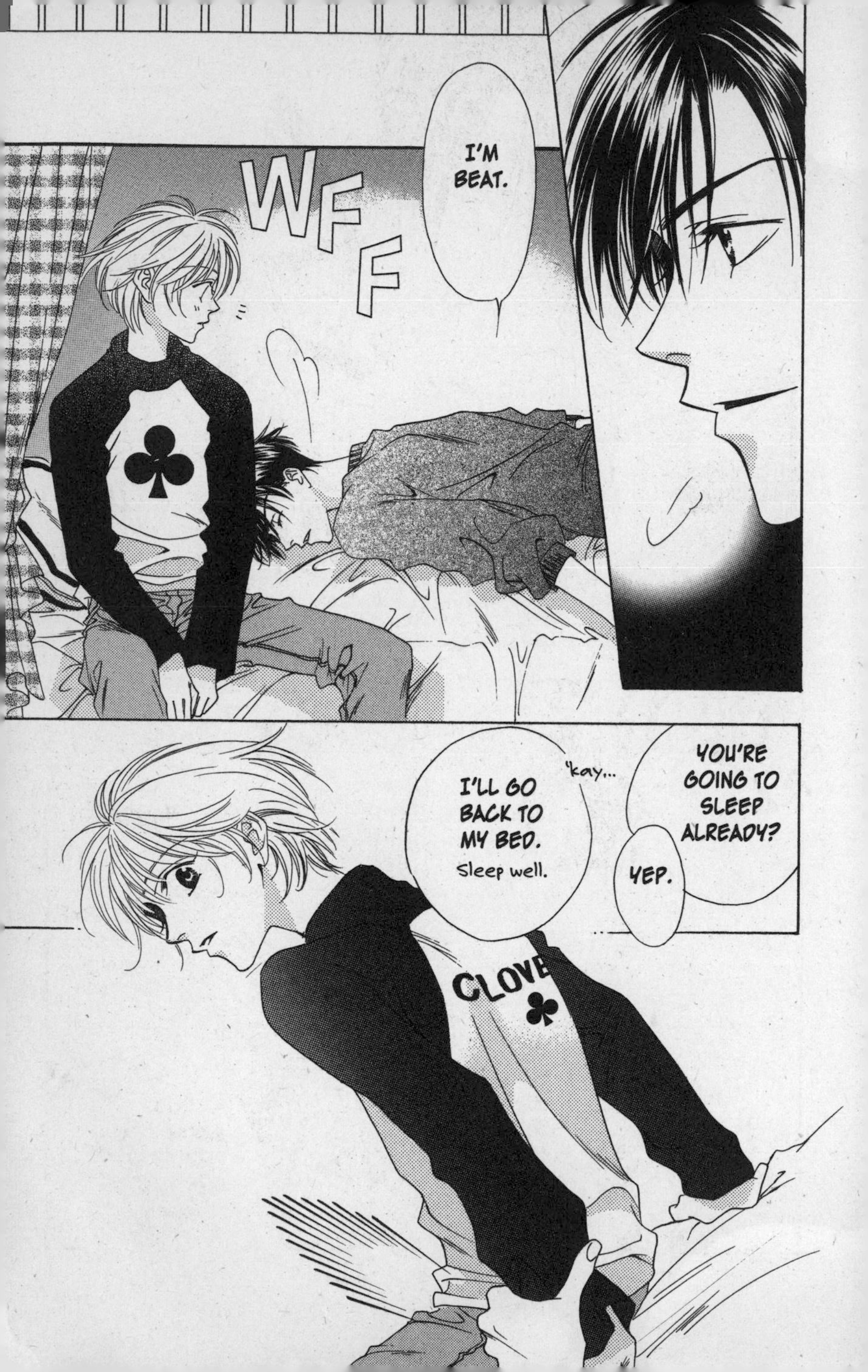
I'M BEAT.
WFF
YOU'RE GOING TO SLEEP ALREADY?
YEP.
'kay...
I'LL GO BACK TO MY BED.
Sleep well.
CLOVE

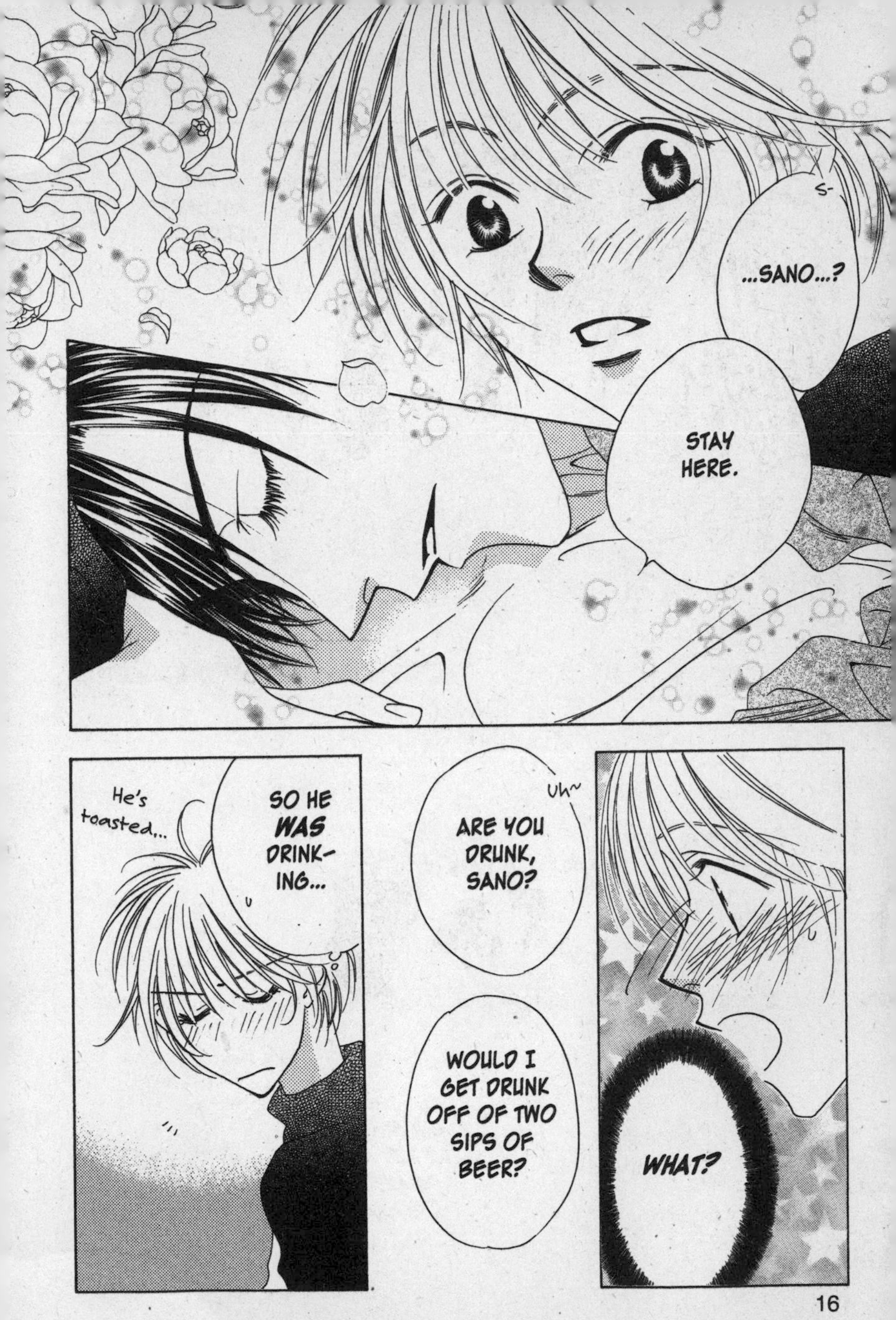
S-
...SANO...?
STAY HERE.
Uh~
ARE YOU DRUNK, SANO?
WOULD I GET DRUNK OFF OF TWO SIPS OF BEER?
WHAT?
SO HE WAS DRINKING...
He's toasted...

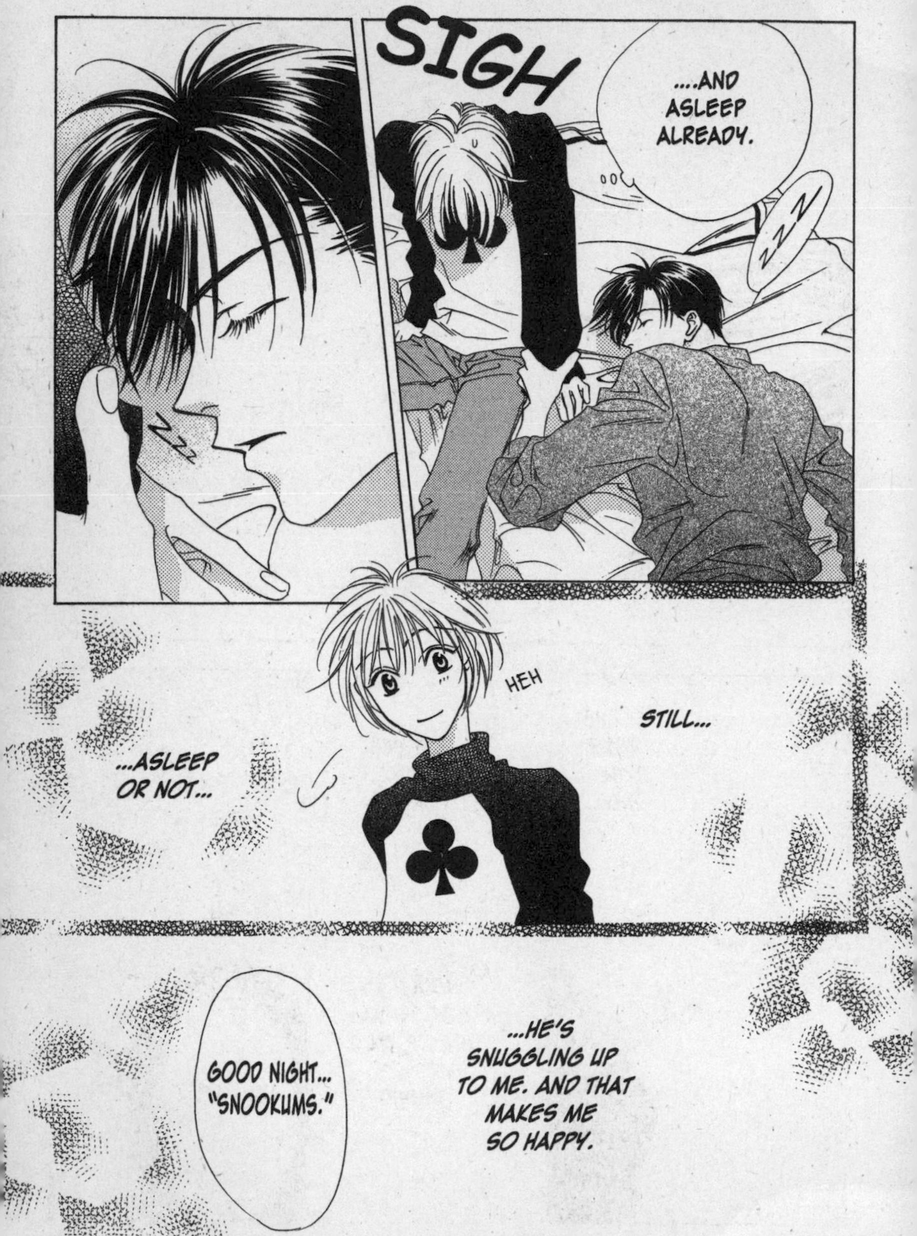
SIGH
....AND ASLEEP ALREADY.
STILL...
HEH
...ASLEEP OR NOT...
...HE'S SNUGGLING UP TO ME. AND THAT MAKES ME SO HAPPY.
GOOD NIGHT... "SNOOKUMS."

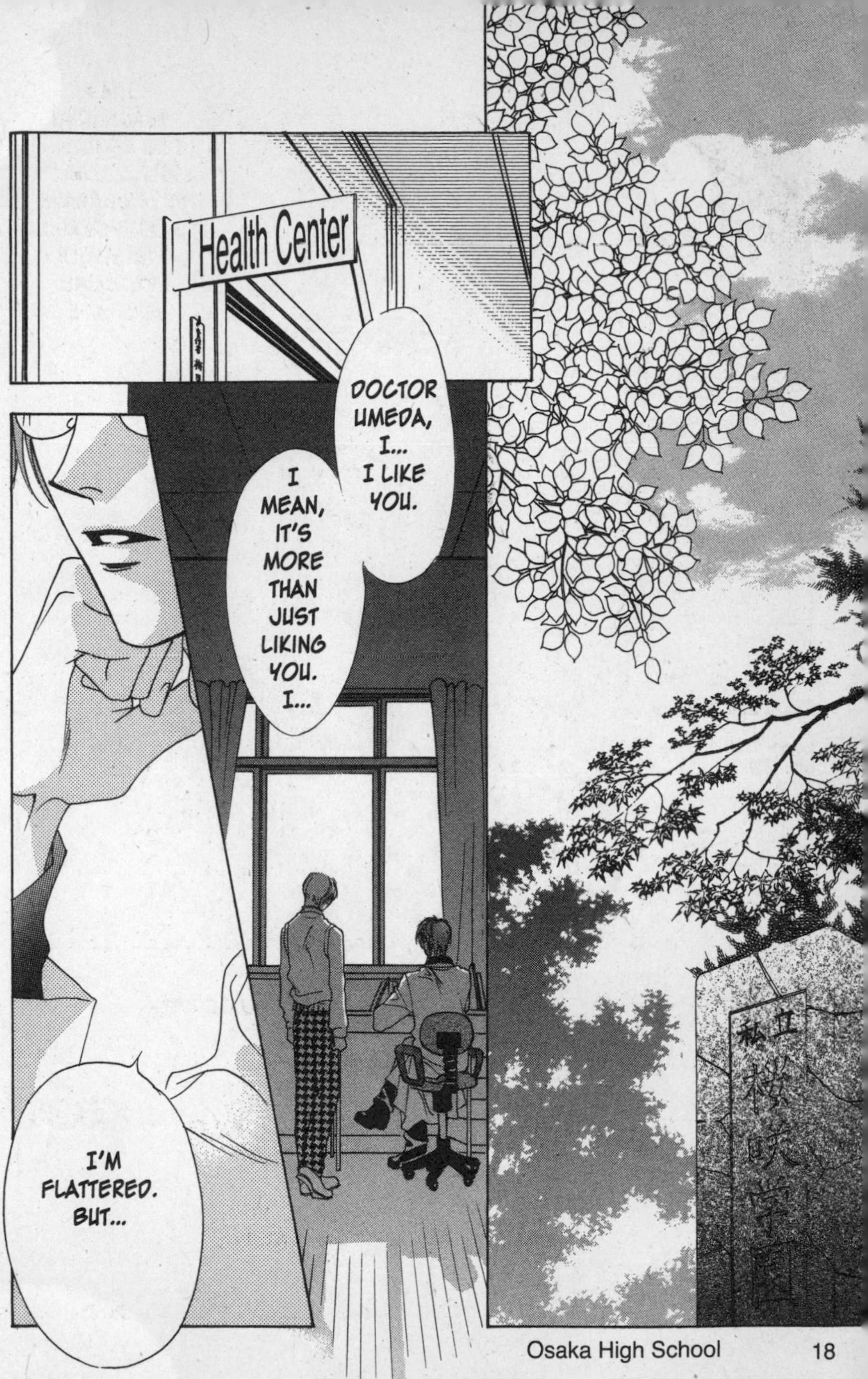
Health Center
DOCTOR UMEDA, I... I LIKE YOU.
I MEAN, IT'S MORE THAN JUST LIKING YOU. I...
I'M FLATTERED. BUT...

Osaka High School

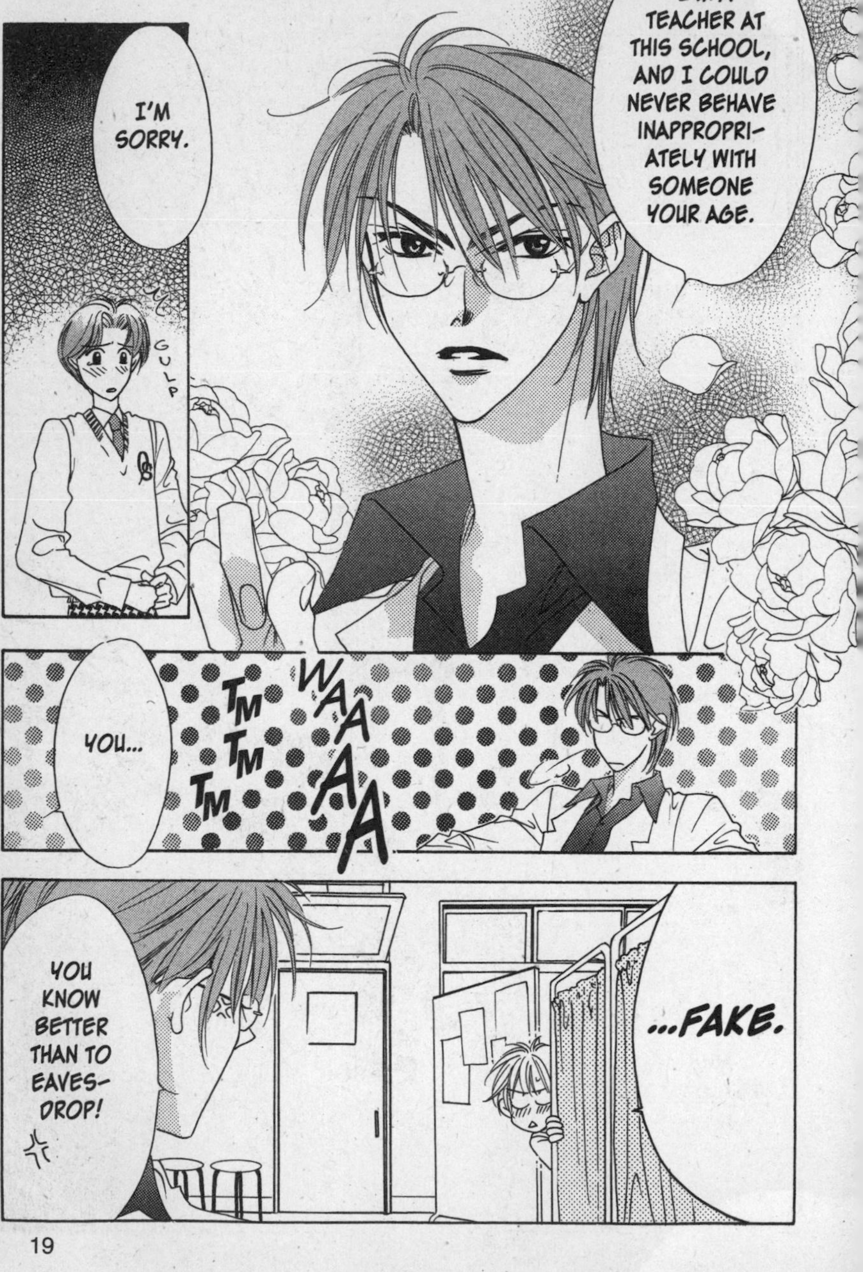
I'M A TEACHER AT THIS SCHOOL, AND I COULD NEVER BEHAVE INAPPROPRI-ATELY WITH SOMEONE YOUR AGE.
I'M SORRY.
GULP
WAAAAA
TM TM TM
YOU...
...FAKE.
YOU KNOW BETTER THAN TO EAVES-DROP!

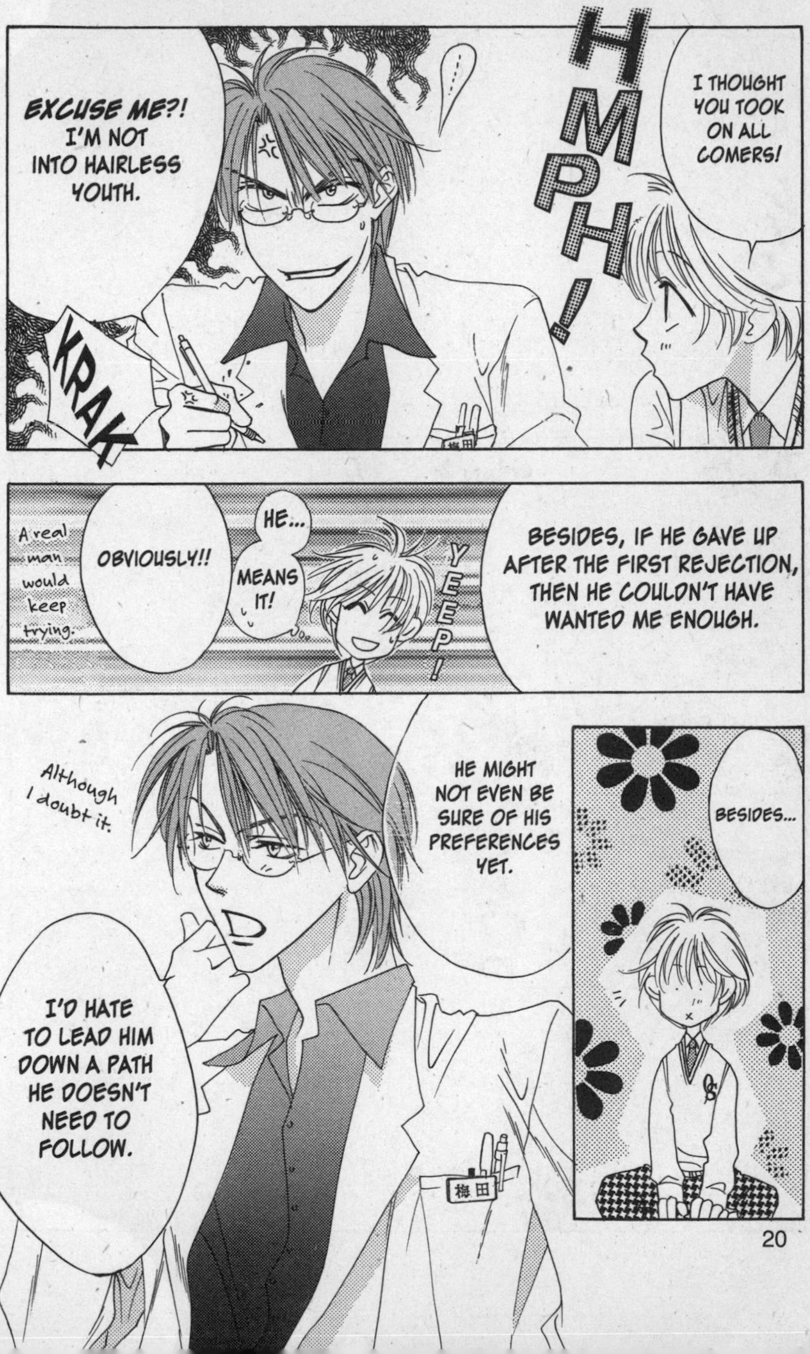
I THOUGHT YOU TOOK ON ALL COMERS!
HMPH!
EXCUSE ME?! I'M NOT INTO HAIRLESS YOUTH.
KRAK
梅田
BESIDES, IF HE GAVE UP AFTER THE FIRST REJECTION, THEN HE COULDN'T HAVE WANTED ME ENOUGH.
YEEP!
HE... MEANS IT!
OBVIOUSLY!!
A real man would keep trying.
BESIDES...
HE MIGHT NOT EVEN BE SURE OF HIS PREFERENCES YET.
Although I doubt it.
I'D HATE TO LEAD HIM DOWN A PATH HE DOESN'T NEED TO FOLLOW.
梅田

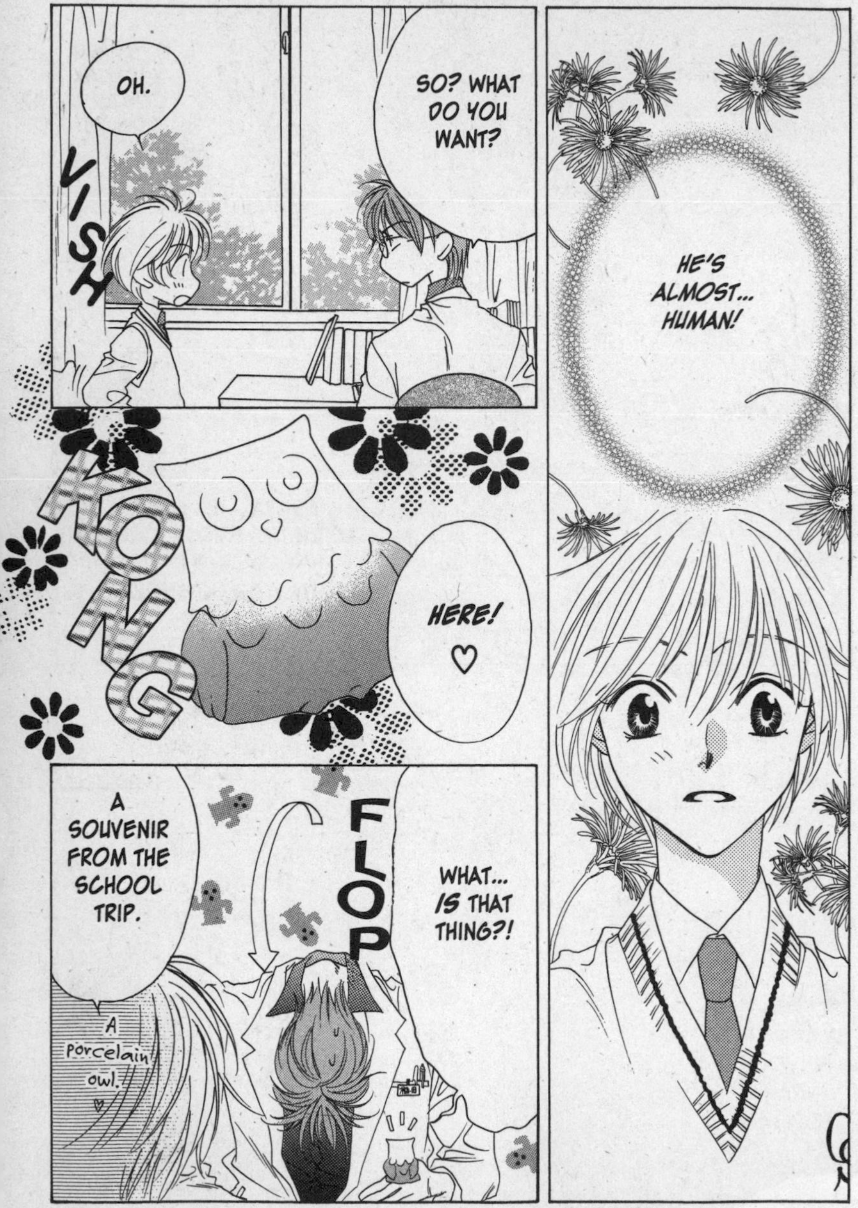
HE'S ALMOST... HUMAN!
SO? WHAT DO YOU WANT?
OH.
VISH
HERE! ♡
KONG
WHAT... IS THAT THING?!
FLOP
A SOUVENIR FROM THE SCHOOL TRIP.
A porcelain owl. ♡

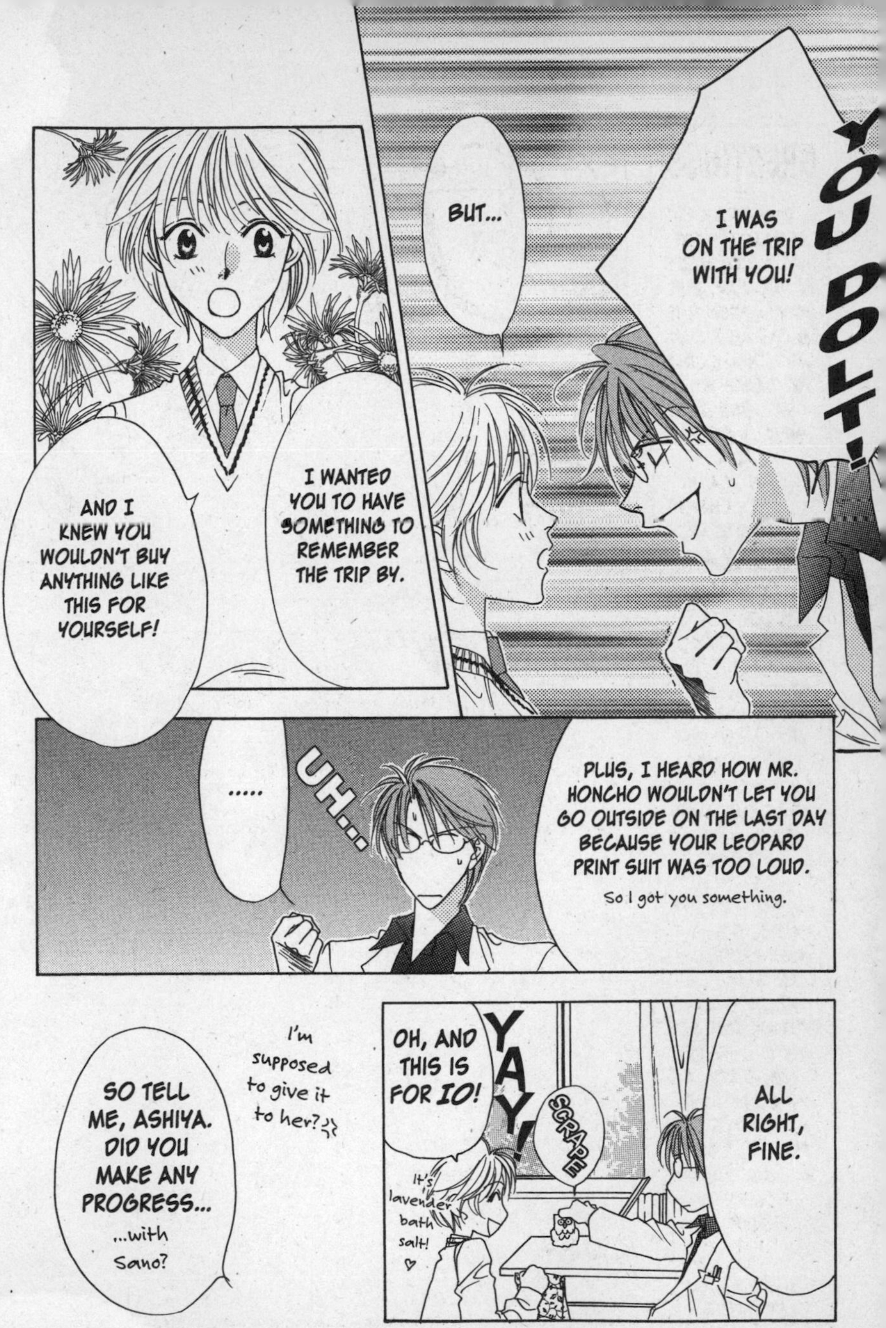
YOU DOLT!
I WAS ON THE TRIP WITH YOU!
BUT...
I WANTED YOU TO HAVE SOMETHING TO REMEMBER THE TRIP BY.
AND I KNEW YOU WOULDN'T BUY ANYTHING LIKE THIS FOR YOURSELF!
PLUS, I HEARD HOW MR. HONCHO WOULDN'T LET YOU GO OUTSIDE ON THE LAST DAY BECAUSE YOUR LEOPARD PRINT SUIT WAS TOO LOUD.
So I got you something.
UH...
.....
ALL RIGHT, FINE.
SCRAPE
YAY!
OH, AND THIS IS FOR IO!
It's lavender bath salt! ♥
I'm supposed to give it to her?
SO TELL ME, ASHIYA. DID YOU MAKE ANY PROGRESS...
...with Sano?

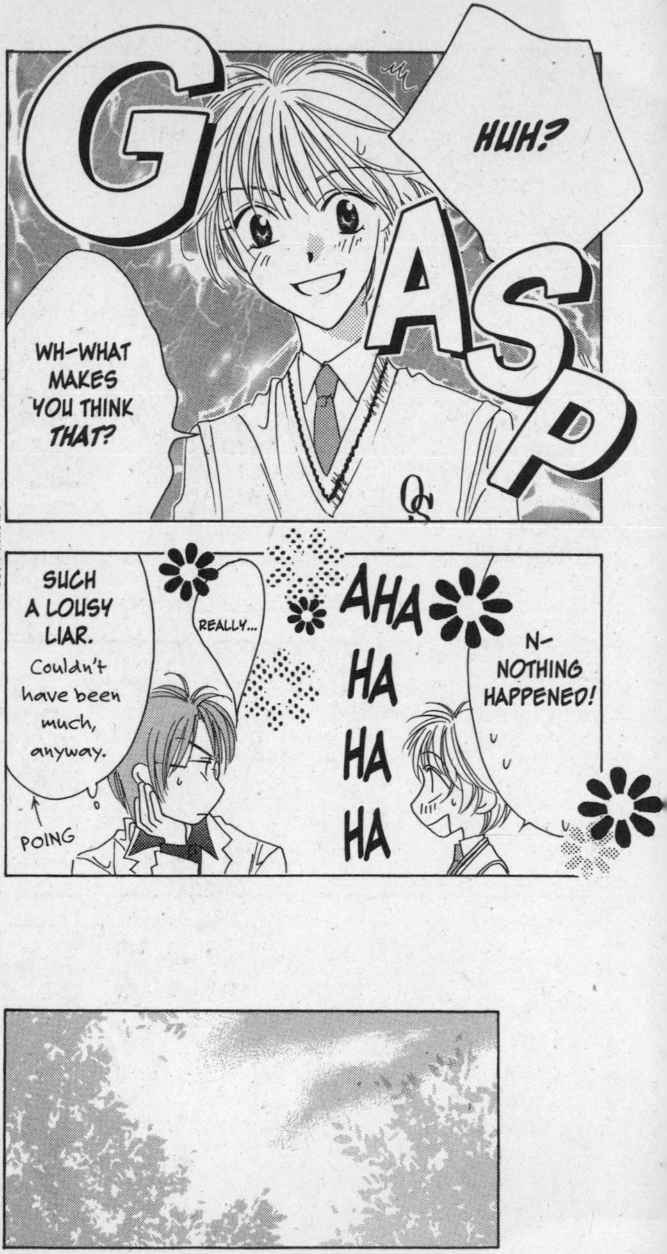
HUH?
GASP
WH-WHAT MAKES YOU THINK *THAT?*
N-NOTHING HAPPENED!
AHA HA HA HA
REALLY...
SUCH A LOUSY LIAR.
Couldn't have been much, anyway.
POING

GREETINGS!

IT'S BOOK 8 ALREADY! NOW THAT WE'VE MADE IT THIS FAR, I'M GONNA PUSH THIS AS FAR AS I CAN. ARE YOU WILLING TO COME WITH ME...BABY?! WAIT...I GOTTA CALM DOWN...CALM DOWN... (HA!) SINCE IT'S ALL ***MANLY MEN*** ← SEXY PHRASE ON THE COVER AND TITLE PAGE, I GUESS I'VE SWITCHED INTO MALE MODE. MIZUKI ON THE BACK COVER IS THE ONLY OASIS OF FEMININITY... HEE-HEE. THIS BACK COVER AND THE ONE IN BOOK 5 ARE ACTUALLY RELATED. IN BOOK 5 IT'S SPRING, AND THIS TIME IT'S WINTER. I GUESS I'LL DO SUMMER AND FALL NEXT. BY THE WAY, I DREW ALL THE BACKGROUNDS BY HAND.

↑ PEOPLE ALWAYS ASK ME ABOUT THAT.

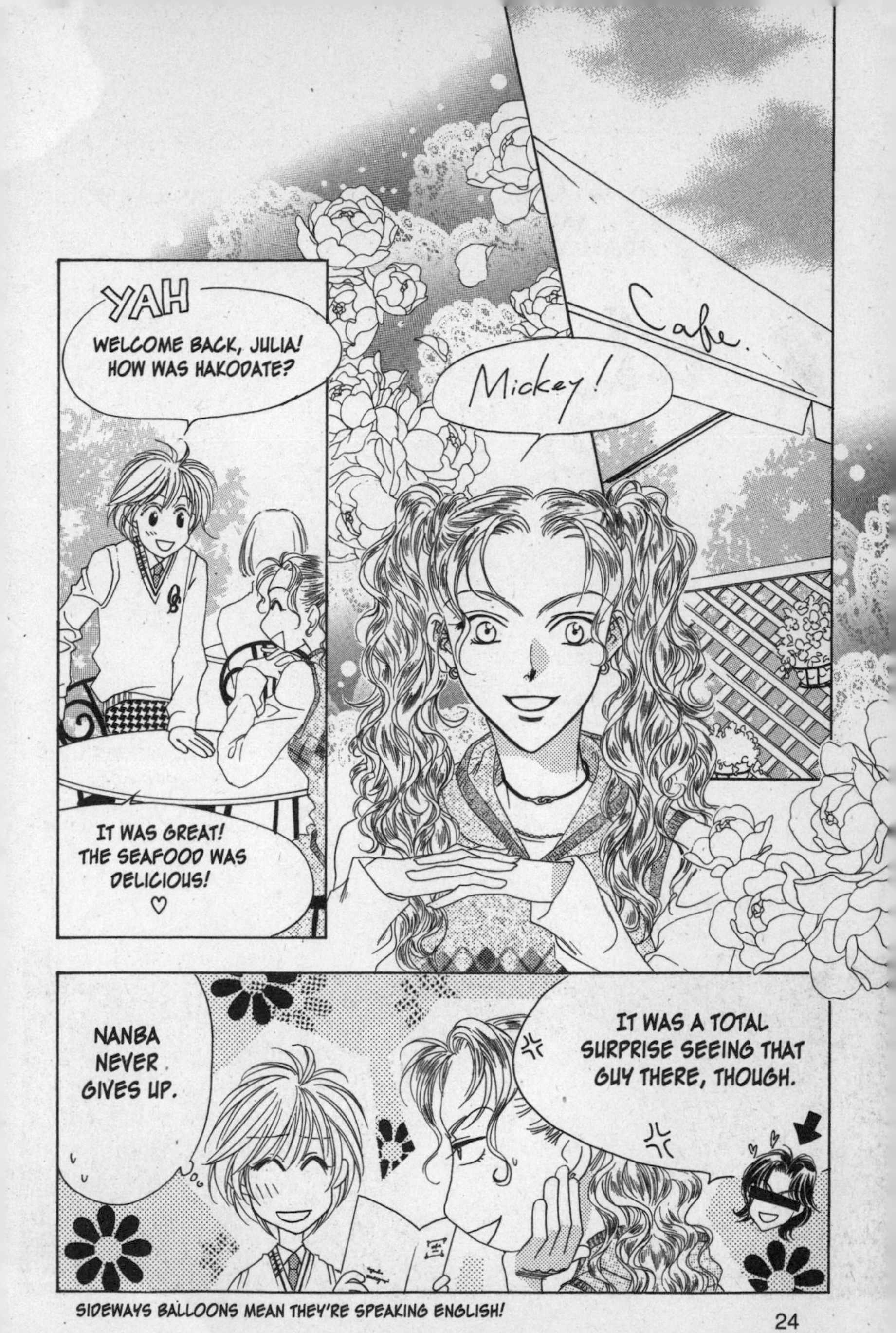
Cafe.
Mickey!
YAH
WELCOME BACK, JULIA! HOW WAS HAKODATE?
IT WAS GREAT! THE SEAFOOD WAS DELICIOUS! ♡
IT WAS A TOTAL SURPRISE SEEING THAT GUY THERE, THOUGH.
NANBA NEVER GIVES UP.

SIDEWAYS BALLOONS MEAN THEY'RE SPEAKING ENGLISH!

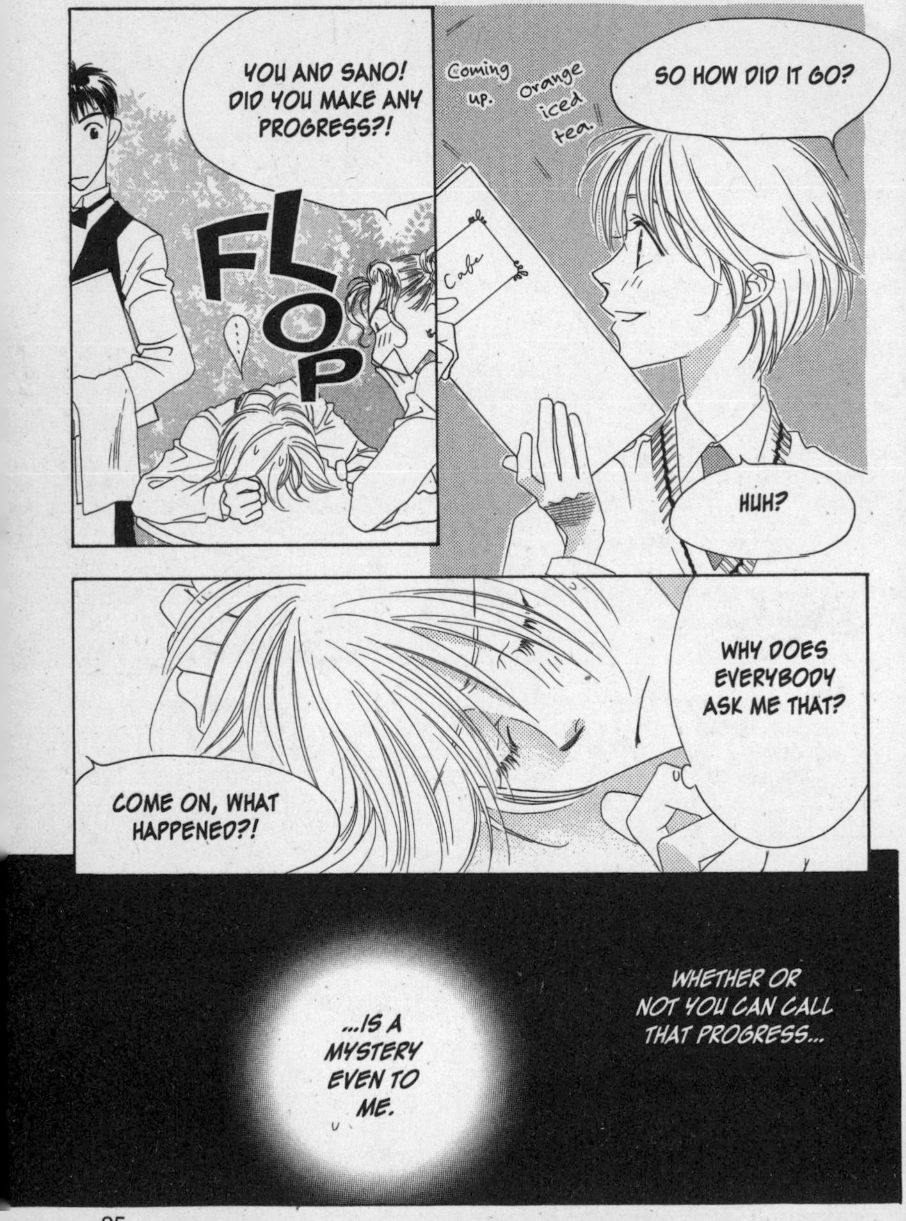
SO HOW DID IT GO?
Coming up. Orange iced tea.
HUH?
YOU AND SANO! DID YOU MAKE ANY PROGRESS?!
FLOP
...
WHY DOES EVERYBODY ASK ME THAT?
COME ON, WHAT HAPPENED?!
WHETHER OR NOT YOU CAN CALL THAT PROGRESS...
...IS A MYSTERY EVEN TO ME.

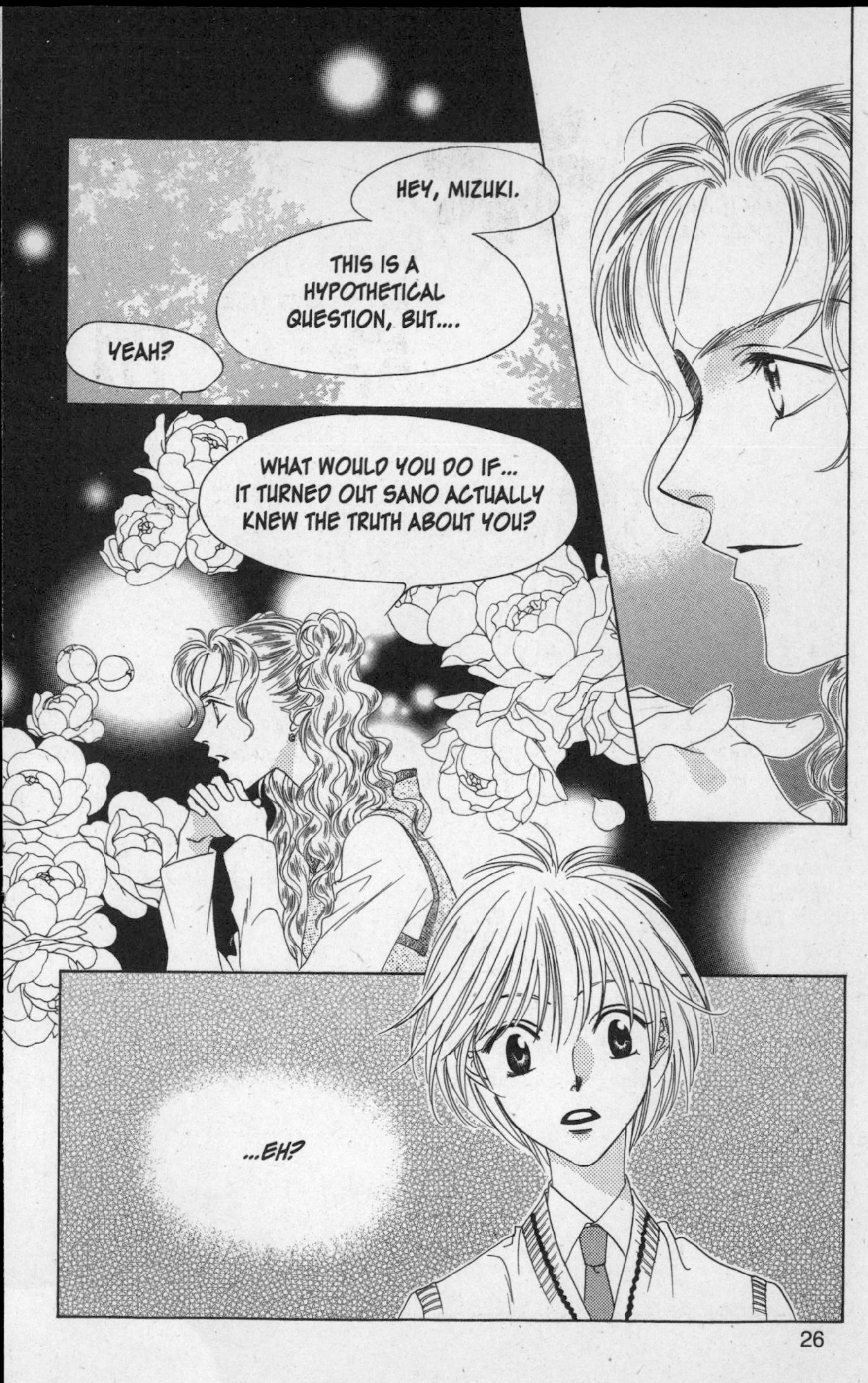
HEY, MIZUKI.
THIS IS A HYPOTHETICAL QUESTION, BUT....
YEAH?
WHAT WOULD YOU DO IF... IT TURNED OUT SANO ACTUALLY KNEW THE TRUTH ABOUT YOU?
...EH?

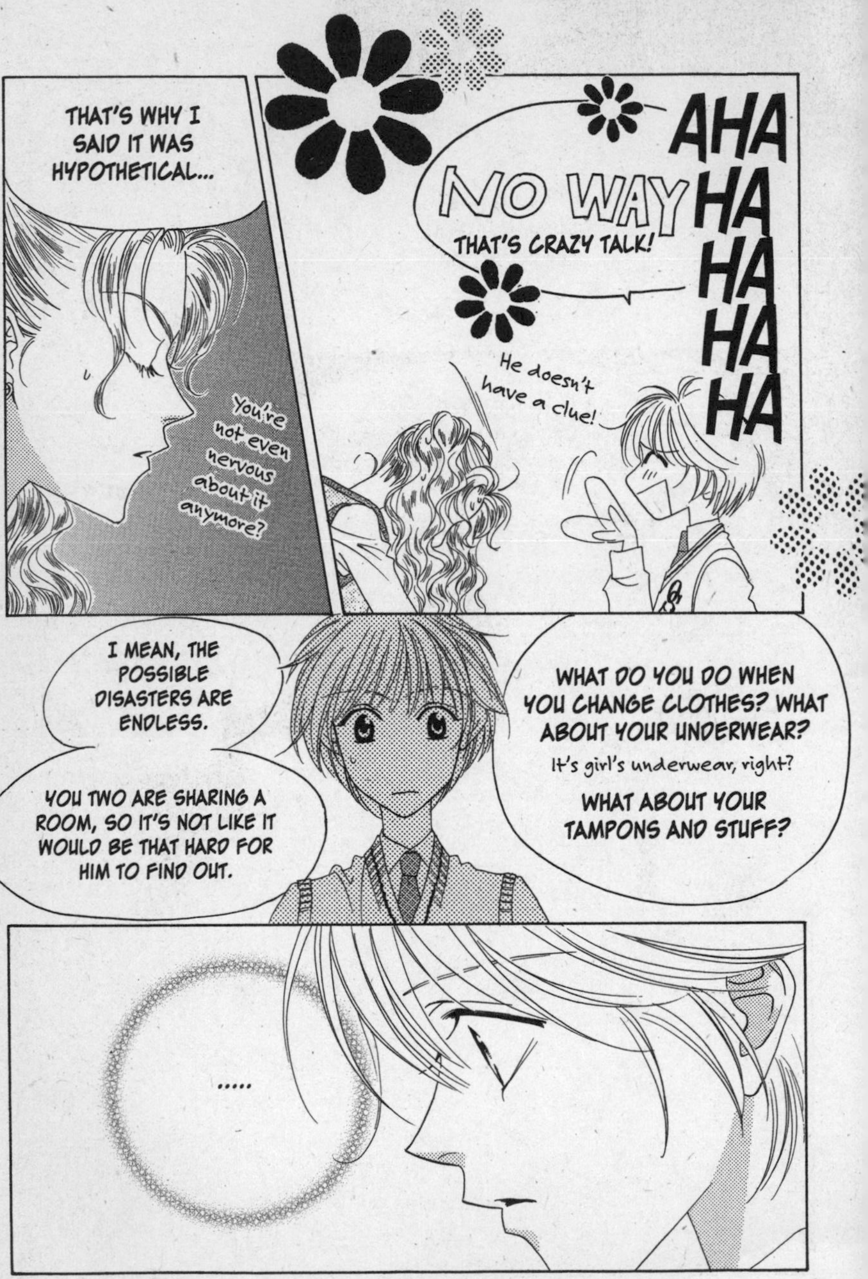
AHAHAHAHAHA
NO WAY
THAT'S CRAZY TALK!
He doesn't have a clue!
THAT'S WHY I SAID IT WAS HYPOTHETICAL...
You're not even nervous about it anymore?
WHAT DO YOU DO WHEN YOU CHANGE CLOTHES? WHAT ABOUT YOUR UNDERWEAR?
It's girl's underwear, right?
WHAT ABOUT YOUR TAMPONS AND STUFF?
I MEAN, THE POSSIBLE DISASTERS ARE ENDLESS.
YOU TWO ARE SHARING A ROOM, SO IT'S NOT LIKE IT WOULD BE THAT HARD FOR HIM TO FIND OUT.
.....

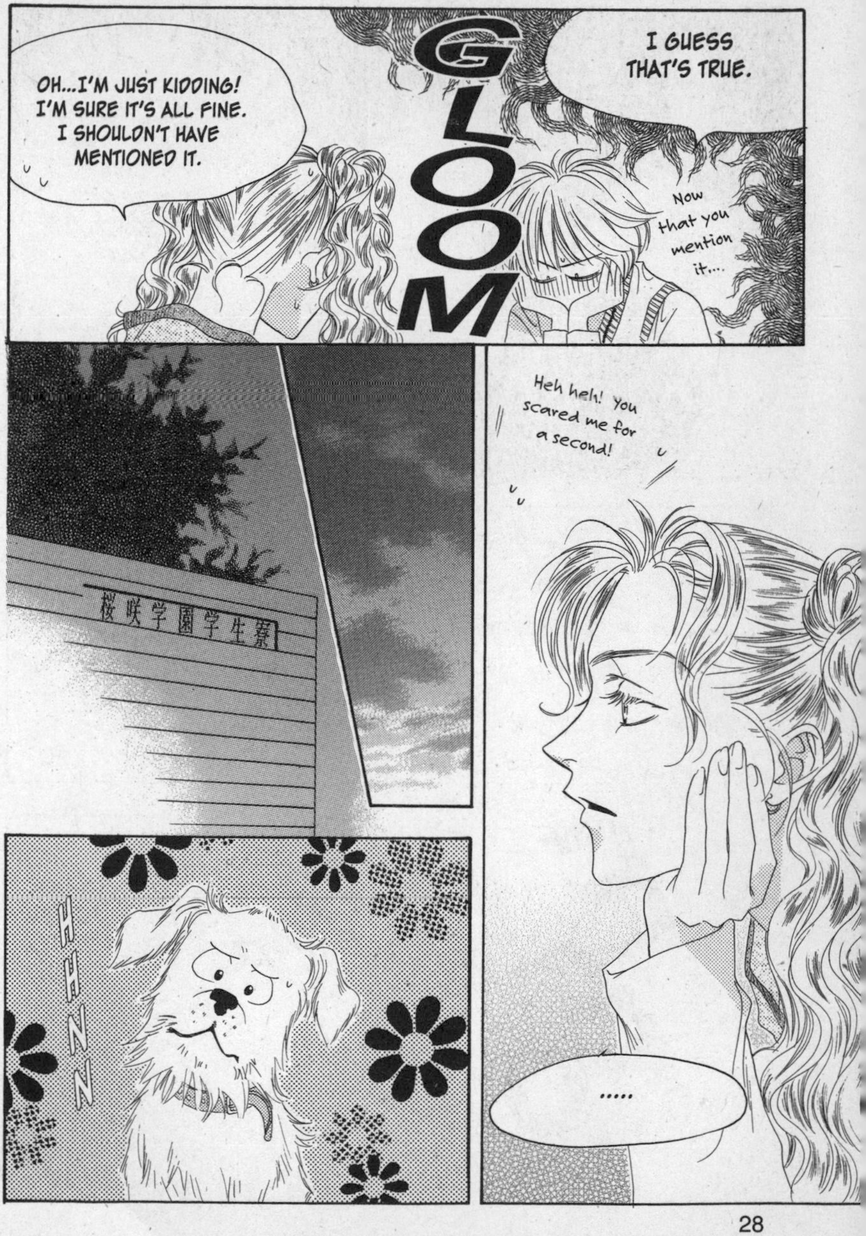
I GUESS THAT'S TRUE.
Now that you mention it....
GLOOM
OH...I'M JUST KIDDING! I'M SURE IT'S ALL FINE. I SHOULDN'T HAVE MENTIONED IT.
Heh heh! You scared me for a second!
.....
桜咲学園学生寮
HHNN

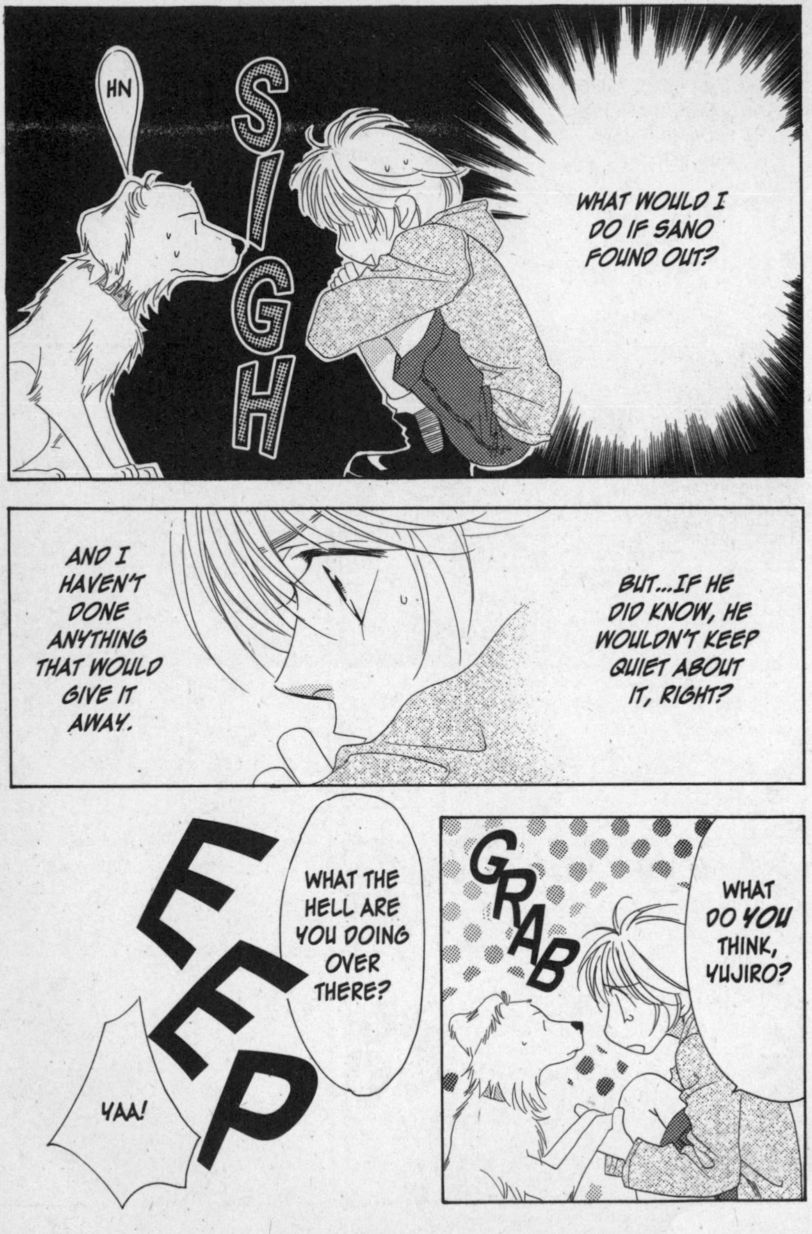
WHAT WOULD I DO IF SANO FOUND OUT?
SIGH
HN
BUT...IF HE DID KNOW, HE WOULDN'T KEEP QUIET ABOUT IT, RIGHT?
AND I HAVEN'T DONE ANYTHING THAT WOULD GIVE IT AWAY.
WHAT DO YOU THINK, YUJIRO?
GRAB
WHAT THE HELL ARE YOU DOING OVER THERE?
EEEP
YAA!

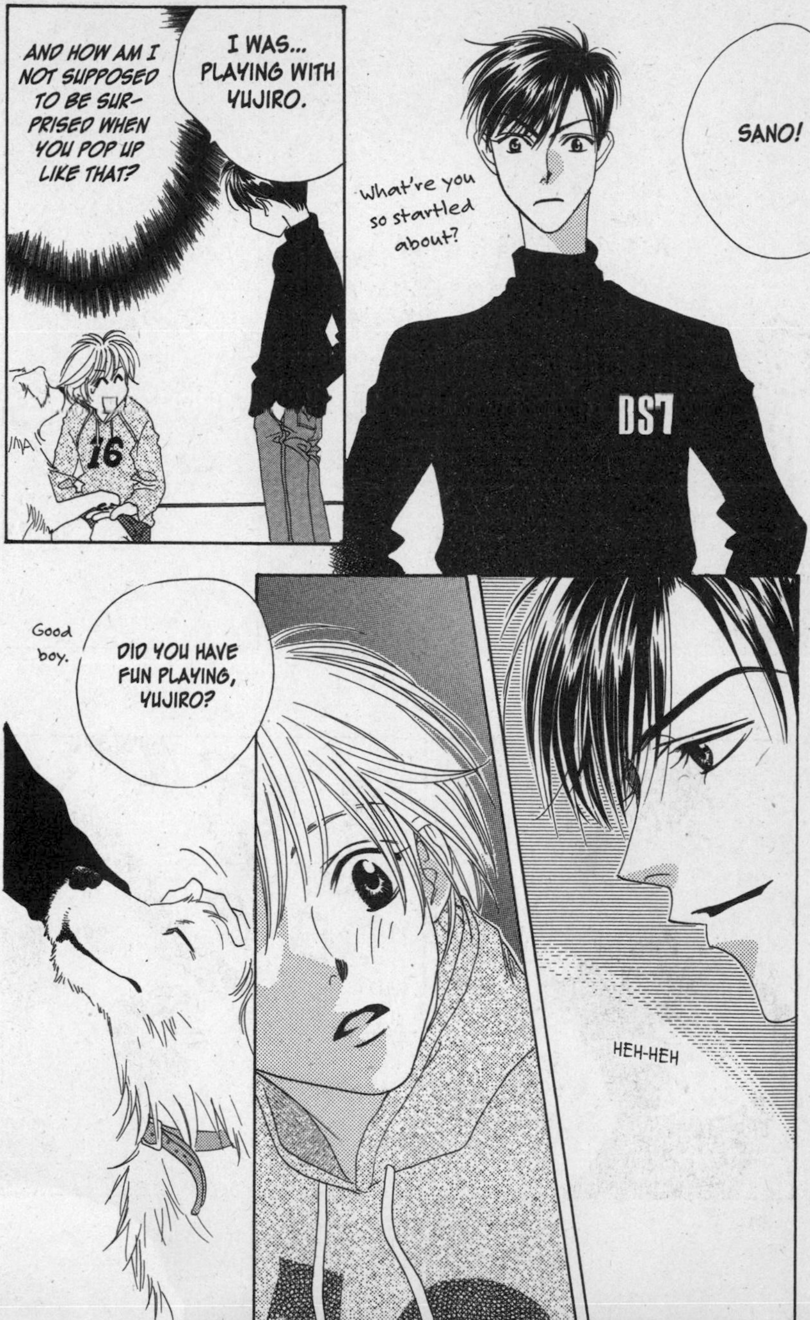
SANO!
What're you so startled about?
I WAS... PLAYING WITH YUJIRO.
AND HOW AM I NOT SUPPOSED TO BE SURPRISED WHEN YOU POP UP LIKE THAT?
HEH-HEH
DID YOU HAVE FUN PLAYING, YUJIRO?
Good boy.

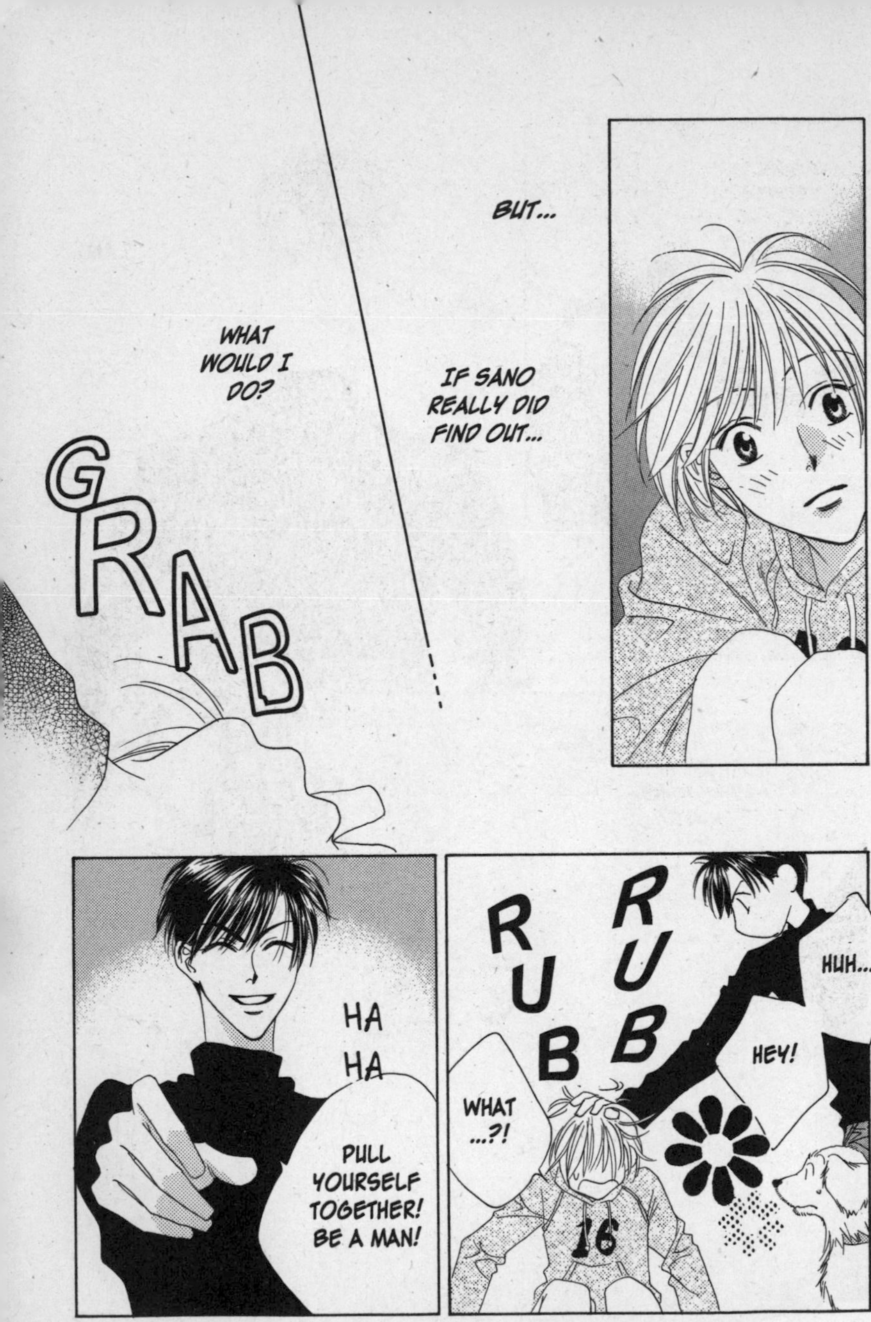
BUT...
IF SANO REALLY DID FIND OUT...
WHAT WOULD I DO?
GRAB
RUB RUB
HUH...
HEY!
WHAT ...?!
HA HA
PULL YOURSELF TOGETHER! BE A MAN!

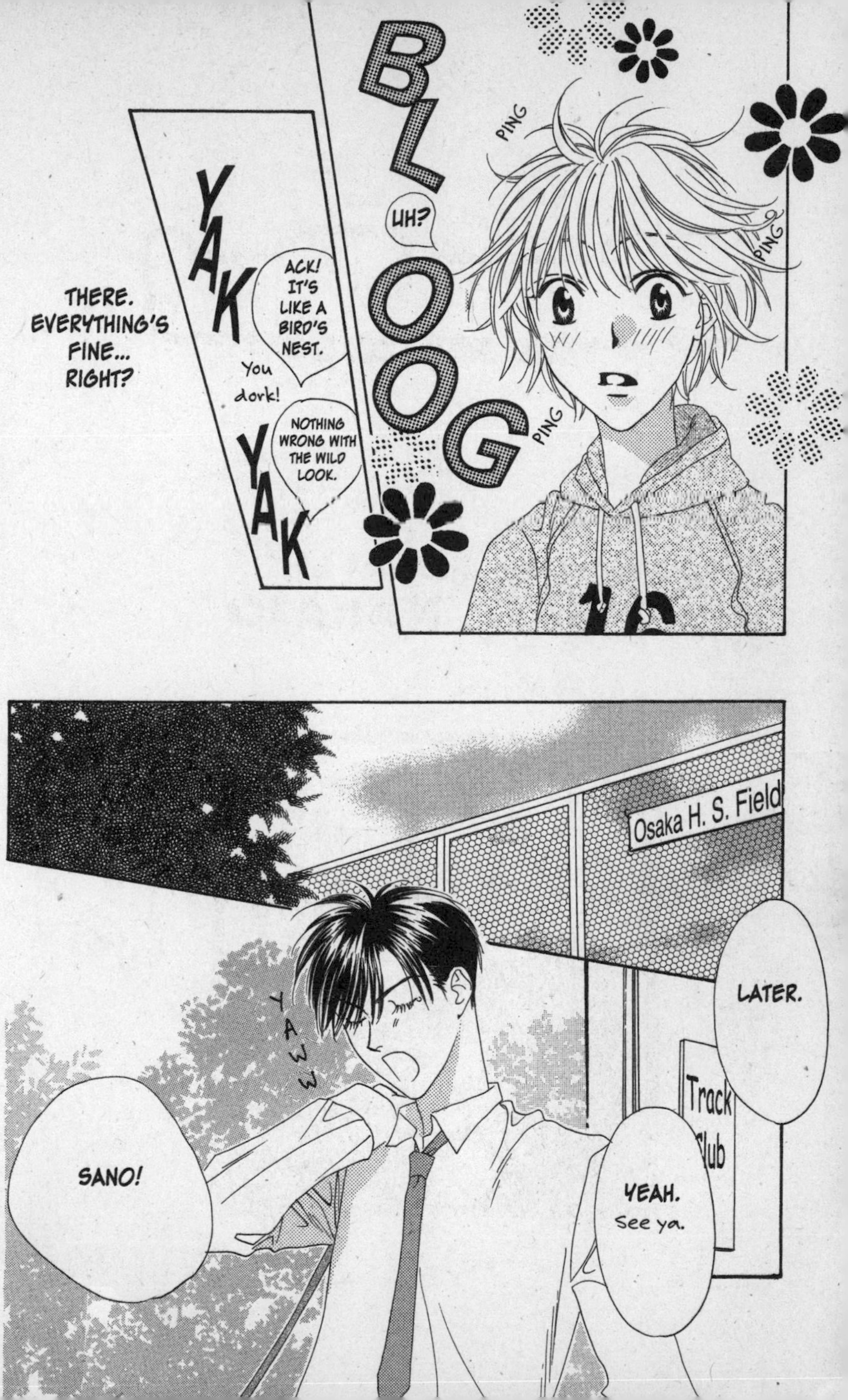
PING
BLOOG
UH?
PING
PING
YAK YAK
ACK! IT'S LIKE A BIRD'S NEST.
You dork!
NOTHING WRONG WITH THE WILD LOOK.
THERE. EVERYTHING'S FINE... RIGHT?
Osaka H. S. Field
LATER.
Track Club
YAWW
YEAH.
See ya.
SANO!

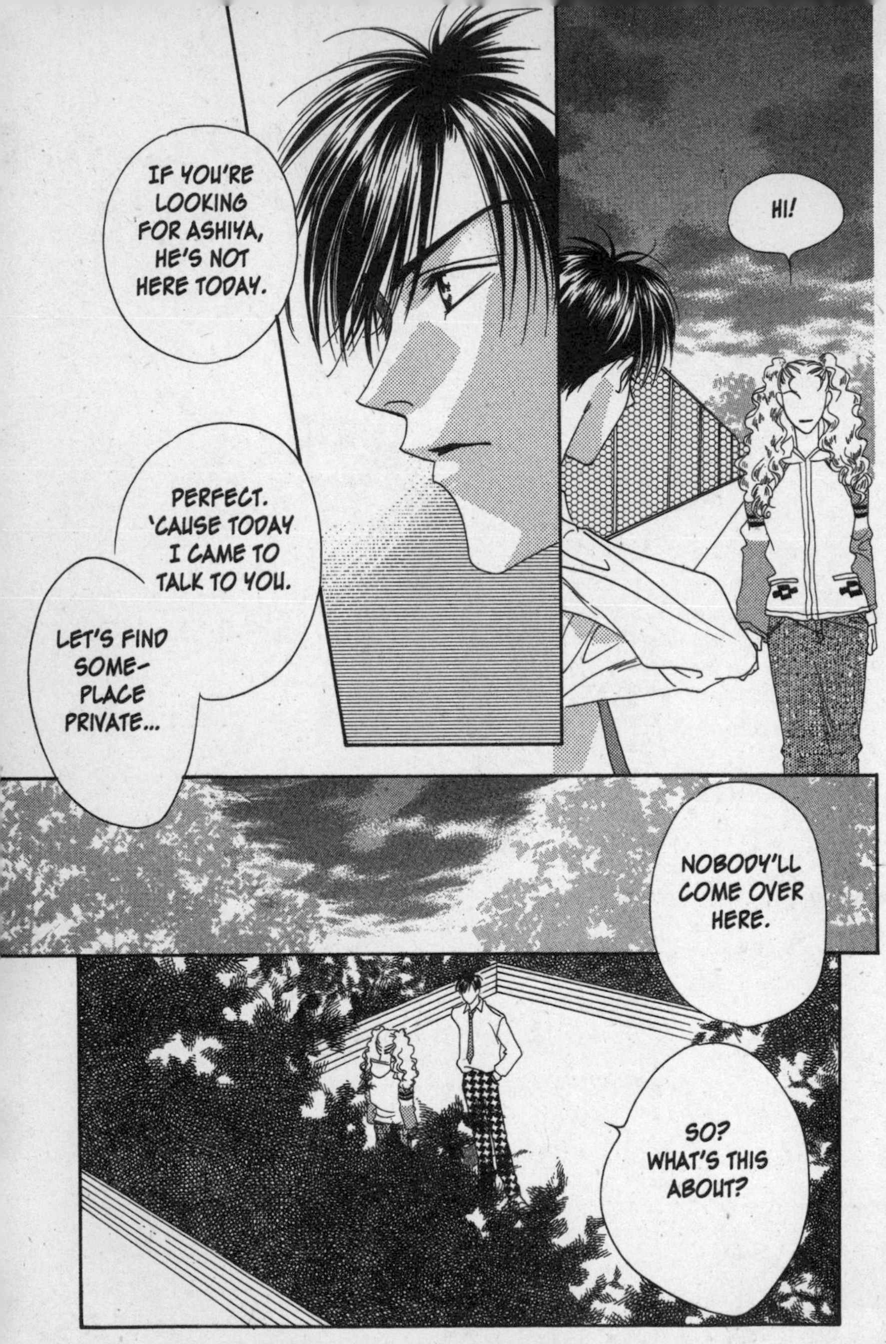
HI!
IF YOU'RE LOOKING FOR ASHIYA, HE'S NOT HERE TODAY.
PERFECT. 'CAUSE TODAY I CAME TO TALK TO YOU.
LET'S FIND SOME-PLACE PRIVATE...
NOBODY'LL COME OVER HERE.
SO? WHAT'S THIS ABOUT?

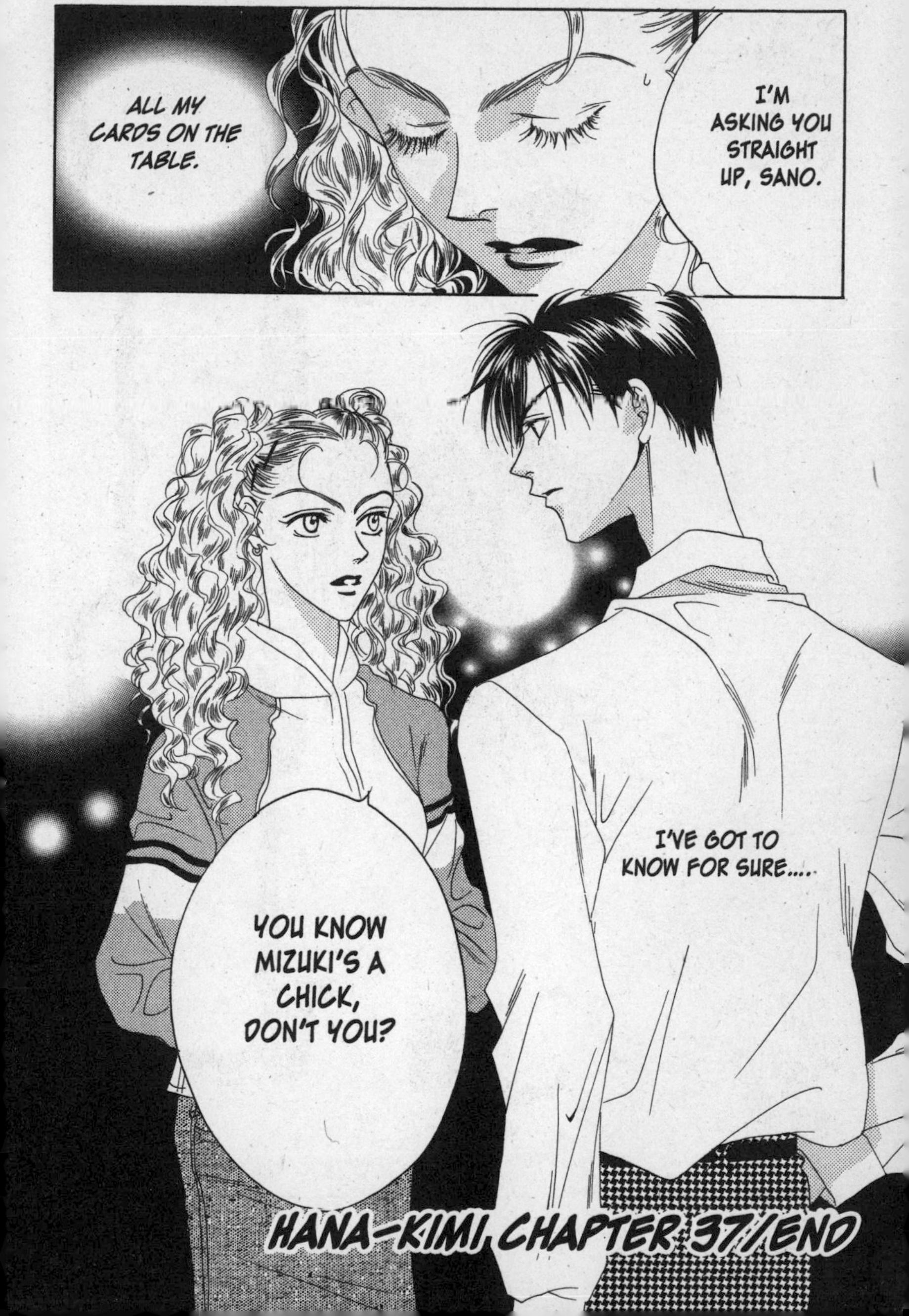
I'M ASKING YOU STRAIGHT UP, SANO.
ALL MY CARDS ON THE TABLE.
I'VE GOT TO KNOW FOR SURE....
YOU KNOW MIZUKI'S A CHICK, DON'T YOU?
HANA-KIMI CHAPTER 37/END

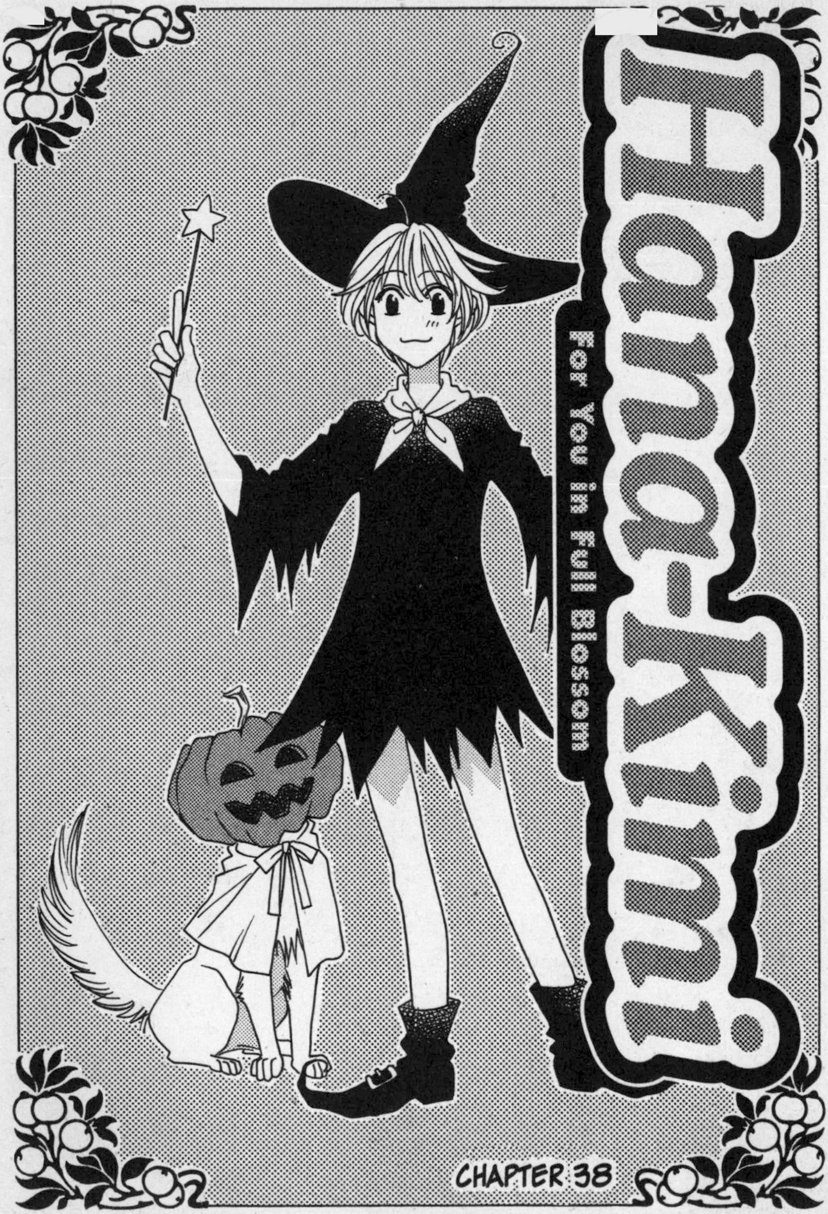
Hana-Kimi
For You in Full Blossom
CHAPTER 38

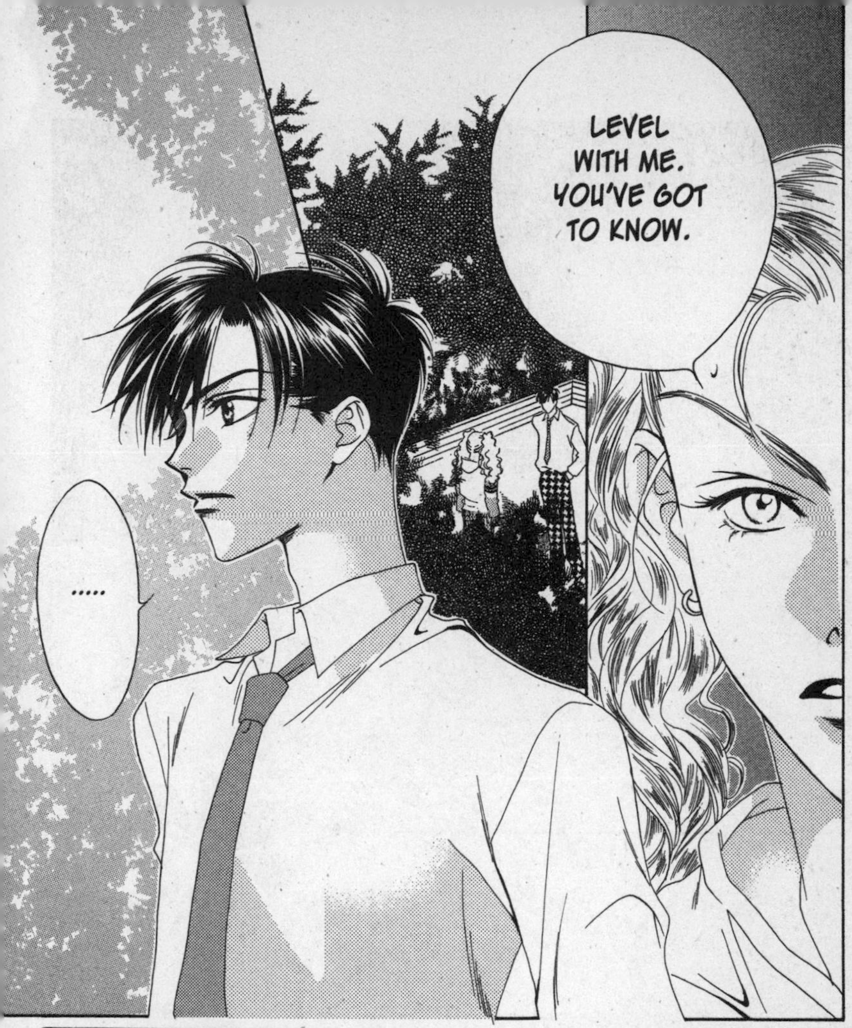
LEVEL WITH ME. YOU'VE GOT TO KNOW.
.....

SHIKI

(Ghoul)

LATELY I'VE BEEN ADDICTED TO READING. RIGHT NOW THIS IS MY FAVORITE -- A LONG NOVEL BY FUYUMI ONO, WHO I'VE MENTIONED BEFORE, AUTHOR OF "JUNI KOKKI" (TWELVE KINGDOMS) AND THE "AKURYO (EVIL SPIRIT) SERIES." HOW LONG IS IT? WELL, IT'S ABOUT AS THICK AS A DICTIONARY, AND THERE ARE TWO VOLUMES. (HA HA!) SINCE THE FIRST VOLUME SETS UP THE CHARACTERS AND LOCALES, I TOOK MY TIME READING IT. BUT ONCE I GOT TO THE SECOND VOLUME, I STARTED READING LIKE I WAS GOING DOWN A ROLLERCOASTER. I WAS SO DESPERATE TO KNOW WHAT HAPPENS NEXT THAT I COULDN'T PUT IT DOWN!

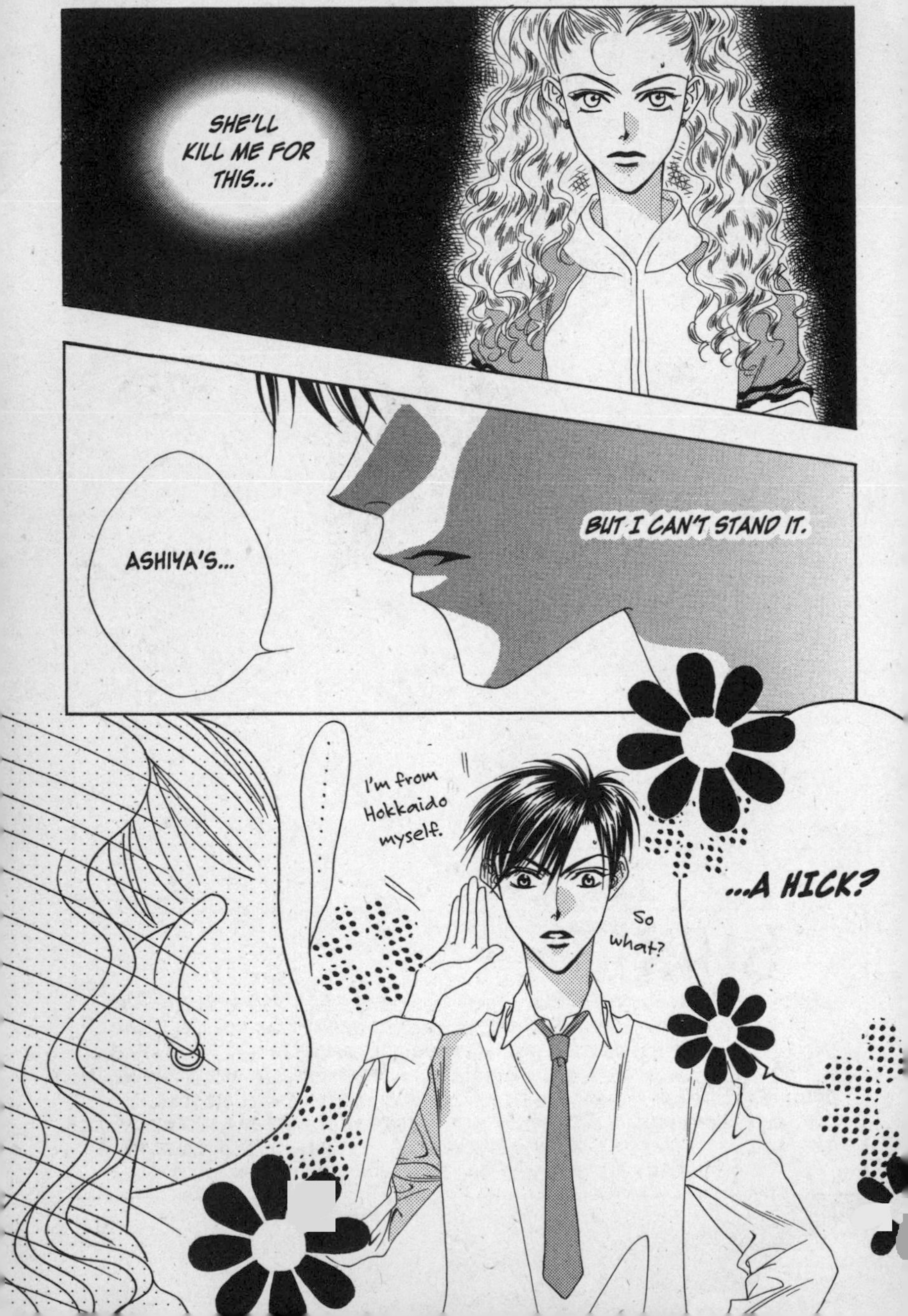
SHE'LL KILL ME FOR THIS...
BUT I CAN'T STAND IT.
ASHIYA'S...
...A HICK?
So what?
I'm from Hokkaido myself.

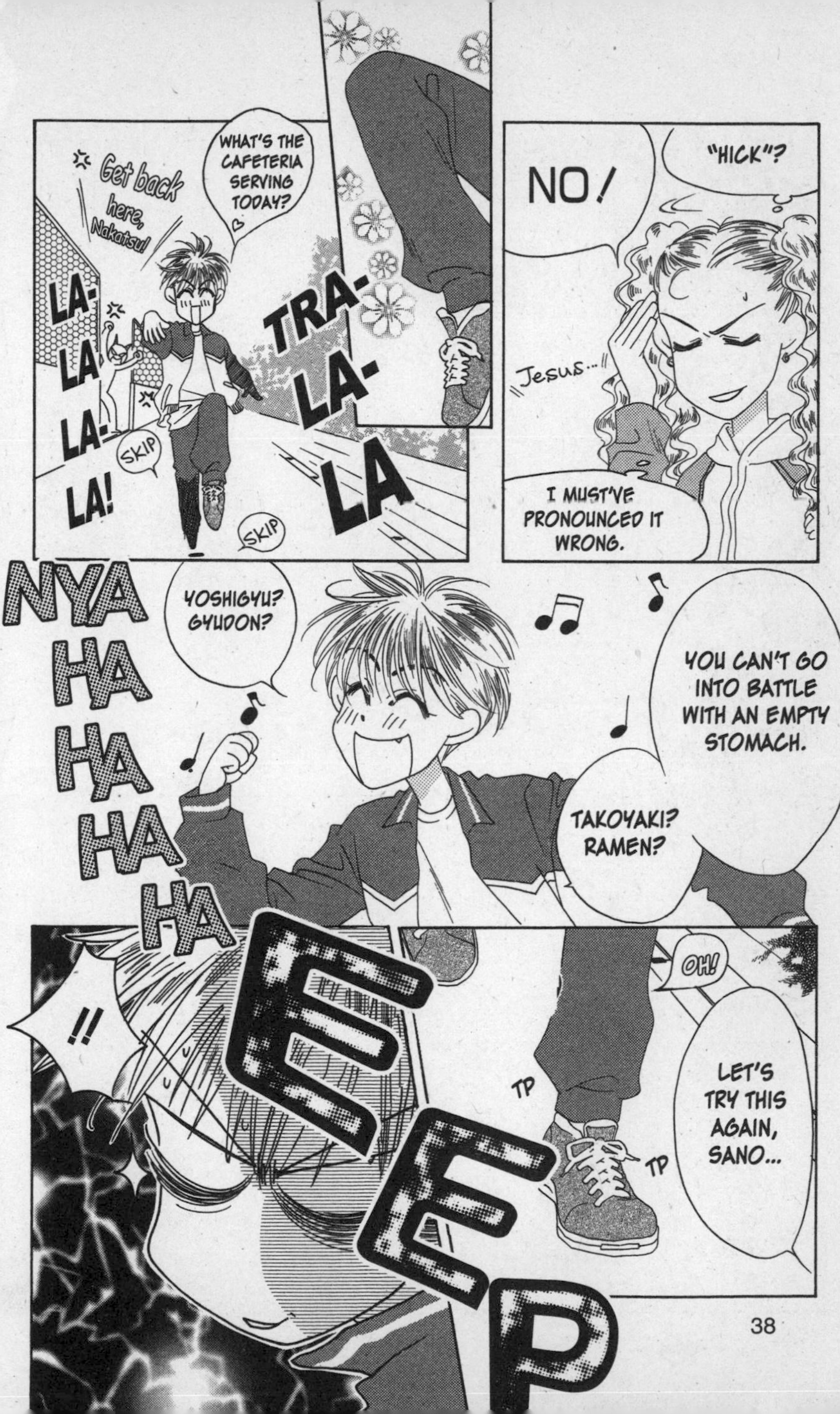
"HICK"?
NO!
Jesus...
I MUST'VE PRONOUNCED IT WRONG.
TRA-LA-LA
Get back here, Nakatsu!
WHAT'S THE CAFETERIA SERVING TODAY?
LA-LA-LA-LA!
SKIP
SKIP
YOU CAN'T GO INTO BATTLE WITH AN EMPTY STOMACH.
TAKOYAKI? RAMEN?
YOSHIGYU? GYUDON?
NYA HA HA HA HA HA
OH!
LET'S TRY THIS AGAIN, SANO...
TP
TP
!!
EEEP

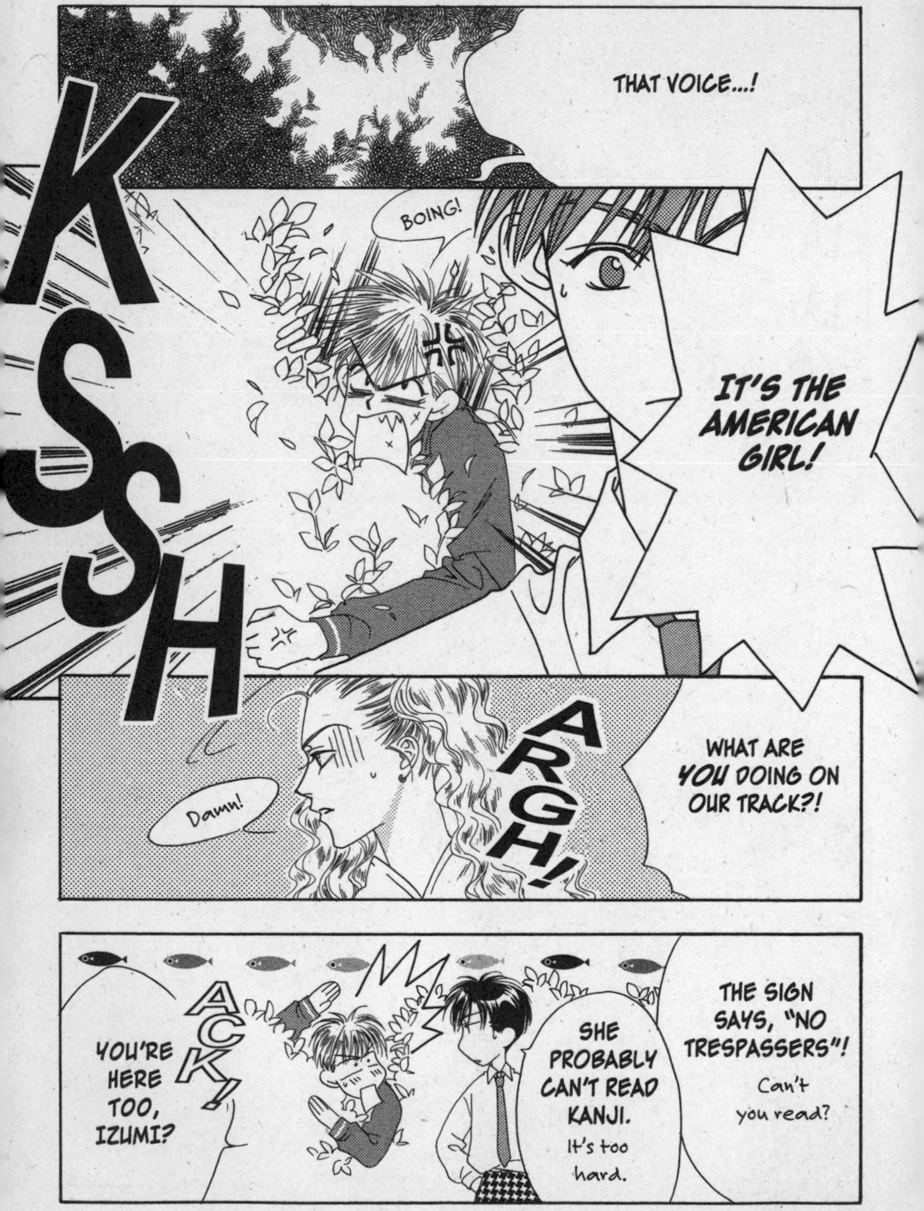
THAT VOICE...!
IT'S THE AMERICAN GIRL!
BOING!
KSSH
WHAT ARE *YOU* DOING ON OUR TRACK?!
ARGH!
Damn!
THE SIGN SAYS, "NO TRESPASSERS"!
Can't you read?
SHE PROBABLY CAN'T READ KANJI.
It's too hard.
ACK!
YOU'RE HERE TOO, IZUMI?

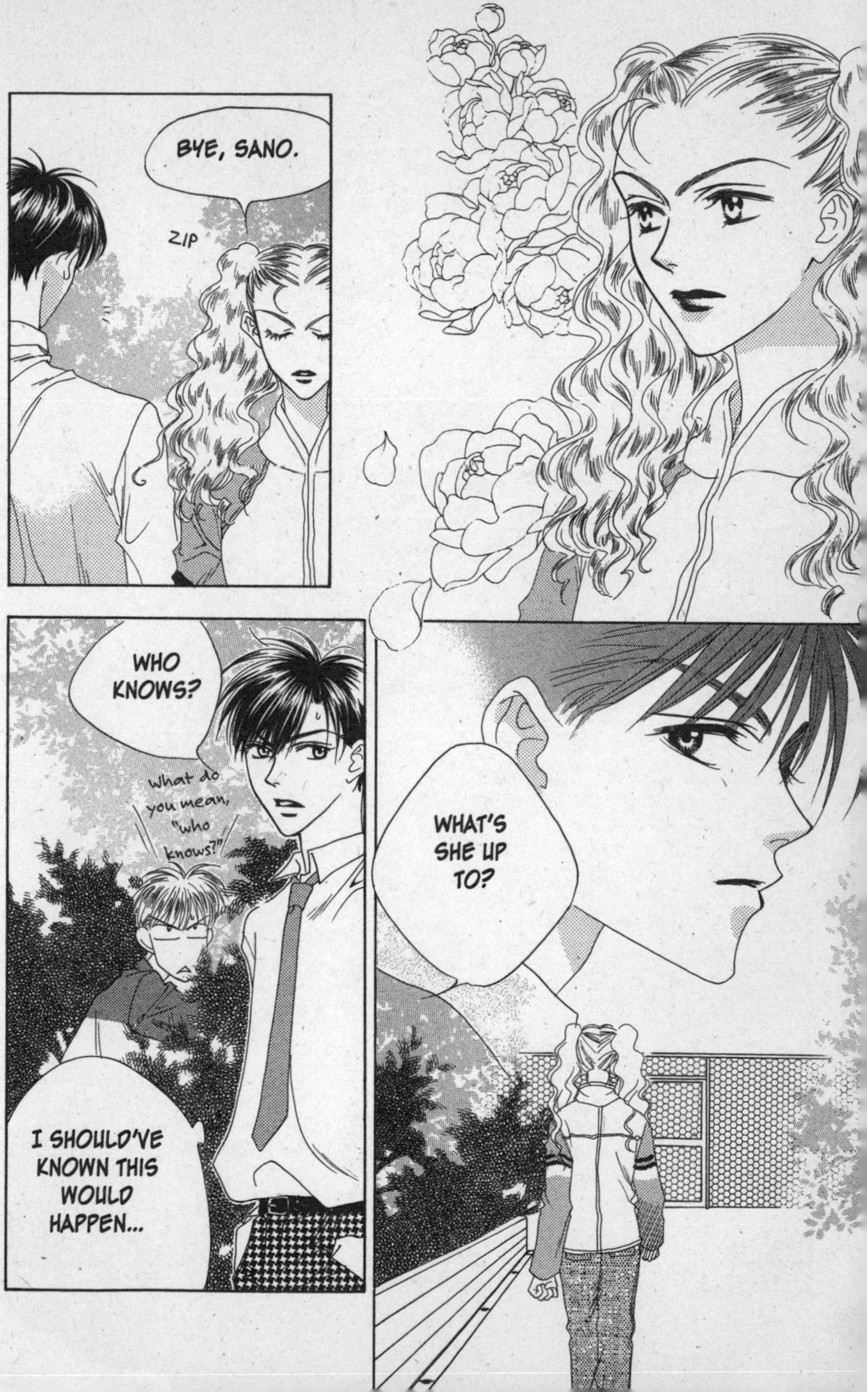
BYE, SANO.
ZIP
WHAT'S SHE UP TO?
WHO KNOWS?
What do you mean, "who knows?"
I SHOULD'VE KNOWN THIS WOULD HAPPEN...

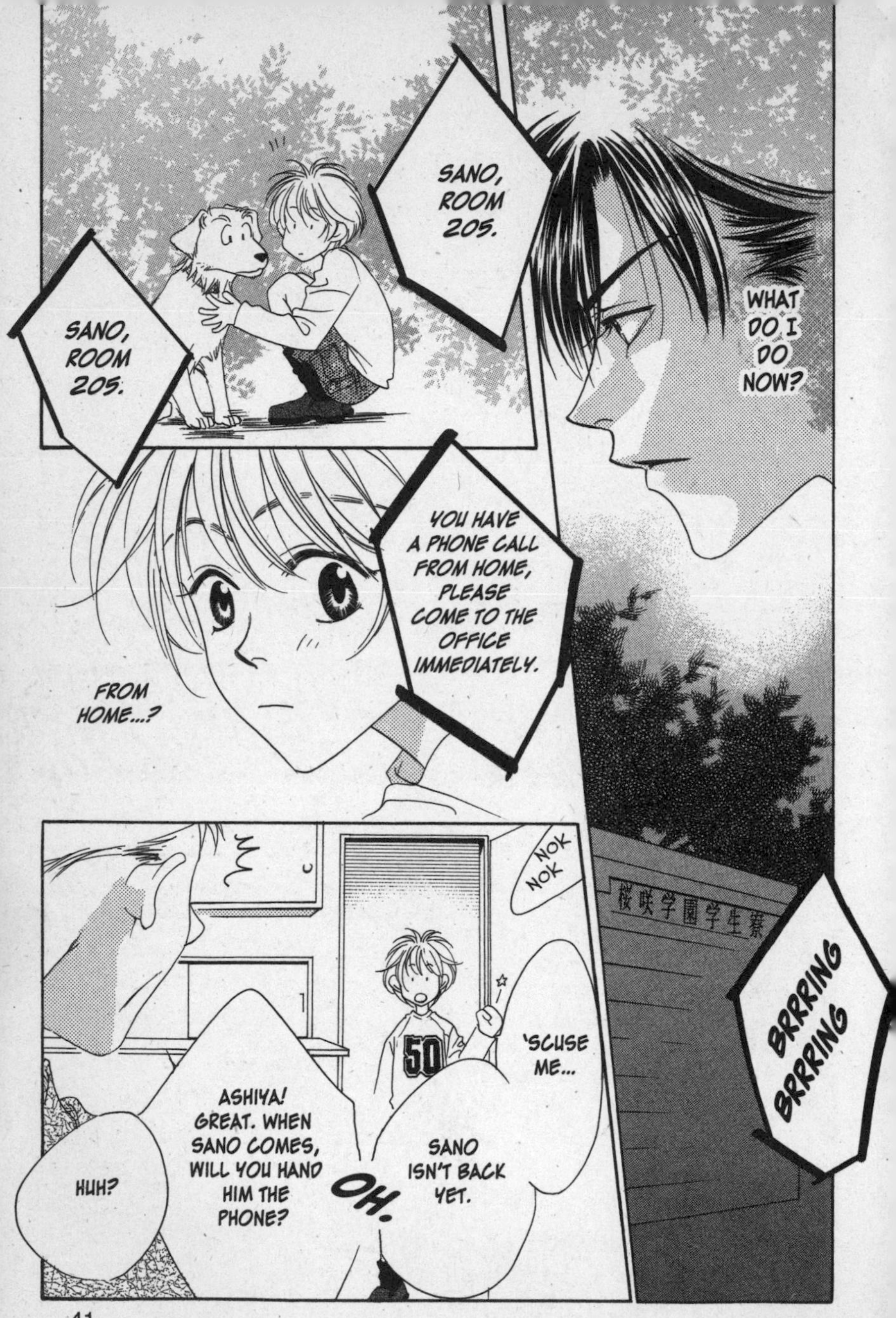
SANO, ROOM 205.
WHAT DO I DO NOW?
桜咲学園学生寮
BRRRING BRRRING
SANO, ROOM 205.
YOU HAVE A PHONE CALL FROM HOME, PLEASE COME TO THE OFFICE IMMEDIATELY.
FROM HOME...?
NOK NOK
'SCUSE ME...
SANO ISN'T BACK YET.
OH.
ASHIYA! GREAT. WHEN SANO COMES, WILL YOU HAND HIM THE PHONE?
HUH?

I HAVE TO GO CHANGE THE LIGHT BULB IN THE EASTERN STEPS, BUT I FORGOT I RAN OUT OF 'EM.
SO I HAVE TO GO BUY ONE, SO YOU'LL FILL IN HERE, RIGHT?
UH... OKAY.
.....
Well, whatever.
OH!
BUT...
WHAT IF IT'S AN EMERGENCY?
MAYBE I SHOULD JUST TELL THEM SANO ISN'T HERE RIGHT NOW.
...UM...

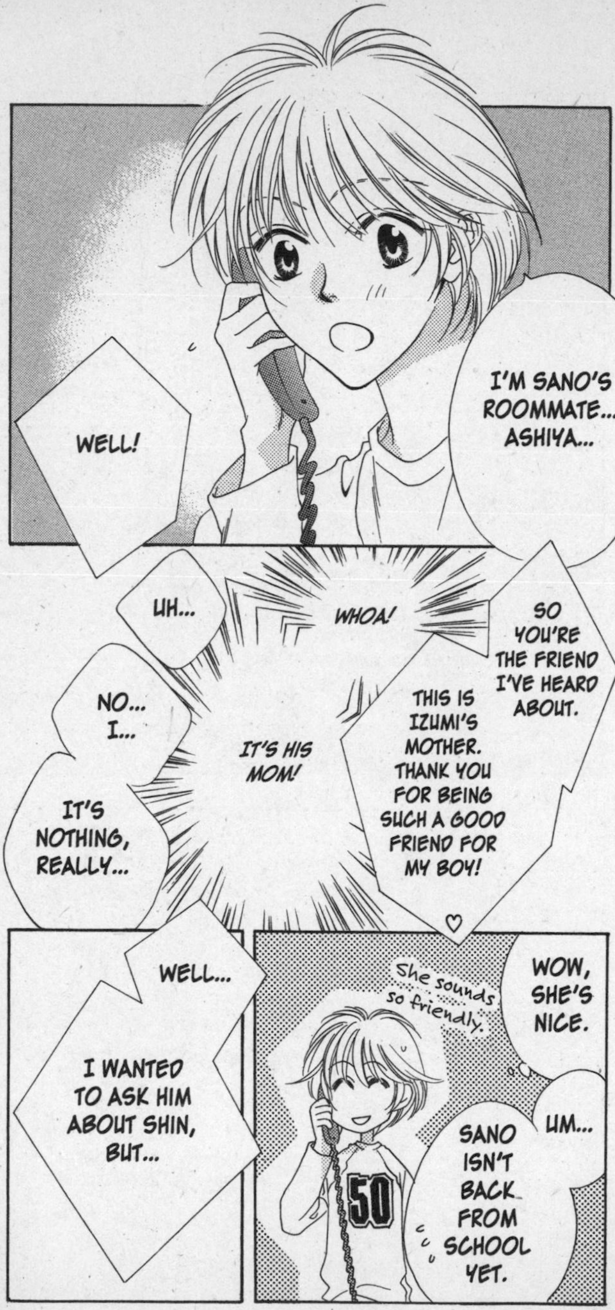
I'M SANO'S ROOMMATE... ASHIYA...
WELL!
SO YOU'RE THE FRIEND I'VE HEARD ABOUT.
THIS IS IZUMI'S MOTHER. THANK YOU FOR BEING SUCH A GOOD FRIEND FOR MY BOY! ♡
WHOA!
IT'S HIS MOM!
UH...
NO... I...
IT'S NOTHING, REALLY...
WOW, SHE'S NICE.
She sounds so friendly.
UM...
SANO ISN'T BACK FROM SCHOOL YET.
WELL...
I WANTED TO ASK HIM ABOUT SHIN, BUT...

WHISPERED SECRETS

THE RIDDLE OF THE BREAST BAND

UM... WHENEVER I MENTION THE VEST MIZUKI WEARS TO HIDE HER CHEST, PEOPLE ASK "WHERE DO THEY SELL THOSE?" BUT IT'S ACTUALLY MY INVENTION AND IT DOESN'T REALLY EXIST. SORRY. I GET MAIL FROM GIRLS IN BANDS WHO ARE MALE IMPERSONATORS AND ACTRESSES WHO PLAY MALE ROLES SAYING, "TELL US!" I DON'T REALLY KNOW, BUT MY FRIEND SAID THEY PROBABLY SELL THOSE IN FEMALE-TO-MALE TRANSVESTITE SHOPS. DUH, MAKES SENSE. I LOOK FORWARD TO HEARING FROM SOMEONE WHO CAN TELL ME WHETHER BREAST BANDS REALLY DO EXIST.

IS "TRANSVESTITE" THE RIGHT WAY TO SAY IT? I'M SORRY IF I OFFENDED ANYONE.

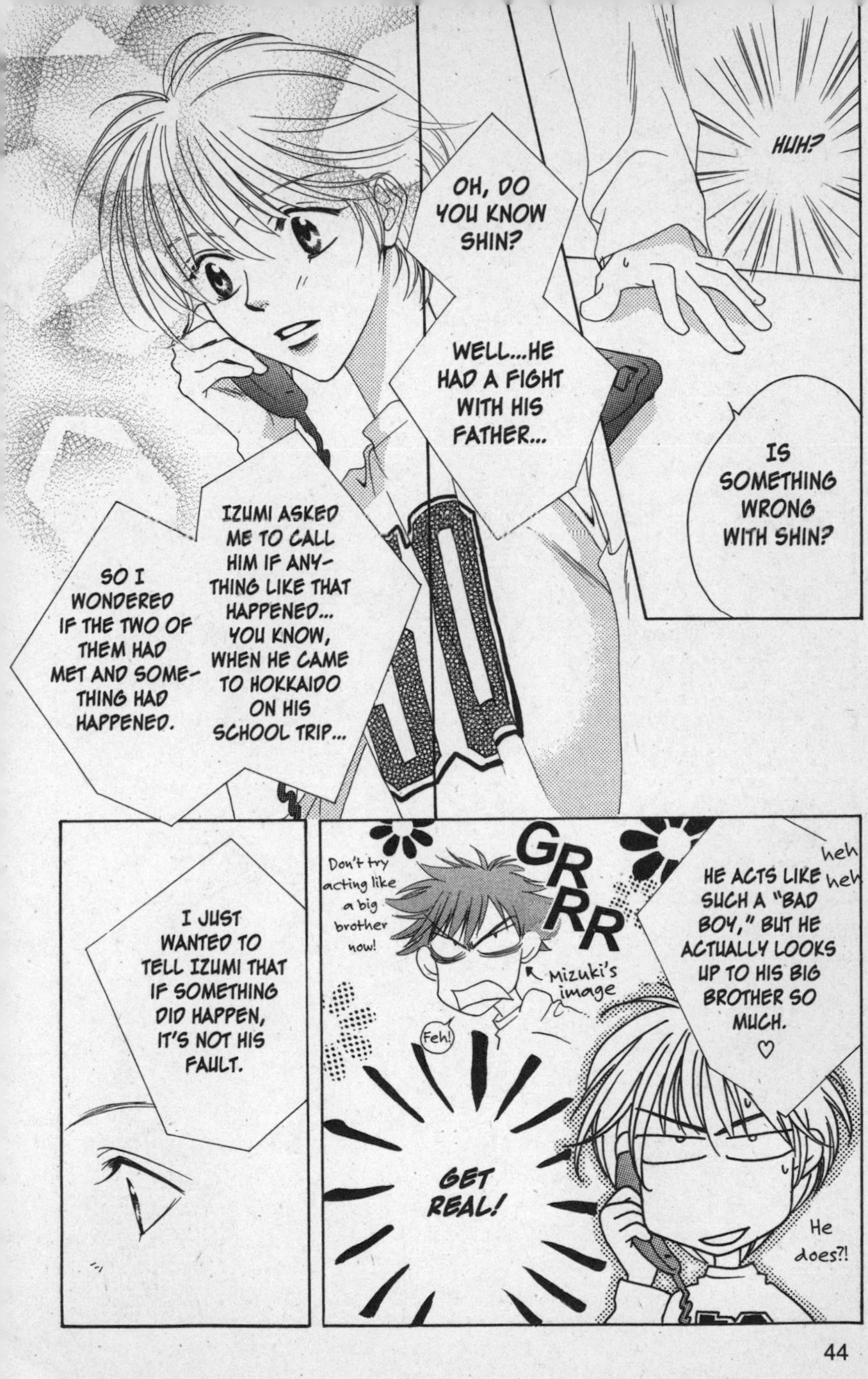
HUH?
IS SOMETHING WRONG WITH SHIN?
OH, DO YOU KNOW SHIN?
WELL...HE HAD A FIGHT WITH HIS FATHER...
IZUMI ASKED ME TO CALL HIM IF ANY-THING LIKE THAT HAPPENED... YOU KNOW, WHEN HE CAME TO HOKKAIDO ON HIS SCHOOL TRIP...
SO I WONDERED IF THE TWO OF THEM HAD MET AND SOME-THING HAD HAPPENED.
heh heh
HE ACTS LIKE SUCH A "BAD BOY," BUT HE ACTUALLY LOOKS UP TO HIS BIG BROTHER SO MUCH. ♡
GRRR
Don't try acting like a big brother now!
Mizuki's image
Feh!
GET REAL!
He does?!
I JUST WANTED TO TELL IZUMI THAT IF SOMETHING DID HAPPEN, IT'S NOT HIS FAULT.

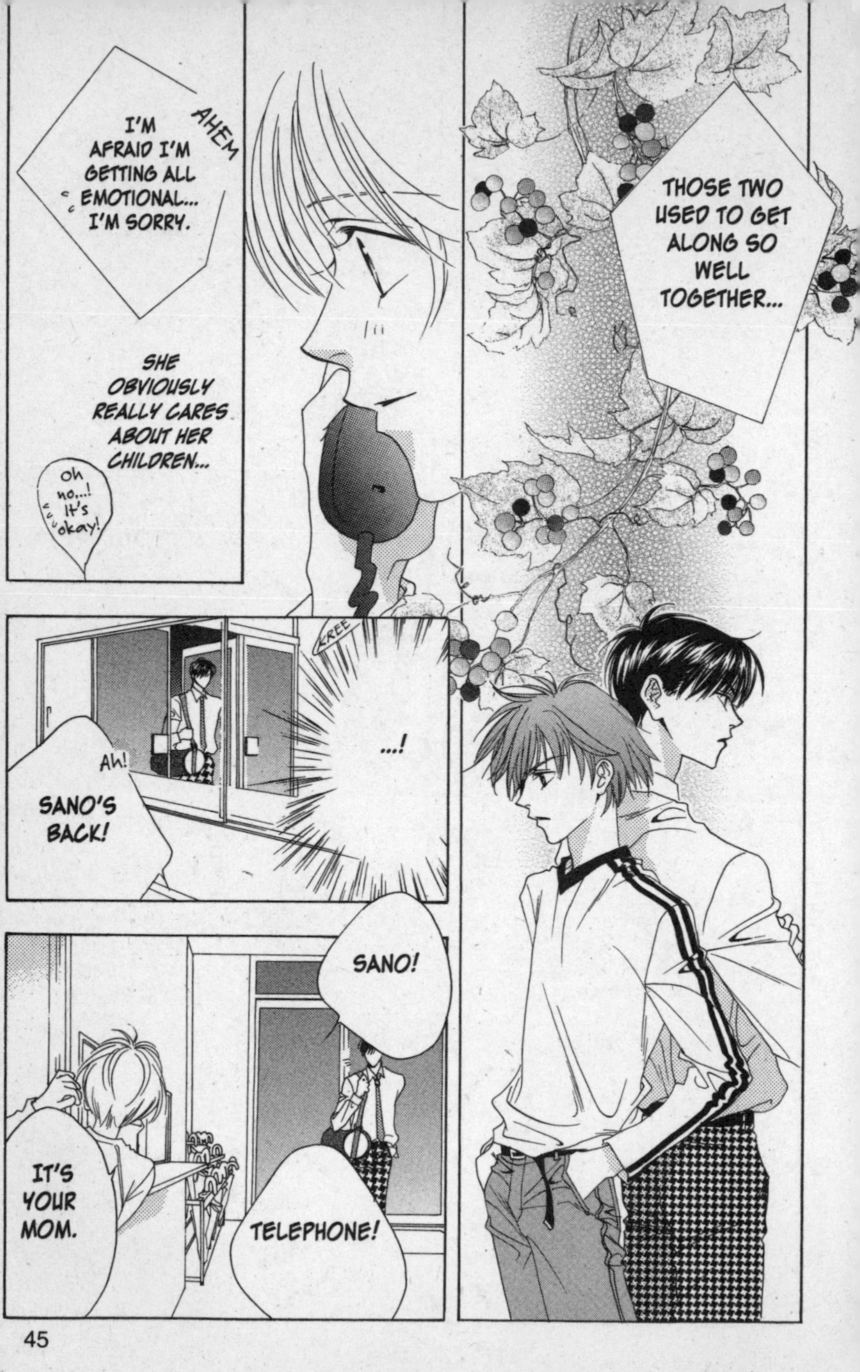
THOSE TWO USED TO GET ALONG SO WELL TOGETHER...
AHEM
I'M AFRAID I'M GETTING ALL EMOTIONAL... I'M SORRY.
SHE OBVIOUSLY REALLY CARES ABOUT HER CHILDREN...
oh no...! It's okay!
KREE
...!
Ah!
SANO'S BACK!
SANO!
TELEPHONE!
IT'S YOUR MOM.

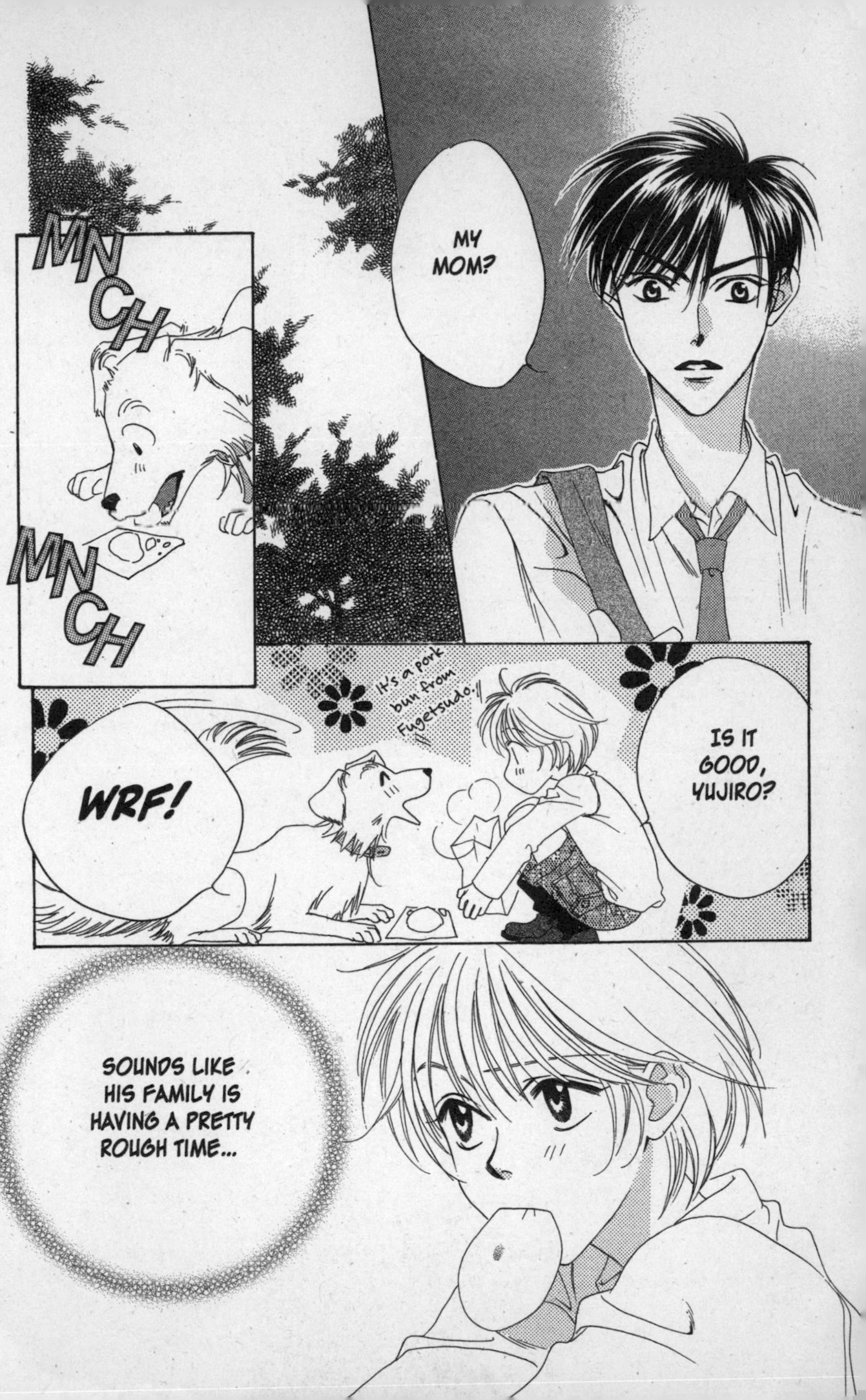
MY MOM?
MNCH
MNCH
IS IT GOOD, YUJIRO?
It's a pork bun from Fugetsudo.
WRF!
SOUNDS LIKE HIS FAMILY IS HAVING A PRETTY ROUGH TIME...

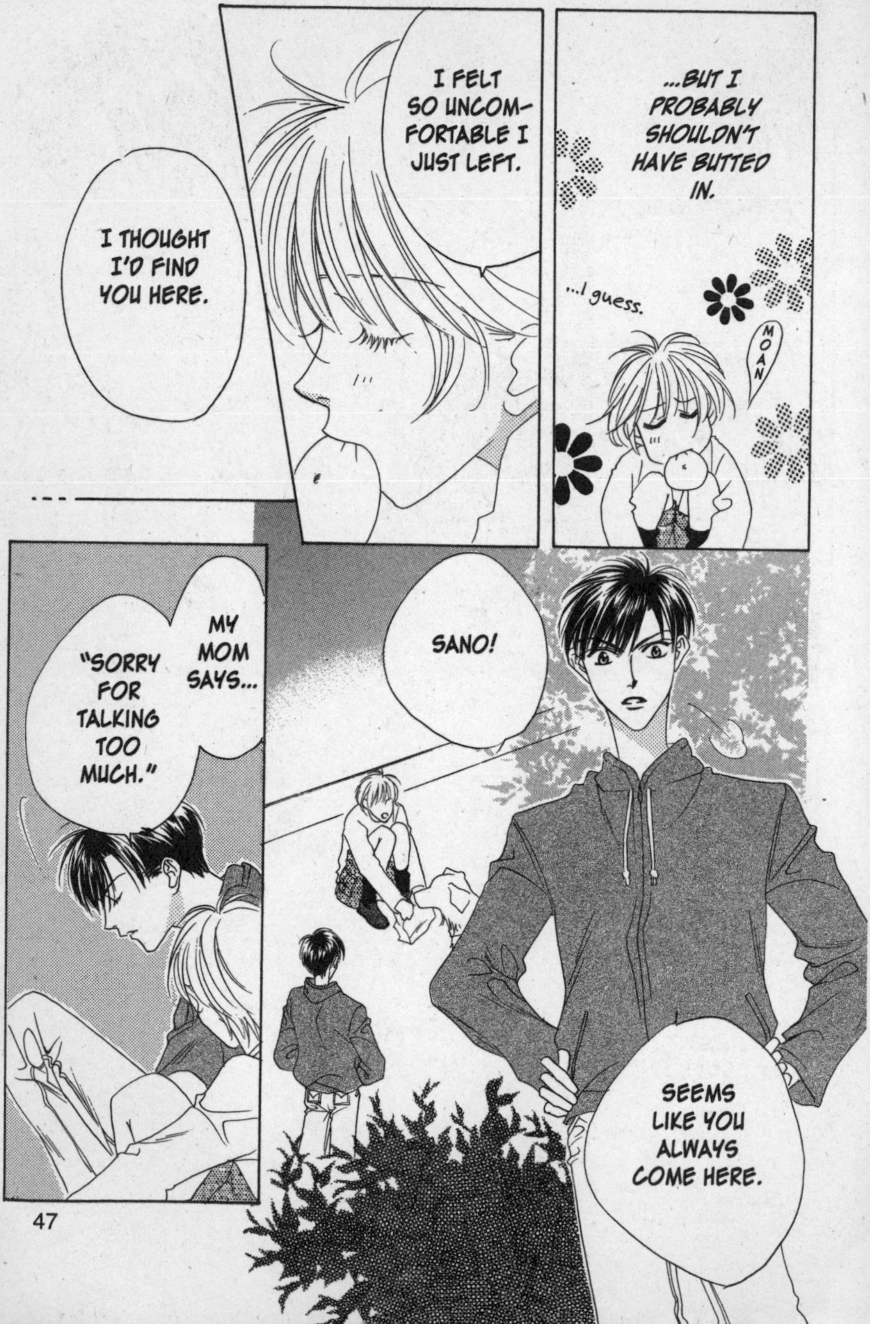
...BUT I PROBABLY SHOULDN'T HAVE BUTTED IN.
...I guess.
MOAN
I FELT SO UNCOM-FORTABLE I JUST LEFT.
I THOUGHT I'D FIND YOU HERE.
SANO!
SEEMS LIKE YOU ALWAYS COME HERE.
MY MOM SAYS...
"SORRY FOR TALKING TOO MUCH."

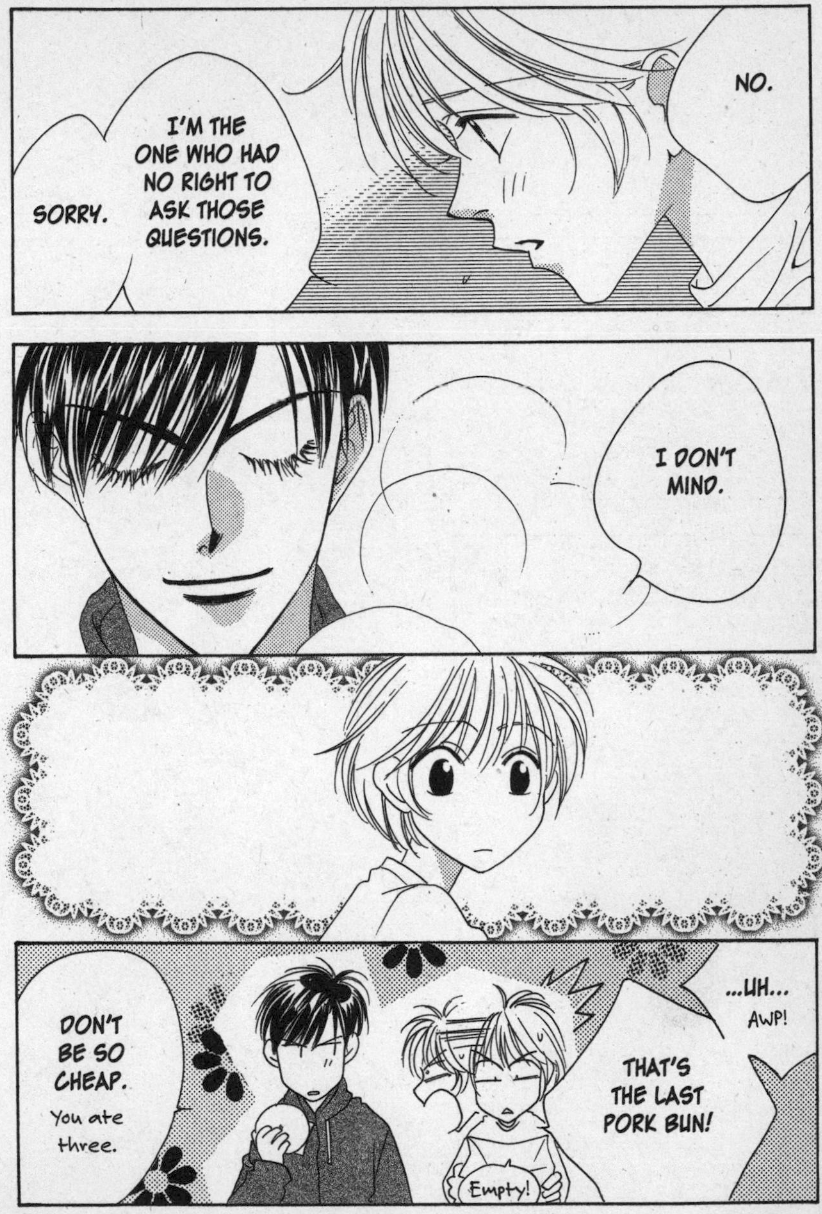
NO.
I'M THE ONE WHO HAD NO RIGHT TO ASK THOSE QUESTIONS.
SORRY.
I DON'T MIND.
...UH...
AWP!
THAT'S THE LAST PORK BUN!
Empty!
DON'T BE SO CHEAP.
You ate three.

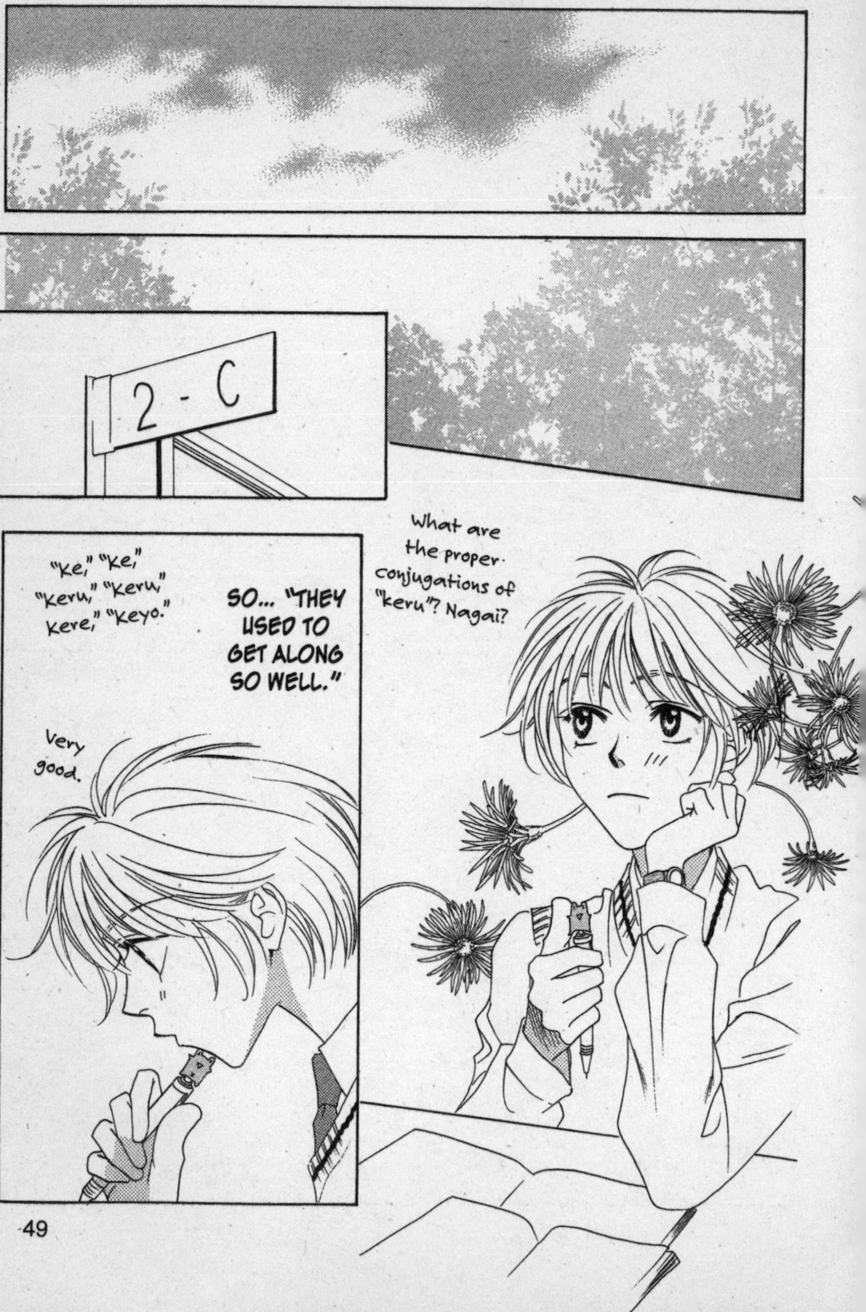
2 - C
What are the proper conjugations of "keru"? Nagai?
"ke," "ke," "keru," "keru," "kere," "keyo."
SO... "THEY USED TO GET ALONG SO WELL."
Very good.

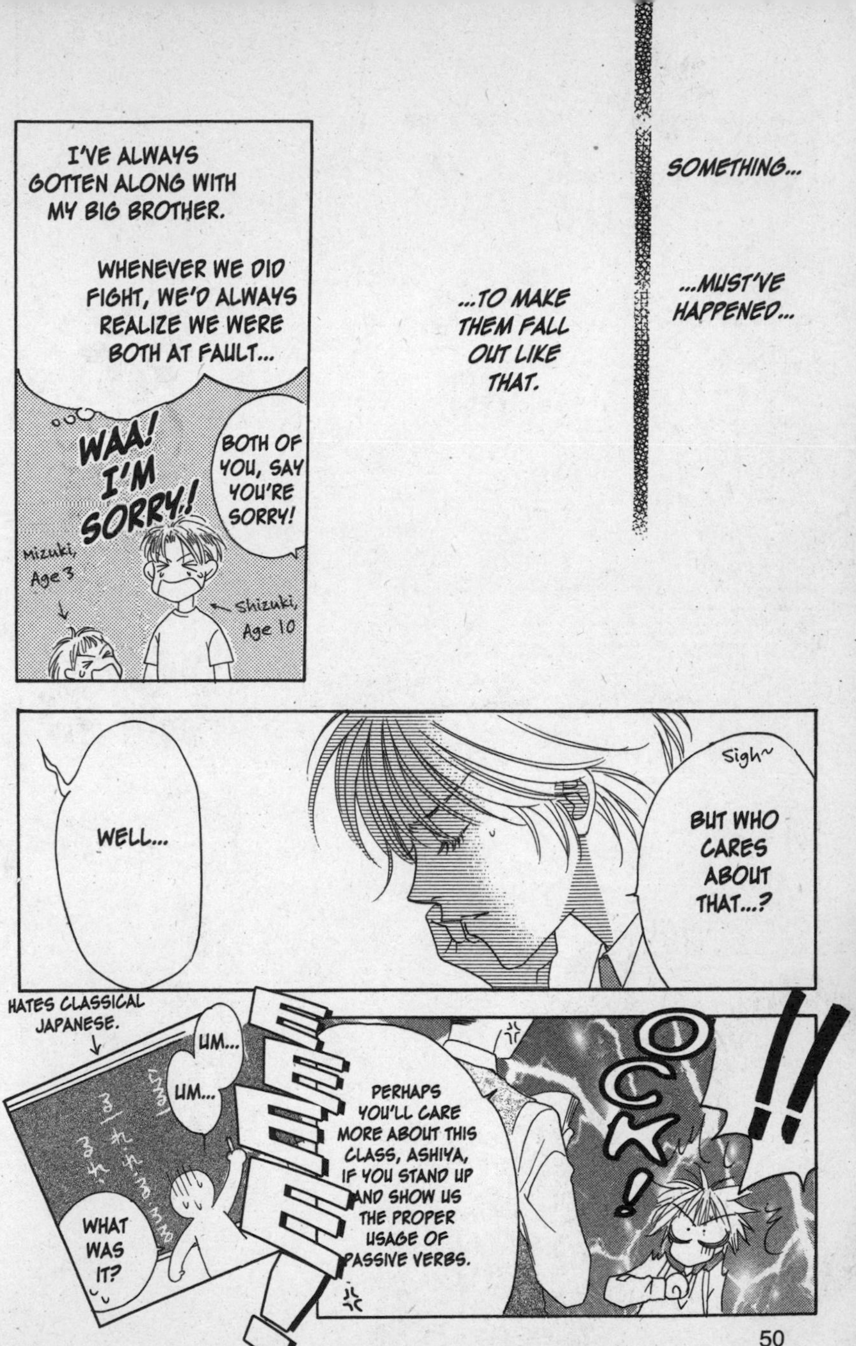
SOMETHING...
...MUST'VE HAPPENED...
...TO MAKE THEM FALL OUT LIKE THAT.
I'VE ALWAYS GOTTEN ALONG WITH MY BIG BROTHER.
WHENEVER WE DID FIGHT, WE'D ALWAYS REALIZE WE WERE BOTH AT FAULT...
BOTH OF YOU, SAY YOU'RE SORRY!
WAA! I'M SORRY!
Mizuki, Age 3
Shizuki, Age 10
Sigh~
BUT WHO CARES ABOUT THAT...?
WELL...
PERHAPS YOU'LL CARE MORE ABOUT THIS CLASS, ASHIYA, IF YOU STAND UP AND SHOW US THE PROPER USAGE OF PASSIVE VERBS.
HATES CLASSICAL JAPANESE.
UM...
UM...
WHAT WAS IT?

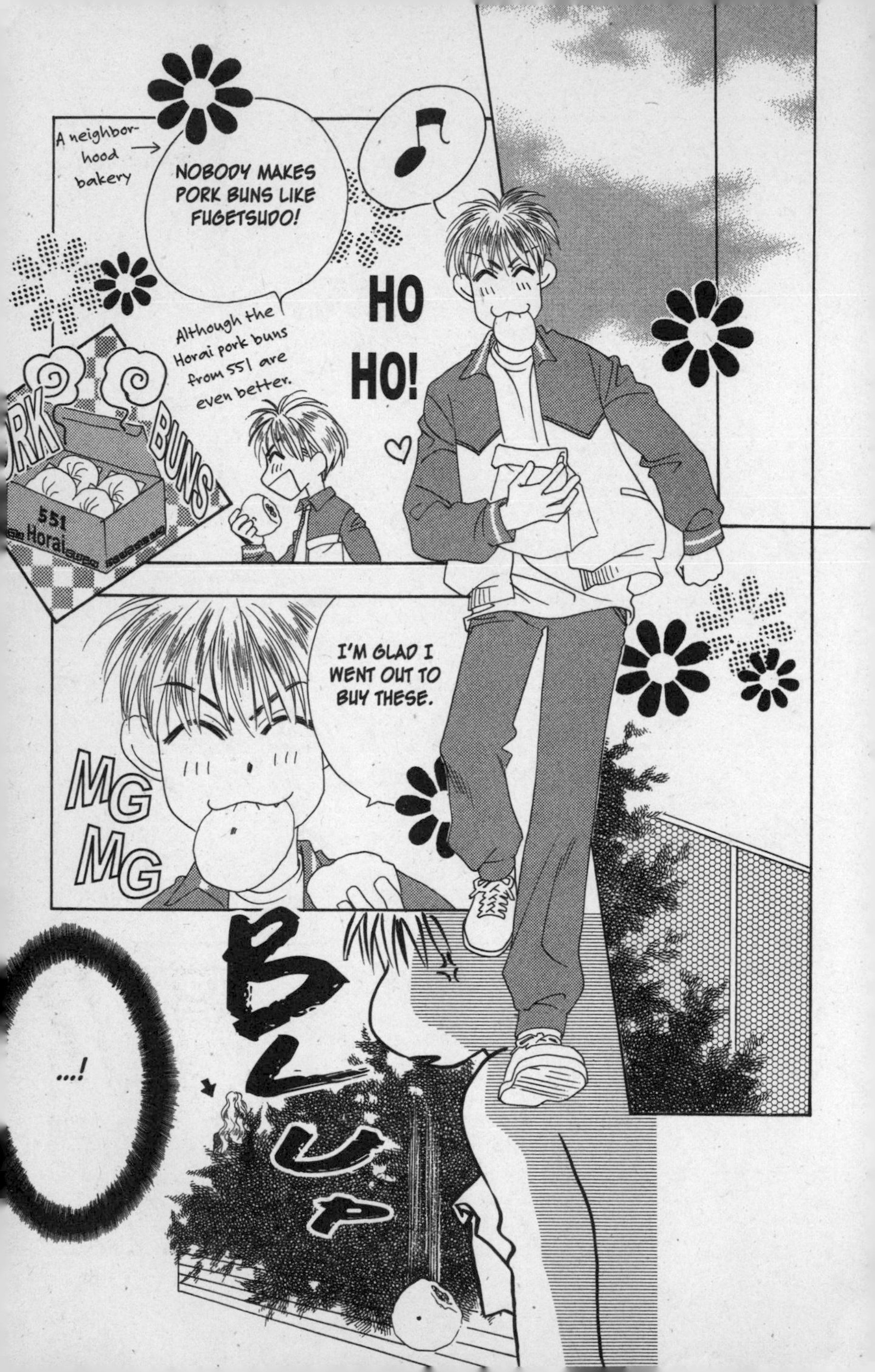
♪
HO HO!
A neighbor-hood bakery
NOBODY MAKES PORK BUNS LIKE FUGETSUDO!
Although the Horai pork buns from 551 are even better.
RK BUNS
551 Horai
I'M GLAD I WENT OUT TO BUY THESE.
MG MG
...!

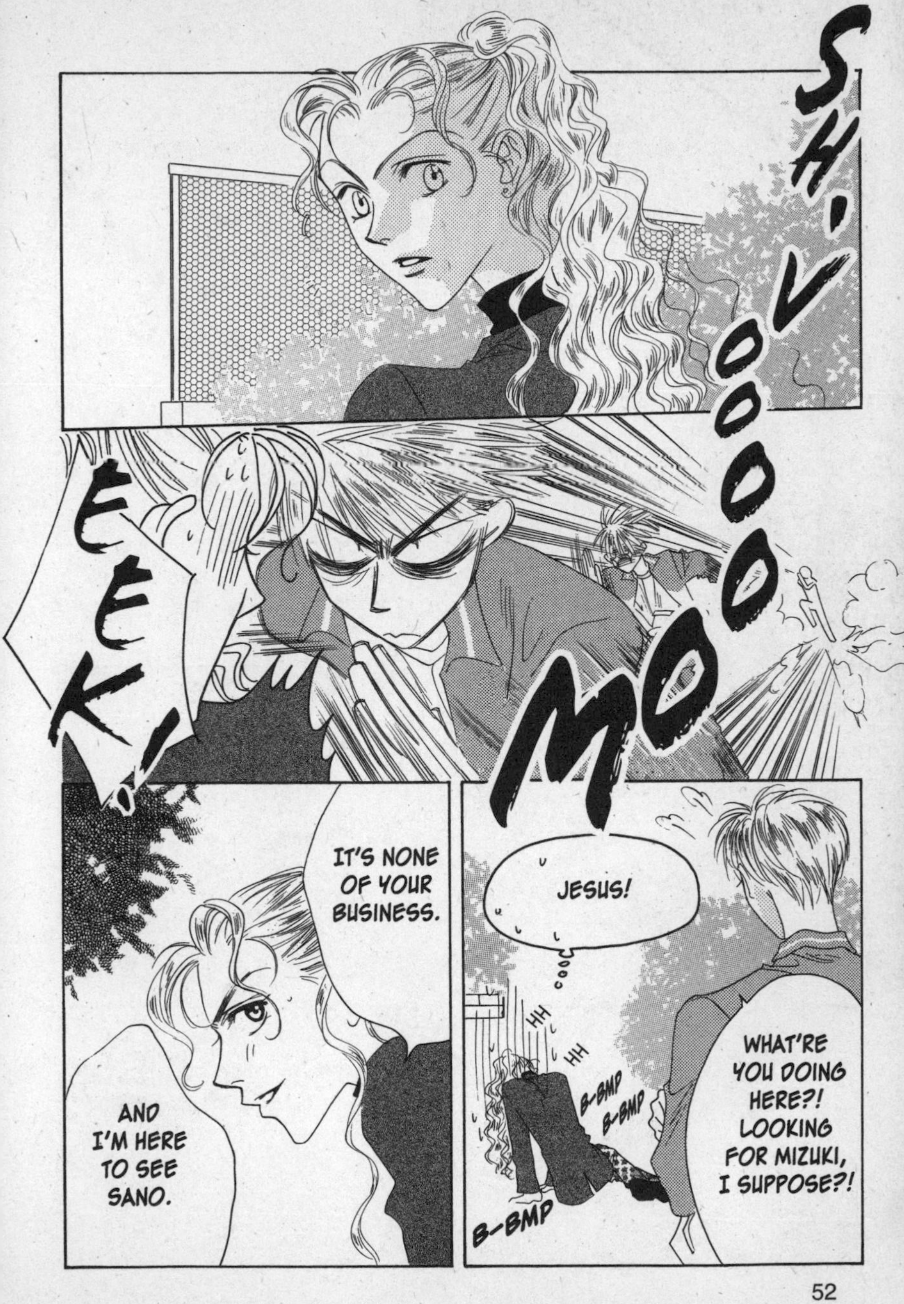
SHIVOOOOMO
EEEK!
WHAT'RE YOU DOING HERE?! LOOKING FOR MIZUKI, I SUPPOSE?!
JESUS!
HH
HH
B-BMP
B-BMP
B-BMP
IT'S NONE OF YOUR BUSINESS.
AND I'M HERE TO SEE SANO.

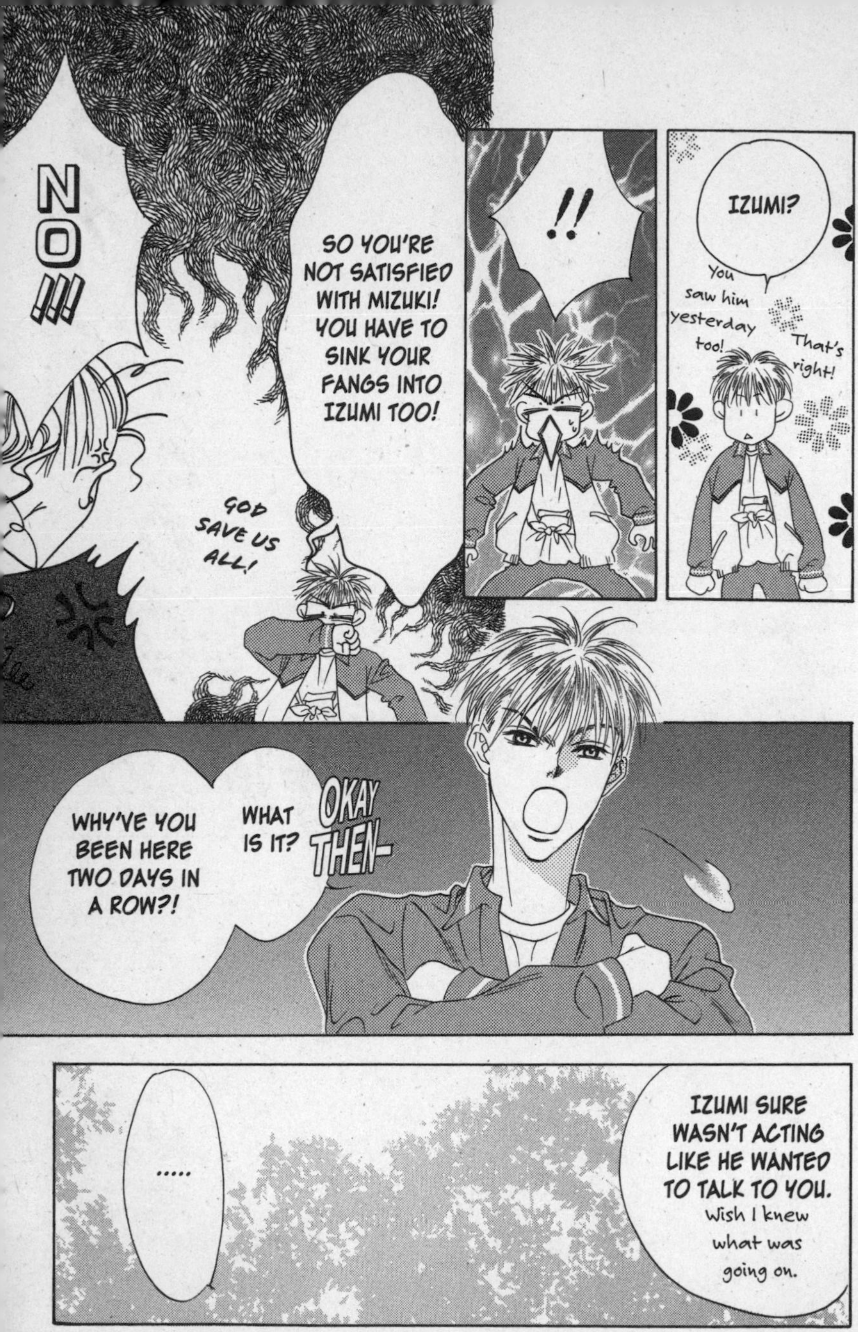
IZUMI?
You saw him yesterday too!
That's right!
!!
SO YOU'RE NOT SATISFIED WITH MIZUKI! YOU HAVE TO SINK YOUR FANGS INTO IZUMI TOO!
NO!!!
GOD SAVE US ALL!
OKAY THEN—
WHAT IS IT?
WHY'VE YOU BEEN HERE TWO DAYS IN A ROW?!
IZUMI SURE WASN'T ACTING LIKE HE WANTED TO TALK TO YOU.
Wish I knew what was going on.
.....

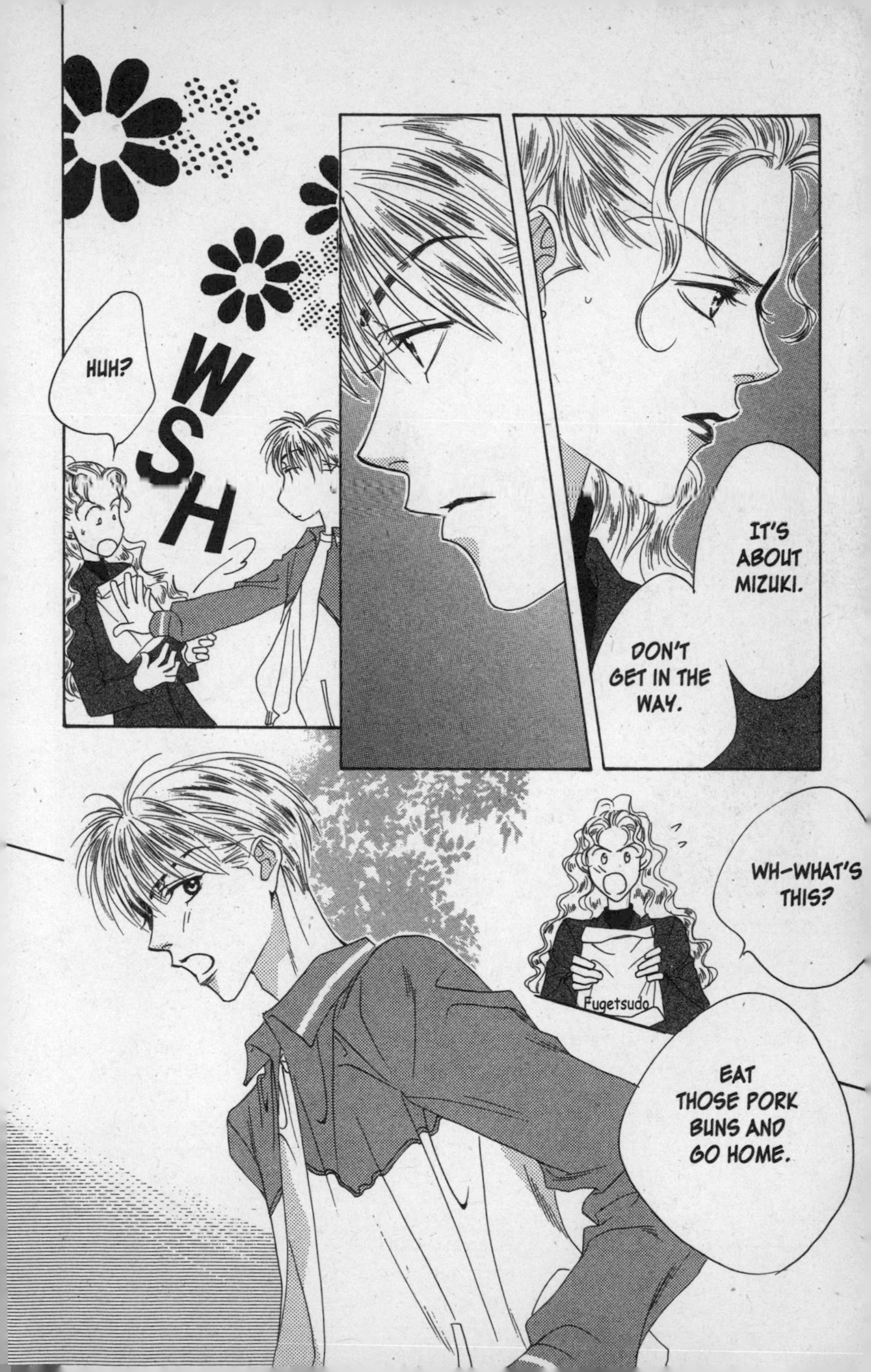
IT'S ABOUT MIZUKI.
DON'T GET IN THE WAY.
HUH?
WSH
WH-WHAT'S THIS?
Fugetsudo
EAT THOSE PORK BUNS AND GO HOME.

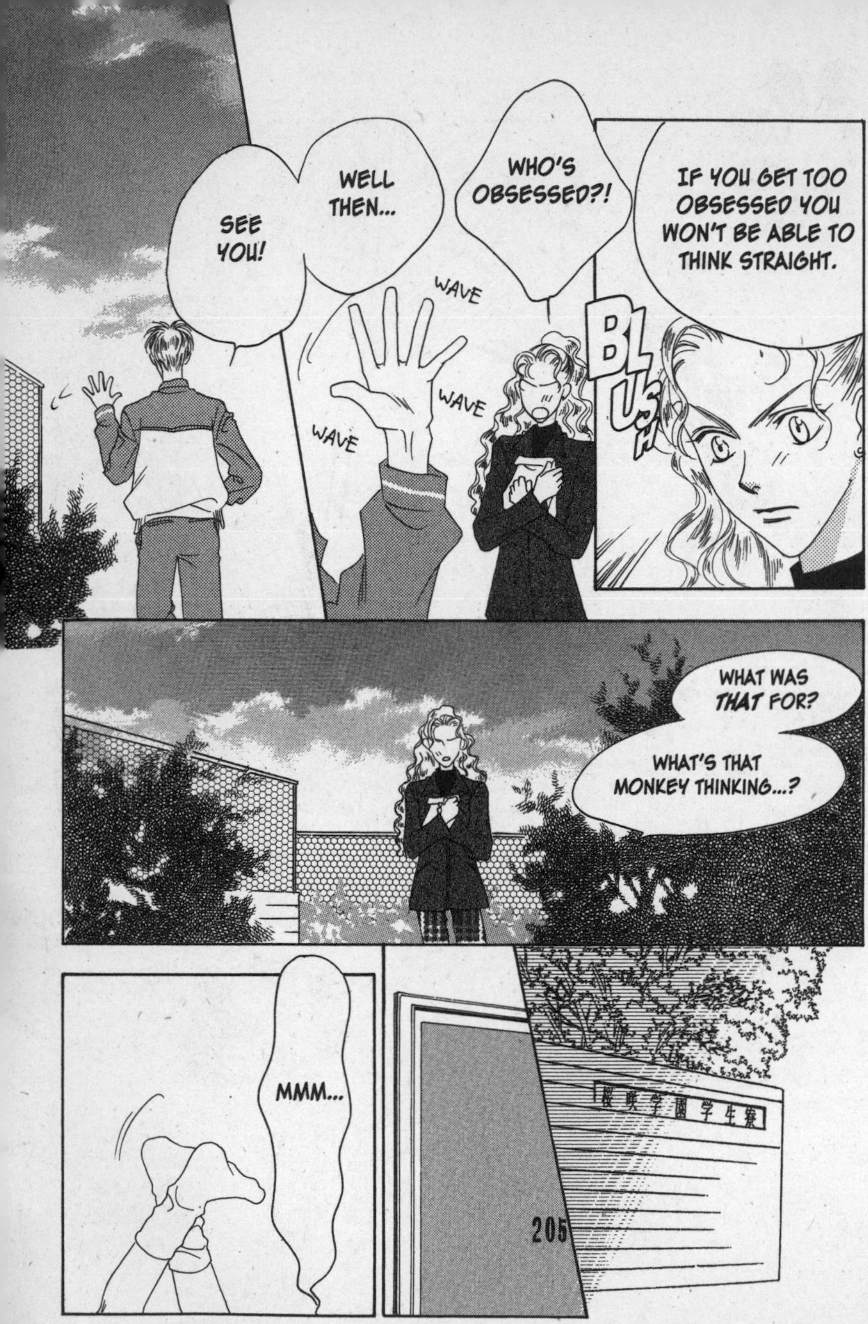
IF YOU GET TOO OBSESSED YOU WON'T BE ABLE TO THINK STRAIGHT.
BLUSH
WHO'S OBSESSED?!
WELL THEN...
WAVE
WAVE
WAVE
SEE YOU!
WHAT WAS *THAT* FOR?
WHAT'S THAT MONKEY THINKING...?
桜咲学園学生寮
205
MMM...

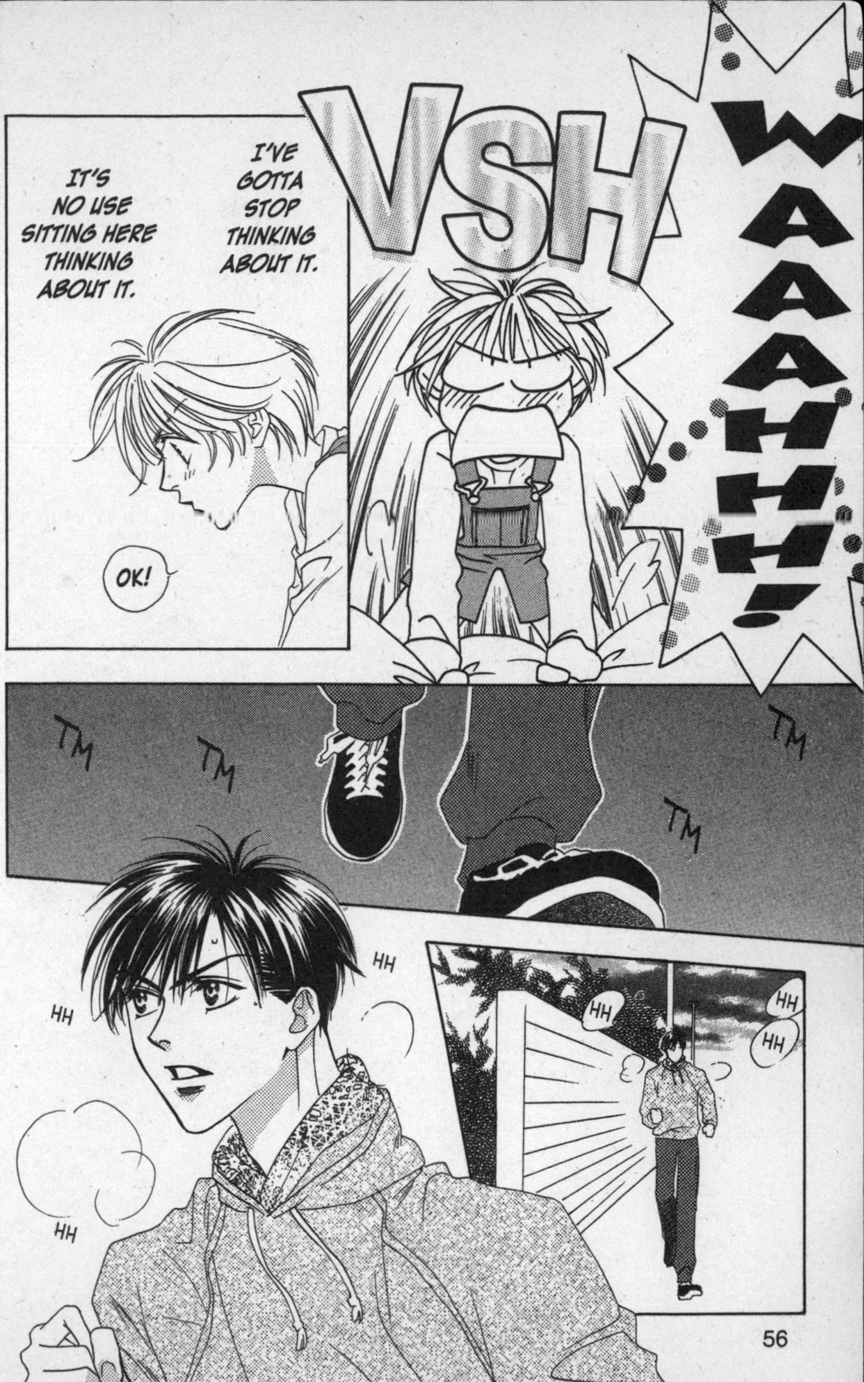
WAAAAHHH!
VSH
I'VE GOTTA STOP THINKING ABOUT IT.
IT'S NO USE SITTING HERE THINKING ABOUT IT.
OK!
TM
TM
TM
TM
HH
HH
HH
HH
HH
HH

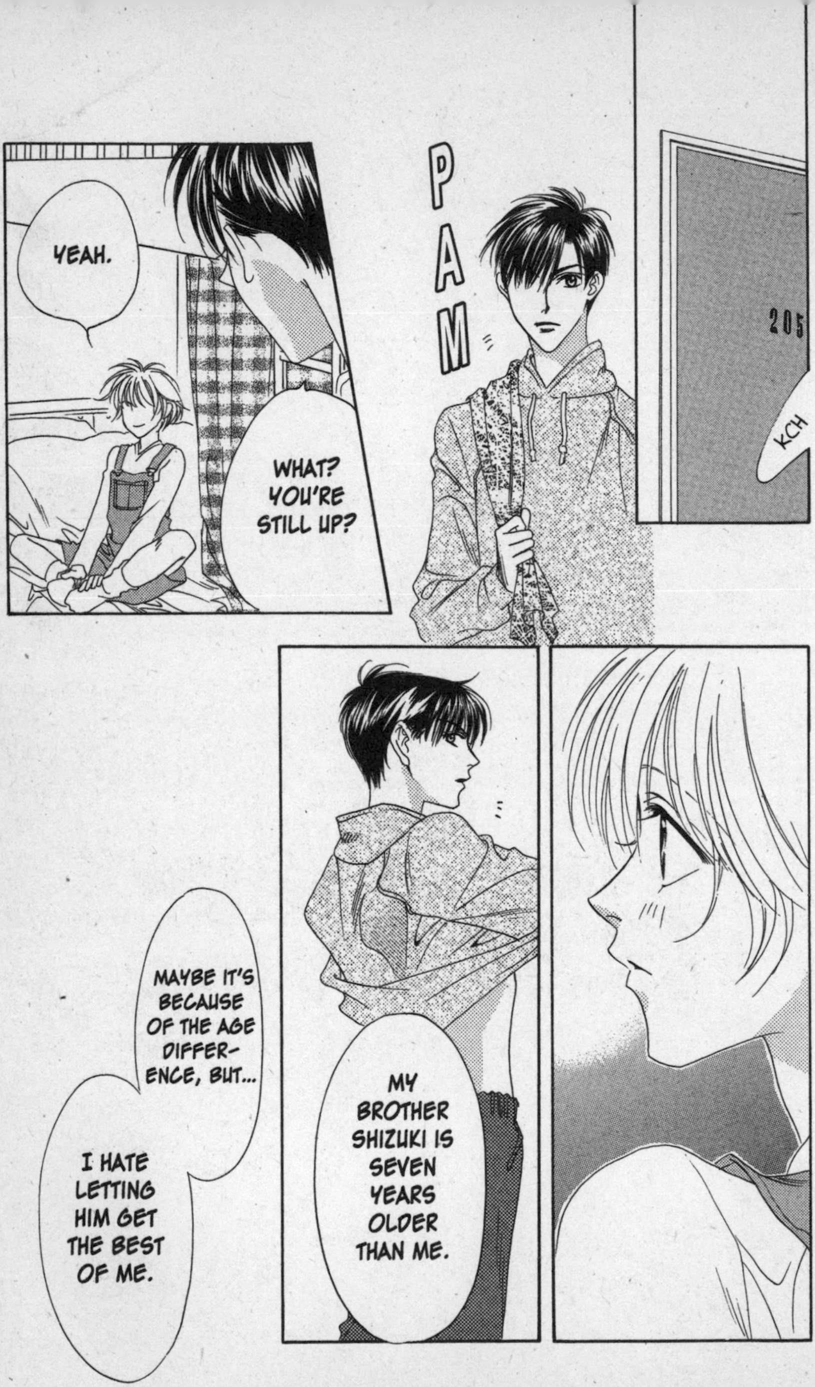
205
KCH
PAM
WHAT? YOU'RE STILL UP?
YEAH.
MY BROTHER SHIZUKI IS SEVEN YEARS OLDER THAN ME.
MAYBE IT'S BECAUSE OF THE AGE DIFFER-ENCE, BUT...
I HATE LETTING HIM GET THE BEST OF ME.

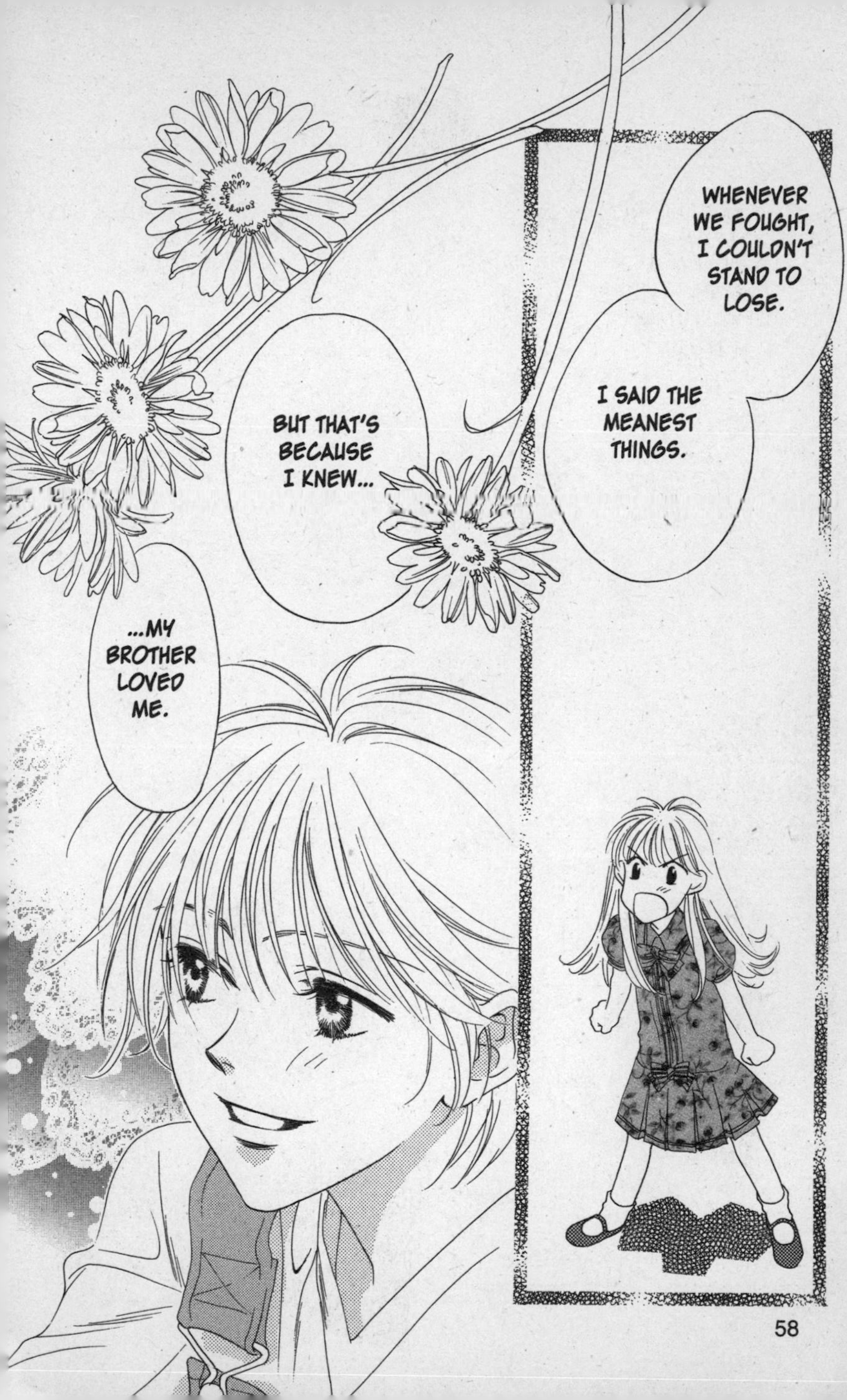
WHENEVER WE FOUGHT, I COULDN'T STAND TO LOSE.
I SAID THE MEANEST THINGS.
BUT THAT'S BECAUSE I KNEW...
...MY BROTHER LOVED ME.

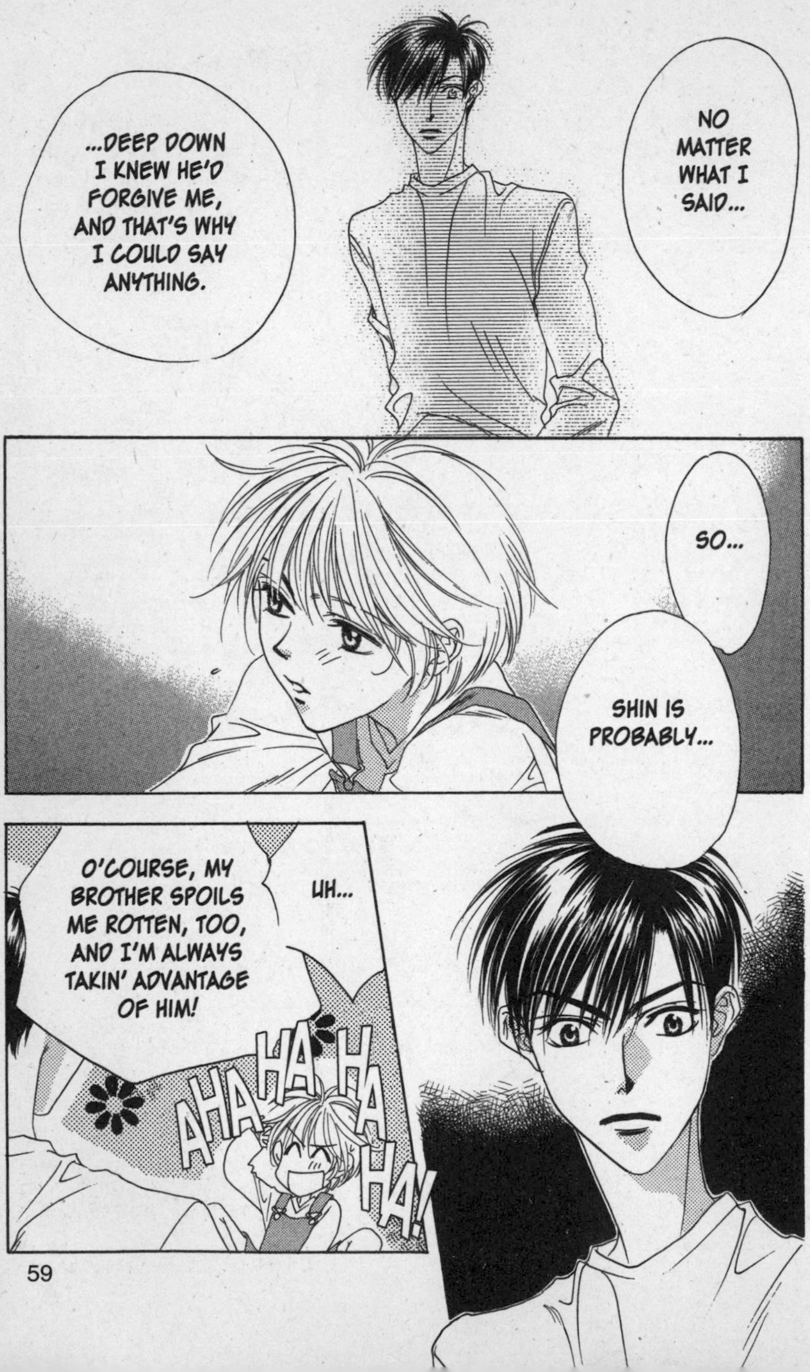
NO MATTER WHAT I SAID...
...DEEP DOWN I KNEW HE'D FORGIVE ME, AND THAT'S WHY I COULD SAY ANYTHING.
SO...
SHIN IS PROBABLY...
UH...
O'COURSE, MY BROTHER SPOILS ME ROTTEN, TOO, AND I'M ALWAYS TAKIN' ADVANTAGE OF HIM!
AHAHAHA HA HA HA!

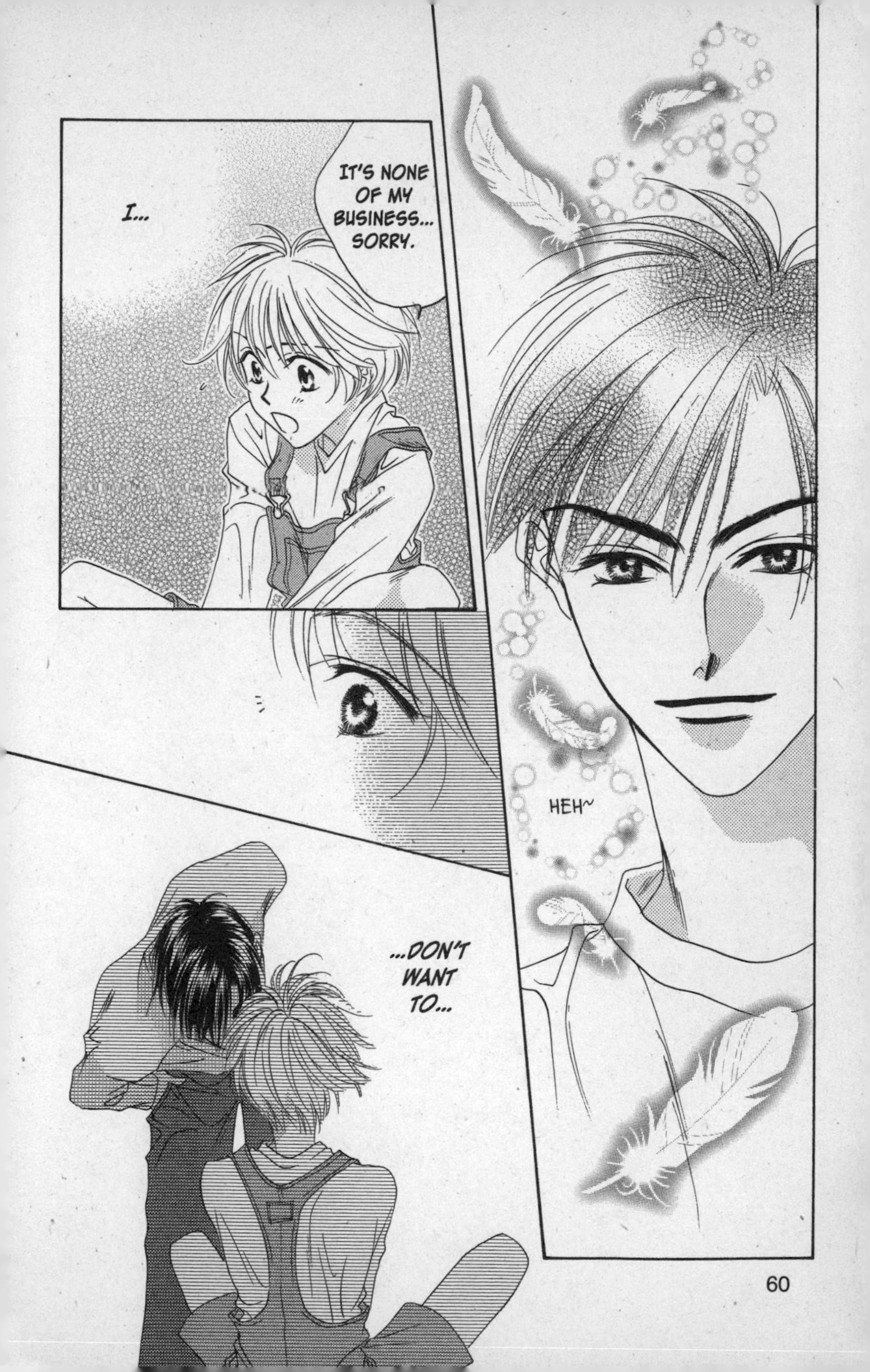
HEH~
IT'S NONE OF MY BUSINESS... SORRY.
I...
...DON'T WANT TO...

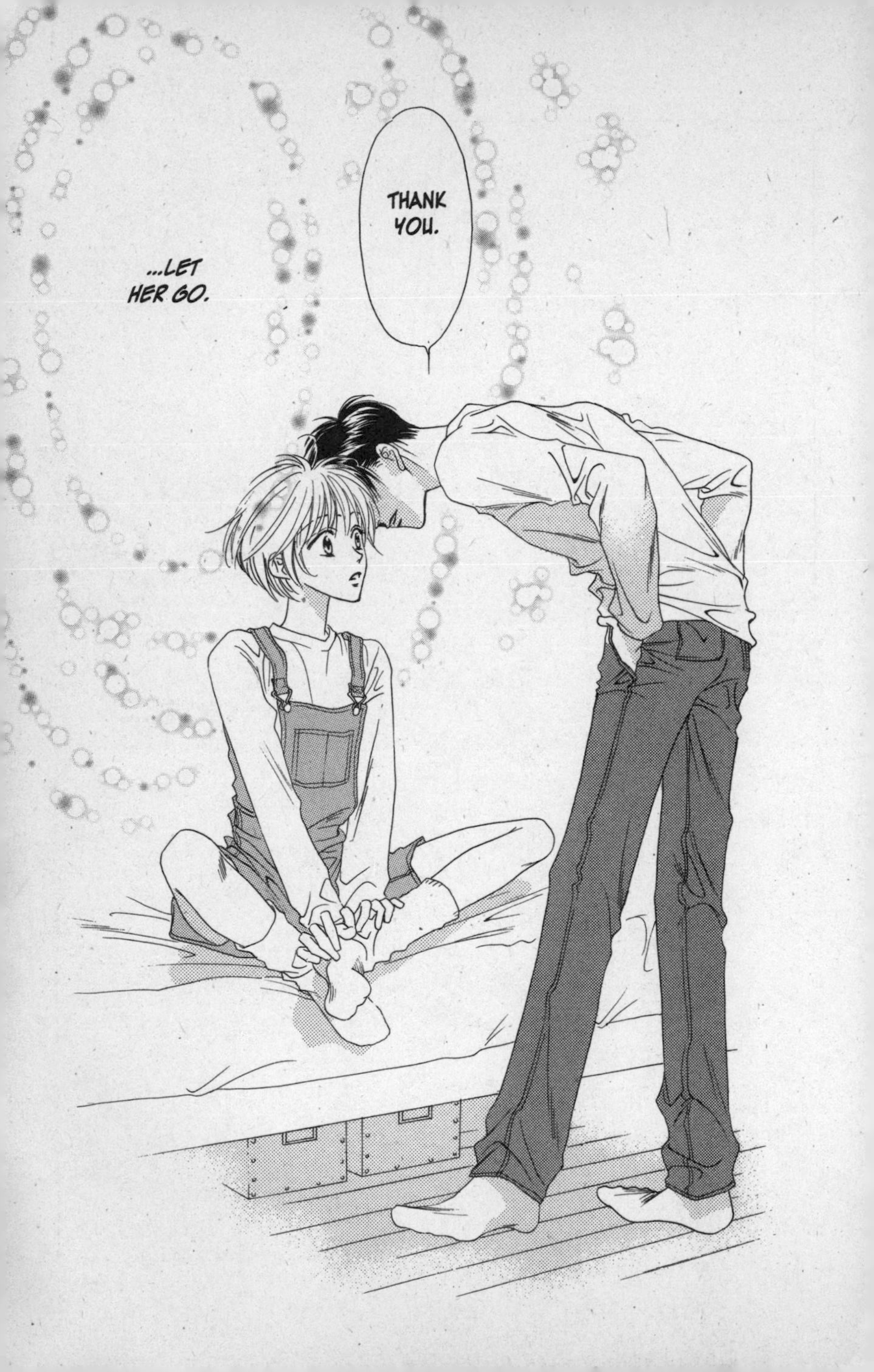
THANK YOU.
...LET HER GO.

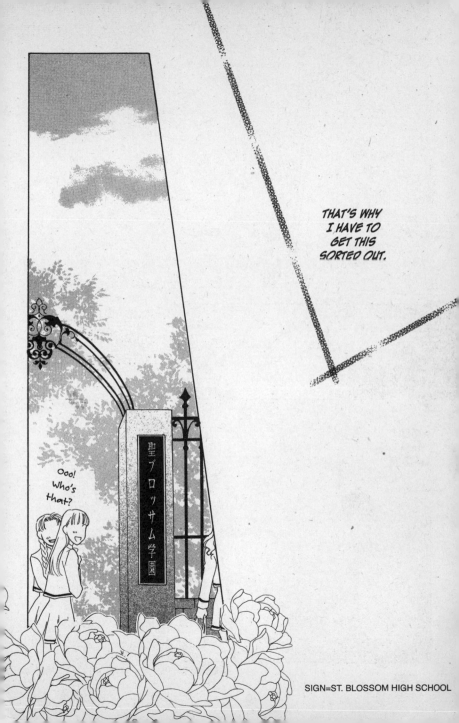

THAT'S WHY I HAVE TO GET THIS SORTED OUT.

Ooo! Who's that?

SIGN=ST. BLOSSOM HIGH SCHOOL

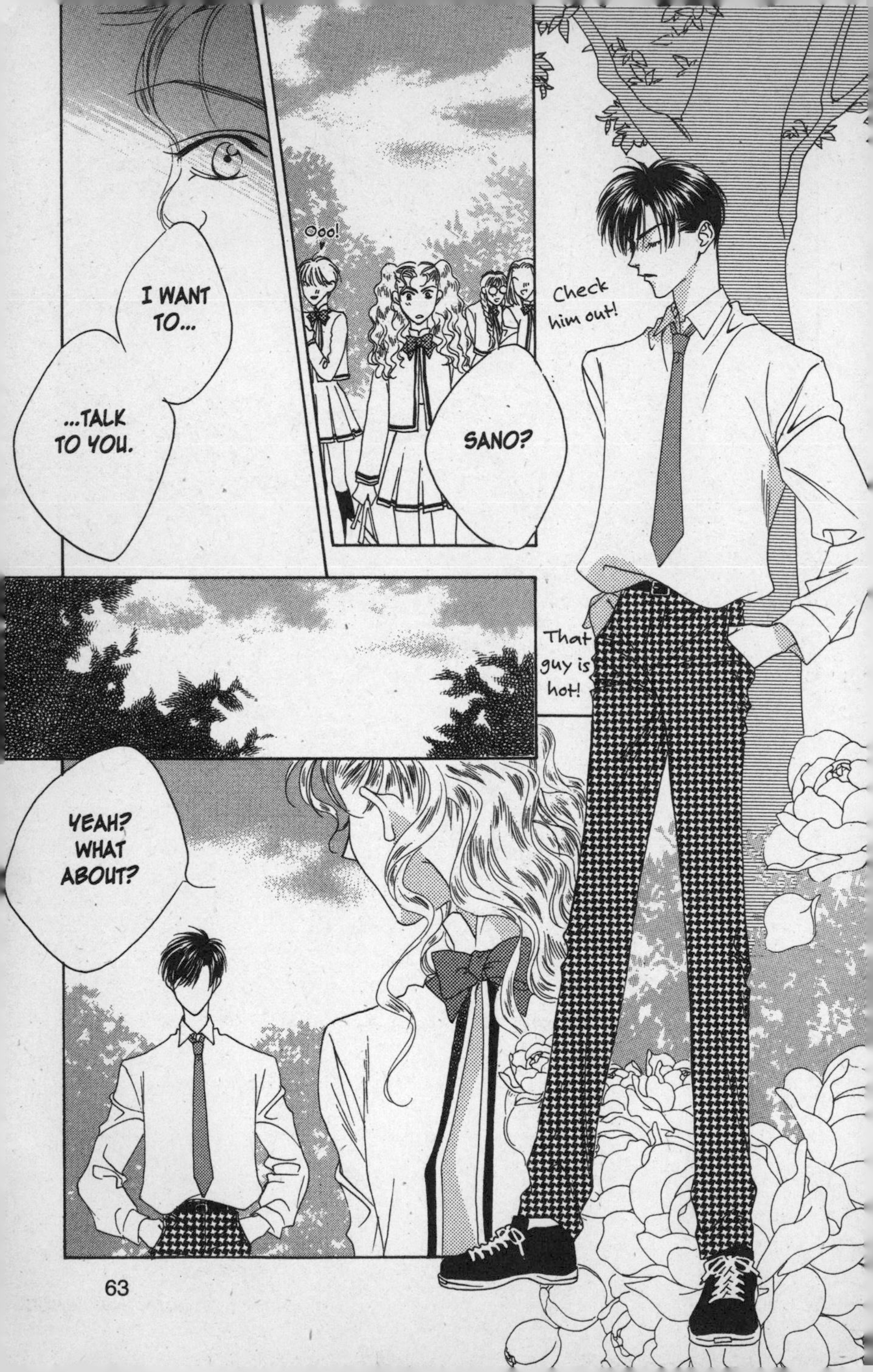
Check him out!
That guy is hot!
Ooo!
SANO?
I WANT TO...
...TALK TO YOU.
YEAH? WHAT ABOUT?

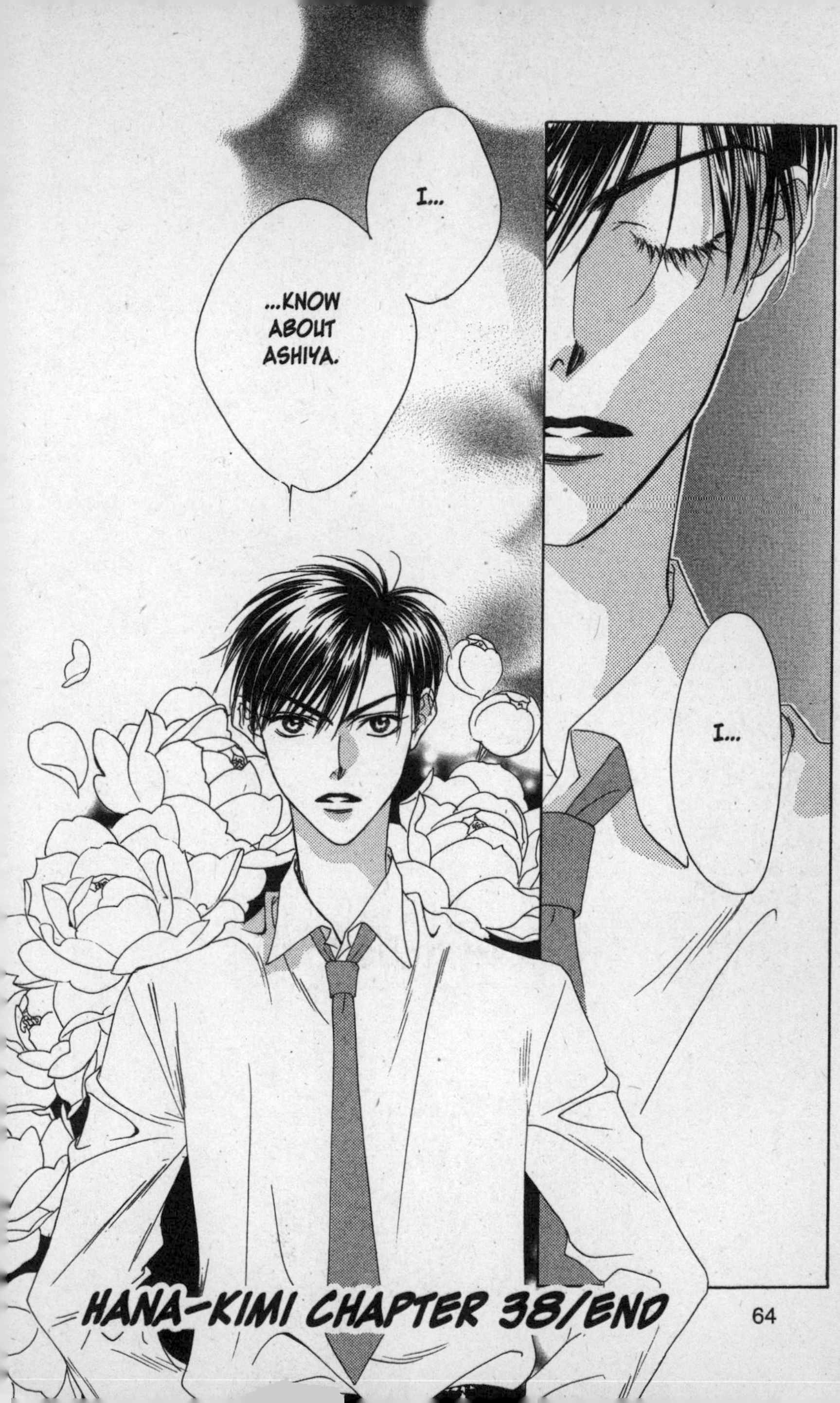
I...
I...
...KNOW ABOUT ASHIYA.
HANA-KIMI CHAPTER 38/END

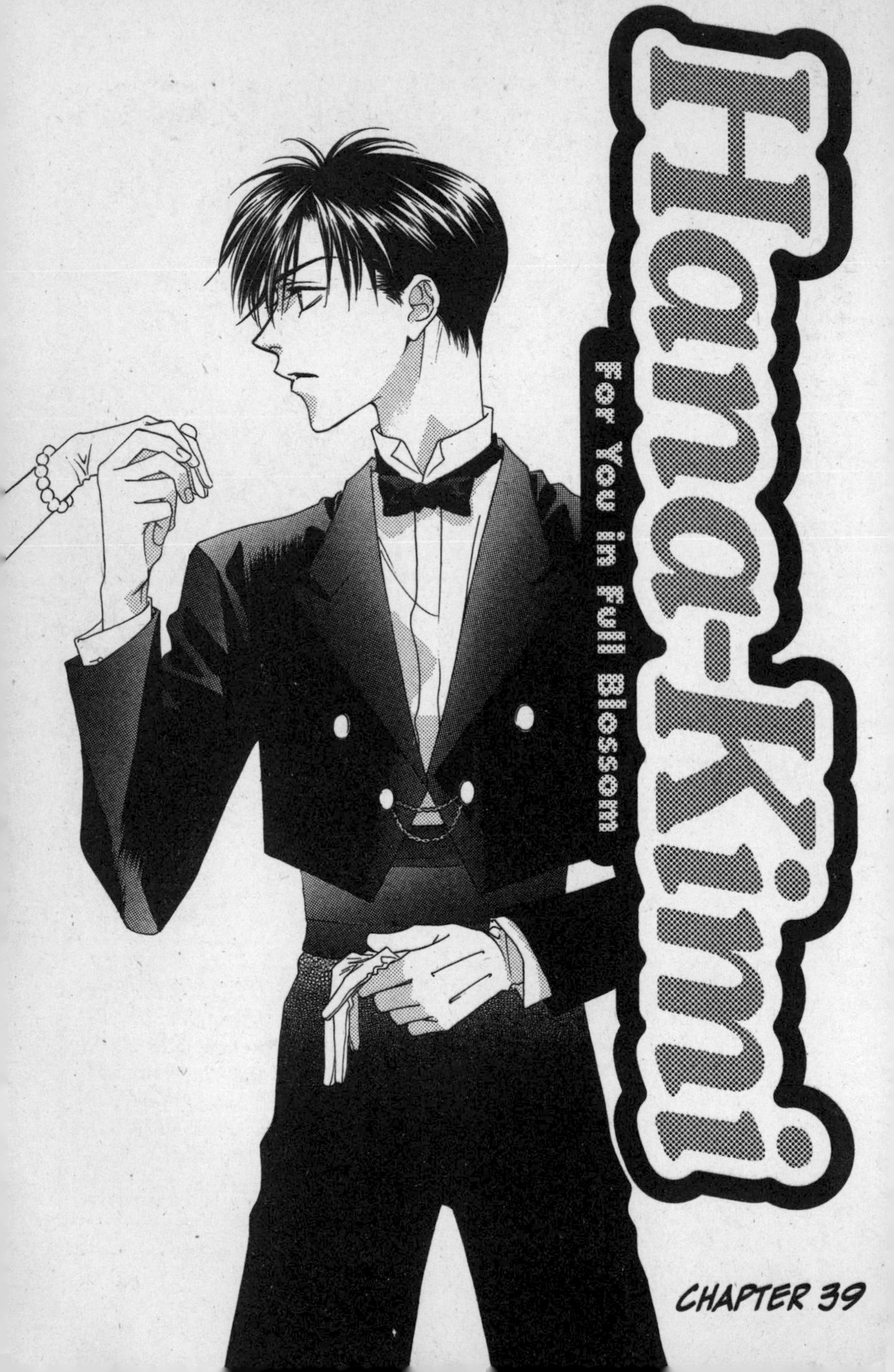
Hana-Kimi
For You in Full Blossom
CHAPTER 39

YOU KNOW?

SHIKI (Part 2)

I'M GLAD I DIDN'T KNOW THE SECRET. I HIGHLY RECOMMEND THESE BOOKS!

ALTHOUGH THEY'RE KIND OF EXPENSIVE...

IF I TELL YOU WHAT HAPPENS IT'LL RUIN IT, SO I WON'T...BUT THERE MIGHT BE A FEW PEOPLE OUT THERE WHO UNDERSTAND THE MEANING OF "SHIKI." I DIDN'T KNOW MYSELF UNTIL A HINT CAME UP IN A CONVERSATION IN THE BOOK. (HEH-HEH!) HINT: IT'S SIMILAR TO WHAT HAPPENS IN THE MOVIE "LOST BOYS."

SEISHIN --SON OF A TEMPLE PRIEST
TOSHIO -- YOUNG DOCTOR AT A CLINIC
SORRY...DRAWINGS ARE BASED ON MY OWN IDEAS.

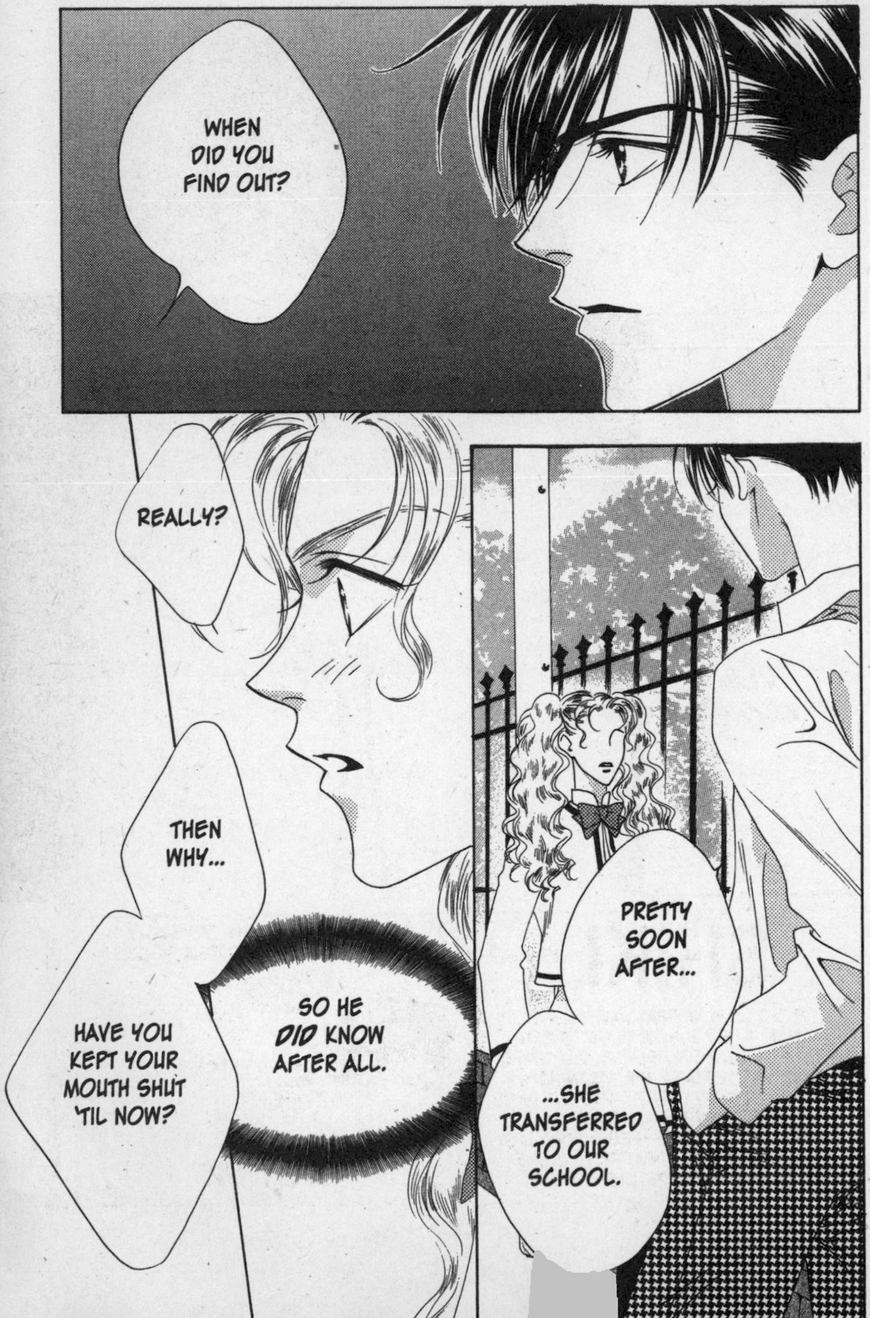
WHEN DID YOU FIND OUT?
PRETTY SOON AFTER...
...SHE TRANSFERRED TO OUR SCHOOL.
REALLY?
THEN WHY...
HAVE YOU KEPT YOUR MOUTH SHUT 'TIL NOW?
SO HE *DID* KNOW AFTER ALL.

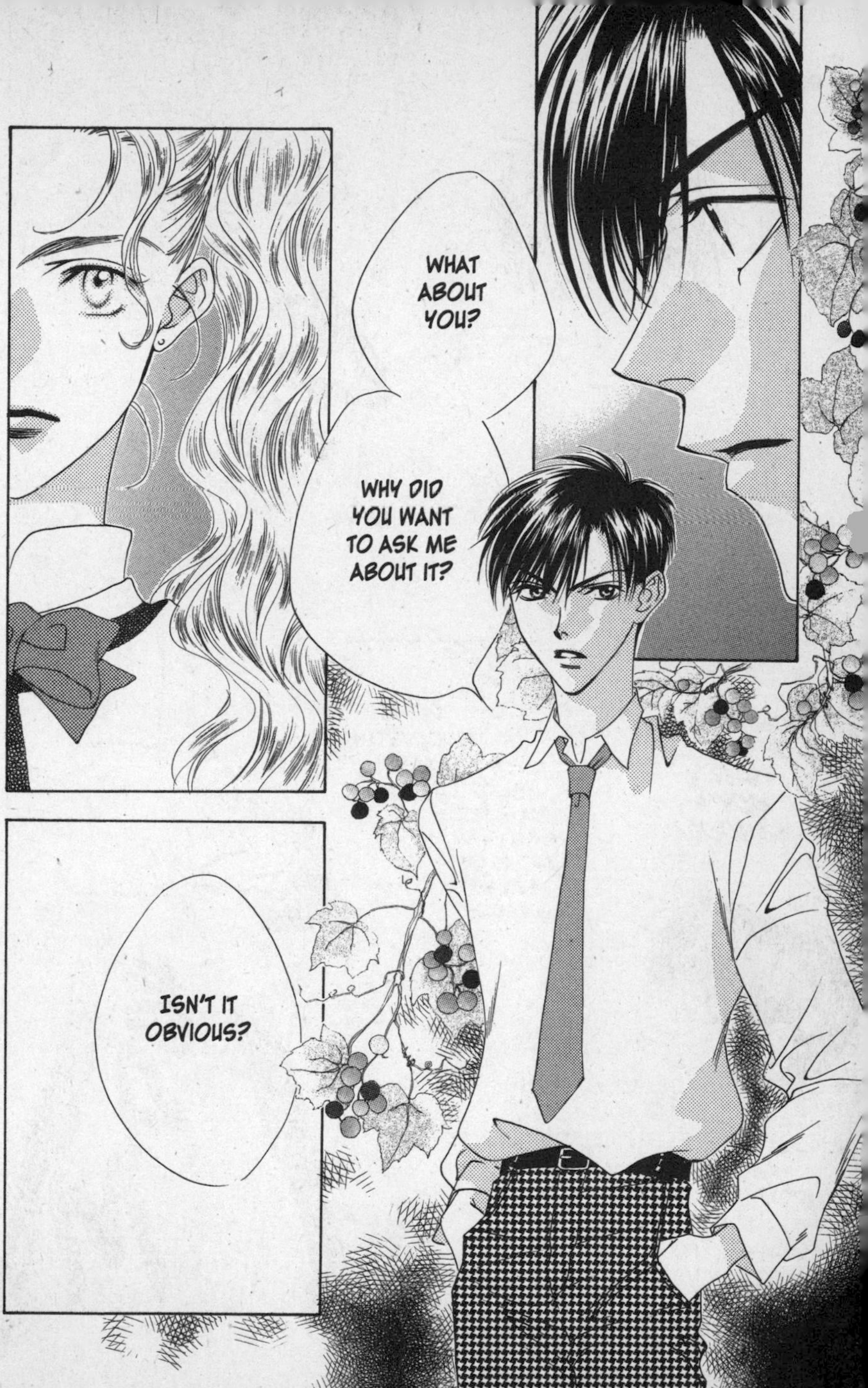
WHAT ABOUT YOU?
WHY DID YOU WANT TO ASK ME ABOUT IT?
ISN'T IT OBVIOUS?

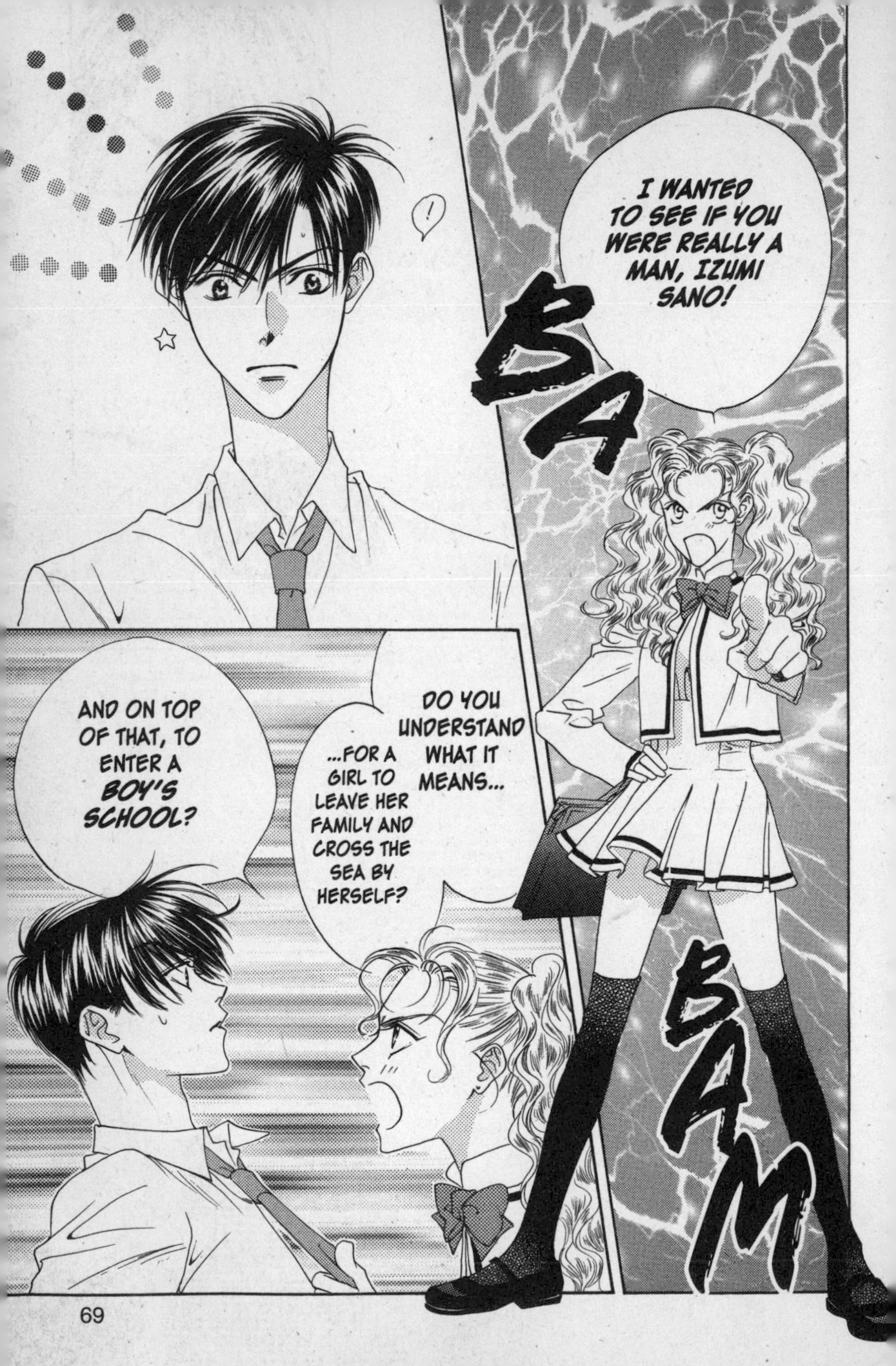
I WANTED TO SEE IF YOU WERE REALLY A MAN, IZUMI SANO!
BA
!
DO YOU UNDERSTAND WHAT IT MEANS...
...FOR A GIRL TO LEAVE HER FAMILY AND CROSS THE SEA BY HERSELF?
AND ON TOP OF THAT, TO ENTER A *BOY'S SCHOOL*?
BAM

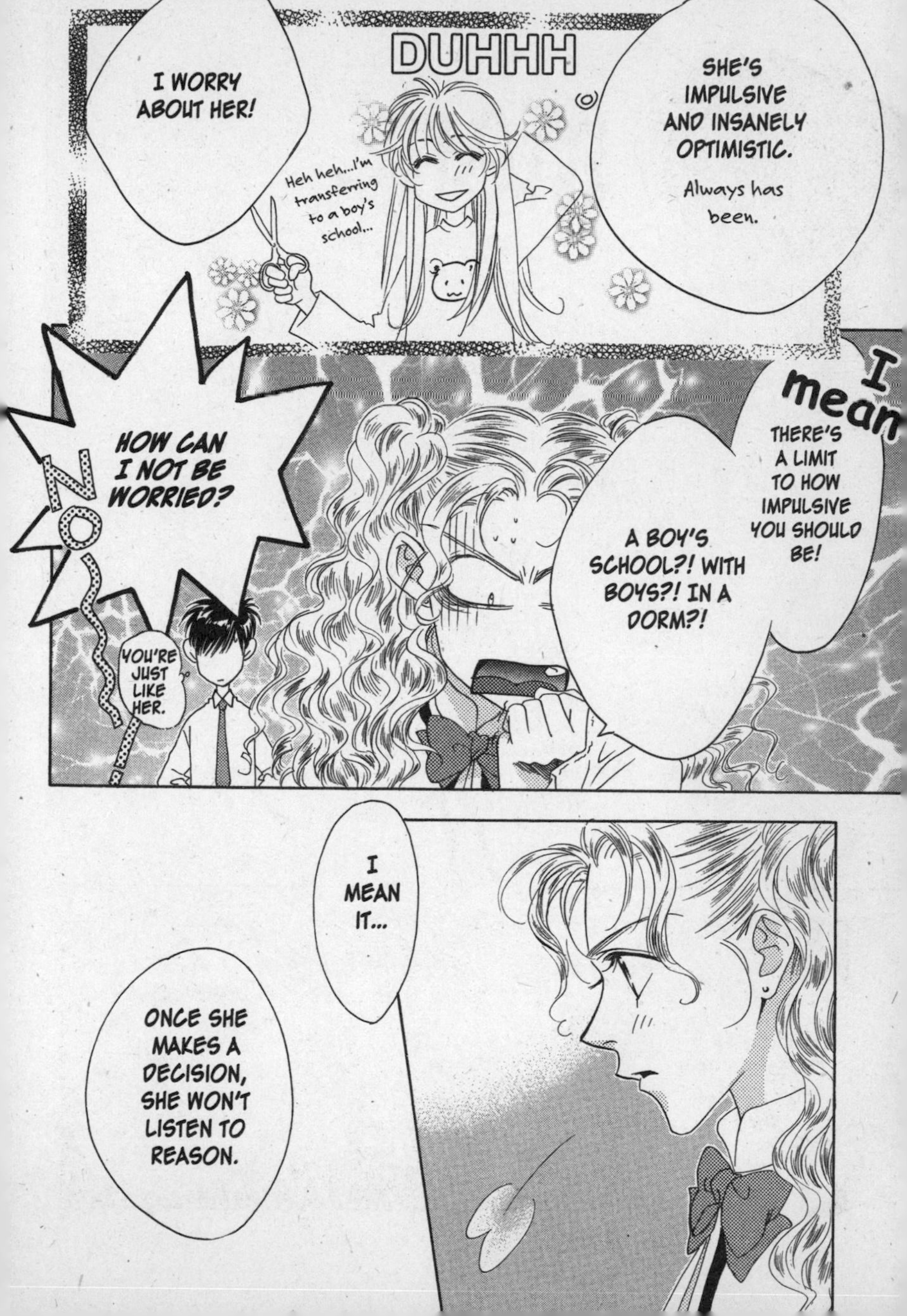
SHE'S IMPULSIVE AND INSANELY OPTIMISTIC.
Always has been.
DUHHH
I WORRY ABOUT HER!
Heh heh...I'm transferring to a boy's school...
I mean
THERE'S A LIMIT TO HOW IMPULSIVE YOU SHOULD BE!
A BOY'S SCHOOL?! WITH BOYS?! IN A DORM?!
HOW CAN I NOT BE WORRIED?
YOU'RE JUST LIKE HER.
I MEAN IT...
ONCE SHE MAKES A DECISION, SHE WON'T LISTEN TO REASON.

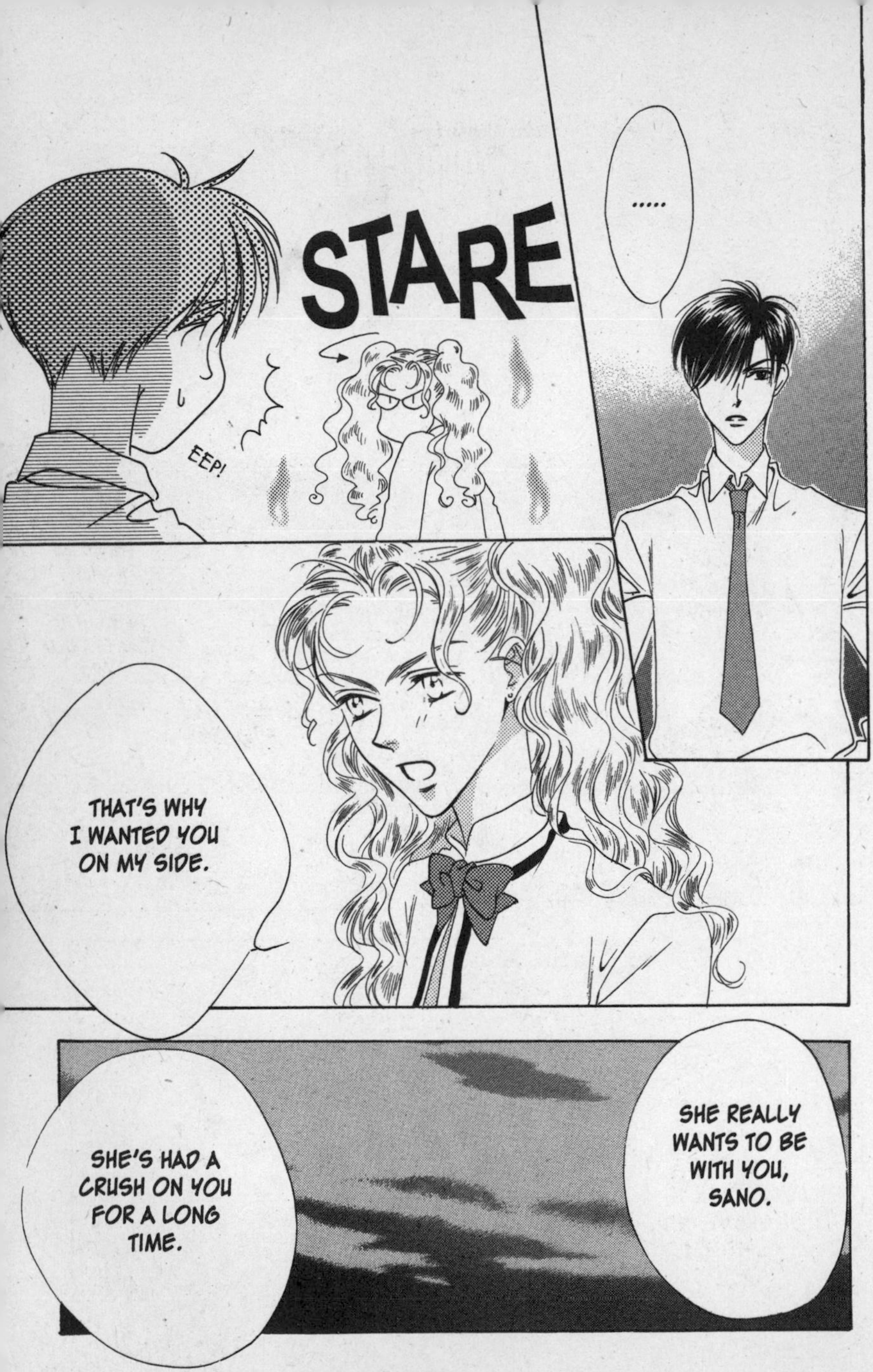
.....
STARE
EEP!
THAT'S WHY I WANTED YOU ON MY SIDE.
SHE REALLY WANTS TO BE WITH YOU, SANO.
SHE'S HAD A CRUSH ON YOU FOR A LONG TIME.

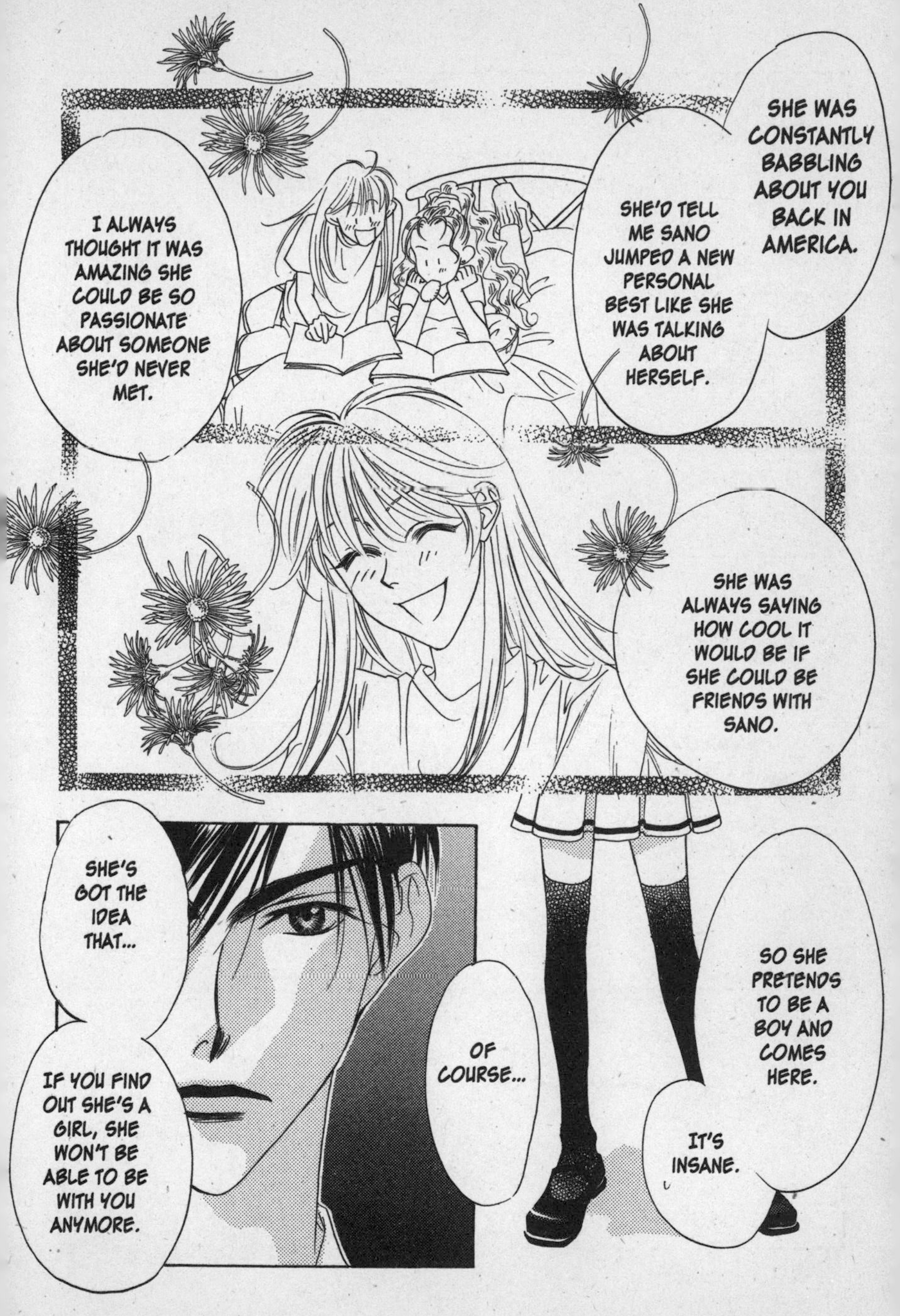
SHE WAS CONSTANTLY BABBLING ABOUT YOU BACK IN AMERICA.
SHE'D TELL ME SANO JUMPED A NEW PERSONAL BEST LIKE SHE WAS TALKING ABOUT HERSELF.
I ALWAYS THOUGHT IT WAS AMAZING SHE COULD BE SO PASSIONATE ABOUT SOMEONE SHE'D NEVER MET.
SHE WAS ALWAYS SAYING HOW COOL IT WOULD BE IF SHE COULD BE FRIENDS WITH SANO.
SO SHE PRETENDS TO BE A BOY AND COMES HERE.
IT'S INSANE.
OF COURSE...
SHE'S GOT THE IDEA THAT...
IF YOU FIND OUT SHE'S A GIRL, SHE WON'T BE ABLE TO BE WITH YOU ANYMORE.

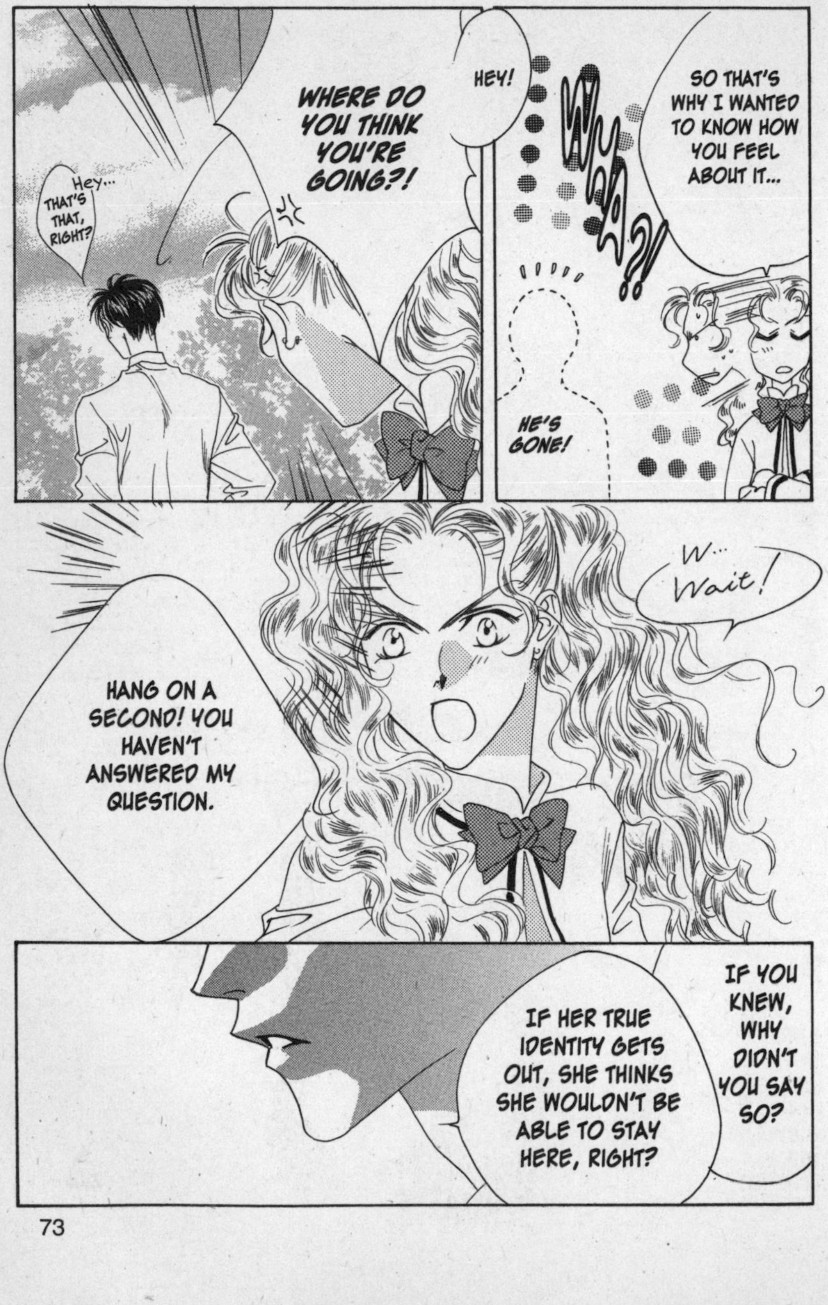

SO THAT'S WHY I WANTED TO KNOW HOW YOU FEEL ABOUT IT...
HE'S GONE!
HEY!
WHERE DO YOU THINK YOU'RE GOING?!
Hey... THAT'S THAT, RIGHT?
W... Wait!
HANG ON A SECOND! YOU HAVEN'T ANSWERED MY QUESTION.
IF YOU KNEW, WHY DIDN'T YOU SAY SO?
IF HER TRUE IDENTITY GETS OUT, SHE THINKS SHE WOULDN'T BE ABLE TO STAY HERE, RIGHT?

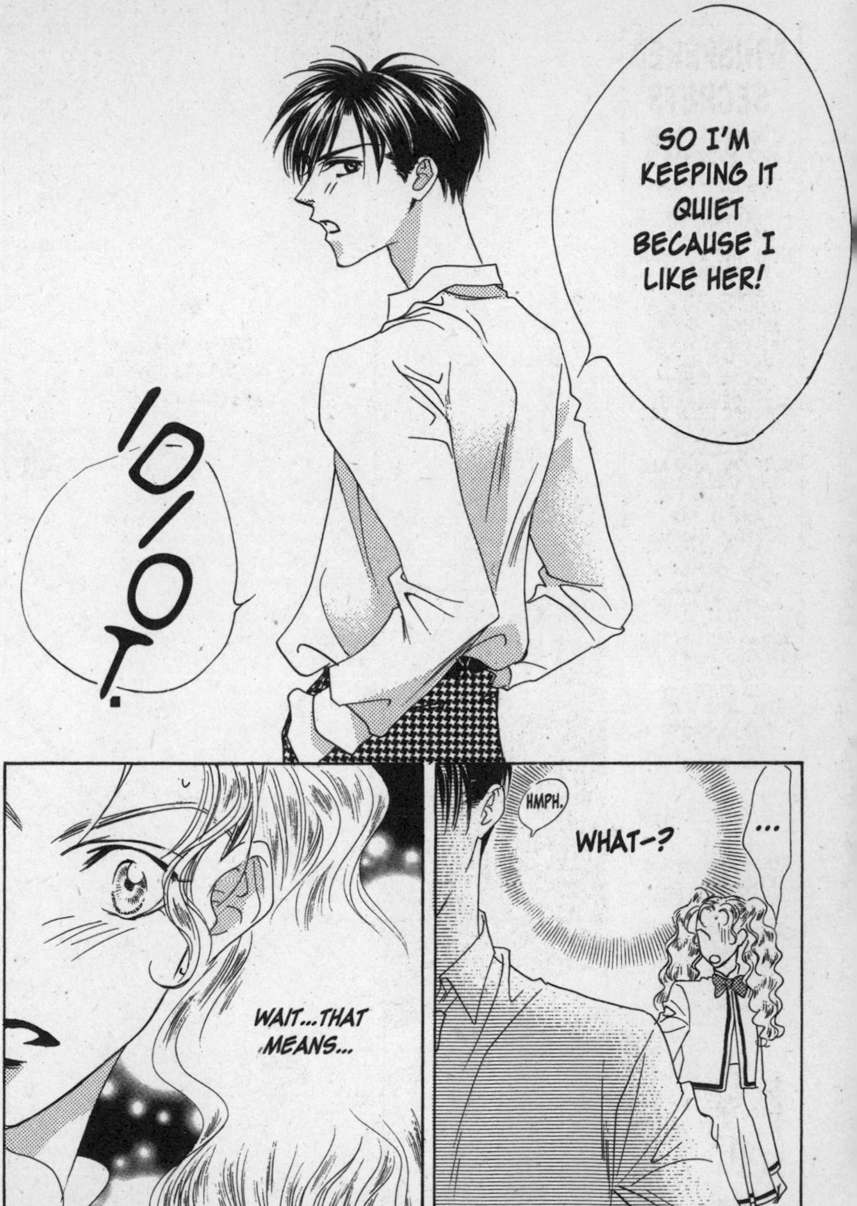
SO I'M KEEPING IT QUIET BECAUSE I LIKE HER!
IDIOT.
...
HMPH.
WHAT-?
WAIT...THAT MEANS...

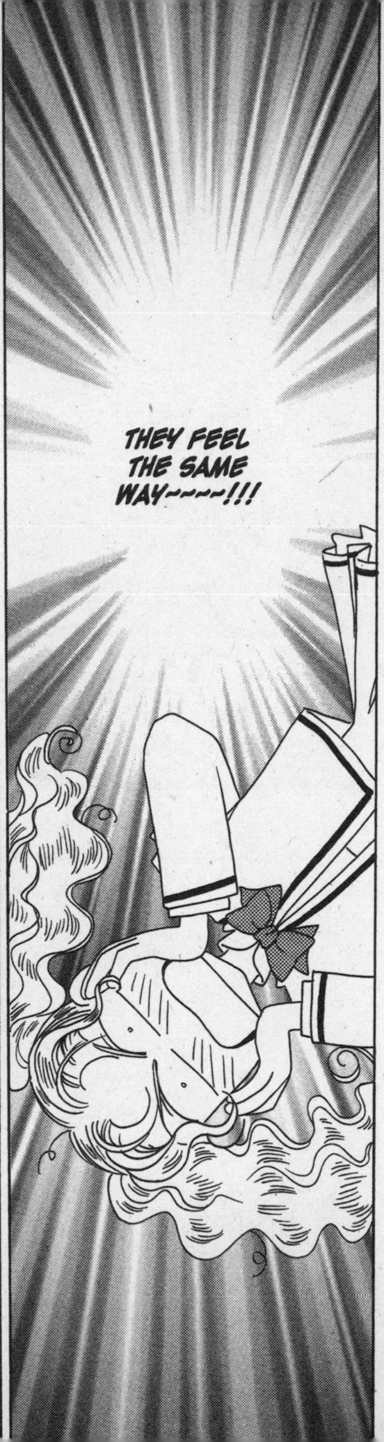
THEY FEEL THE SAME WAY~~~~!!!

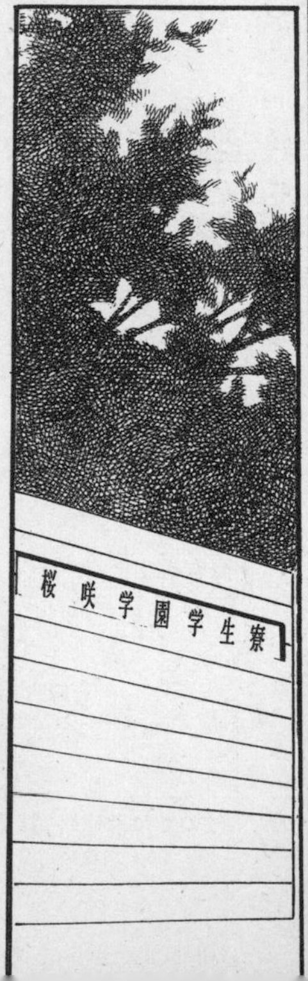
「桜咲学園学生寮」

WHISPERED SECRETS

(WELCOME TO KOREA)

IT'S OUT! FIRST CAME THE TAIWANESE VERSION AND NOW THE KOREAN VERSION OF "HANA-KIMI"! YAHOO! AS OF MARCH, 1999, THE FIRST THREE BOOKS HAVE BEEN PUBLISHED. IT'S BIGGER THAN THE JAPANESE TANKOBON EDITION, AND ALL THE DIALOGUE AND EFFECTS ARE IN THE KOREAN HANGUL ALPHABET. (OBVIOUSLY.) THE HANGUL CHARACTERS ARE THE MOST ADVANCED IN THE WORLD WHEN IT COMES TO EXPRESSING SPECIFIC PRONUNCIATIONS. THE TITLE IN KOREAN IS:

「아름디운 그대애 게」

INTERESTINGLY ENOUGH, THE LOVE SCENES AND SEXY SHOTS, WHETHER OF MEN OR WOMEN, ARE CENSORED IN KOREA.

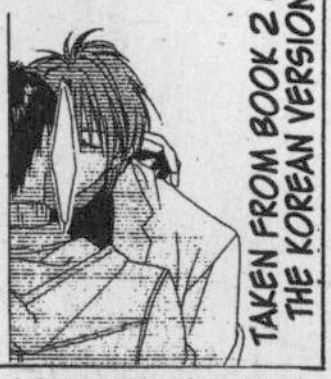

TAKEN FROM BOOK 2 OF THE KOREAN VERSION.

COMPARE THIS WITH YOUR OWN BOOK 2! (HEE!)

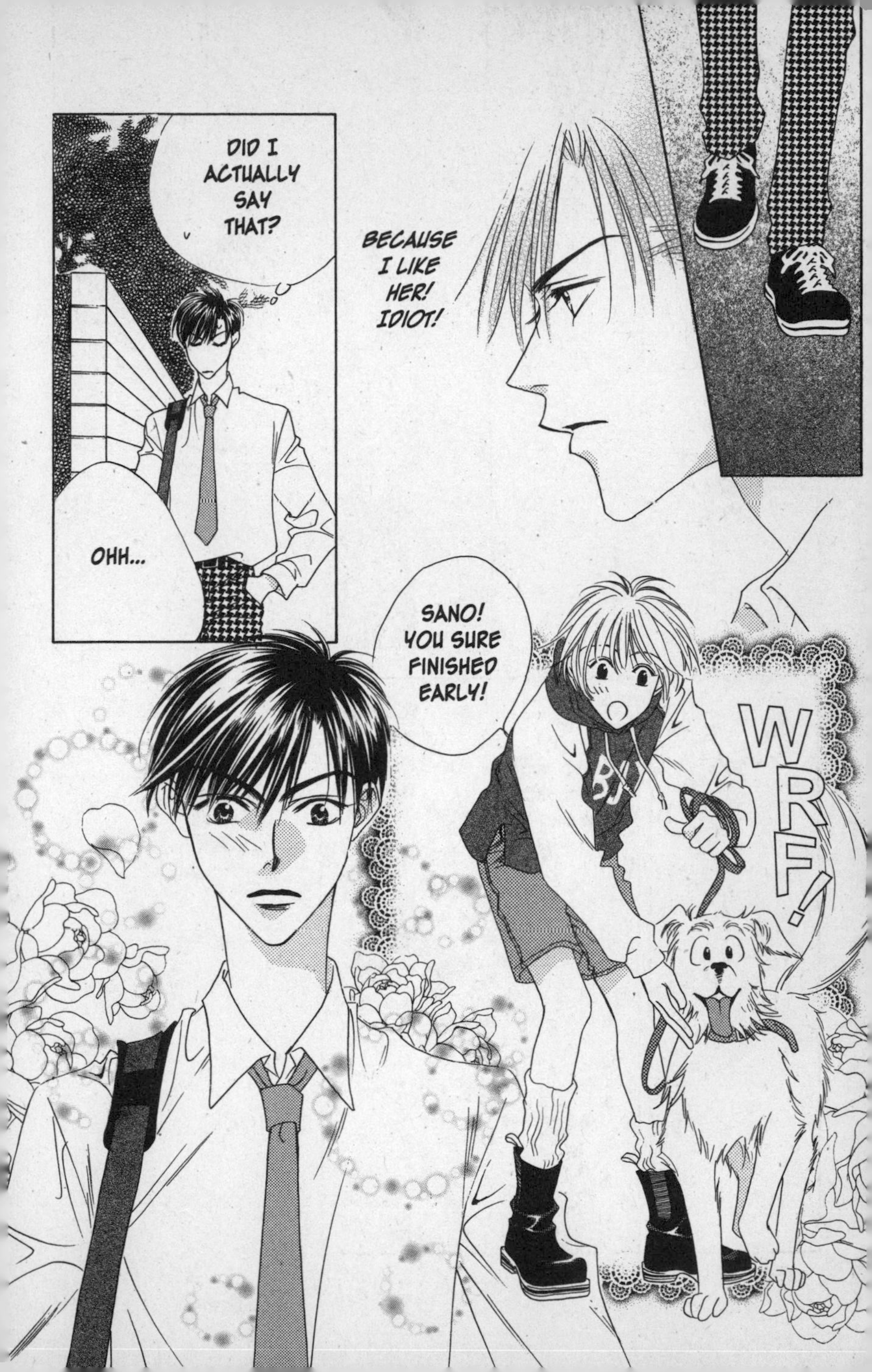
BECAUSE I LIKE HER! IDIOT!
DID I ACTUALLY SAY THAT?
OHH...
WRF!
SANO! YOU SURE FINISHED EARLY!

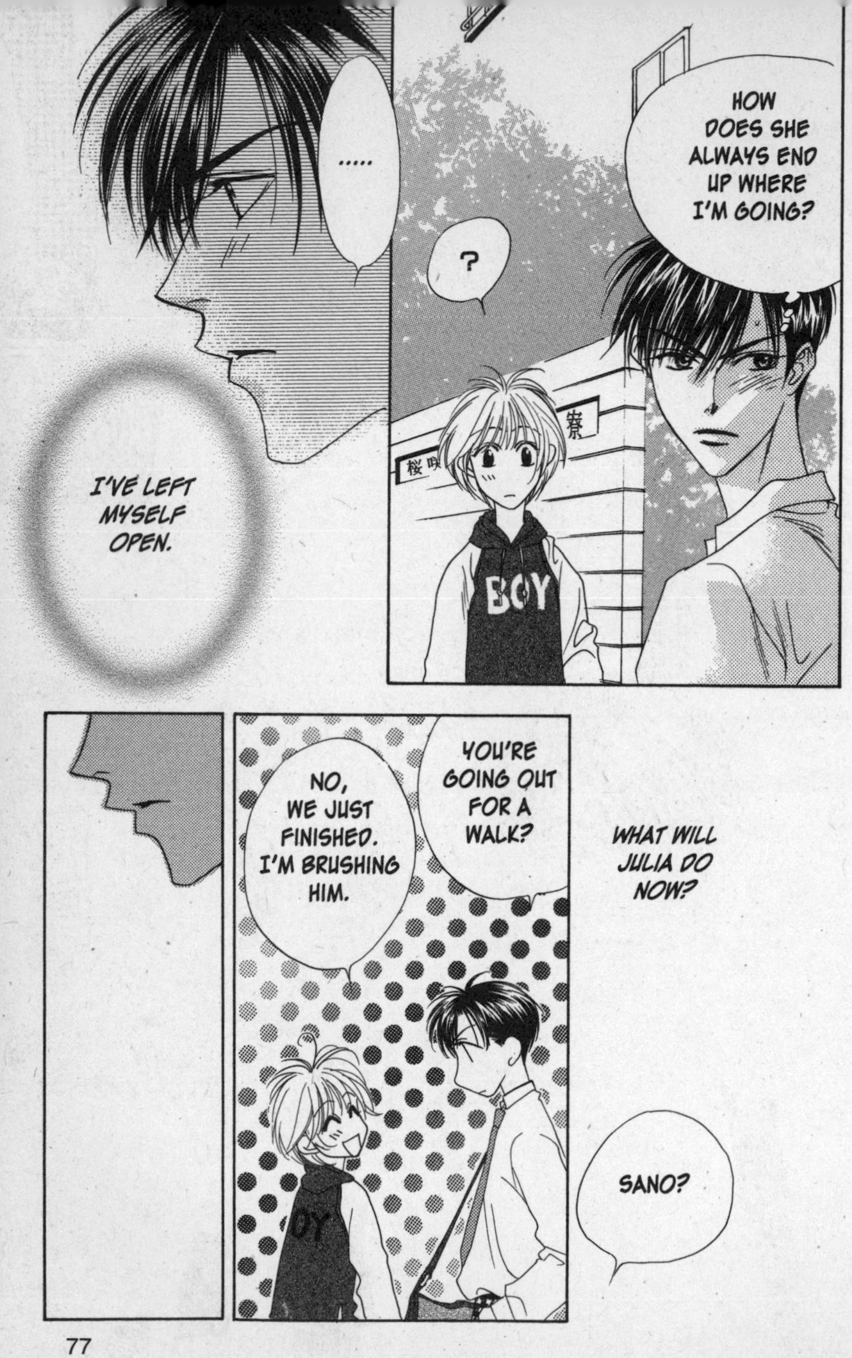
HOW DOES SHE ALWAYS END UP WHERE I'M GOING?
?
.....
I'VE LEFT MYSELF OPEN.
WHAT WILL JULIA DO NOW?
SANO?
YOU'RE GOING OUT FOR A WALK?
NO, WE JUST FINISHED. I'M BRUSHING HIM.

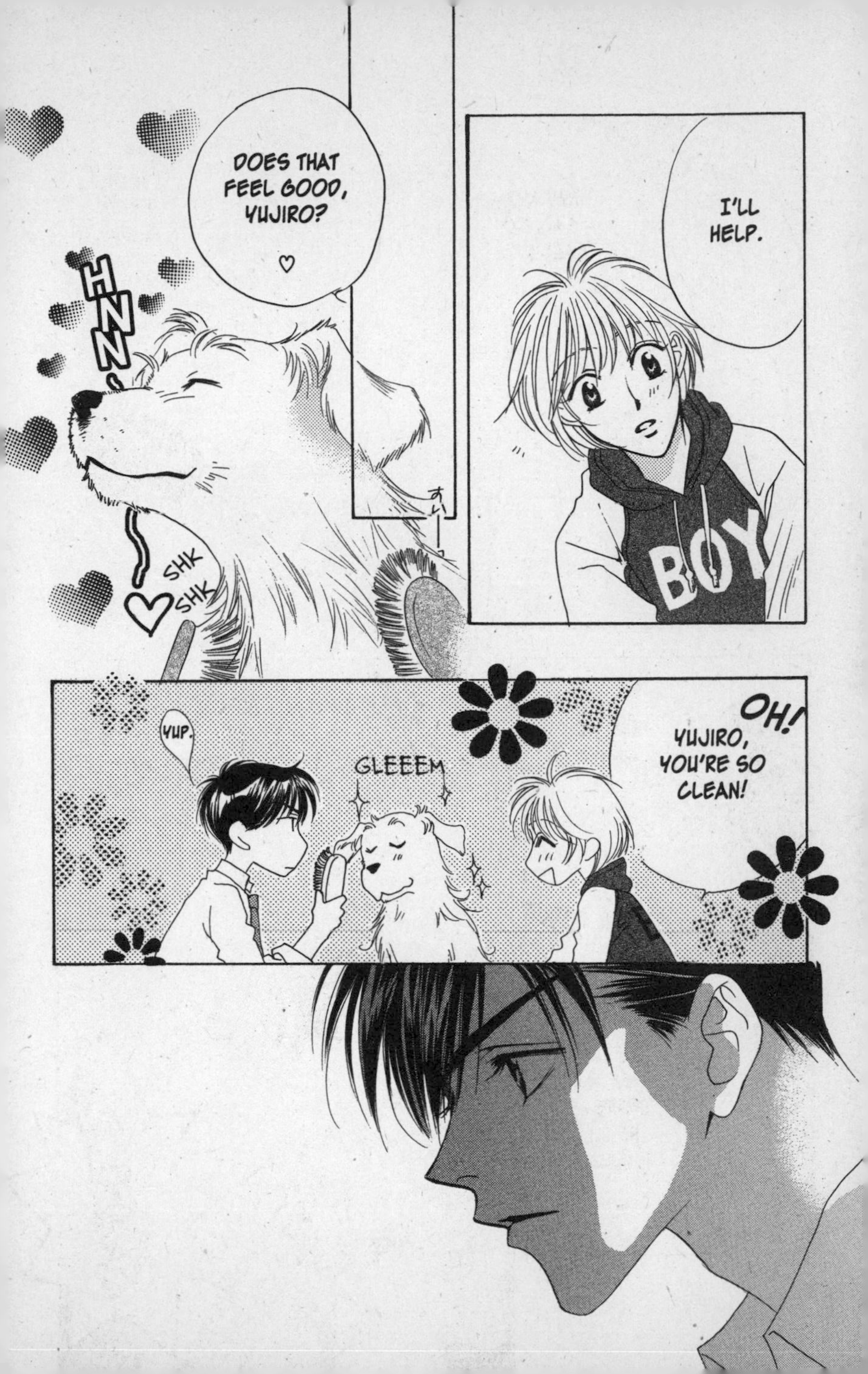
I'LL HELP.
DOES THAT FEEL GOOD, YUJIRO? ♡
HNN
SHK SHK
OH! YUJIRO, YOU'RE SO CLEAN!
GLEEEM
YUP.

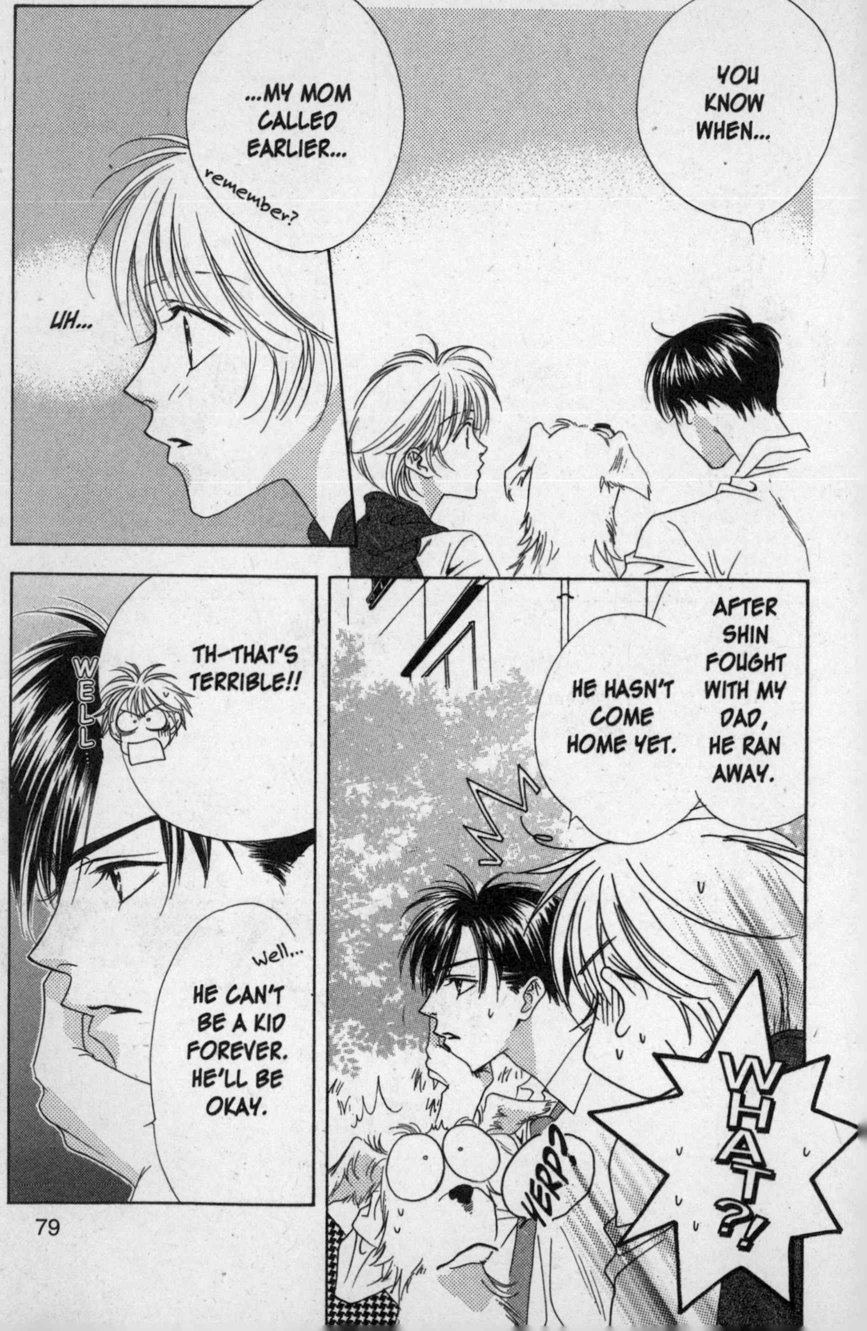
YOU KNOW WHEN...
...MY MOM CALLED EARLIER...
remember?
UH...
AFTER SHIN FOUGHT WITH MY DAD, HE RAN AWAY.
HE HASN'T COME HOME YET.
WHAT?!
YERP?
TH-THAT'S TERRIBLE!!
WELL...
well...
HE CAN'T BE A KID FOREVER. HE'LL BE OKAY.

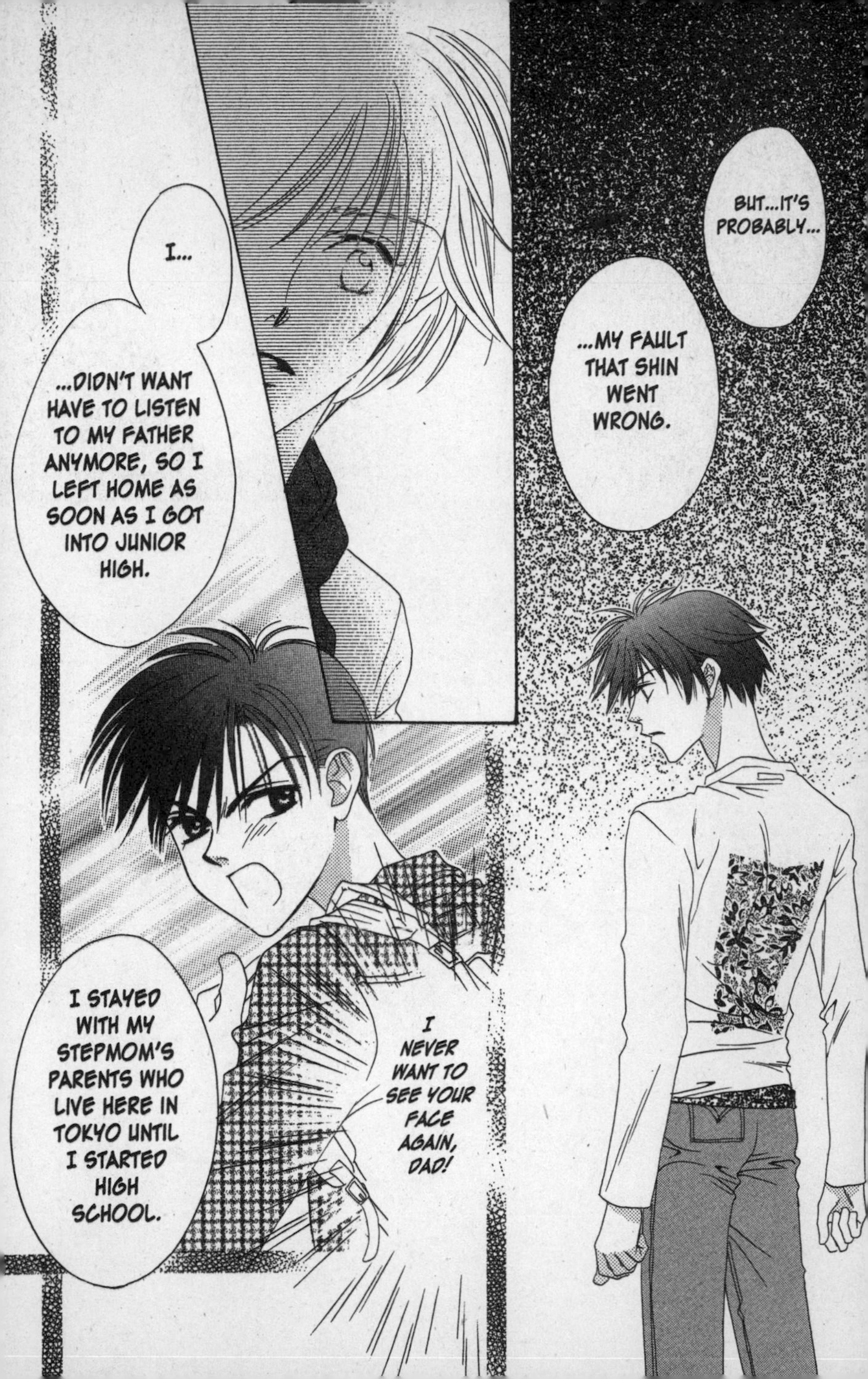
BUT...IT'S PROBABLY...
...MY FAULT THAT SHIN WENT WRONG.
I...
...DIDN'T WANT HAVE TO LISTEN TO MY FATHER ANYMORE, SO I LEFT HOME AS SOON AS I GOT INTO JUNIOR HIGH.
I NEVER WANT TO SEE YOUR FACE AGAIN, DAD!
I STAYED WITH MY STEPMOM'S PARENTS WHO LIVE HERE IN TOKYO UNTIL I STARTED HIGH SCHOOL.

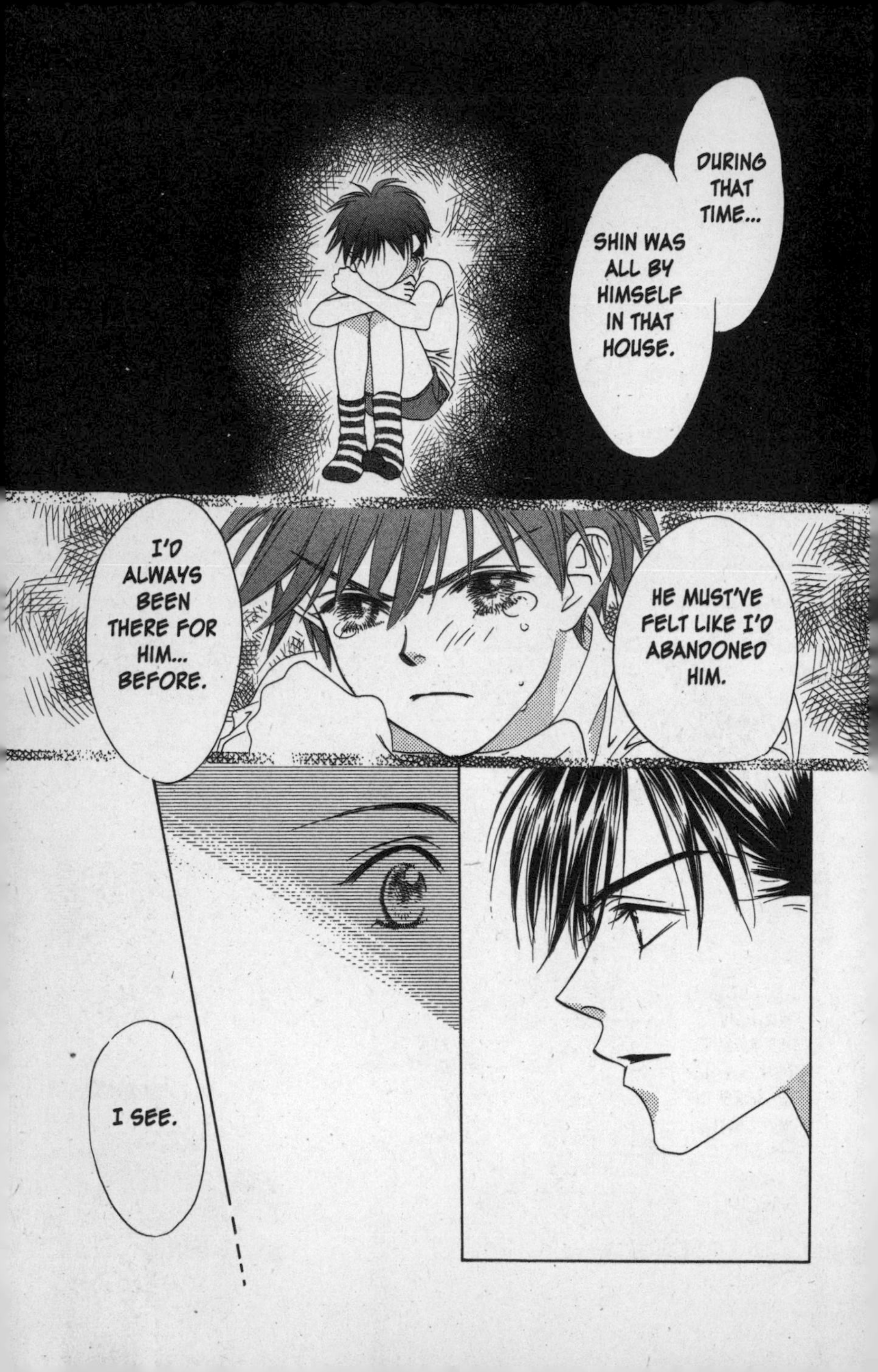
DURING THAT TIME...
SHIN WAS ALL BY HIMSELF IN THAT HOUSE.
HE MUST'VE FELT LIKE I'D ABANDONED HIM.
I'D ALWAYS BEEN THERE FOR HIM... BEFORE.
I SEE.

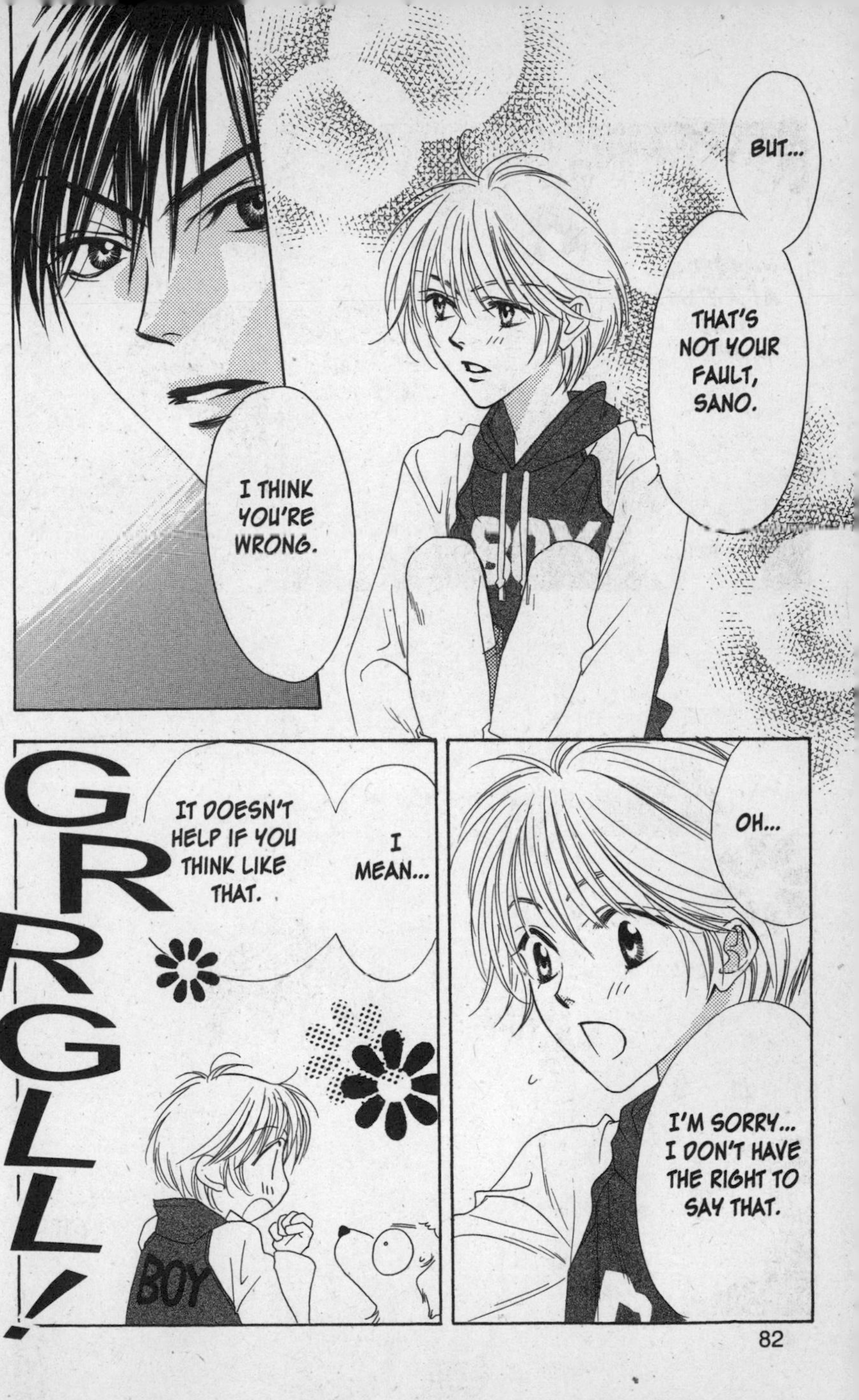
BUT...
THAT'S NOT YOUR FAULT, SANO.
I THINK YOU'RE WRONG.
OH...
I'M SORRY... I DON'T HAVE THE RIGHT TO SAY THAT.
I MEAN...
IT DOESN'T HELP IF YOU THINK LIKE THAT.
GRRGLL!
BOY

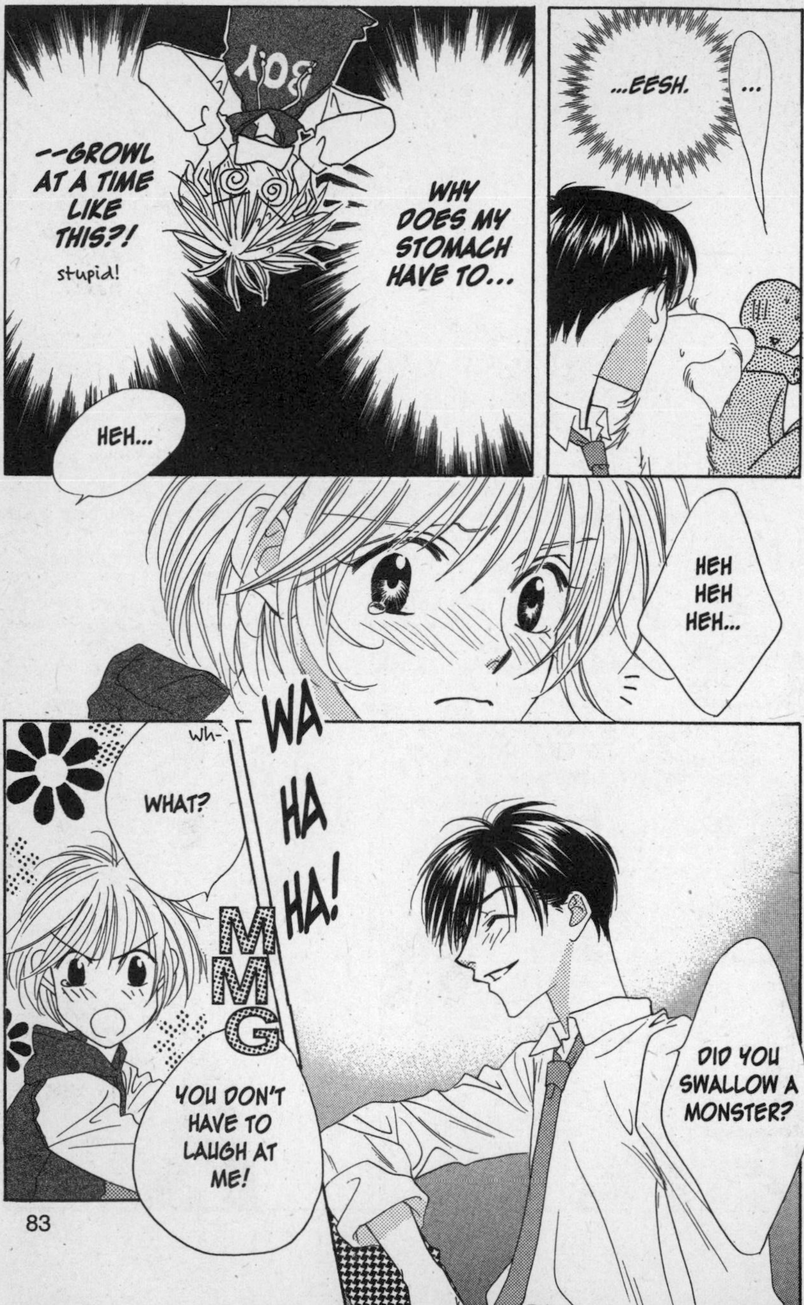
...EESH.
...
WHY DOES MY STOMACH HAVE TO...
--GROWL AT A TIME LIKE THIS?!
stupid!
HEH...
HEH HEH HEH...
DID YOU SWALLOW A MONSTER?
WA HA HA!
Wh-
WHAT?
MMG
YOU DON'T HAVE TO LAUGH AT ME!

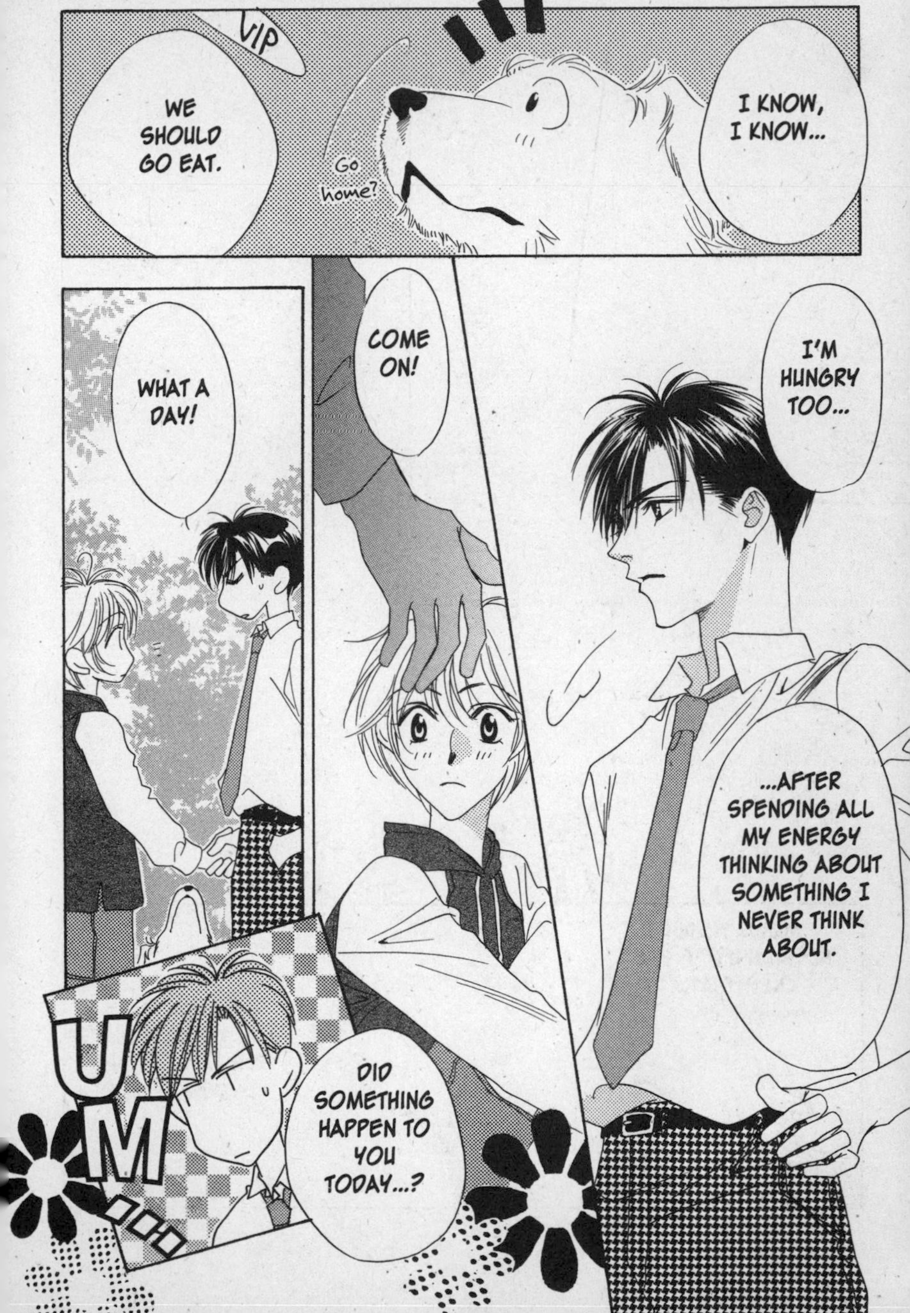
I KNOW, I KNOW...
Go home?
VIP
WE SHOULD GO EAT.
I'M HUNGRY TOO...
...AFTER SPENDING ALL MY ENERGY THINKING ABOUT SOMETHING I NEVER THINK ABOUT.
COME ON!
WHAT A DAY!
UM...
DID SOMETHING HAPPEN TO YOU TODAY...?

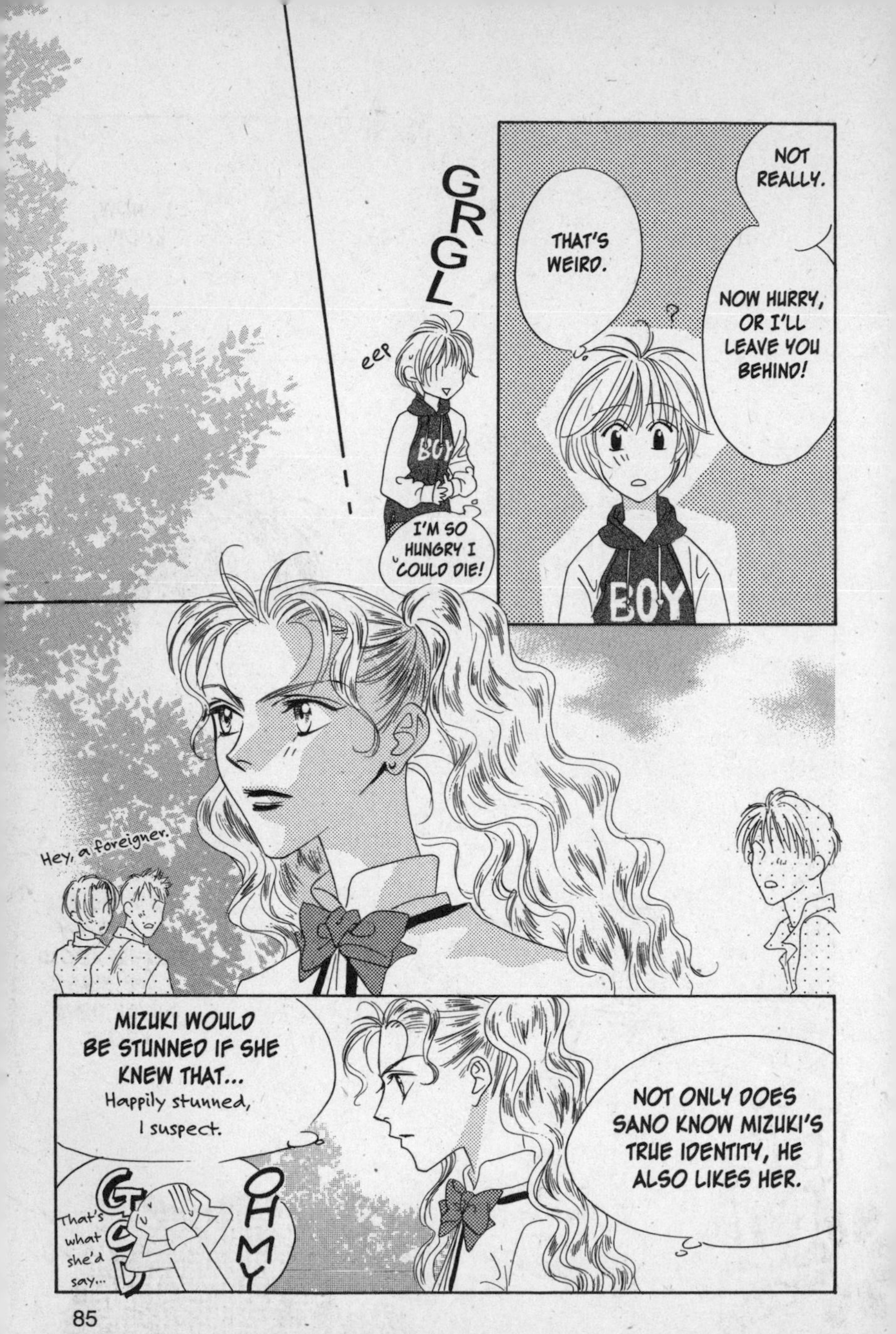
NOT REALLY.
THAT'S WEIRD.
NOW HURRY, OR I'LL LEAVE YOU BEHIND!
GRGL
eep
I'M SO HUNGRY I COULD DIE!
Hey, a foreigner.
NOT ONLY DOES SANO KNOW MIZUKI'S TRUE IDENTITY, HE ALSO LIKES HER.
MIZUKI WOULD BE STUNNED IF SHE KNEW THAT...
Happily stunned, I suspect.
OH MY
GOD
That's what she'd say...

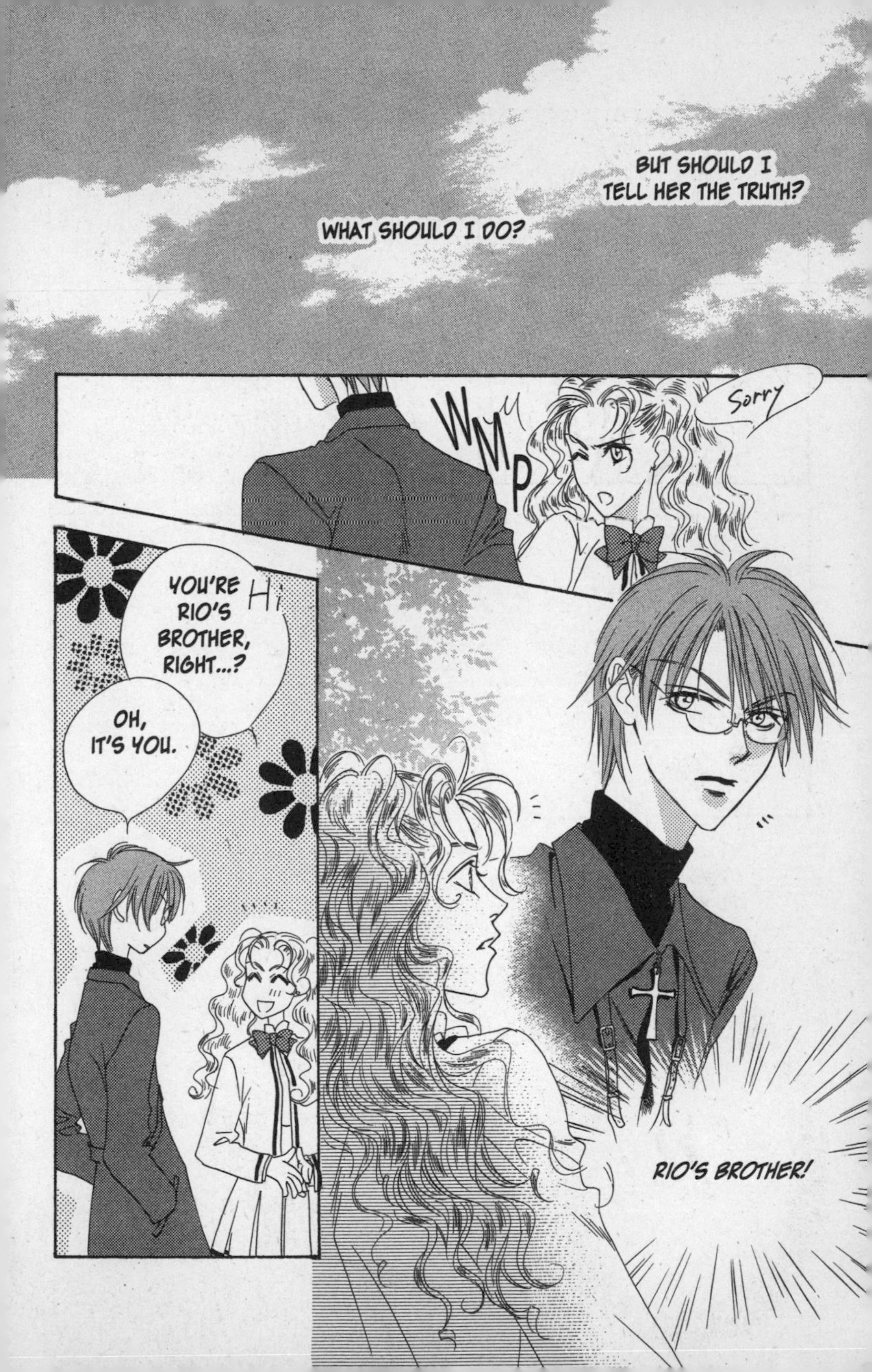
BUT SHOULD I TELL HER THE TRUTH?
WHAT SHOULD I DO?
Sorry
WUMP
RIO'S BROTHER!
Hi
YOU'RE RIO'S BROTHER, RIGHT...?
OH, IT'S YOU.

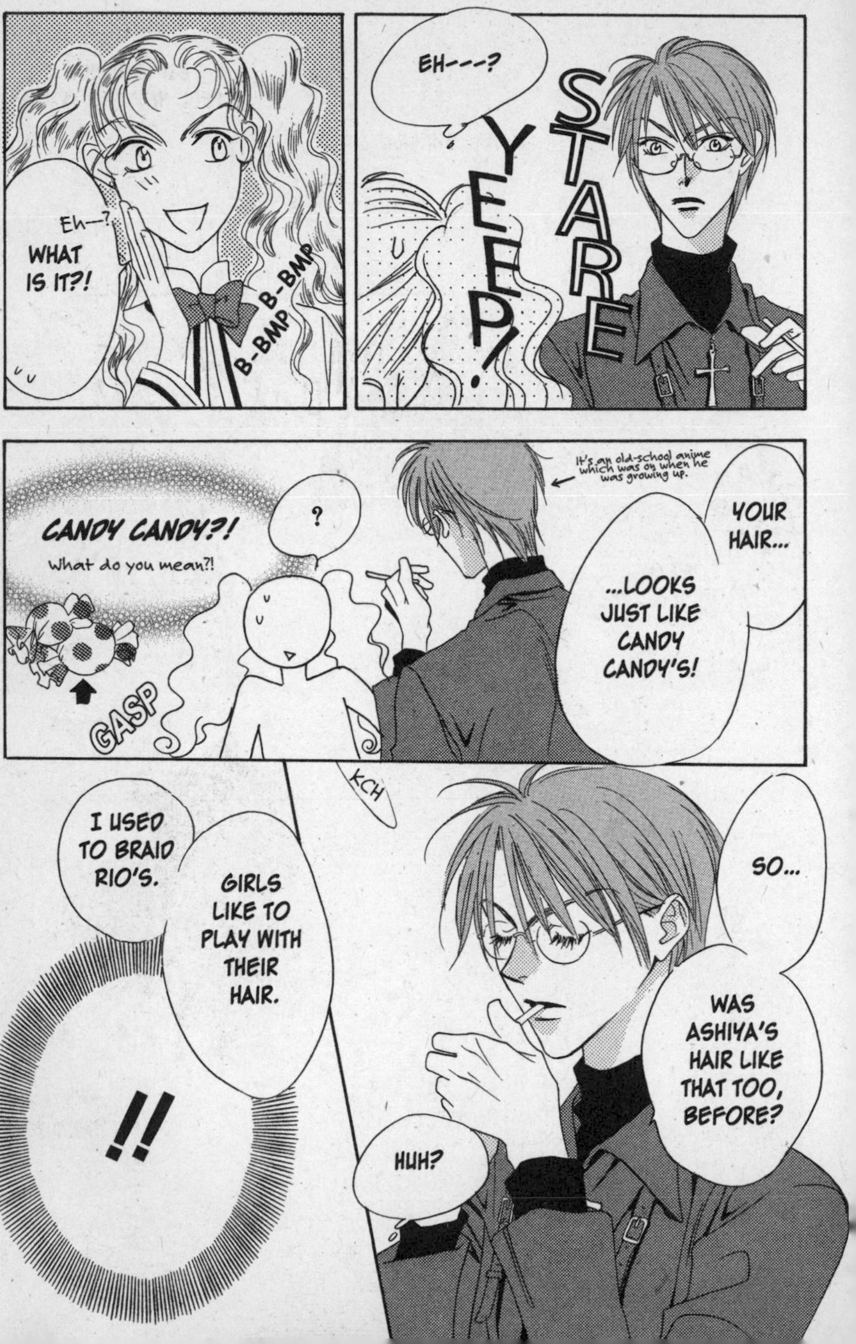

EH---?
STARE
YEEP!
Eh--?
WHAT IS IT?!
B-BMP B-BMP
YOUR HAIR...
...LOOKS JUST LIKE CANDY CANDY'S!
It's an old-school anime which was on when he was growing up.
?
CANDY CANDY?!
What do you mean?!
GASP
SO...
WAS ASHIYA'S HAIR LIKE THAT TOO, BEFORE?
HUH?
KCH
GIRLS LIKE TO PLAY WITH THEIR HAIR.
I USED TO BRAID RIO'S.
!!

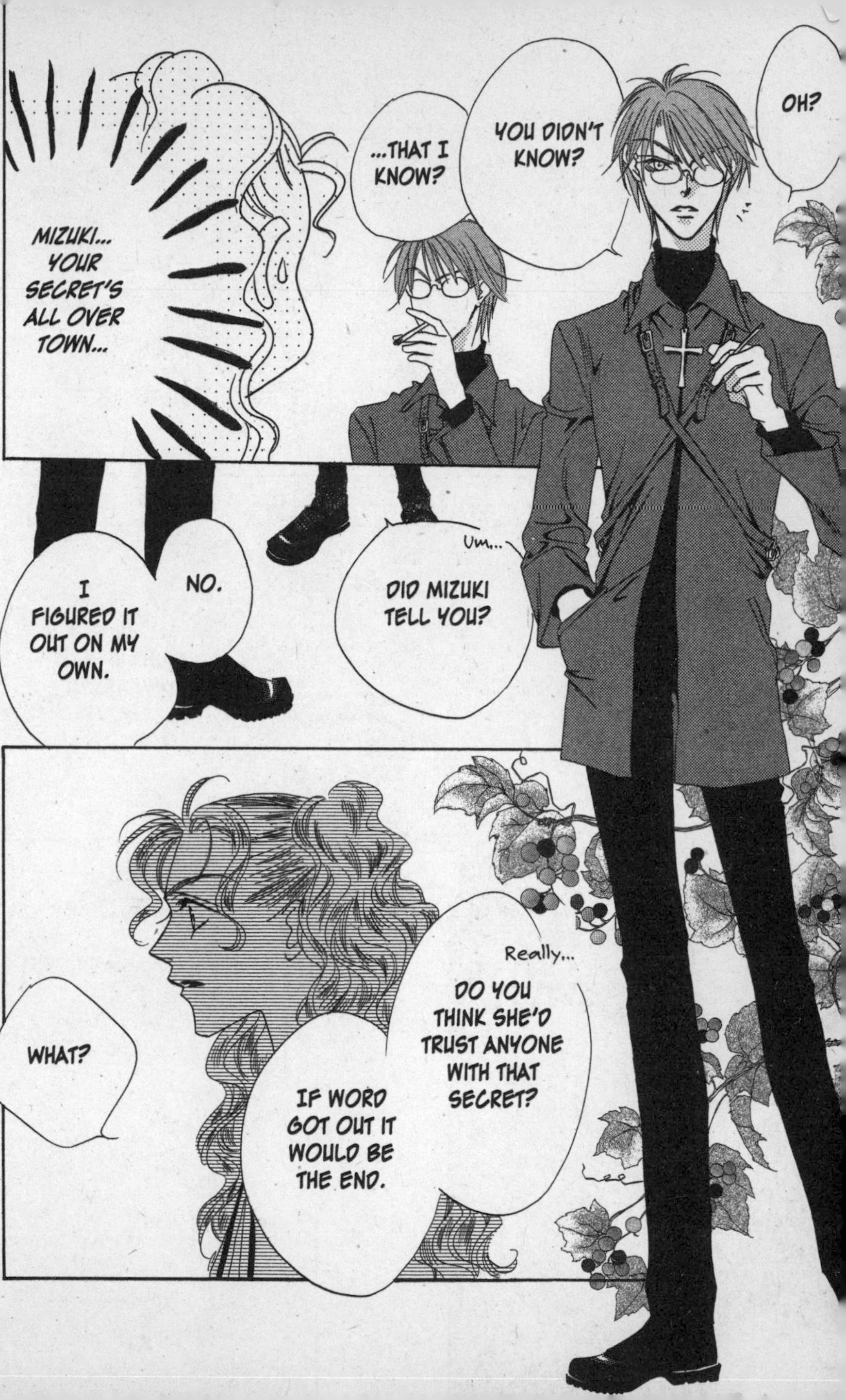
OH?
YOU DIDN'T KNOW?
...THAT I KNOW?
MIZUKI... YOUR SECRET'S ALL OVER TOWN...
Um...
DID MIZUKI TELL YOU?
NO.
I FIGURED IT OUT ON MY OWN.
Really...
DO YOU THINK SHE'D TRUST ANYONE WITH THAT SECRET?
IF WORD GOT OUT IT WOULD BE THE END.
WHAT?

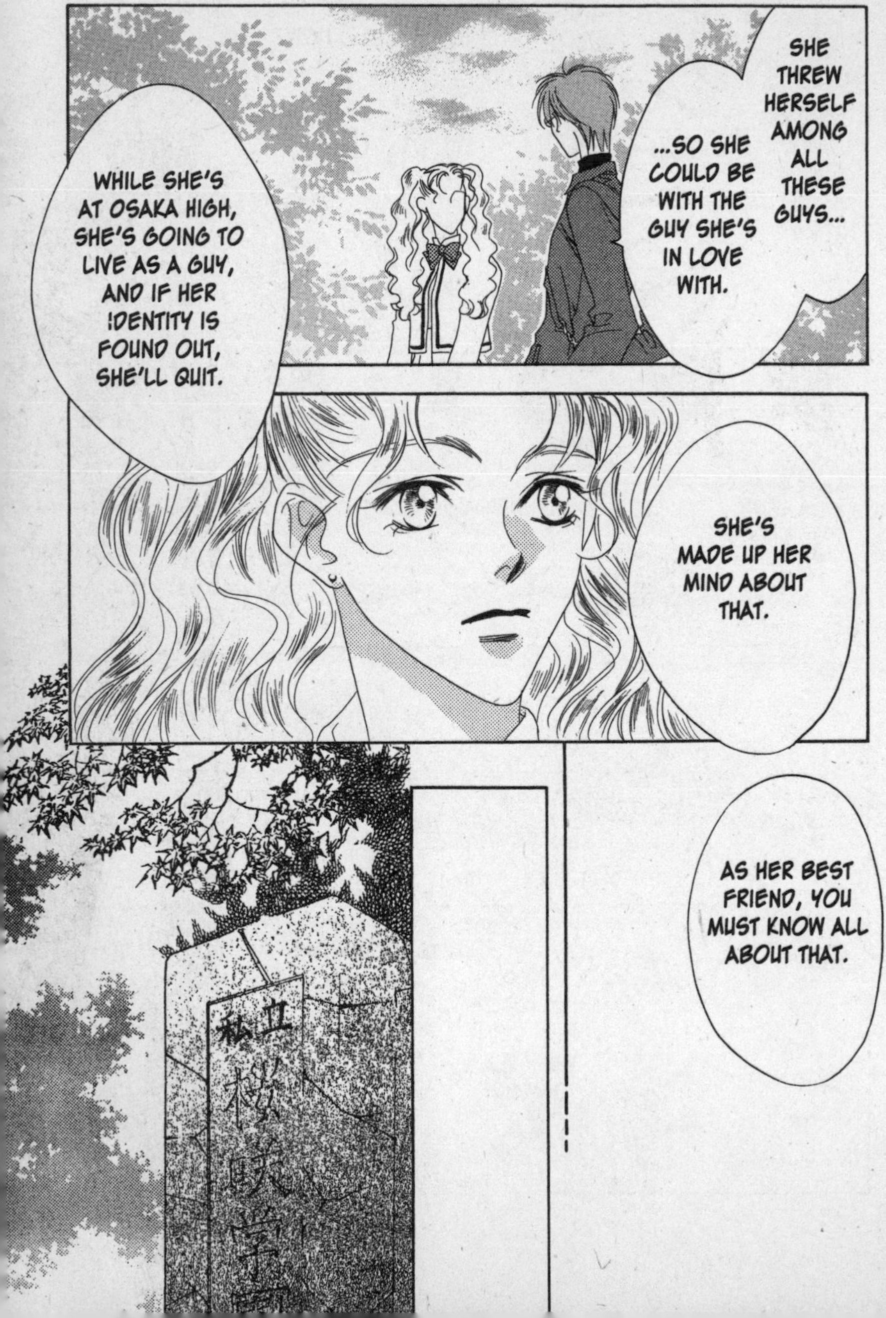
SHE THREW HERSELF AMONG ALL THESE GUYS...
...SO SHE COULD BE WITH THE GUY SHE'S IN LOVE WITH.
WHILE SHE'S AT OSAKA HIGH, SHE'S GOING TO LIVE AS A GUY, AND IF HER IDENTITY IS FOUND OUT, SHE'LL QUIT.
SHE'S MADE UP HER MIND ABOUT THAT.
AS HER BEST FRIEND, YOU MUST KNOW ALL ABOUT THAT.
私立

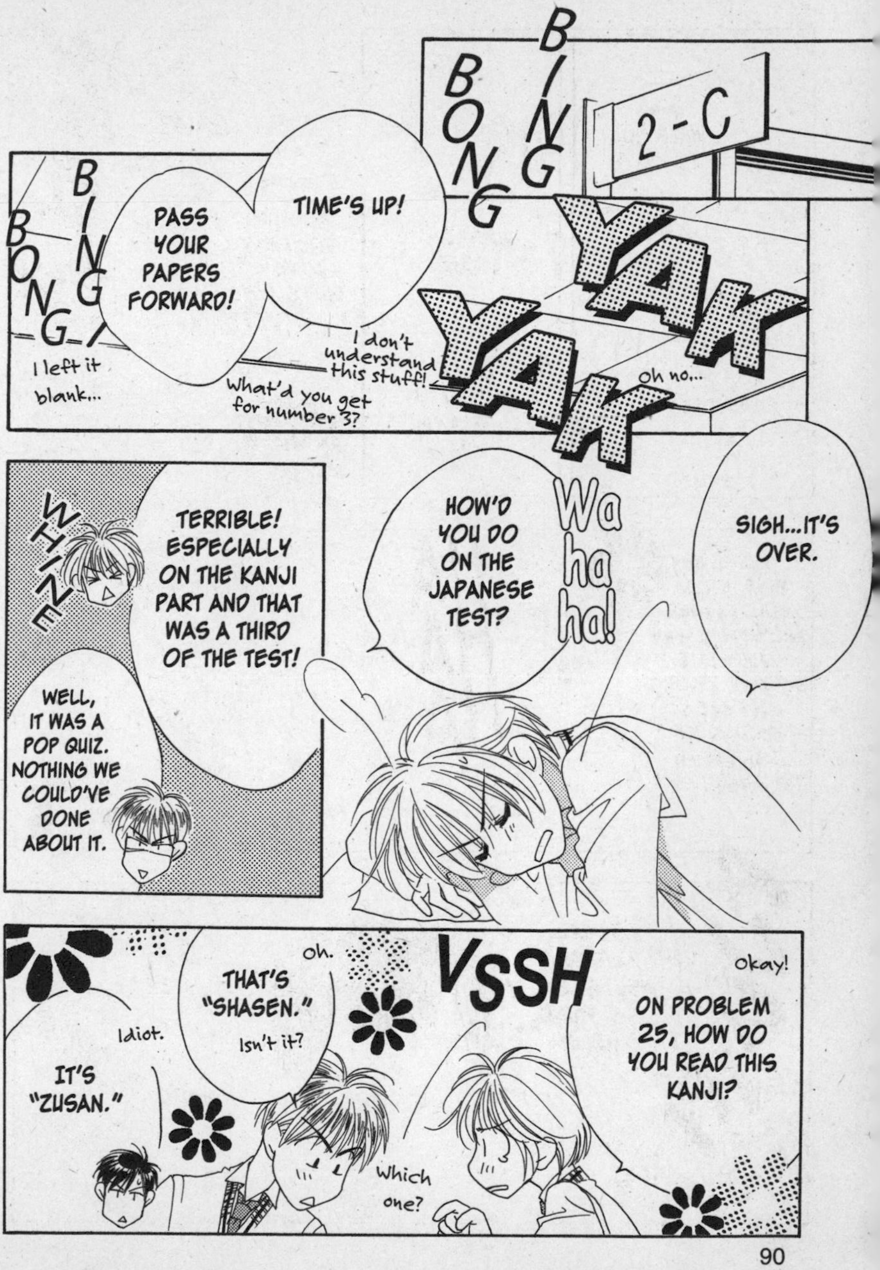
BING BONG
TIME'S UP!
PASS YOUR PAPERS FORWARD!
BING BONG
YAK YAK
oh no...
I don't understand this stuff!
What'd you get for number 3?
I left it blank...
SIGH...IT'S OVER.
Wa ha ha!
HOW'D YOU DO ON THE JAPANESE TEST?
WHINE
TERRIBLE! ESPECIALLY ON THE KANJI PART AND THAT WAS A THIRD OF THE TEST!
WELL, IT WAS A POP QUIZ. NOTHING WE COULD'VE DONE ABOUT IT.
Okay!
ON PROBLEM 25, HOW DO YOU READ THIS KANJI?
VSSH
Which one?
oh.
THAT'S "SHASEN."
Isn't it?
Idiot.
IT'S "ZUSAN."

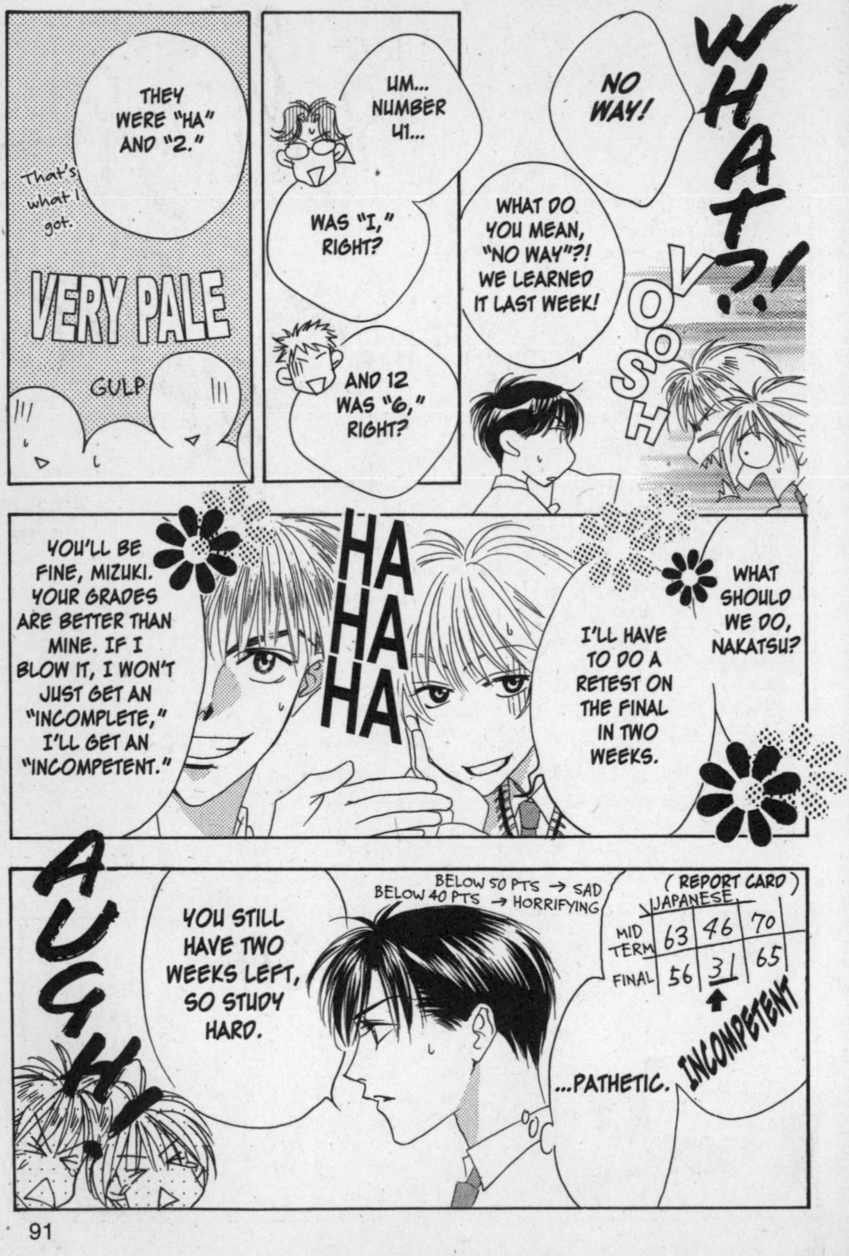
WHAT?!
NO WAY!
WHAT DO YOU MEAN, "NO WAY"?! WE LEARNED IT LAST WEEK!
VOOSH
UM... NUMBER 41...
WAS "I," RIGHT?
AND 12 WAS "6," RIGHT?
THEY WERE "HA" AND "2."
That's what I got.
VERY PALE
GULP
WHAT SHOULD WE DO, NAKATSU?
I'LL HAVE TO DO A RETEST ON THE FINAL IN TWO WEEKS.
HAHAHA
YOU'LL BE FINE, MIZUKI. YOUR GRADES ARE BETTER THAN MINE. IF I BLOW IT, I WON'T JUST GET AN "INCOMPLETE," I'LL GET AN "INCOMPETENT."
(REPORT CARD)
JAPANESE
MID TERM 63 46 70
FINAL 56 31 65
INCOMPETENT
...PATHETIC.
BELOW 50 PTS → SAD
BELOW 40 PTS → HORRIFYING
YOU STILL HAVE TWO WEEKS LEFT, SO STUDY HARD.
AUGH!

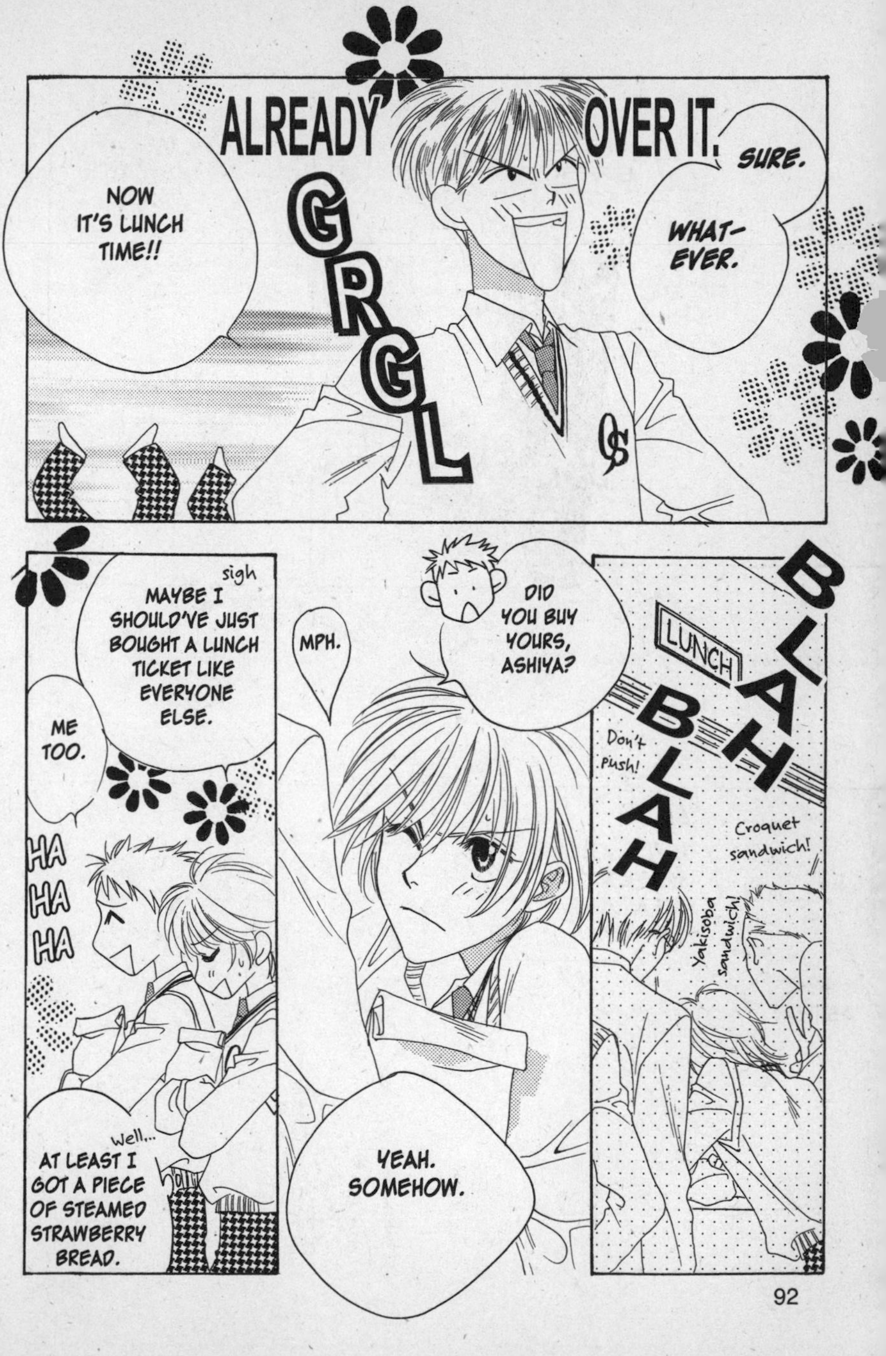
SURE. WHATEVER.
ALREADY OVER IT.
GRGL
NOW IT'S LUNCH TIME!!
BLAH BLAH
LUNCH
BLAH BLAH
Don't push!
Croquet sandwich!
Yakisoba sandwich!
DID YOU BUY YOURS, ASHIYA?
MPH.
YEAH. SOMEHOW.
sigh
MAYBE I SHOULD'VE JUST BOUGHT A LUNCH TICKET LIKE EVERYONE ELSE.
ME TOO.
HA HA HA
well...
AT LEAST I GOT A PIECE OF STEAMED STRAWBERRY BREAD.

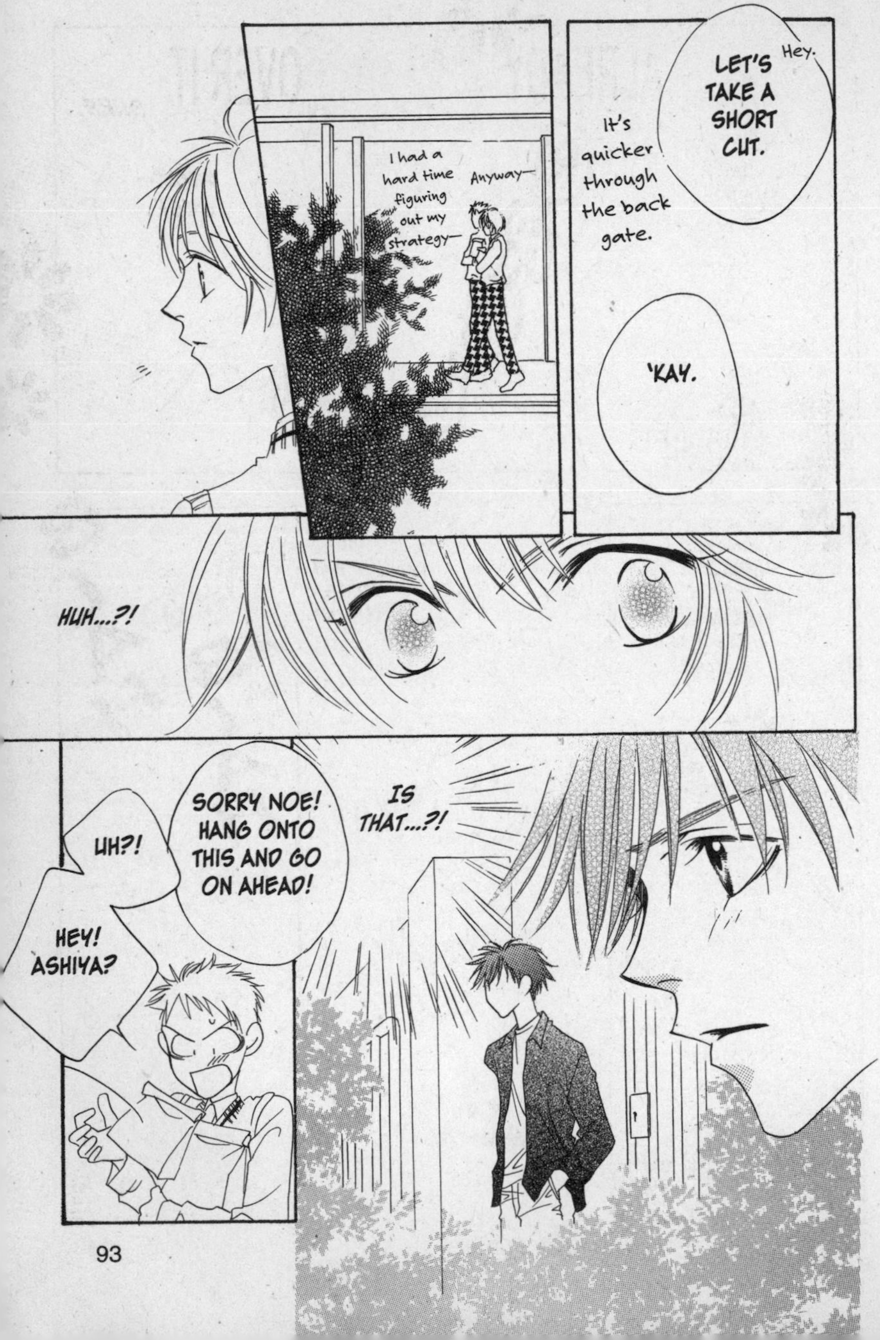
Hey.
LET'S TAKE A SHORT CUT.
It's quicker through the back gate.
'KAY.
I had a hard time figuring out my strategy—
Anyway—
HUH...?!
IS THAT...?!
SORRY NOE! HANG ONTO THIS AND GO ON AHEAD!
UH?!
HEY! ASHIYA?

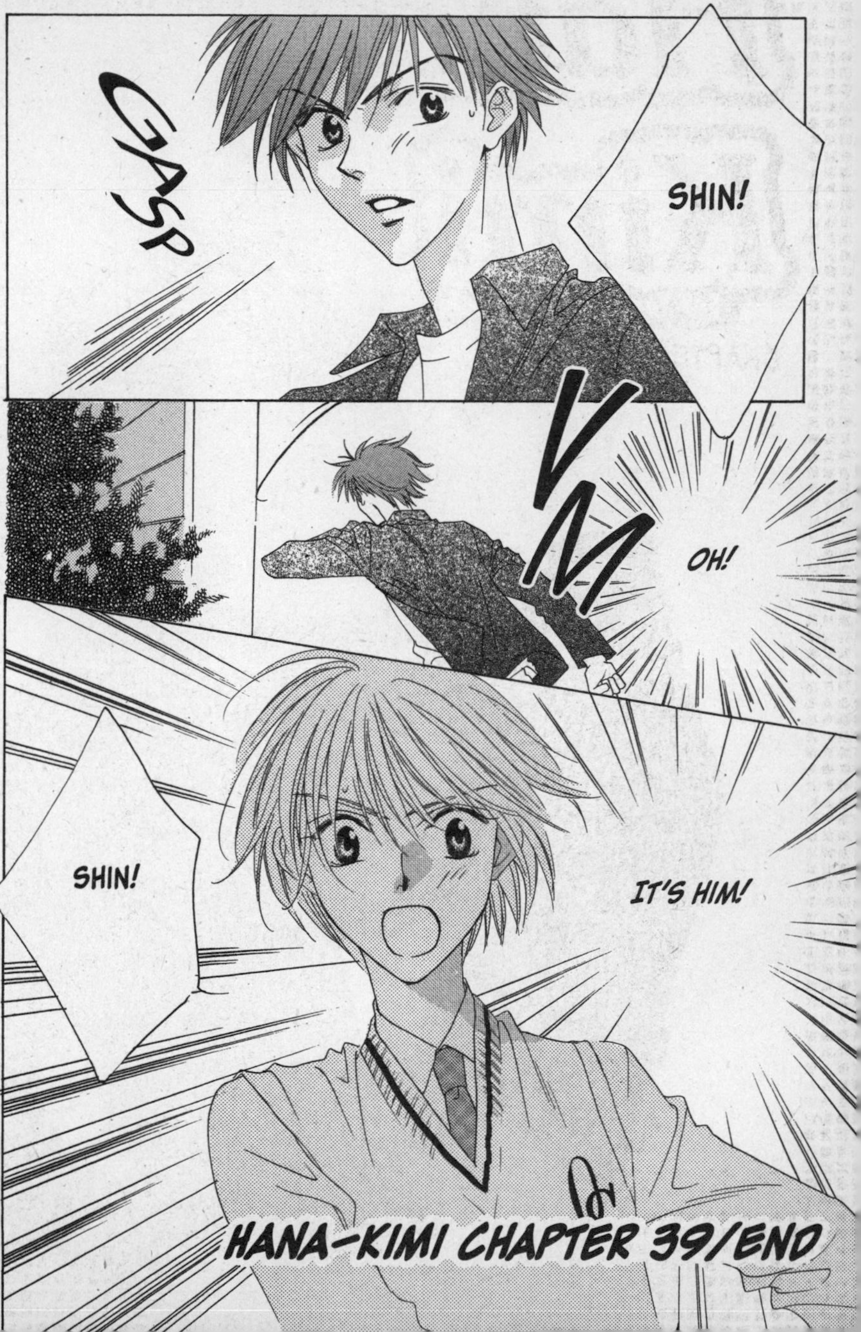
SHIN!
GASP
VM
OH!
IT'S HIM!
SHIN!
HANA-KIMI CHAPTER 39/END

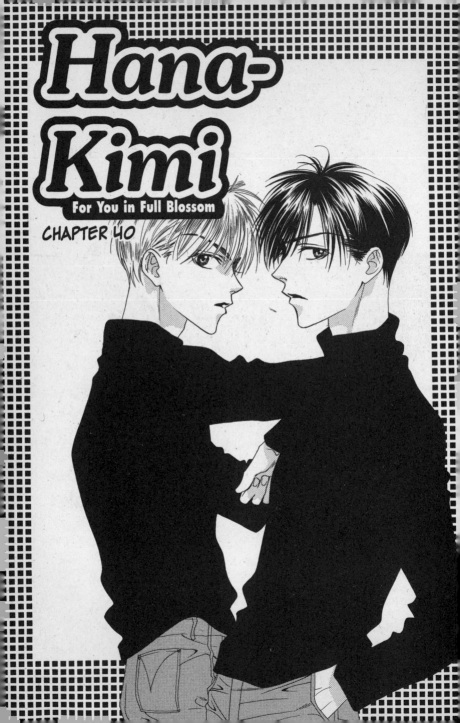

Hana-Kimi

For You in Full Blossom

CHAPTER 40

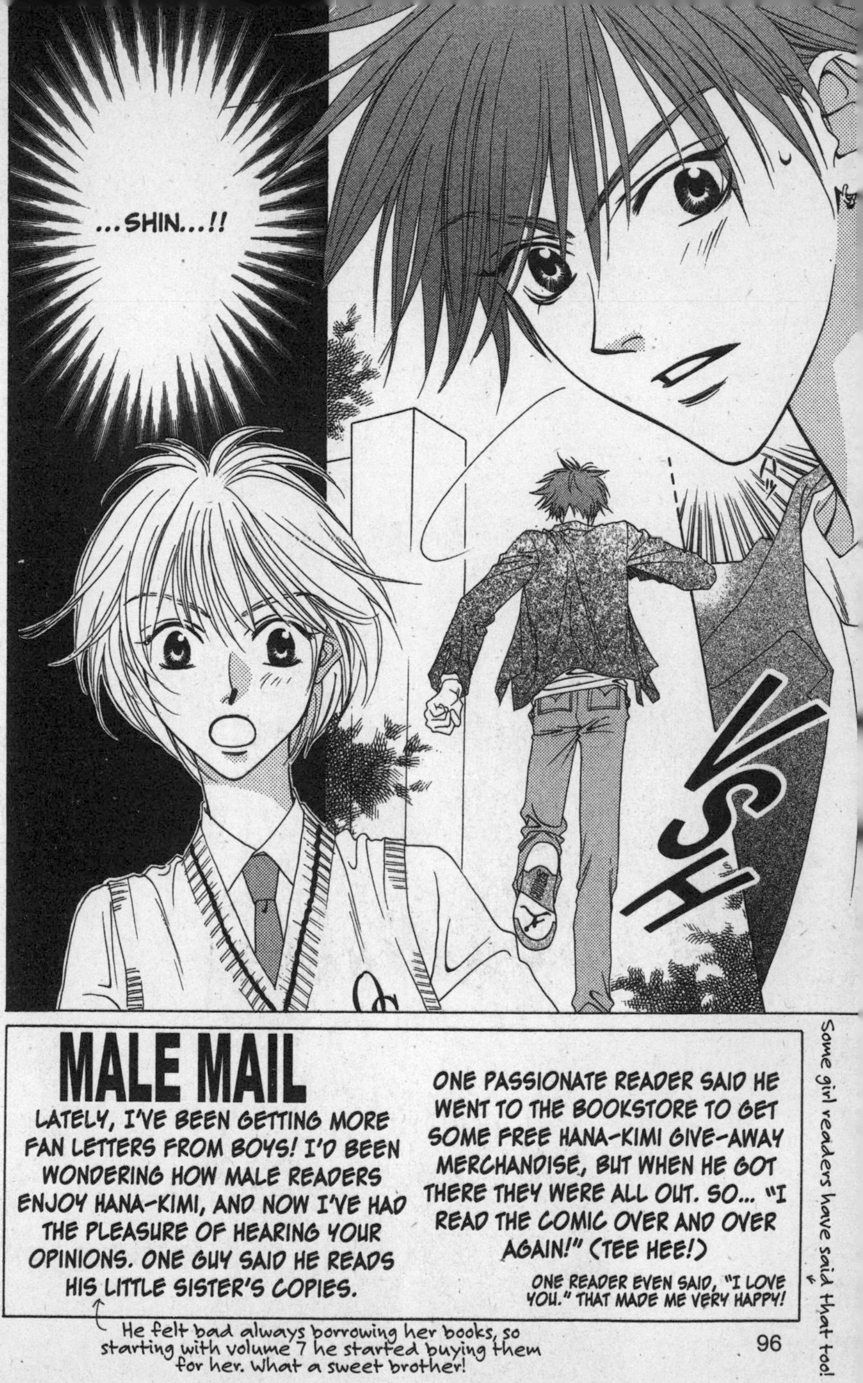
VSSH
...SHIN...!!

MALE MAIL

LATELY, I'VE BEEN GETTING MORE FAN LETTERS FROM BOYS! I'D BEEN WONDERING HOW MALE READERS ENJOY HANA-KIMI, AND NOW I'VE HAD THE PLEASURE OF HEARING YOUR OPINIONS. ONE GUY SAID HE READS HIS LITTLE SISTER'S COPIES.

← He felt bad always borrowing her books, so starting with volume 7 he started buying them for her. What a sweet brother!

ONE PASSIONATE READER SAID HE WENT TO THE BOOKSTORE TO GET SOME FREE HANA-KIMI GIVE-AWAY MERCHANDISE, BUT WHEN HE GOT THERE THEY WERE ALL OUT. SO... "I READ THE COMIC OVER AND OVER AGAIN!" (TEE HEE!)

ONE READER EVEN SAID, "I LOVE YOU." THAT MADE ME VERY HAPPY!

Some girl readers have said that too!

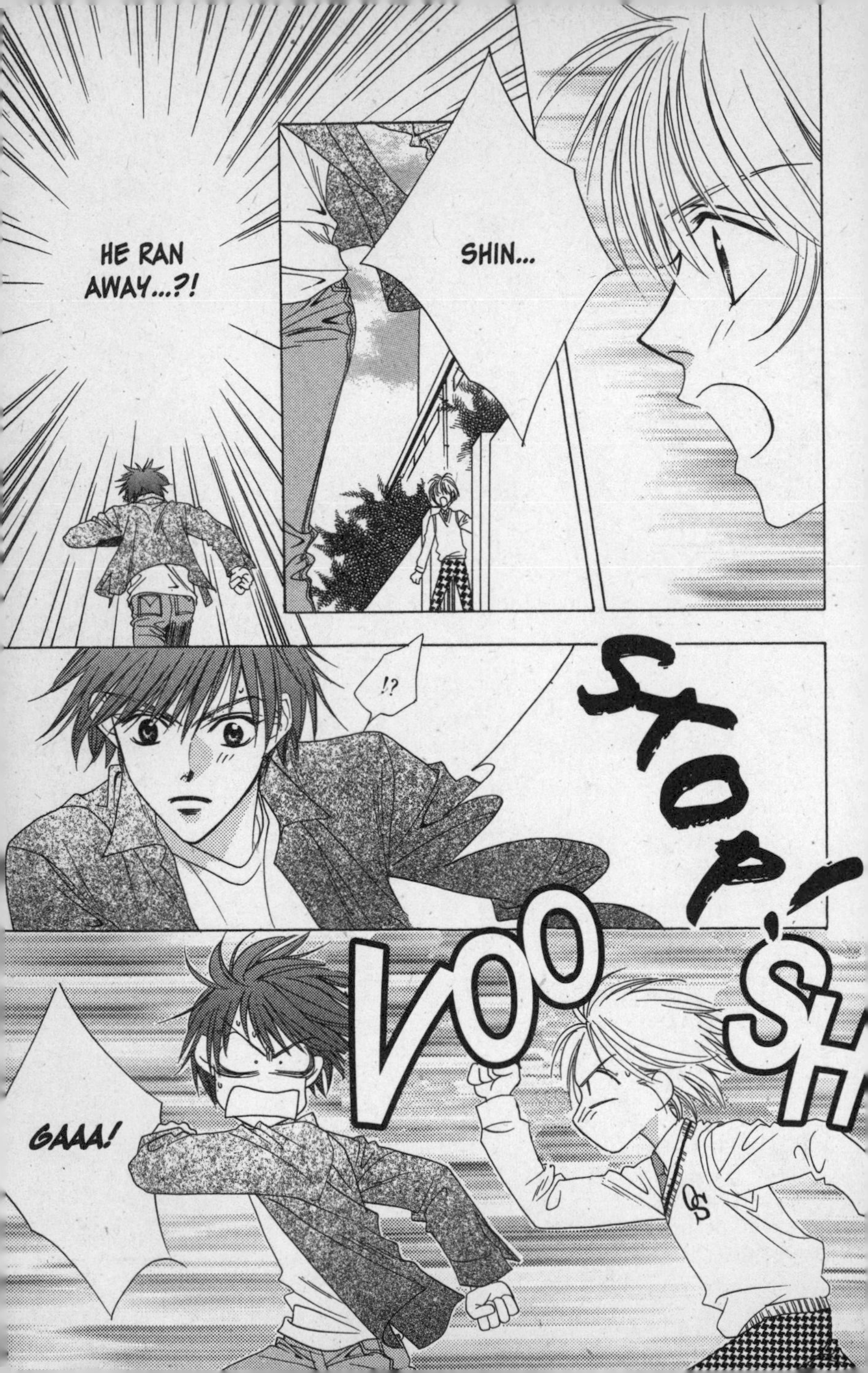
SHIN...
HE RAN AWAY...?!
STOP!
!?
VOOSH
GAAA!

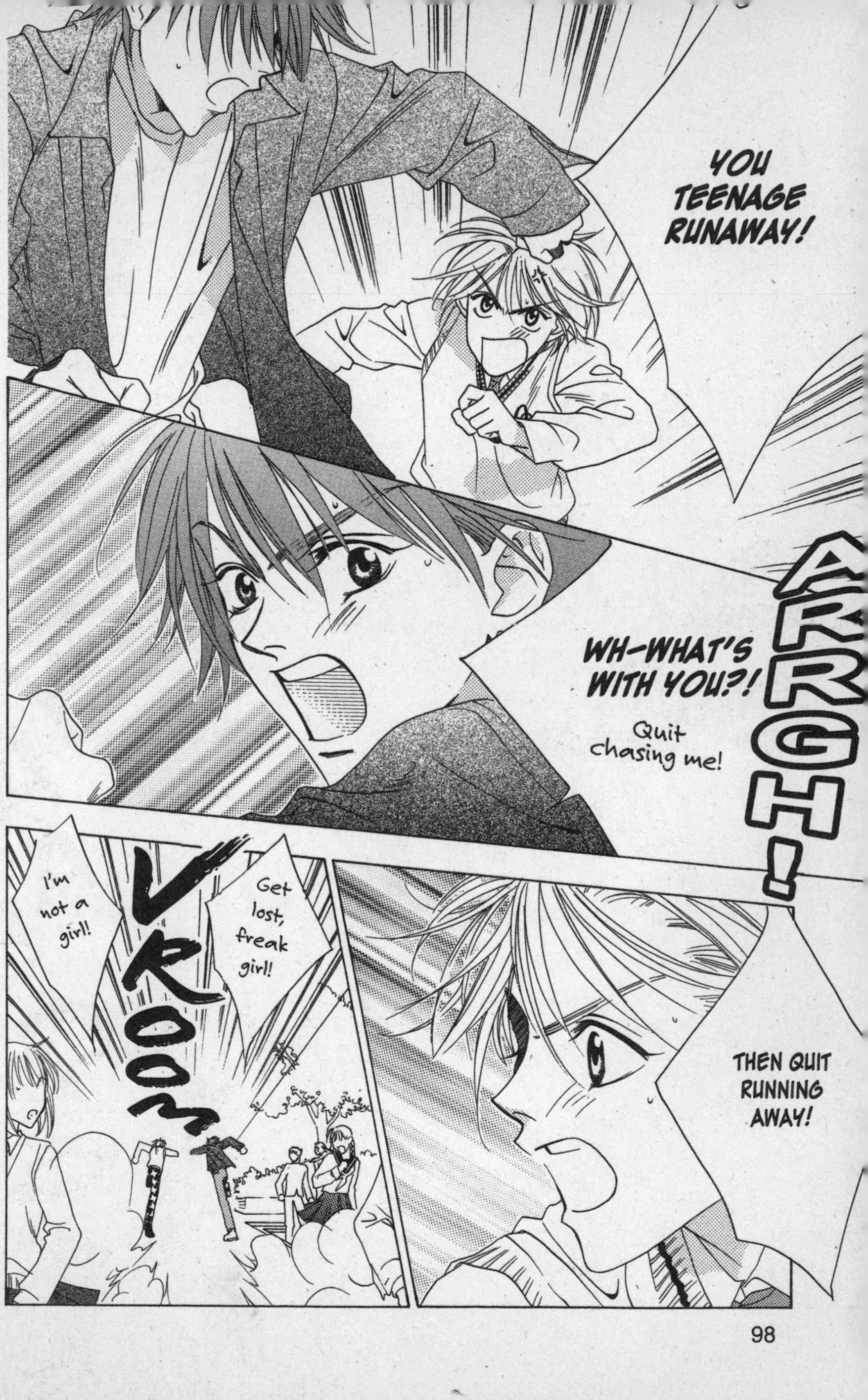
YOU TEENAGE RUNAWAY!
ARGH!
WH-WHAT'S WITH YOU?!
Quit chasing me!
THEN QUIT RUNNING AWAY!
Get lost, freak girl!
I'm not a girl!
VROOM

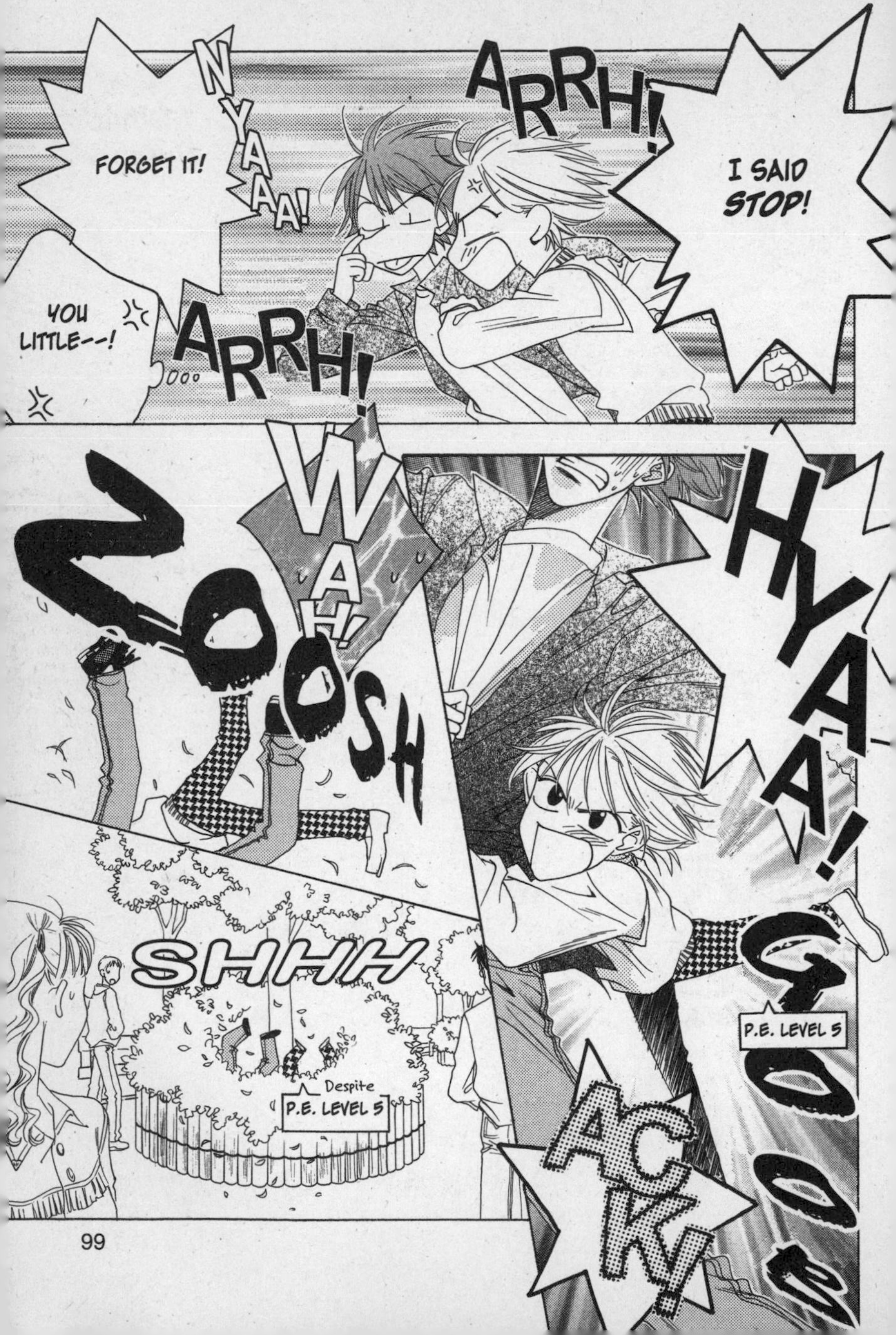
I SAID STOP!
ARRH!
NYAAA!
FORGET IT!
ARRH!
YOU LITTLE--!
HYAA!
GOOO
P.E. LEVEL 5
ACK!
WAH!
ZOOSH
SHHH
Despite
P.E. LEVEL 5

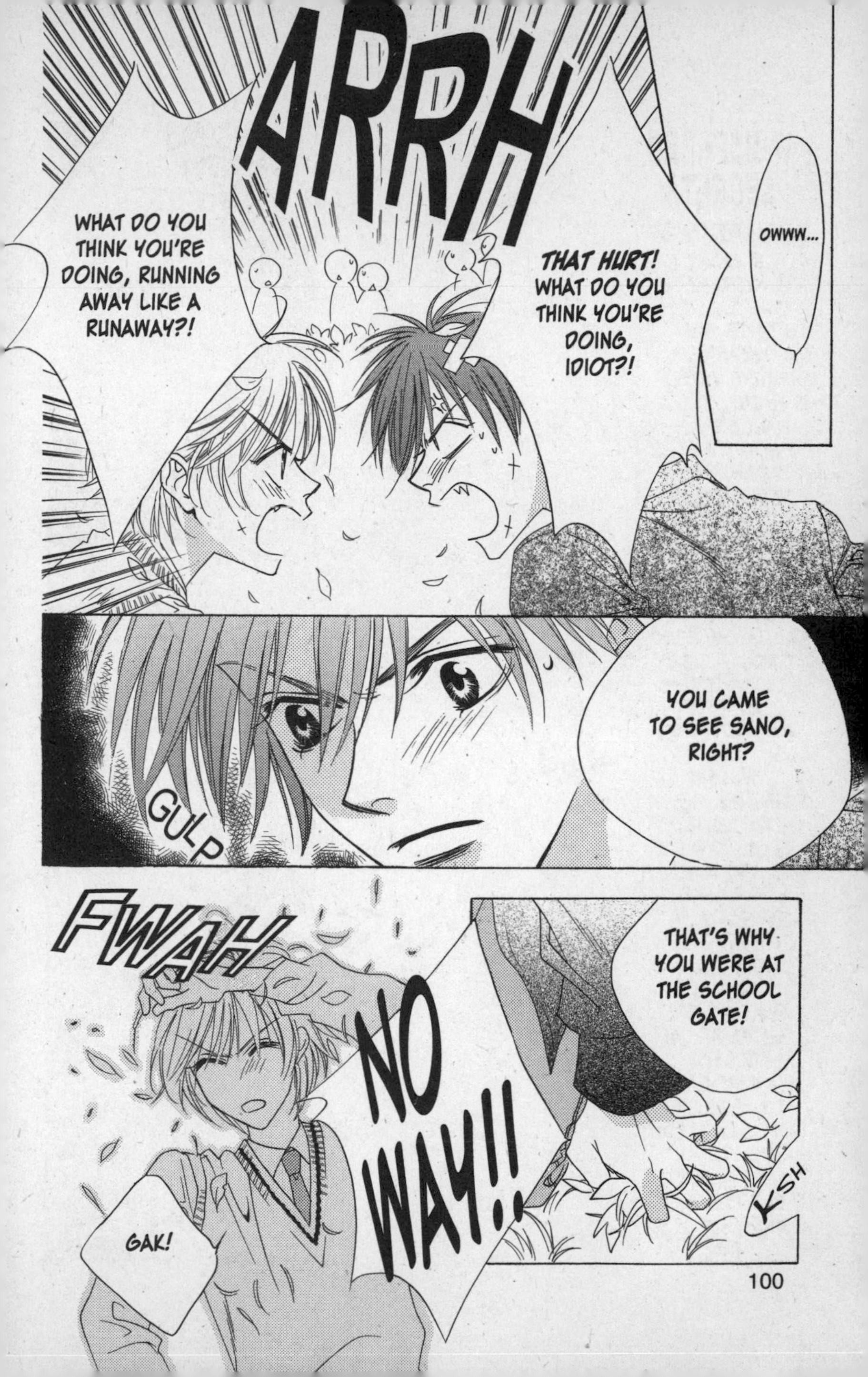
OWWW...
ARRH
THAT HURT! WHAT DO YOU THINK YOU'RE DOING, IDIOT?!
WHAT DO YOU THINK YOU'RE DOING, RUNNING AWAY LIKE A RUNAWAY?!
YOU CAME TO SEE SANO, RIGHT?
GULP
THAT'S WHY YOU WERE AT THE SCHOOL GATE!
KSH
NO WAY!!
FWAH
GAK!

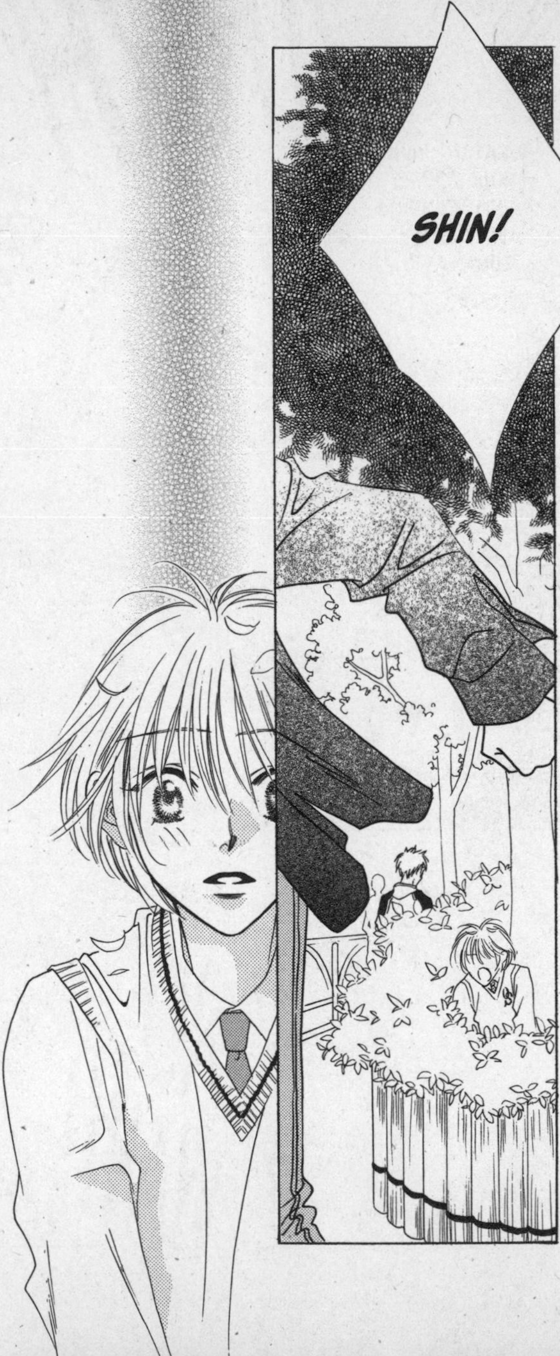
SHIN!

WHISPERED SECRETS

PLAYSTATION

I BOUGHT A PLAYSTATION! YAY! I GOT IT FOR THE "HOUSHIN ENGI" VIDEO GAME, BUT I HAVEN'T FINISHED IT YET. I MEAN, WHEN YOU GET INTO IT YOU CAN PLAY FOR FIVE OR SIX HOURS AT A TIME. SO UNLESS I HAVE A LOT OF FREE TIME, FORGET IT. I'M TRYING TO KEEP MYSELF FROM GETTING TOO CAUGHT UP...HEH-HEH. NOW I REALLY WANT "DANCE DANCE REVOLUTION," BUT IT'S SOLD OUT. OH, AND THANK YOU SO MUCH TO THE PERSON WHO SENT ME THE "BLACK MATRIX" GAME! I'M THRILLED AND GRATEFUL. I'LL TRY TO FIND A GUIDE BOOK FOR IT AND GIVE IT A TRY.

桜咲学園学生寮

AND THAT...

...IS HOW I LET HIM GET AWAY.

I'M SO ASHAMED.

I can't believe him!

YEAH...

WELL...

AT LEAST I KNOW HE'S OKAY. DON'T WORRY ABOUT IT.

SIGH

I'M SORRY.

102

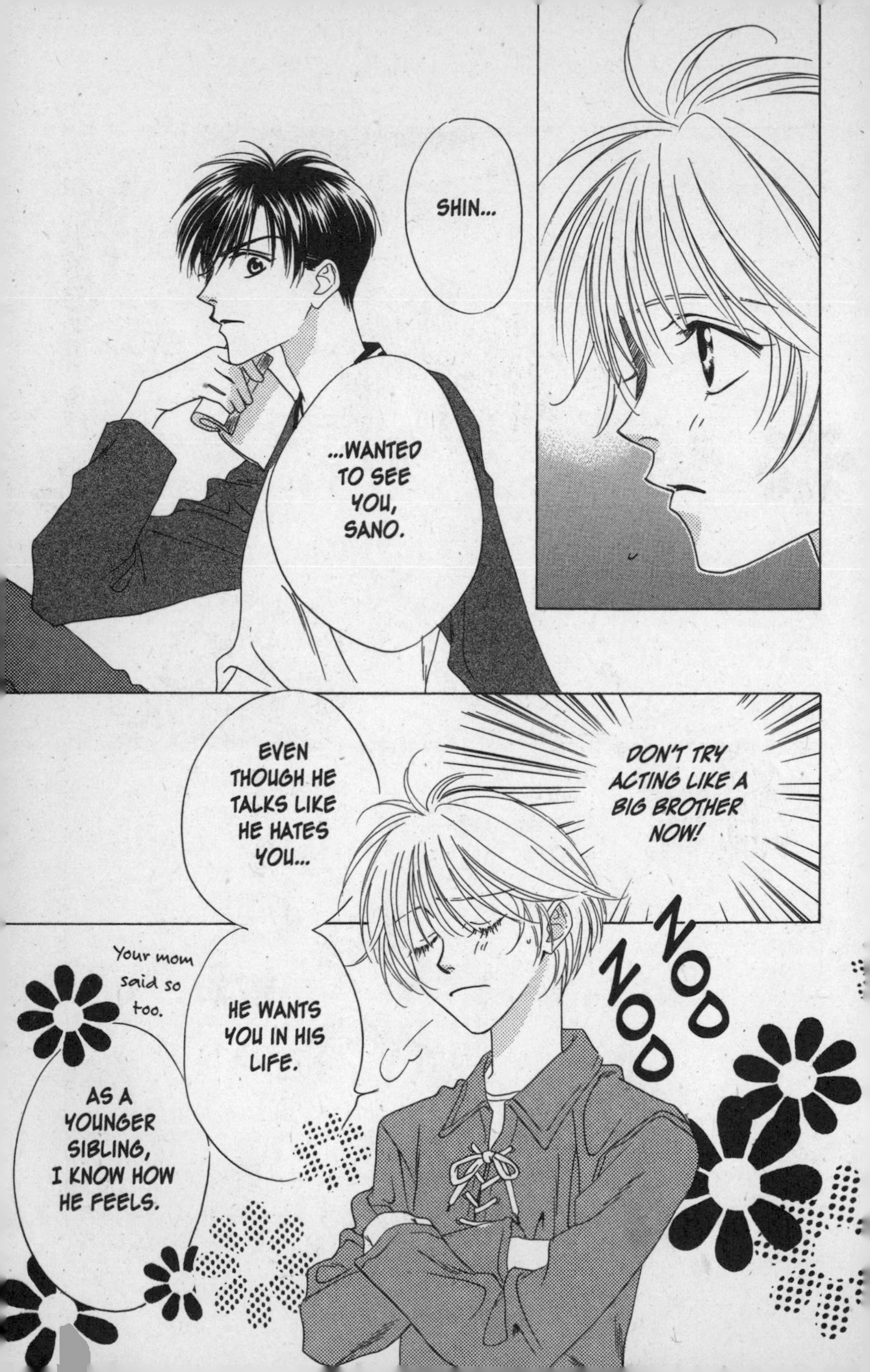
SHIN...
...WANTED TO SEE YOU, SANO.
DON'T TRY ACTING LIKE A BIG BROTHER NOW!
EVEN THOUGH HE TALKS LIKE HE HATES YOU...
NOD NOD
HE WANTS YOU IN HIS LIFE.
Your mom said so too.
AS A YOUNGER SIBLING, I KNOW HOW HE FEELS.

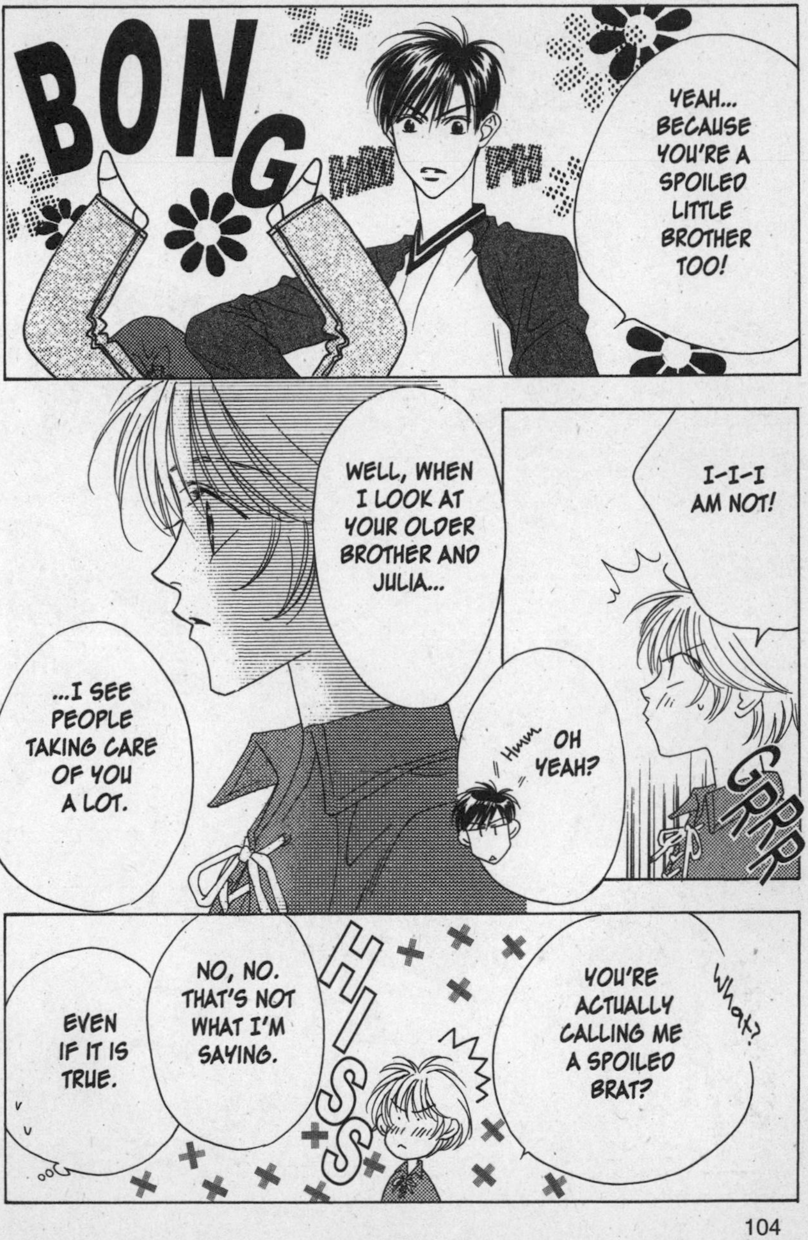
BONG
HMMPH
YEAH... BECAUSE YOU'RE A SPOILED LITTLE BROTHER TOO!
I-I-I AM NOT!
GRRR
WELL, WHEN I LOOK AT YOUR OLDER BROTHER AND JULIA...
Hmm
OH YEAH?
...I SEE PEOPLE TAKING CARE OF YOU A LOT.
What?
YOU'RE ACTUALLY CALLING ME A SPOILED BRAT?
HISS
NO, NO. THAT'S NOT WHAT I'M SAYING.
EVEN IF IT IS TRUE.

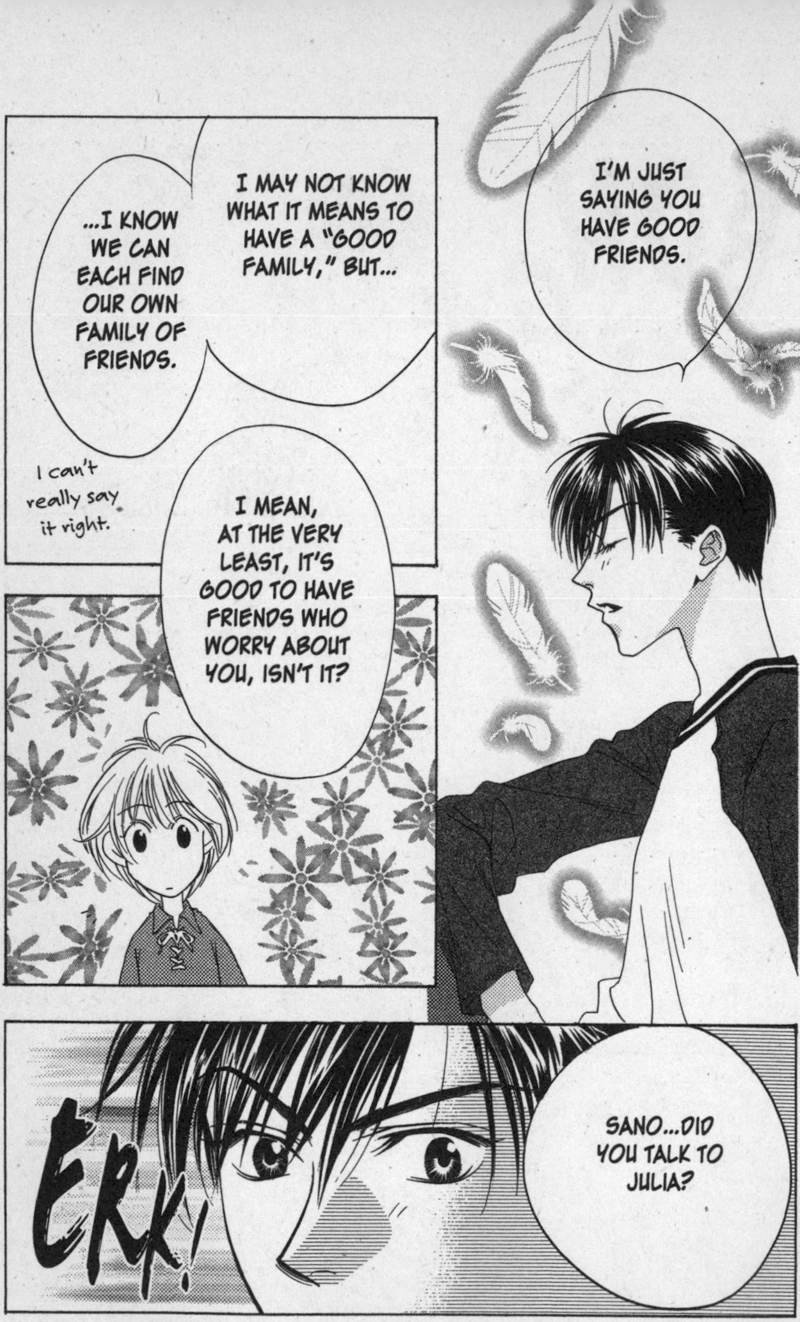
I'M JUST SAYING YOU HAVE GOOD FRIENDS.
I MAY NOT KNOW WHAT IT MEANS TO HAVE A "GOOD FAMILY," BUT...
...I KNOW WE CAN EACH FIND OUR OWN FAMILY OF FRIENDS.
I can't really say it right.
I MEAN, AT THE VERY LEAST, IT'S GOOD TO HAVE FRIENDS WHO WORRY ABOUT YOU, ISN'T IT?
SANO...DID YOU TALK TO JULIA?
ERK!

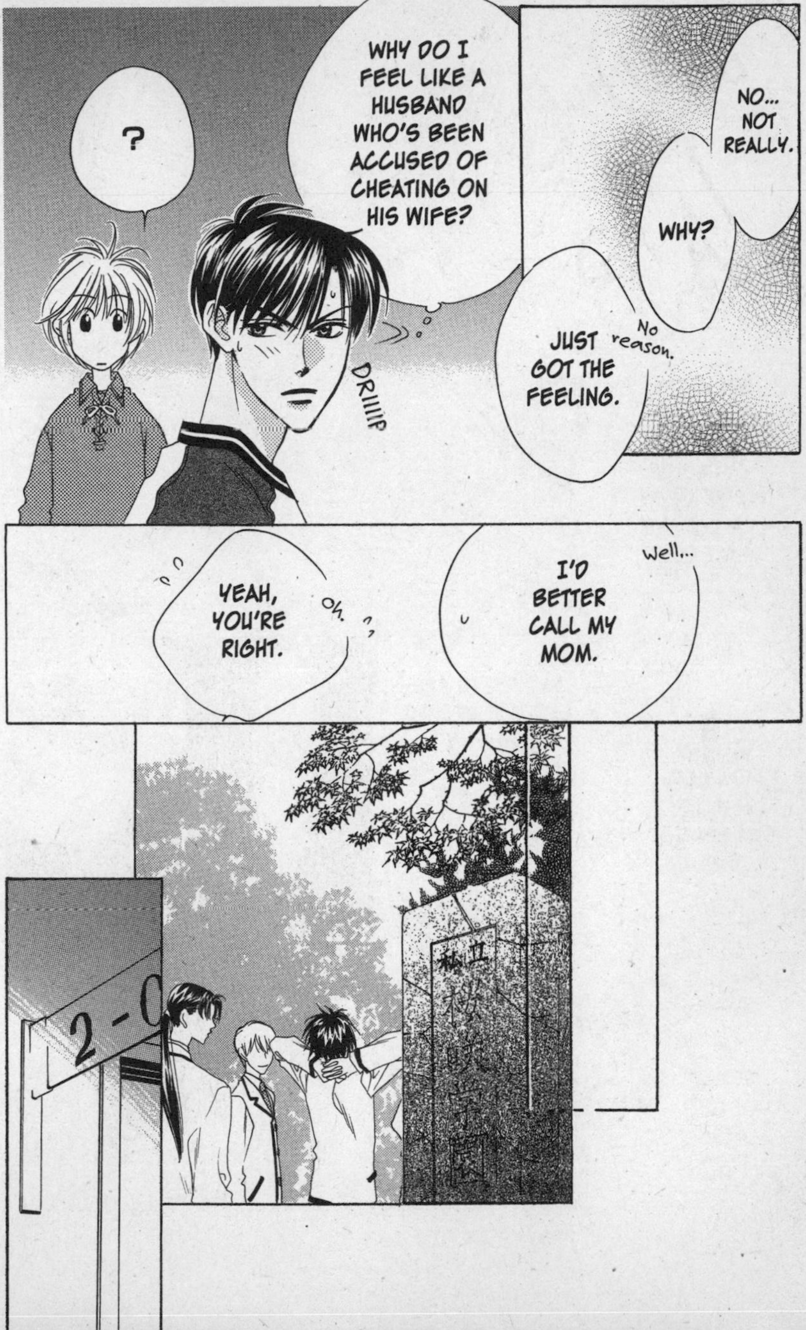
NO... NOT REALLY.
WHY?
No reason.
JUST GOT THE FEELING.
WHY DO I FEEL LIKE A HUSBAND WHO'S BEEN ACCUSED OF CHEATING ON HIS WIFE?
?
DRIIIIP
Well...
I'D BETTER CALL MY MOM.
Oh.
YEAH, YOU'RE RIGHT.

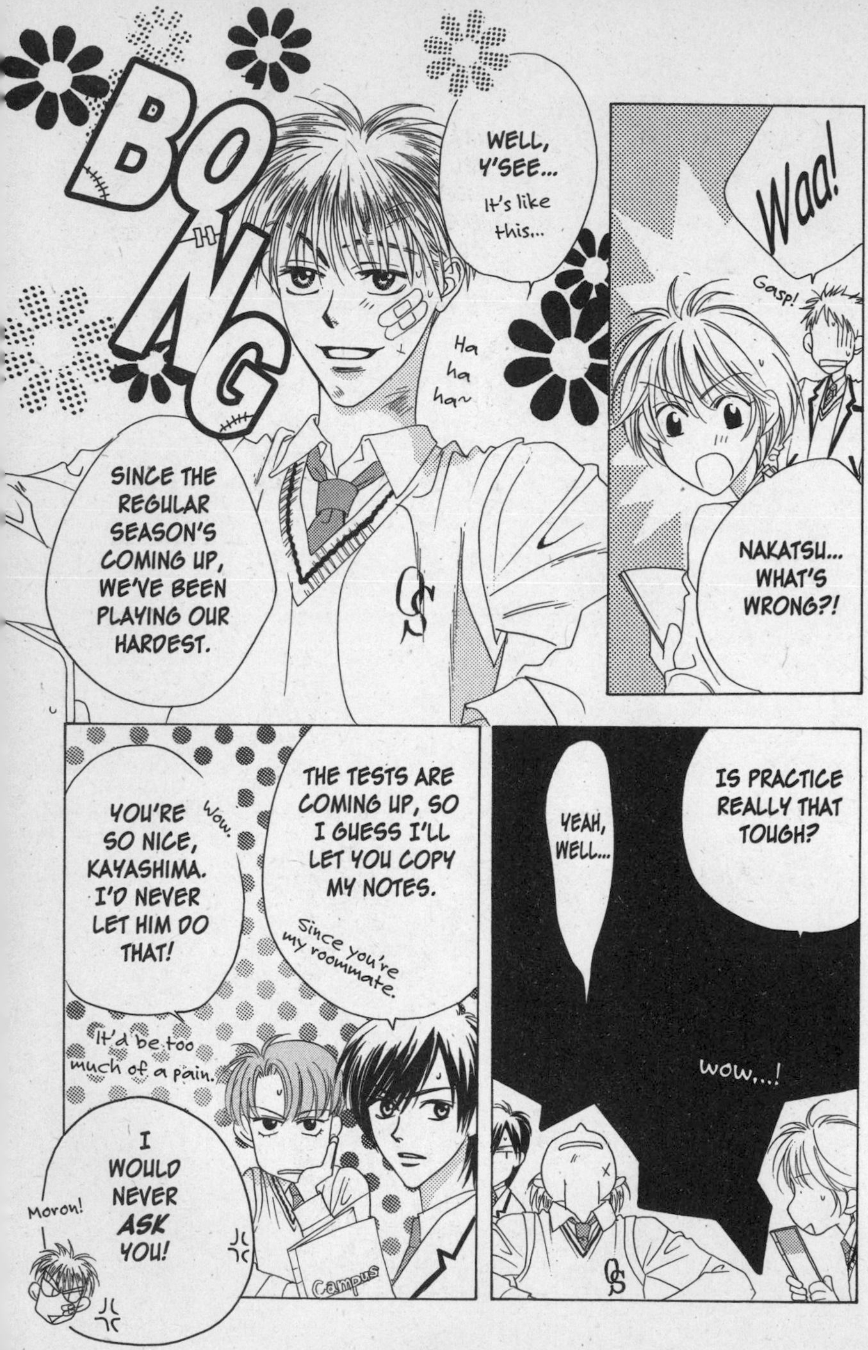
Waa!
Gasp!
NAKATSU... WHAT'S WRONG?!
BONG
WELL, Y'SEE...
It's like this...
Ha ha ha~
SINCE THE REGULAR SEASON'S COMING UP, WE'VE BEEN PLAYING OUR HARDEST.
IS PRACTICE REALLY THAT TOUGH?
YEAH, WELL...
wow...!
THE TESTS ARE COMING UP, SO I GUESS I'LL LET YOU COPY MY NOTES.
Since you're my roommate.
YOU'RE SO NICE, KAYASHIMA. I'D NEVER LET HIM DO THAT!
Wow.
It'd be too much of a pain.
I WOULD NEVER ASK YOU!
Moron!
Campus

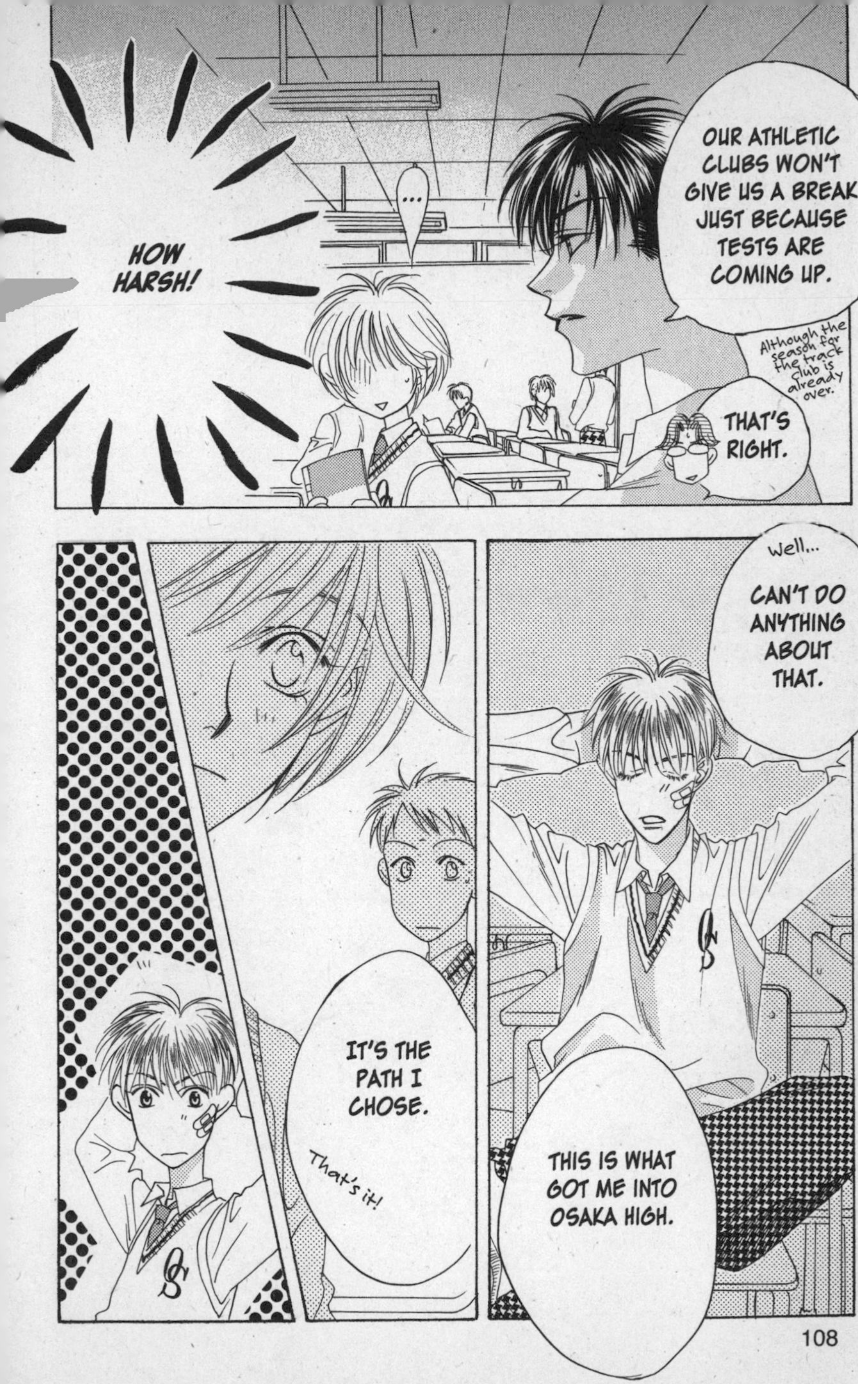
OUR ATHLETIC CLUBS WON'T GIVE US A BREAK JUST BECAUSE TESTS ARE COMING UP.
Although the season for the track club is already over.
THAT'S RIGHT.
...
HOW HARSH!
Well...
CAN'T DO ANYTHING ABOUT THAT.
THIS IS WHAT GOT ME INTO OSAKA HIGH.
IT'S THE PATH I CHOSE.
That's it!

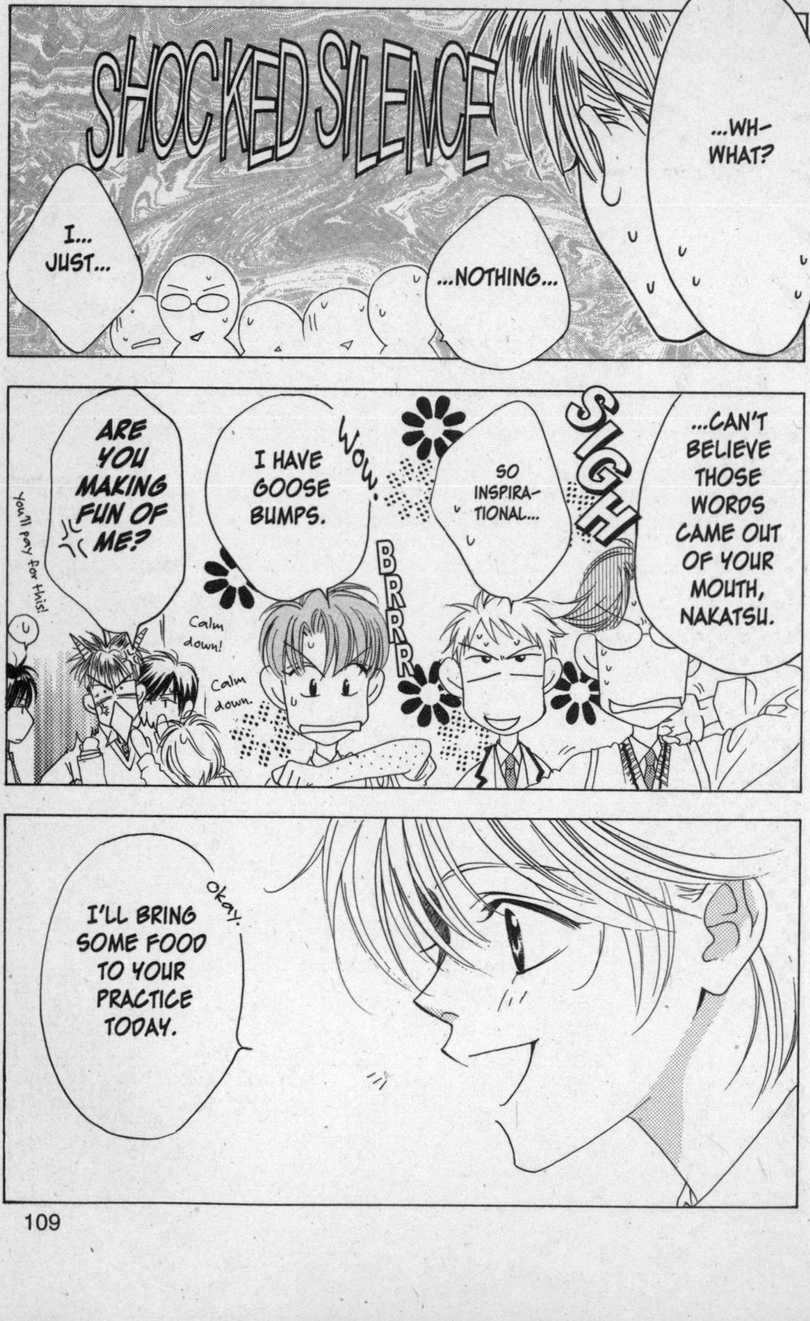
...WH-WHAT?
SHOCKED SILENCE
...NOTHING...
I... JUST...
...CAN'T BELIEVE THOSE WORDS CAME OUT OF YOUR MOUTH, NAKATSU.
SIGH
SO INSPIRA-TIONAL...
BRRRR
WOW.
I HAVE GOOSE BUMPS.
Calm down.
Calm down!
ARE YOU MAKING FUN OF ME?
You'll pay for this!
Okay.
I'LL BRING SOME FOOD TO YOUR PRACTICE TODAY.

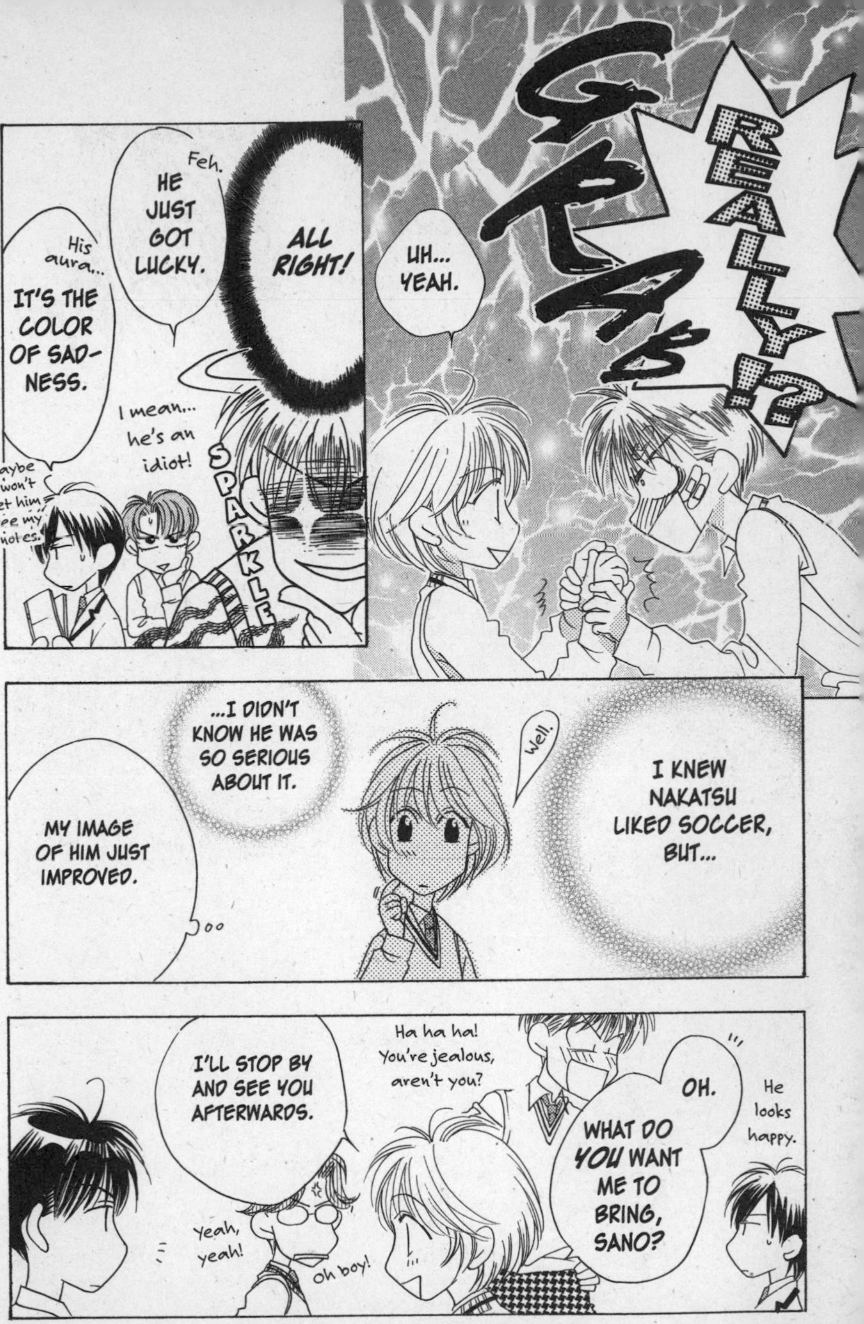
GRAB
REALLY!?
UH... YEAH.
ALL RIGHT!
SPARKLE
Feh.
HE JUST GOT LUCKY.
I mean... he's an idiot!
His aura...
IT'S THE COLOR OF SAD-NESS.
Maybe I won't let him see my notes.
I KNEW NAKATSU LIKED SOCCER, BUT...
Well.
...I DIDN'T KNOW HE WAS SO SERIOUS ABOUT IT.
MY IMAGE OF HIM JUST IMPROVED.
He looks happy.
OH.
WHAT DO YOU WANT ME TO BRING, SANO?
Ha ha ha! You're jealous, aren't you?
I'LL STOP BY AND SEE YOU AFTERWARDS.
Oh boy!
Yeah, yeah!

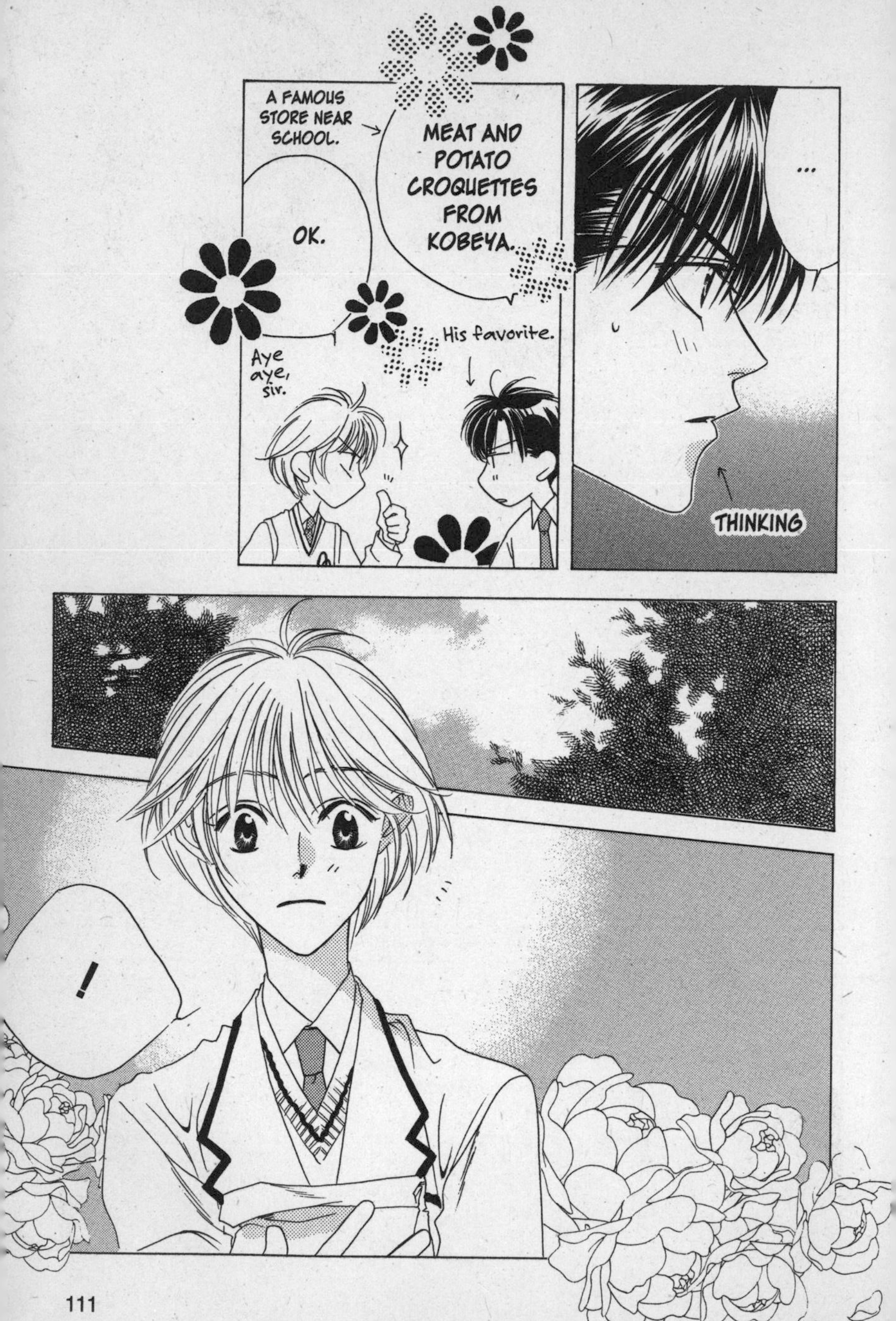
...
THINKING
MEAT AND POTATO CROQUETTES FROM KOBEYA.
A FAMOUS STORE NEAR SCHOOL.
OK.
His favorite.
Aye aye, sir.
!

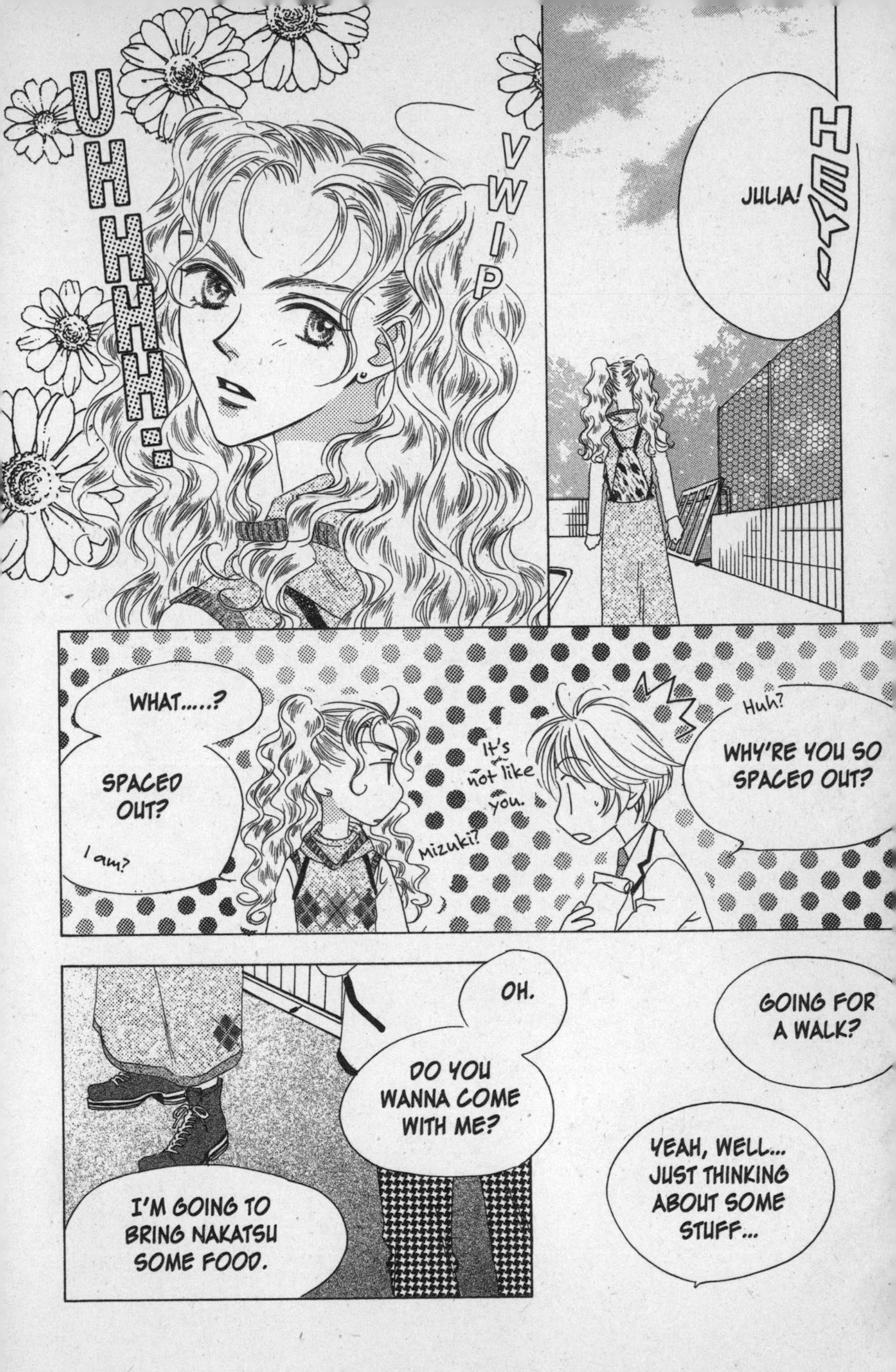
HEY!
JULIA!
UHHHHH!!
VWIP
Huh?
WHY'RE YOU SO SPACED OUT?
It's not like you.
Mizuki?
WHAT.....?
SPACED OUT?
I am?
GOING FOR A WALK?
YEAH, WELL... JUST THINKING ABOUT SOME STUFF...
OH.
DO YOU WANNA COME WITH ME?
I'M GOING TO BRING NAKATSU SOME FOOD.

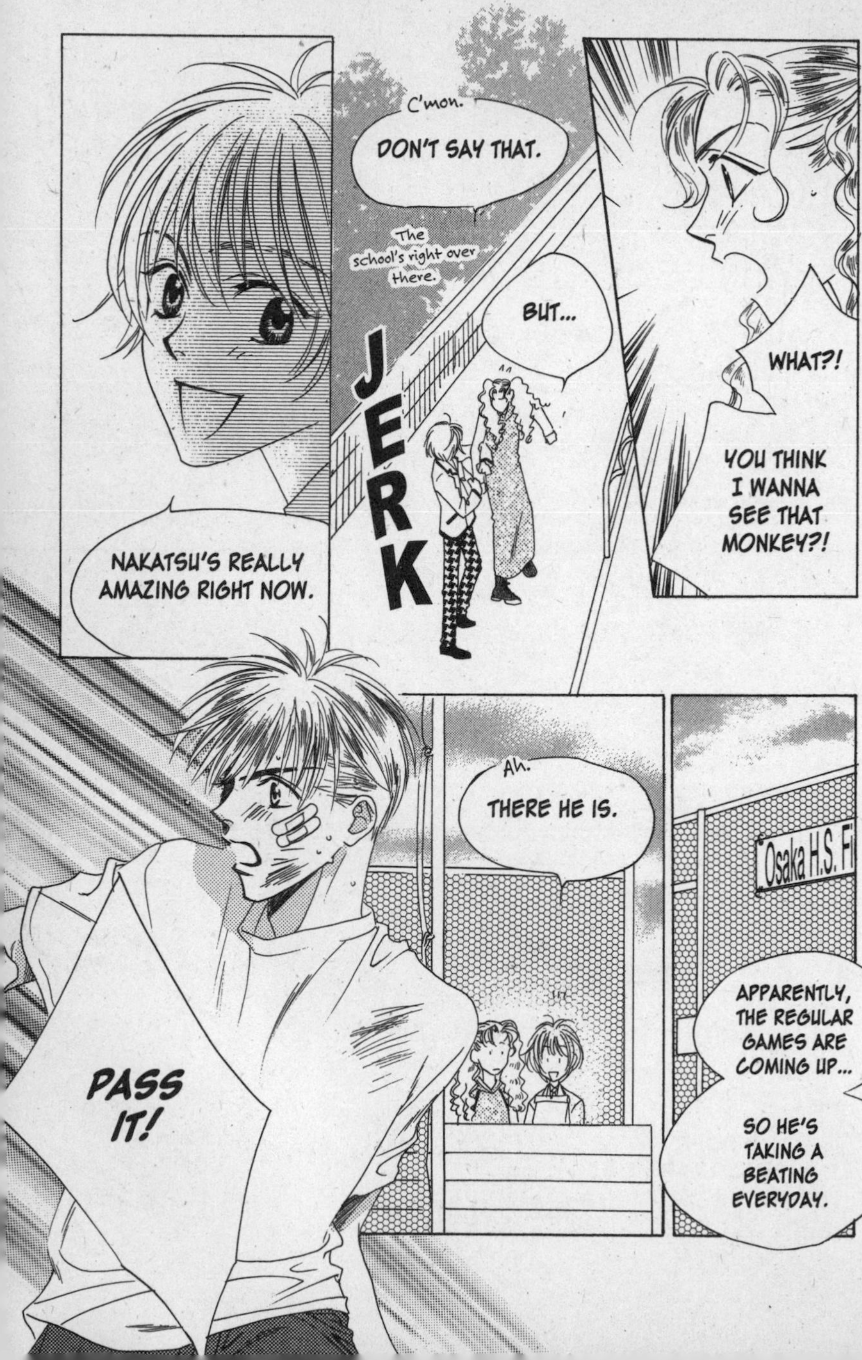

WHAT?!
YOU THINK I WANNA SEE THAT MONKEY?!
C'mon.
DON'T SAY THAT.
The school's right over there.
BUT...
JERK
NAKATSU'S REALLY AMAZING RIGHT NOW.
Osaka H.S. Fi
APPARENTLY, THE REGULAR GAMES ARE COMING UP...
SO HE'S TAKING A BEATING EVERYDAY.
Ah.
THERE HE IS.
PASS IT!

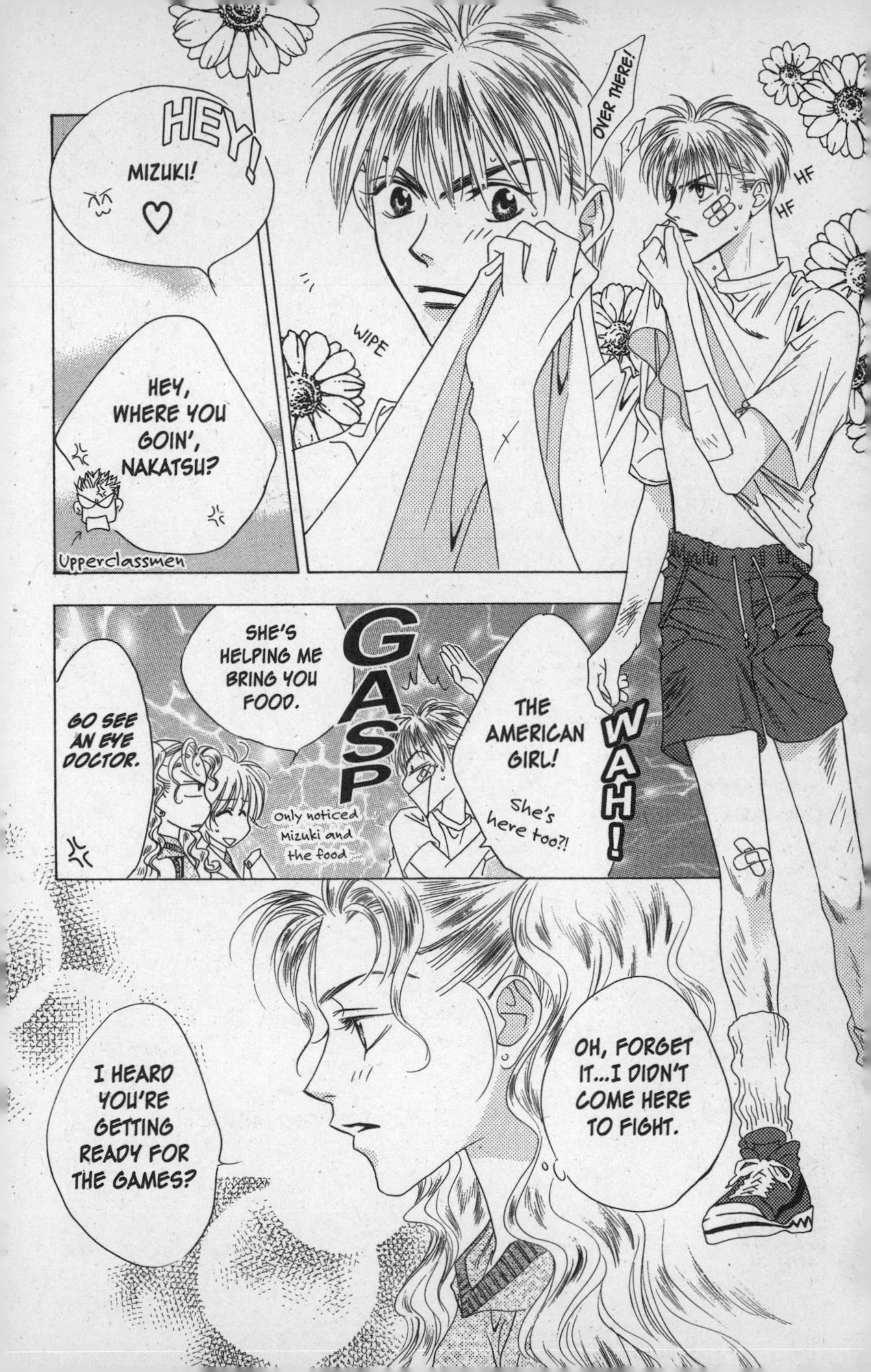
HF
HF
OVER THERE!
WIPE
HEY!
MIZUKI! ♥
HEY, WHERE YOU GOIN', NAKATSU?
Upperclassmen
WAH!
THE AMERICAN GIRL!
She's here too?!
GASP
SHE'S HELPING ME BRING YOU FOOD.
Only noticed Mizuki and the food
GO SEE AN EYE DOCTOR.
OH, FORGET IT...I DIDN'T COME HERE TO FIGHT.
I HEARD YOU'RE GETTING READY FOR THE GAMES?

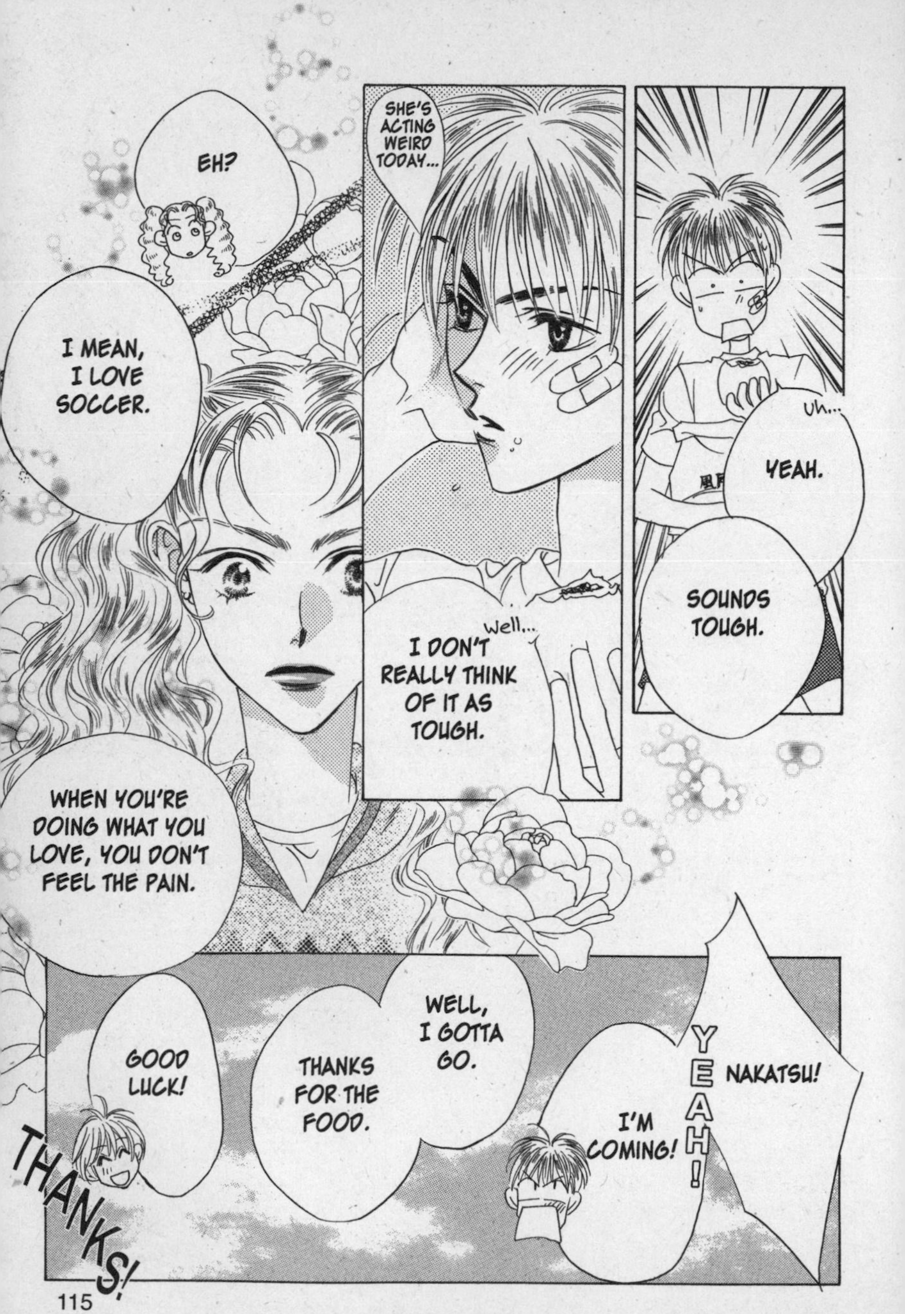
Uh...
YEAH.
SOUNDS TOUGH.
SHE'S ACTING WEIRD TODAY...
Well...
I DON'T REALLY THINK OF IT AS TOUGH.
EH?
I MEAN, I LOVE SOCCER.
WHEN YOU'RE DOING WHAT YOU LOVE, YOU DON'T FEEL THE PAIN.
NAKATSU!
YEAH!
I'M COMING!
WELL, I GOTTA GO.
THANKS FOR THE FOOD.
GOOD LUCK!
THANKS!

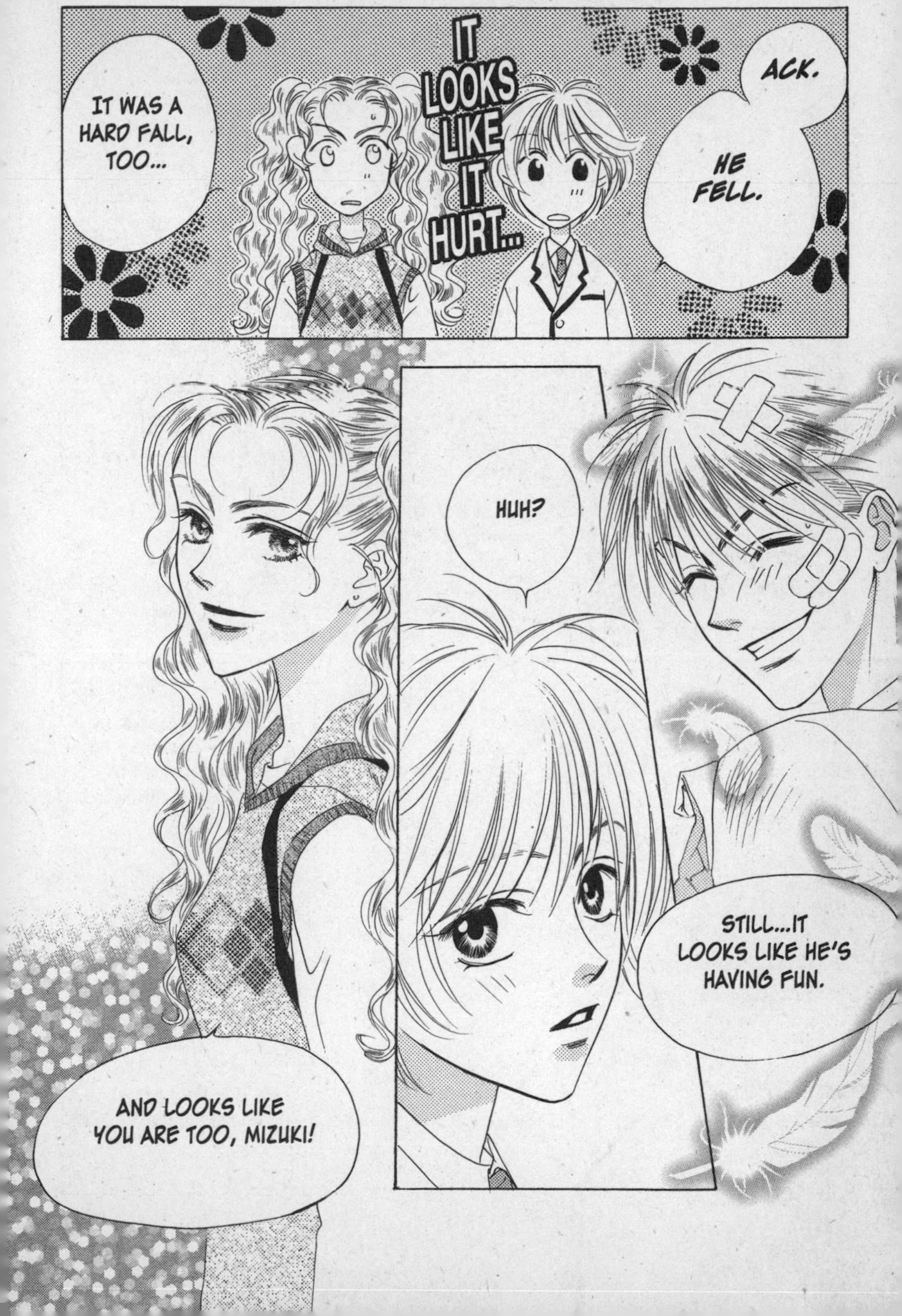
ACK.
HE FELL.
IT LOOKS LIKE IT HURT...
IT WAS A HARD FALL, TOO...
STILL...IT LOOKS LIKE HE'S HAVING FUN.
HUH?
AND LOOKS LIKE YOU ARE TOO, MIZUKI!

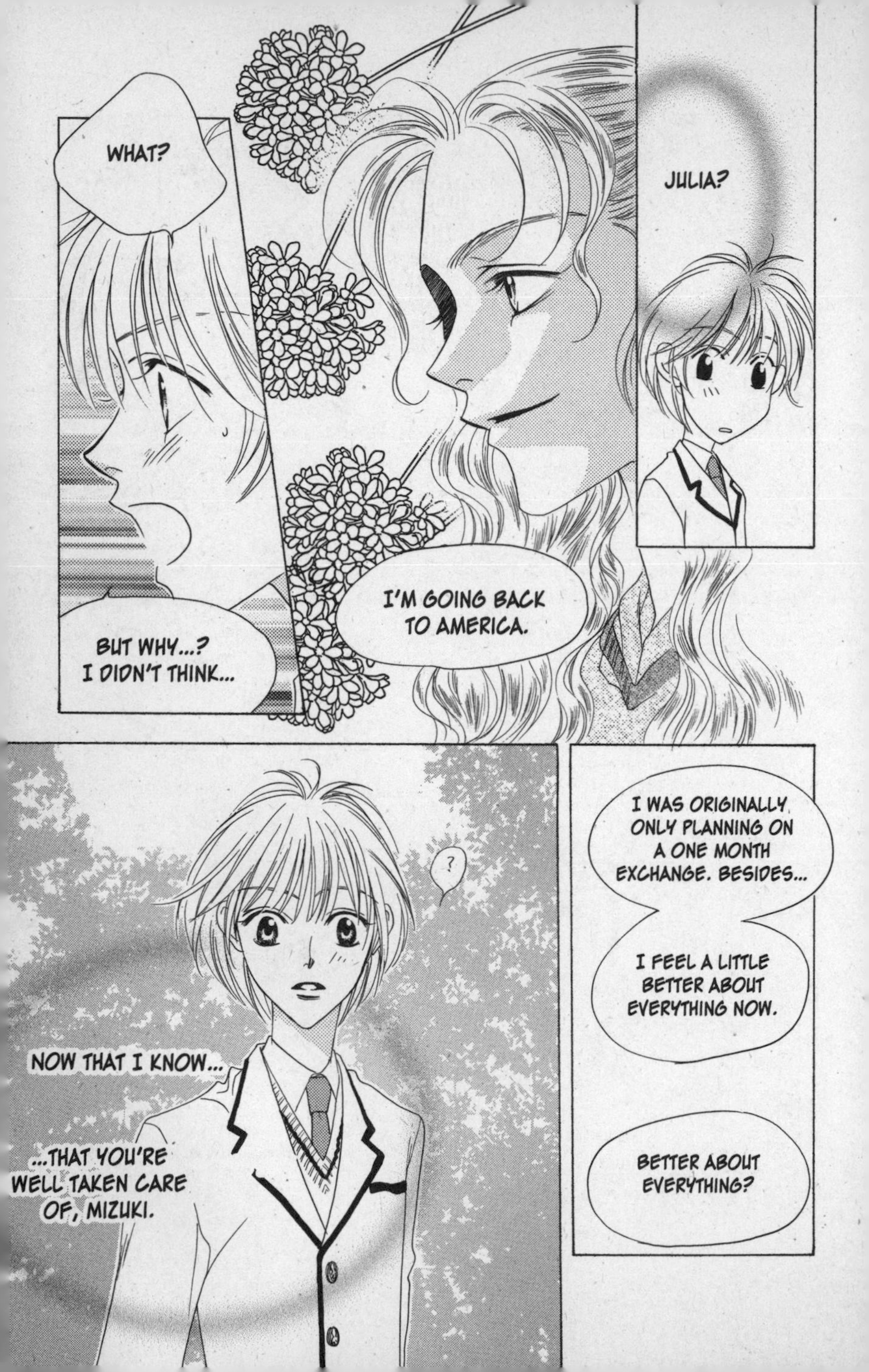
JULIA?
I'M GOING BACK TO AMERICA.
WHAT?
BUT WHY...? I DIDN'T THINK...
I WAS ORIGINALLY ONLY PLANNING ON A ONE MONTH EXCHANGE. BESIDES...
I FEEL A LITTLE BETTER ABOUT EVERYTHING NOW.
BETTER ABOUT EVERYTHING?
?
NOW THAT I KNOW...
...THAT YOU'RE WELL TAKEN CARE OF, MIZUKI.

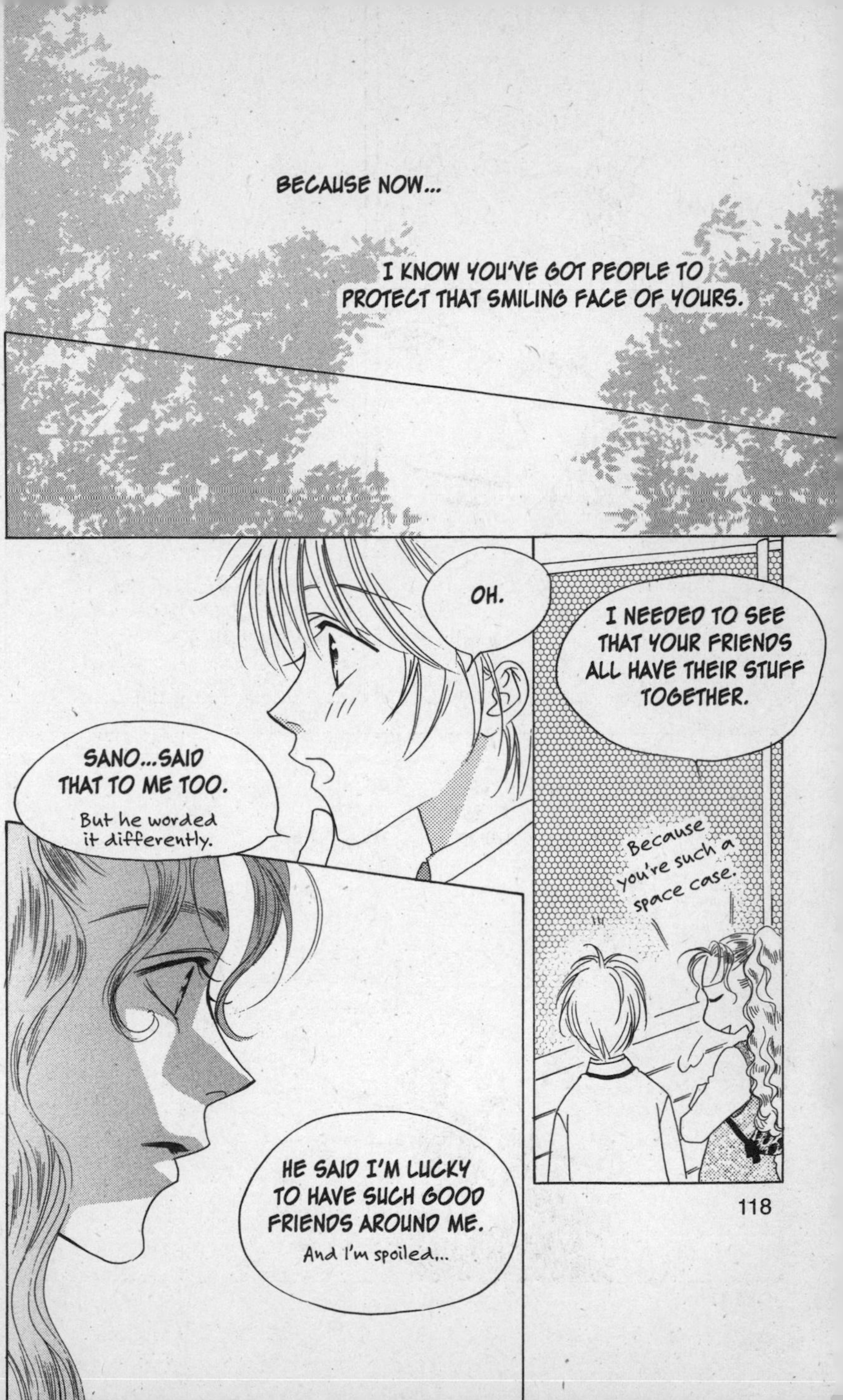
BECAUSE NOW...
I KNOW YOU'VE GOT PEOPLE TO PROTECT THAT SMILING FACE OF YOURS.
I NEEDED TO SEE THAT YOUR FRIENDS ALL HAVE THEIR STUFF TOGETHER.
Because you're such a space case.
OH.
SANO...SAID THAT TO ME TOO. But he worded it differently.
HE SAID I'M LUCKY TO HAVE SUCH GOOD FRIENDS AROUND ME. And I'm spoiled...

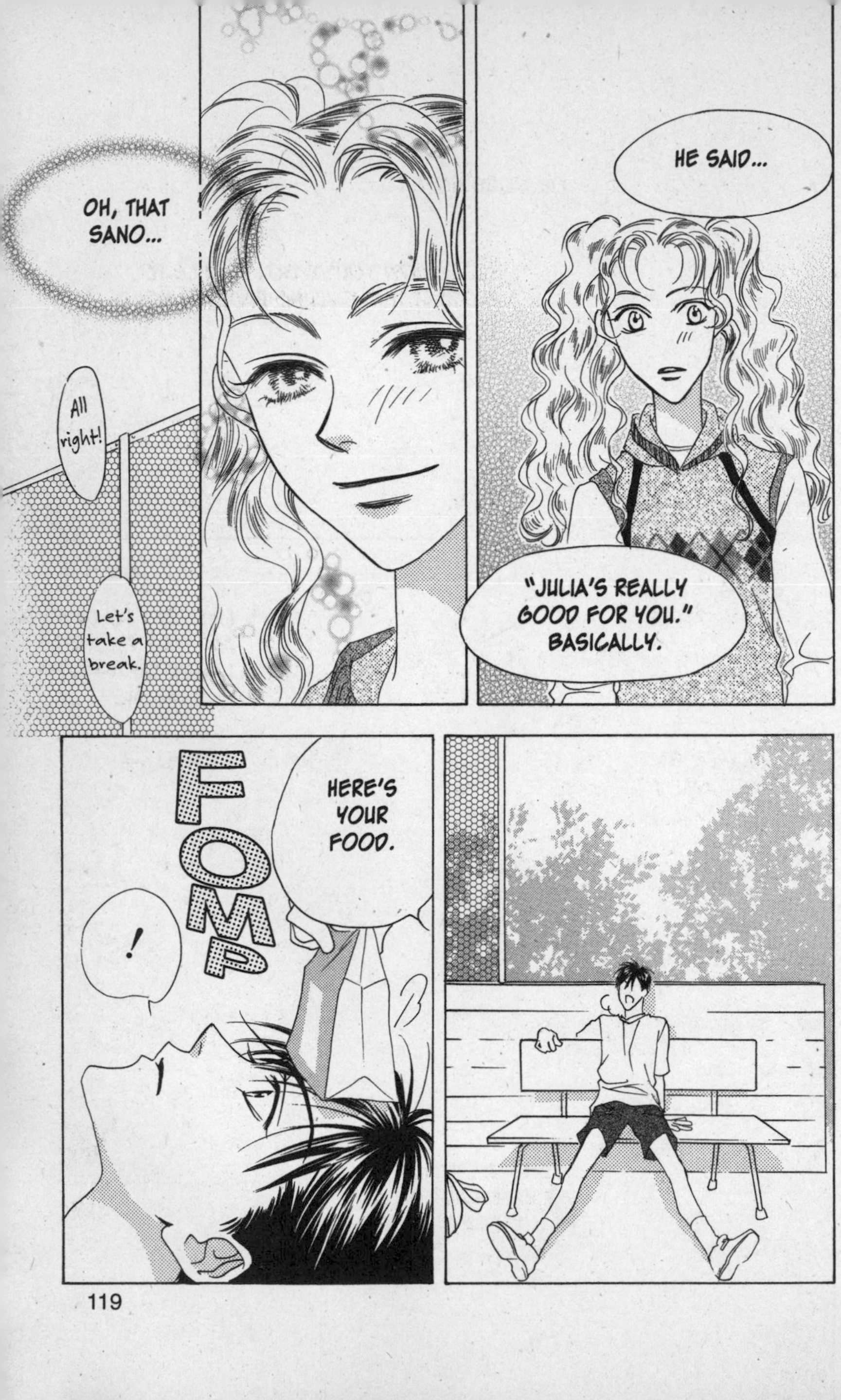
HE SAID...
"JULIA'S REALLY GOOD FOR YOU." BASICALLY.
OH, THAT SANO...
All right!
Let's take a break.
HERE'S YOUR FOOD.
FOMP
!

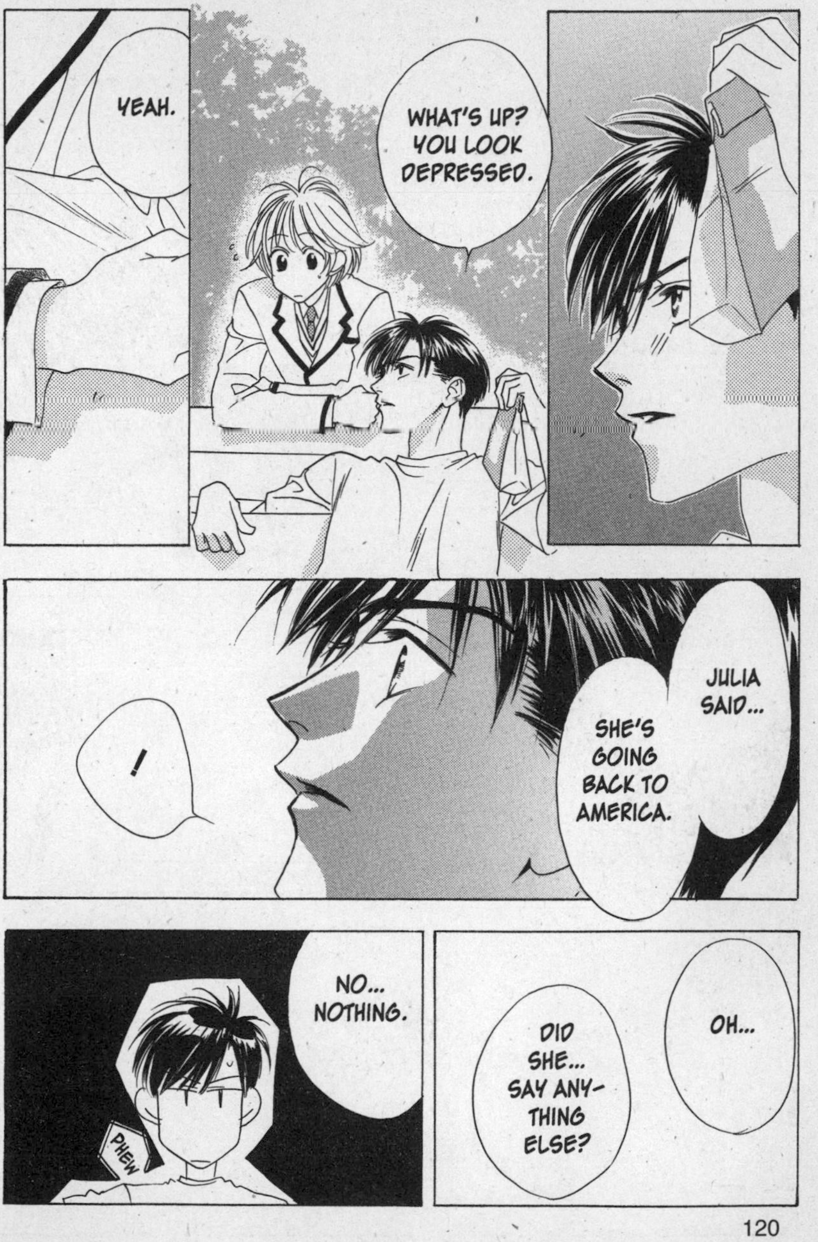
WHAT'S UP? YOU LOOK DEPRESSED.
YEAH.
JULIA SAID...
SHE'S GOING BACK TO AMERICA.
!
OH...
DID SHE... SAY ANY-THING ELSE?
NO... NOTHING.
PHEW

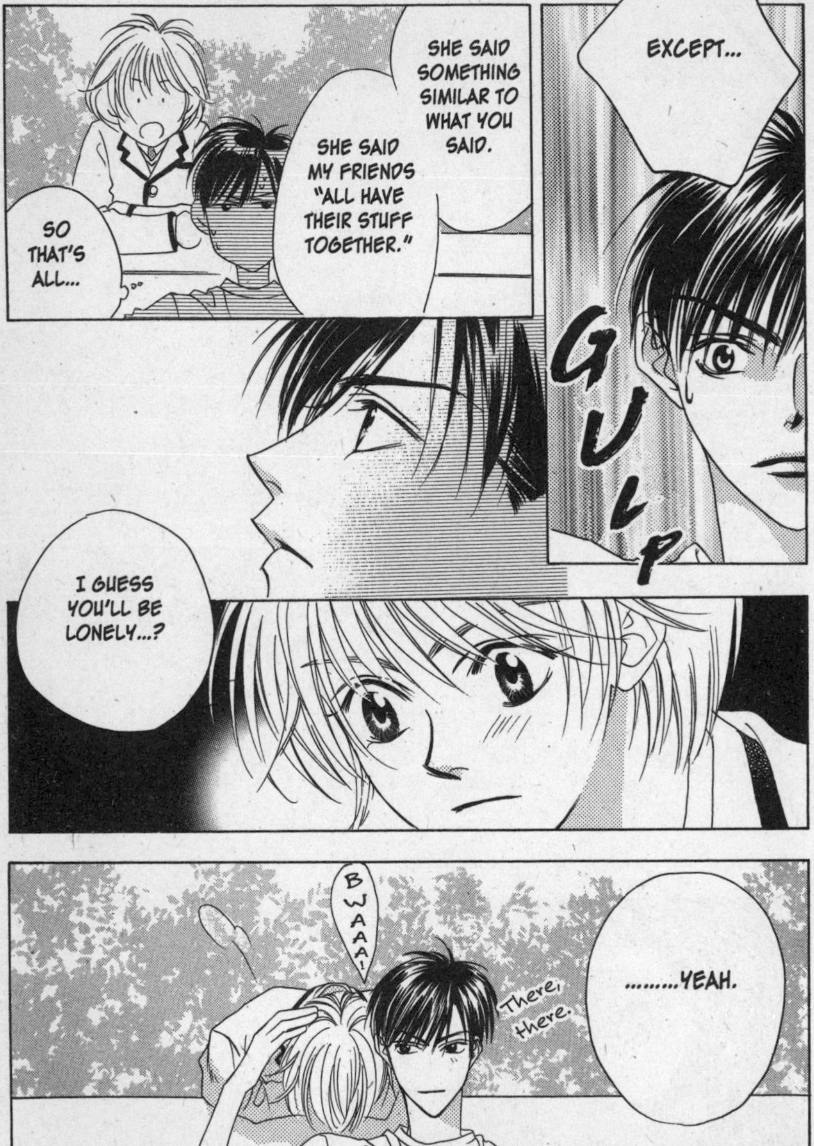
EXCEPT...
GULP
SHE SAID SOMETHING SIMILAR TO WHAT YOU SAID.
SHE SAID MY FRIENDS "ALL HAVE THEIR STUFF TOGETHER."
SO THAT'S ALL...
I GUESS YOU'LL BE LONELY...?
.........YEAH.
There, there.
BWAAA!

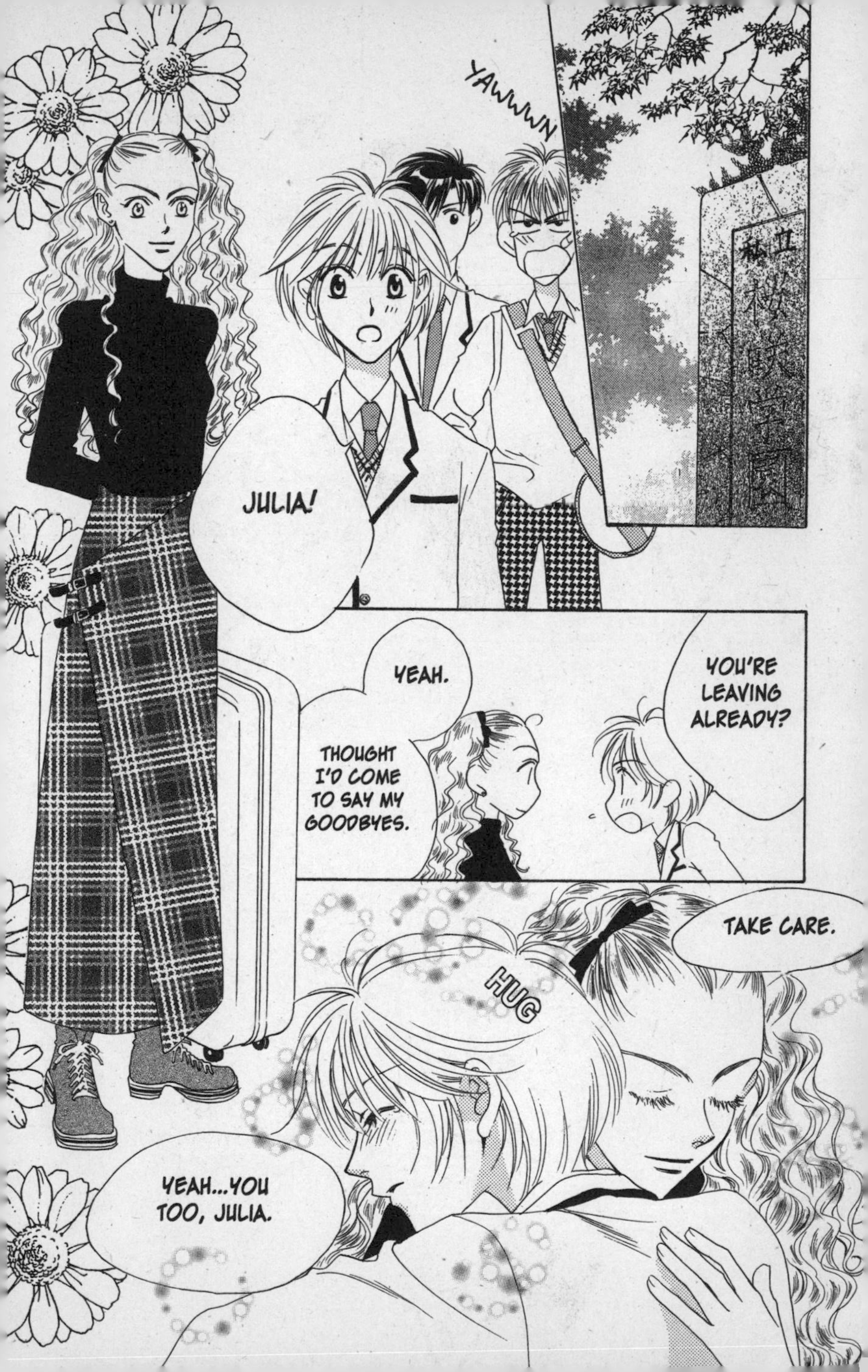
私立
桜咲学園
YAWWWN
JULIA!
YOU'RE LEAVING ALREADY?
YEAH.
THOUGHT I'D COME TO SAY MY GOODBYES.
TAKE CARE.
HUG
YEAH...YOU TOO, JULIA.

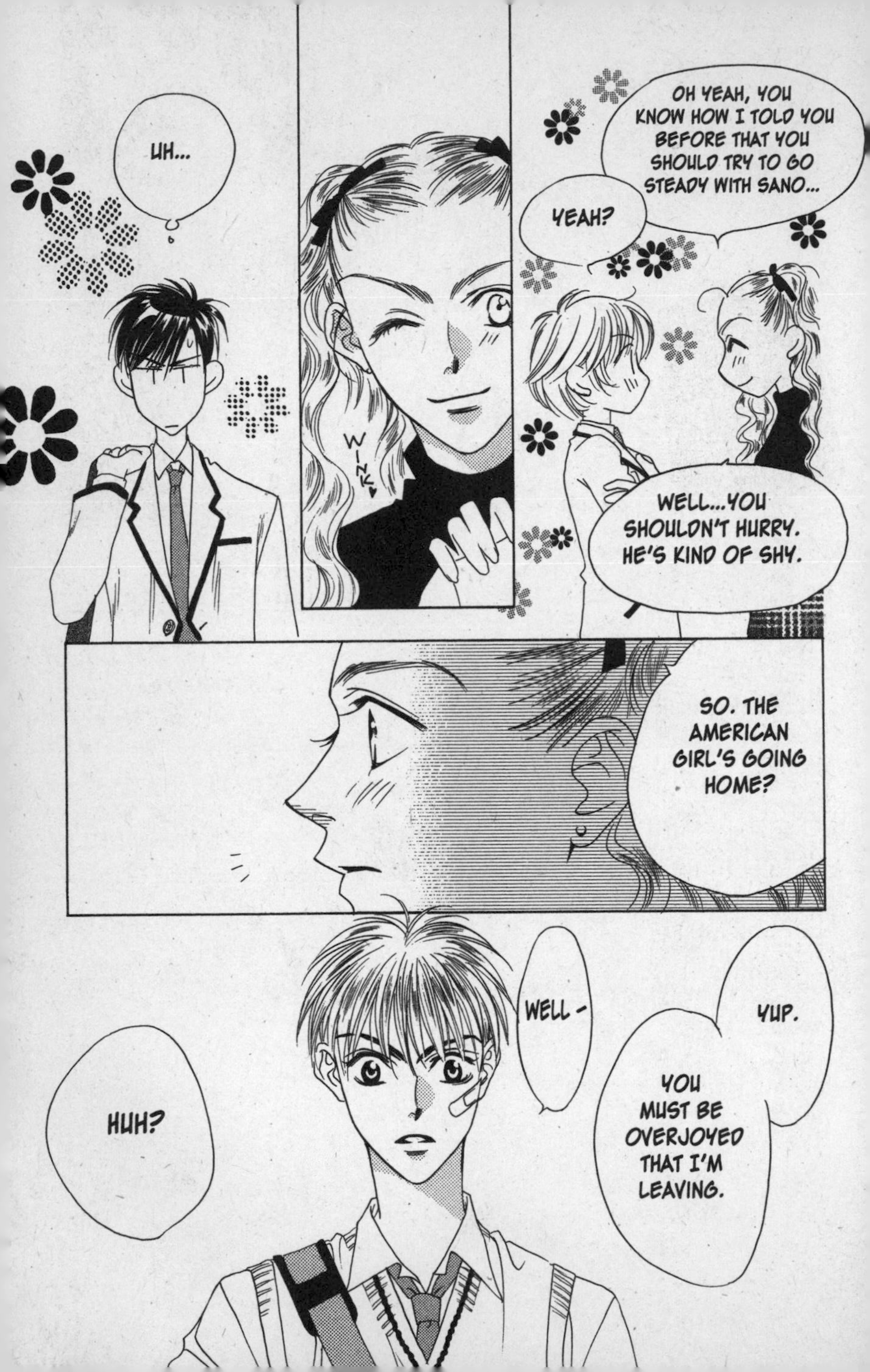
OH YEAH, YOU KNOW HOW I TOLD YOU BEFORE THAT YOU SHOULD TRY TO GO STEADY WITH SANO...
YEAH?
WELL...YOU SHOULDN'T HURRY. HE'S KIND OF SHY.
WINK
UH...
SO. THE AMERICAN GIRL'S GOING HOME?
YUP.
YOU MUST BE OVERJOYED THAT I'M LEAVING.
WELL -
HUH?

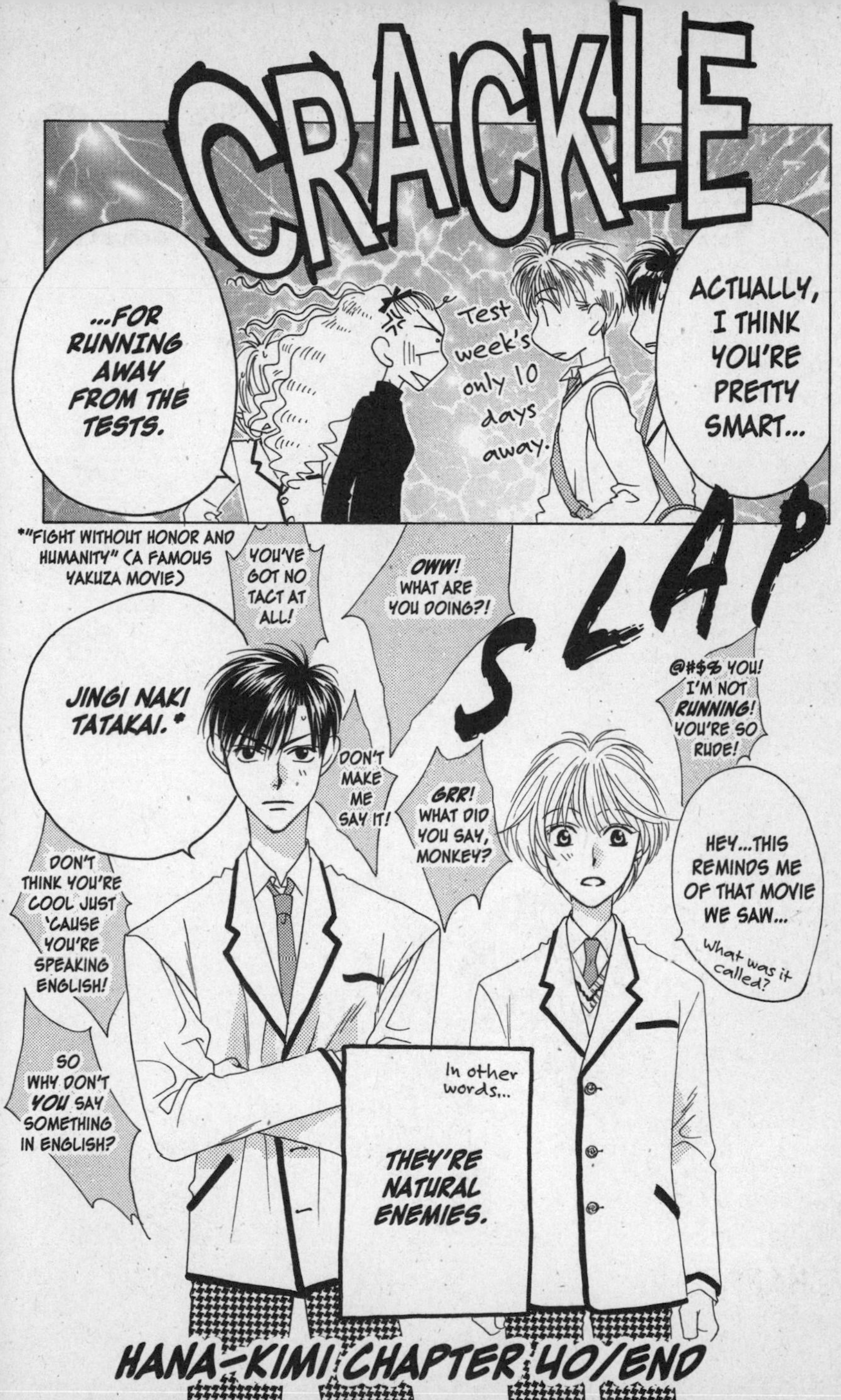
CRACKLE
ACTUALLY, I THINK YOU'RE PRETTY SMART...
Test week's only 10 days away.
...FOR RUNNING AWAY FROM THE TESTS.
SLAP
@#$% YOU! I'M NOT RUNNING! YOU'RE SO RUDE!
OWW! WHAT ARE YOU DOING?!
YOU'VE GOT NO TACT AT ALL!
JINGI NAKI TATAKAI.*
HEY...THIS REMINDS ME OF THAT MOVIE WE SAW...
What was it called?
GRR! WHAT DID YOU SAY, MONKEY?
DON'T MAKE ME SAY IT!
DON'T THINK YOU'RE COOL JUST 'CAUSE YOU'RE SPEAKING ENGLISH!
SO WHY DON'T YOU SAY SOMETHING IN ENGLISH?
In other words...
THEY'RE NATURAL ENEMIES.
*"FIGHT WITHOUT HONOR AND HUMANITY" (A FAMOUS YAKUZA MOVIE)
HANA-KIMI CHAPTER 40/END

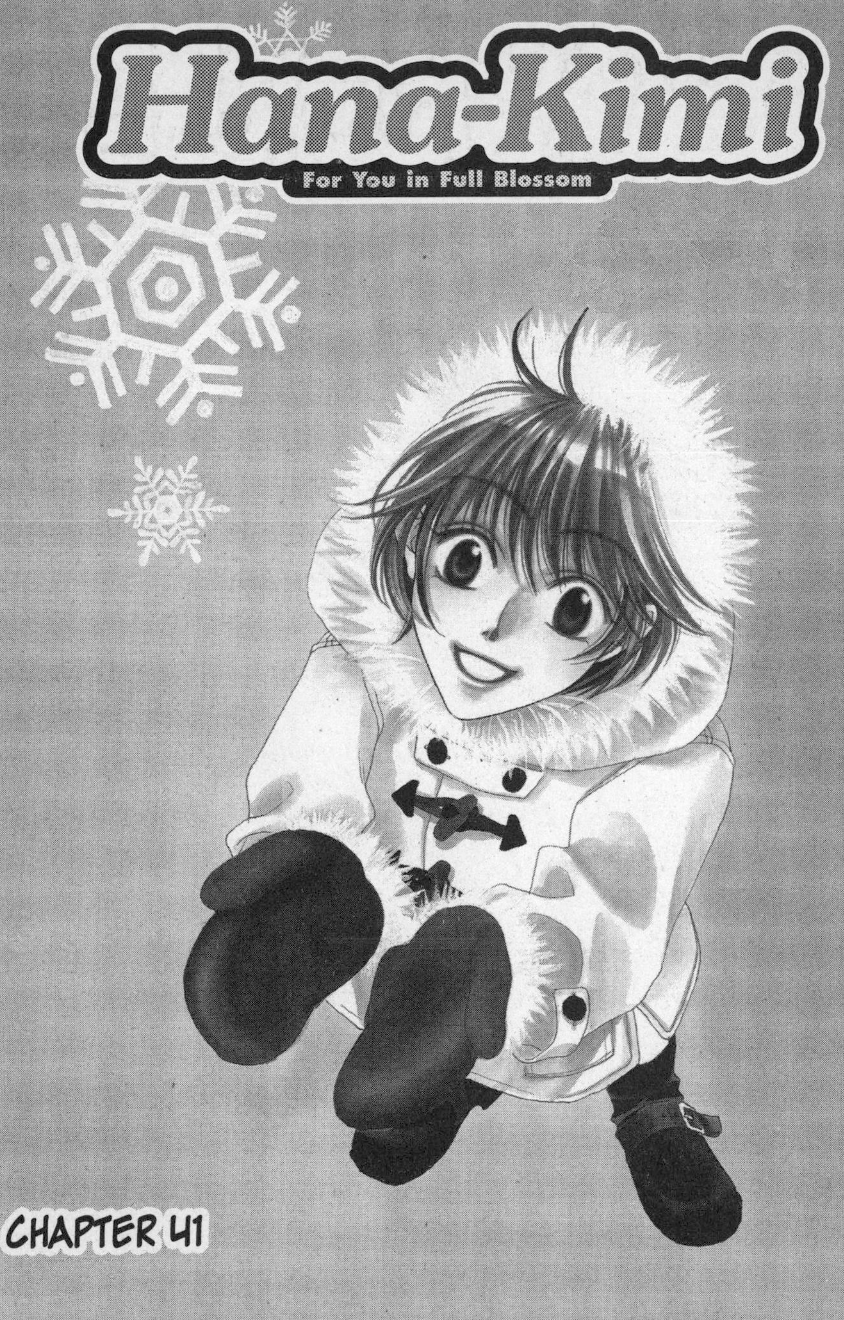
Hana-Kimi
For You in Full Blossom
CHAPTER 41

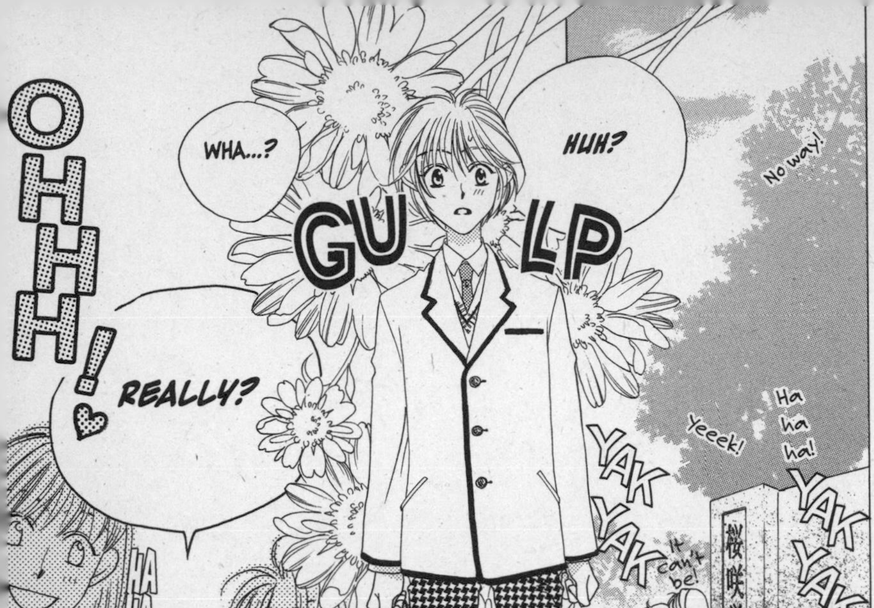
No way!
HUH?
WHA...?
GULP
Ha ha ha!
Yeeek!
YAK YAK YAK
YAK YAK YAK
It can't be!
桜咲学園
Hee hee!
OHHHH!
REALLY?
HA HA HA!
sweat sweat
WHEEE!

ROMEO NO AOI SORA

(Romeo's Blue Skies)

I LOVED THIS ANIME!♡ EVER SINCE I WAS A KID, I'VE ALWAYS LIKED THE ANIME SHOW "SEKAI MEISAKU GEKIJO" (WORLD MASTERPIECE THEATER). BUT I CAN'T BELIEVE I'VE GOTTEN SO INTO IT AS AN ADULT. I HAVEN'T BEEN INTO ANYTHING THIS HEAVILY SINCE "MAKIBA NO SHOJO KATRI" (KATRI, GIRL OF THE MEADOWS). I EVEN READ THE BOOK IT WAS BASED ON, "DIE SCHWARZEN BRÜDER" (THE BLACK BROTHERS) BY LISA TETZNER, AND I BOUGHT ALL THE TV EPISODES ON VIDEO. RECENTLY, THEY WERE REBROADCASTING THE SERIES IN THE KANSAI AREA (AT 8 AM), SO MY ASSISTANTS AND I STARTED OUR OWN ROMEO BOOM. I LOVE IT!

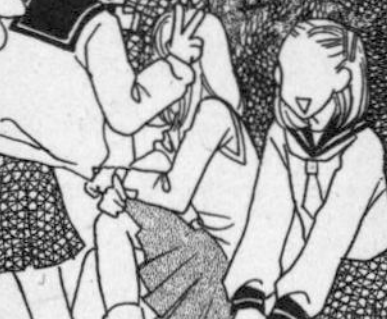
TV
Alfredo!
SOBB

I LOVE IT! I LOVE IT! I SHOULD SHUT UP, ALREADY!

IKKYU-SAN!

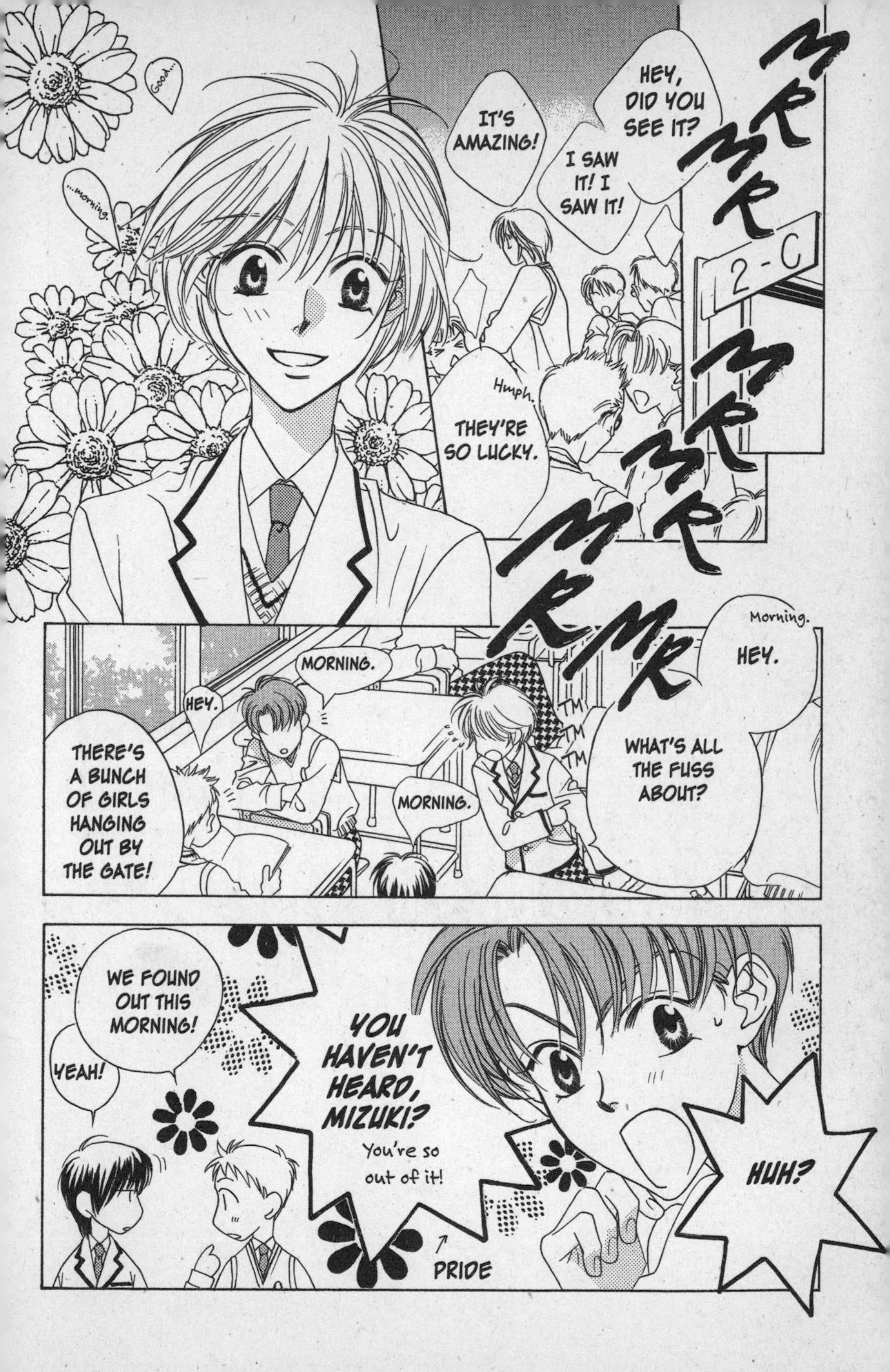
MR MR MR MR MR MR
2-C
HEY, DID YOU SEE IT?
IT'S AMAZING!
I SAW IT! I SAW IT!
Hmph.
THEY'RE SO LUCKY.
Good...
...morning.
Morning.
HEY.
TM TM TM
WHAT'S ALL THE FUSS ABOUT?
MORNING.
MORNING.
HEY.
THERE'S A BUNCH OF GIRLS HANGING OUT BY THE GATE!
HUH?
YOU HAVEN'T HEARD, MIZUKI?
You're so out of it!
PRIDE
WE FOUND OUT THIS MORNING!
YEAH!

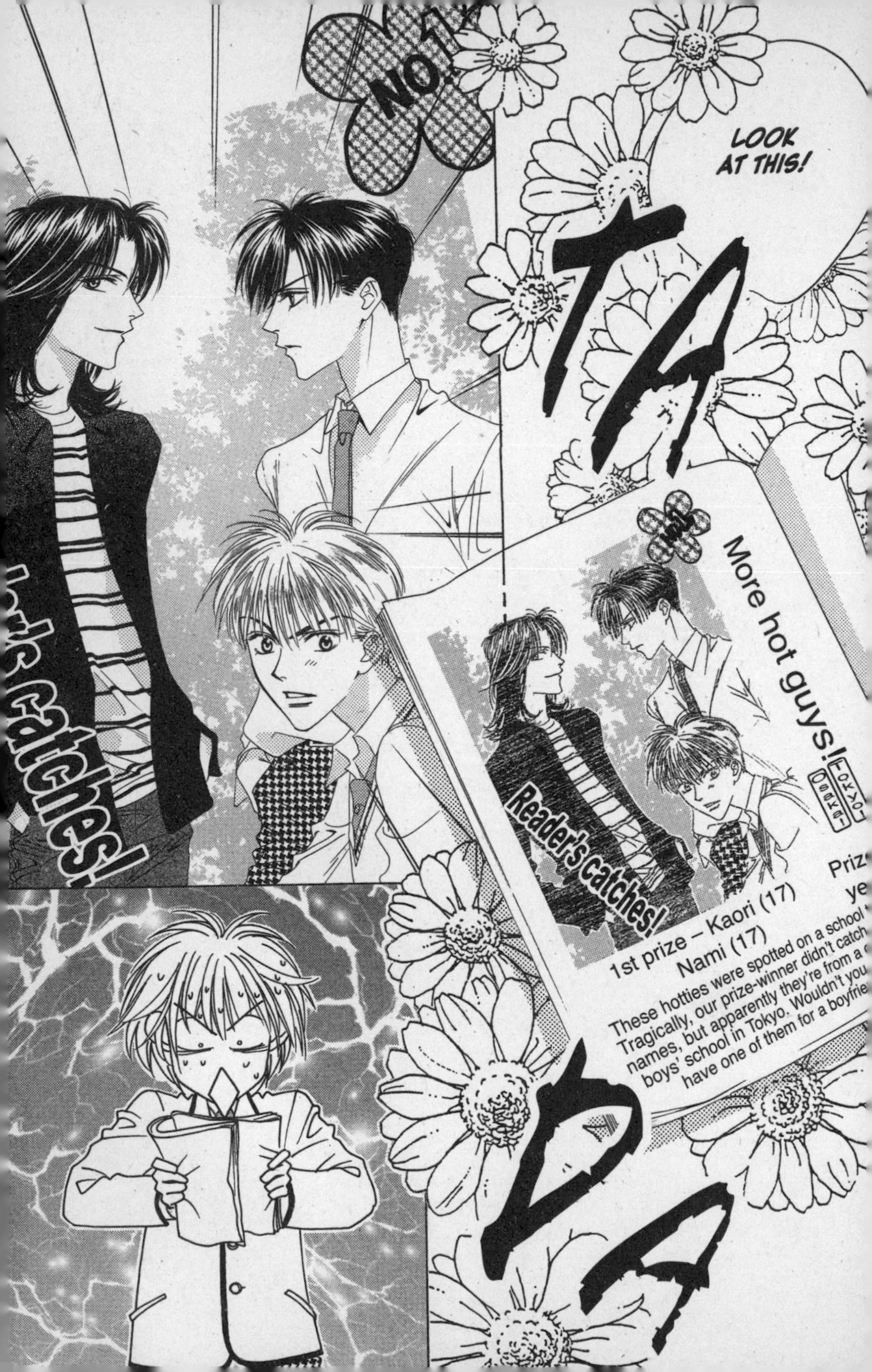
LOOK AT THIS!
TA
NO.1
More hot guys!
TOKYO
Osaka
Reader's catches!
Prize
1st prize – Kaori (17)
Nami (17)
These hotties were spotted on a school
Tragically, our prize-winner didn't catch
names, but apparently they're from a
boys' school in Tokyo. Wouldn't you
have one of them for a boyfrie
der's catches!
DA

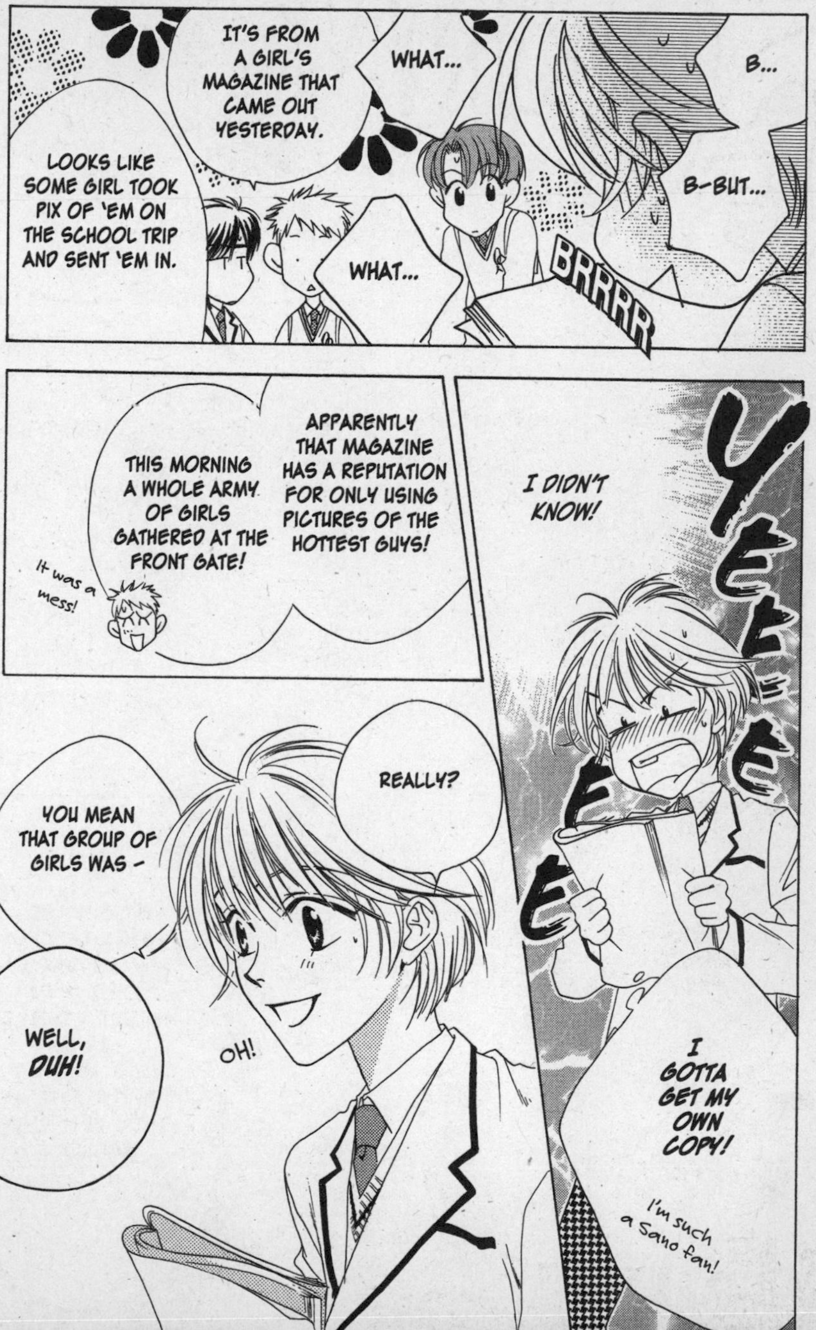
B...
B-BUT...
WHAT...
IT'S FROM A GIRL'S MAGAZINE THAT CAME OUT YESTERDAY.
BRRRR
WHAT...
LOOKS LIKE SOME GIRL TOOK PIX OF 'EM ON THE SCHOOL TRIP AND SENT 'EM IN.
YEEEEEE
I DIDN'T KNOW!
I GOTTA GET MY OWN COPY!
I'm such a Sano fan!
APPARENTLY THAT MAGAZINE HAS A REPUTATION FOR ONLY USING PICTURES OF THE HOTTEST GUYS!
THIS MORNING A WHOLE ARMY OF GIRLS GATHERED AT THE FRONT GATE!
It was a mess!
REALLY?
YOU MEAN THAT GROUP OF GIRLS WAS -
OH!
WELL, DUH!

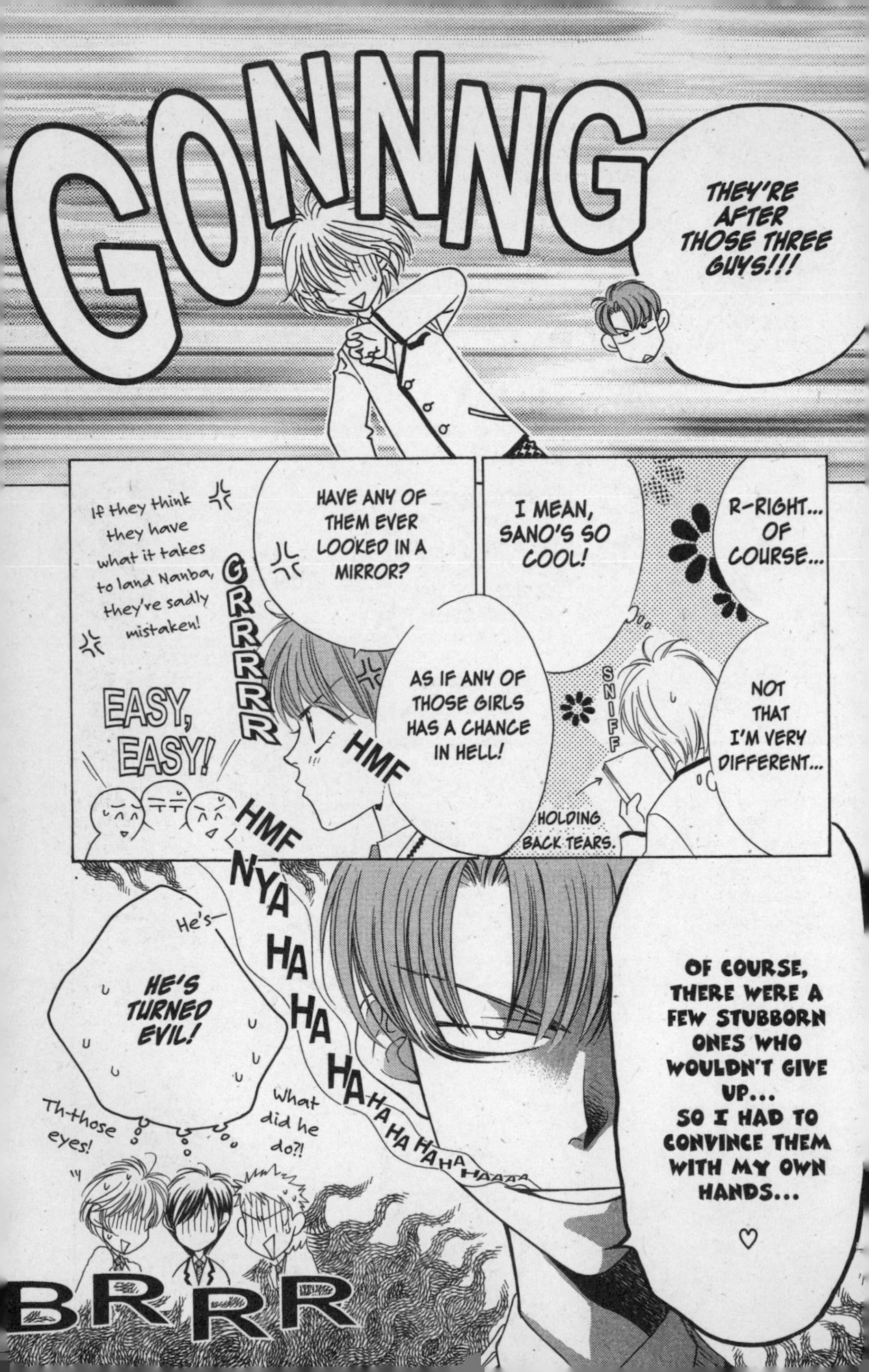
GONNNG
THEY'RE AFTER THOSE THREE GUYS!!!
R-RIGHT... OF COURSE...
I MEAN, SANO'S SO COOL!
NOT THAT I'M VERY DIFFERENT...
SNIFF
HOLDING BACK TEARS.
HAVE ANY OF THEM EVER LOOKED IN A MIRROR?
If they think they have what it takes to land Nanba, they're sadly mistaken!
GRRRRRR
AS IF ANY OF THOSE GIRLS HAS A CHANCE IN HELL!
HMF
HMF
EASY, EASY!
OF COURSE, THERE WERE A FEW STUBBORN ONES WHO WOULDN'T GIVE UP... SO I HAD TO CONVINCE THEM WITH MY OWN HANDS... ♡
NYA HA HA HA HA HA HA HA HA HAAAA
He's—
HE'S TURNED EVIL!
What did he do?!
Th-those eyes!
BRRRR

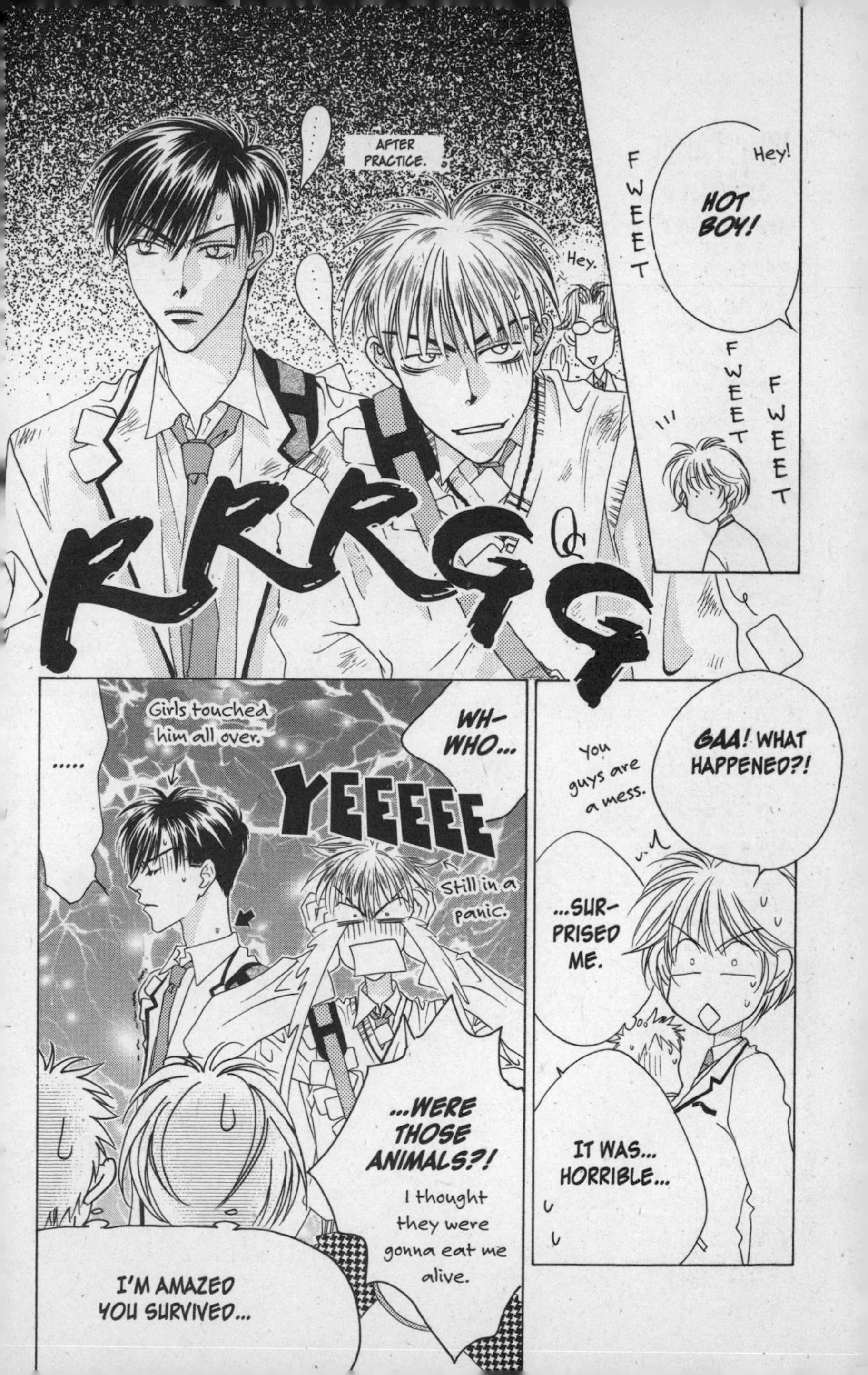
FWEET
Hey!
HOT BOY!
FWEET
FWEET
AFTER PRACTICE.
...
...
Hey.
RRRGG
GAA! WHAT HAPPENED?!
You guys are a mess.
...SUR-PRISED ME.
IT WAS... HORRIBLE...
WH-WHO...
YEEEEE
Still in a panic.
...WERE THOSE ANIMALS?!
I thought they were gonna eat me alive.
Girls touched him all over.
.....
I'M AMAZED YOU SURVIVED...

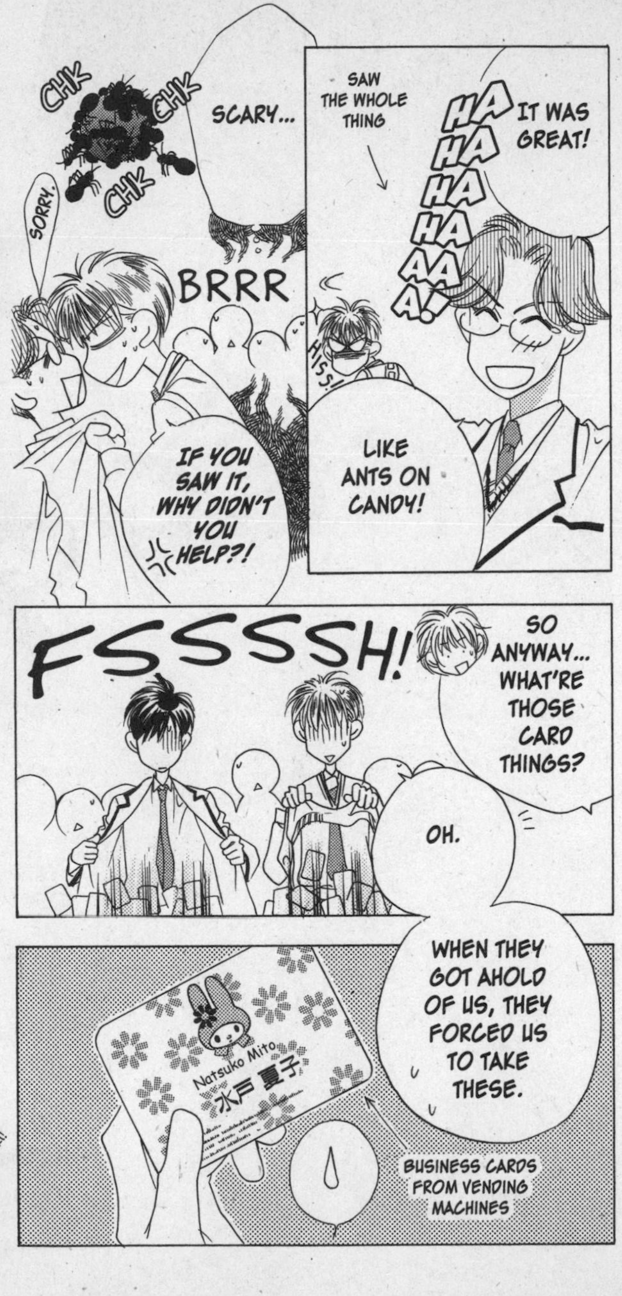
HA HA HA HA AA A!
IT WAS GREAT!
SAW THE WHOLE THING
HISS!
LIKE ANTS ON CANDY!
SCARY...
CHK
CHK
CHK
SORRY.
BRRR
IF YOU SAW IT, WHY DIDN'T YOU HELP?!
SO ANYWAY... WHAT'RE THOSE CARD THINGS?
FSSSSH!
OH.
WHEN THEY GOT AHOLD OF US, THEY FORCED US TO TAKE THESE.
Natsuko Mito
水戸夏子
BUSINESS CARDS FROM VENDING MACHINES

WHISPERED SECRETS

WEISS LIVE

I WENT TO WEISS'S LAST LIVE CONCERT ON DECEMBER 26TH IN OSAKA. PEOPLE KEEP ASKING ME "WHAT WAS IT LIKE?" I GOT THE TICKETS KIND OF BY ACCIDENT AND I WAS WONDERING WHAT A VOICE ACTOR'S CONCERT MIGHT BE LIKE. IT WAS AMAZING! I NEVER REALIZED JUST HOW POPULAR VOICE ACTORS ARE. IN A WAY, IT'S ALMOST LIKE A "VISUAL BAND"'S LIVE SHOW. I WAS WATCHING FROM A THIRD FLOOR SEAT THROUGH MY OPERA GLASSES, BUT I WAS OVERWHELMED BY HOW PASSIONATE THE FANS ARE! (HA HA!) IT WAS REALLY FUN.

YAY, YOUJI! AYA! OMI! KEN!

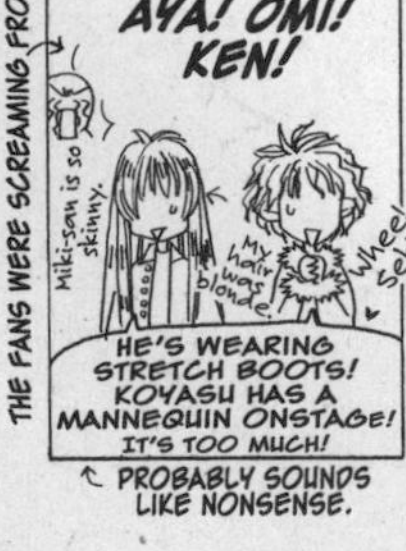
THE FANS WERE SCREAMING FROM BEHIND US.
Miki-san is so skinny.
My hair was blonde.
Whee! seki!
HE'S WEARING STRETCH BOOTS! KOYASU HAS A MANNEQUIN ONSTAGE! IT'S TOO MUCH!

↖ PROBABLY SOUNDS LIKE NONSENSE.

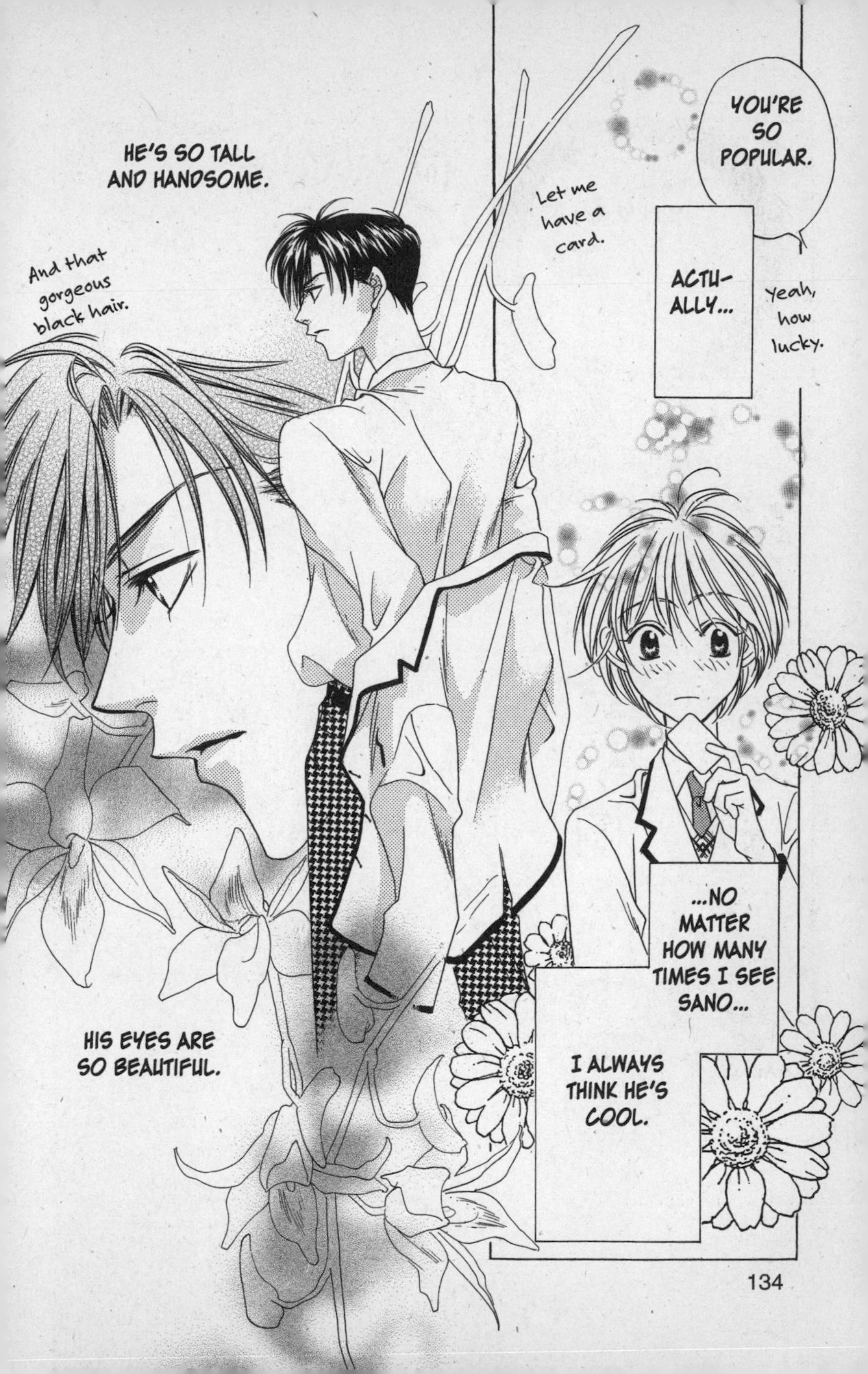
YOU'RE SO POPULAR.
ACTU-ALLY...
Yeah, how lucky.
...NO MATTER HOW MANY TIMES I SEE SANO...
I ALWAYS THINK HE'S COOL.
Let me have a card.
HE'S SO TALL AND HANDSOME.
And that gorgeous black hair.
HIS EYES ARE SO BEAUTIFUL.

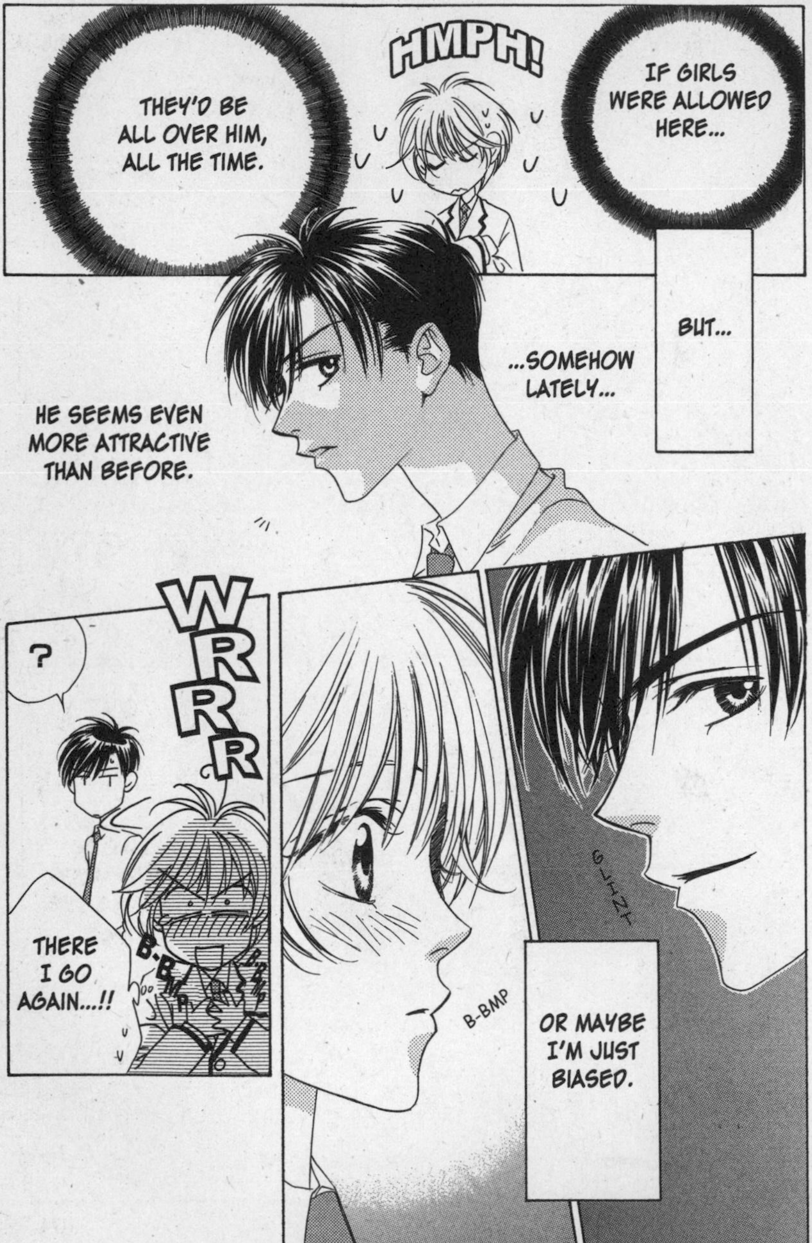
IF GIRLS WERE ALLOWED HERE...
HMPH!
THEY'D BE ALL OVER HIM, ALL THE TIME.
BUT...
...SOMEHOW LATELY...
HE SEEMS EVEN MORE ATTRACTIVE THAN BEFORE.
GLINT
OR MAYBE I'M JUST BIASED.
B-BMP
WRRR
?
THERE I GO AGAIN...!!
B-BMP

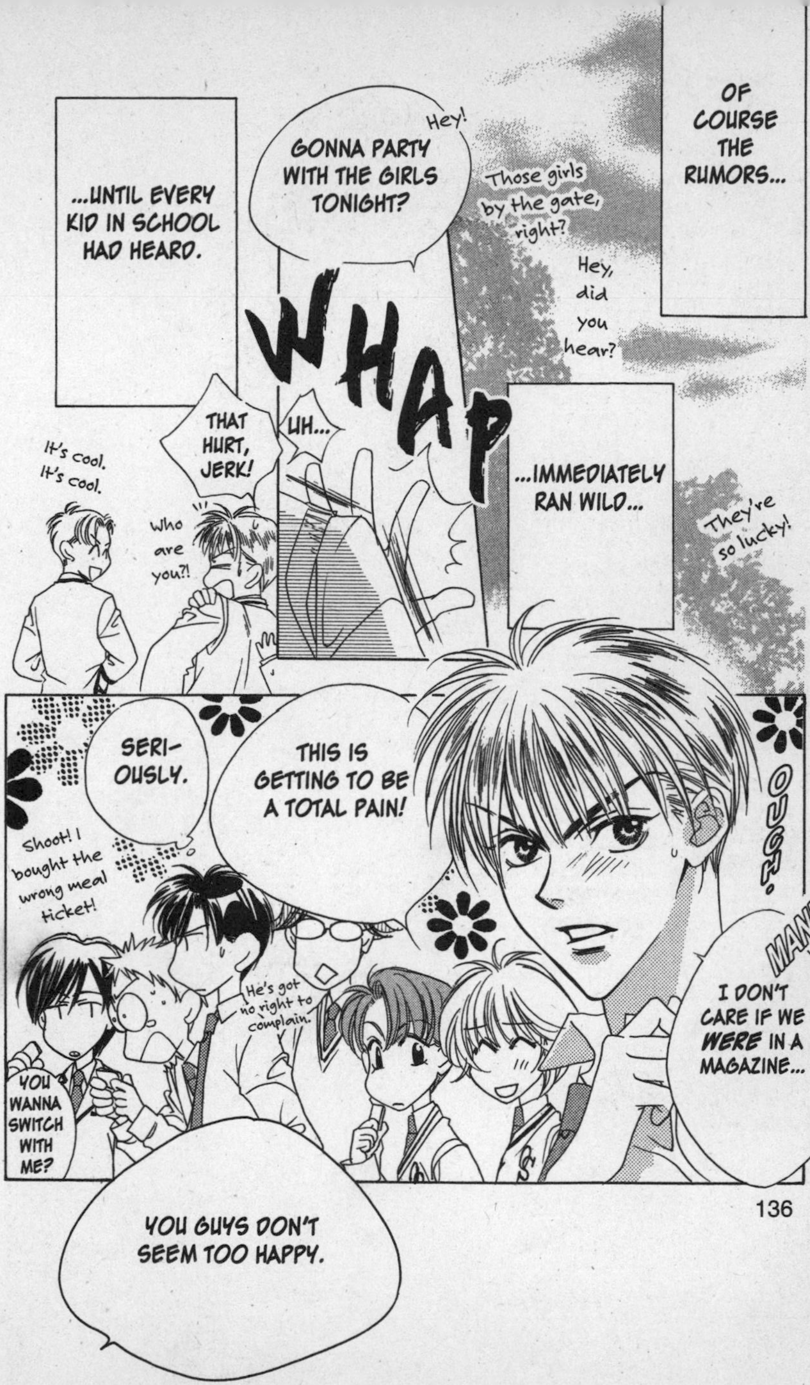
OF COURSE THE RUMORS...
Hey, did you hear?
Those girls by the gate, right?
...IMMEDIATELY RAN WILD...
They're so lucky!
Hey!
GONNA PARTY WITH THE GIRLS TONIGHT?
WHAP
UH...
...UNTIL EVERY KID IN SCHOOL HAD HEARD.
THAT HURT, JERK!
Who are you?!
It's cool. It's cool.
OUCH!
MAN!
I DON'T CARE IF WE WERE IN A MAGAZINE...
THIS IS GETTING TO BE A TOTAL PAIN!
He's got no right to complain.
SERIOUSLY.
Shoot! I bought the wrong meal ticket!
YOU WANNA SWITCH WITH ME?
YOU GUYS DON'T SEEM TOO HAPPY.

*SIGNS= "A" SET LUNCH, OMELET RICE, TEMPURA

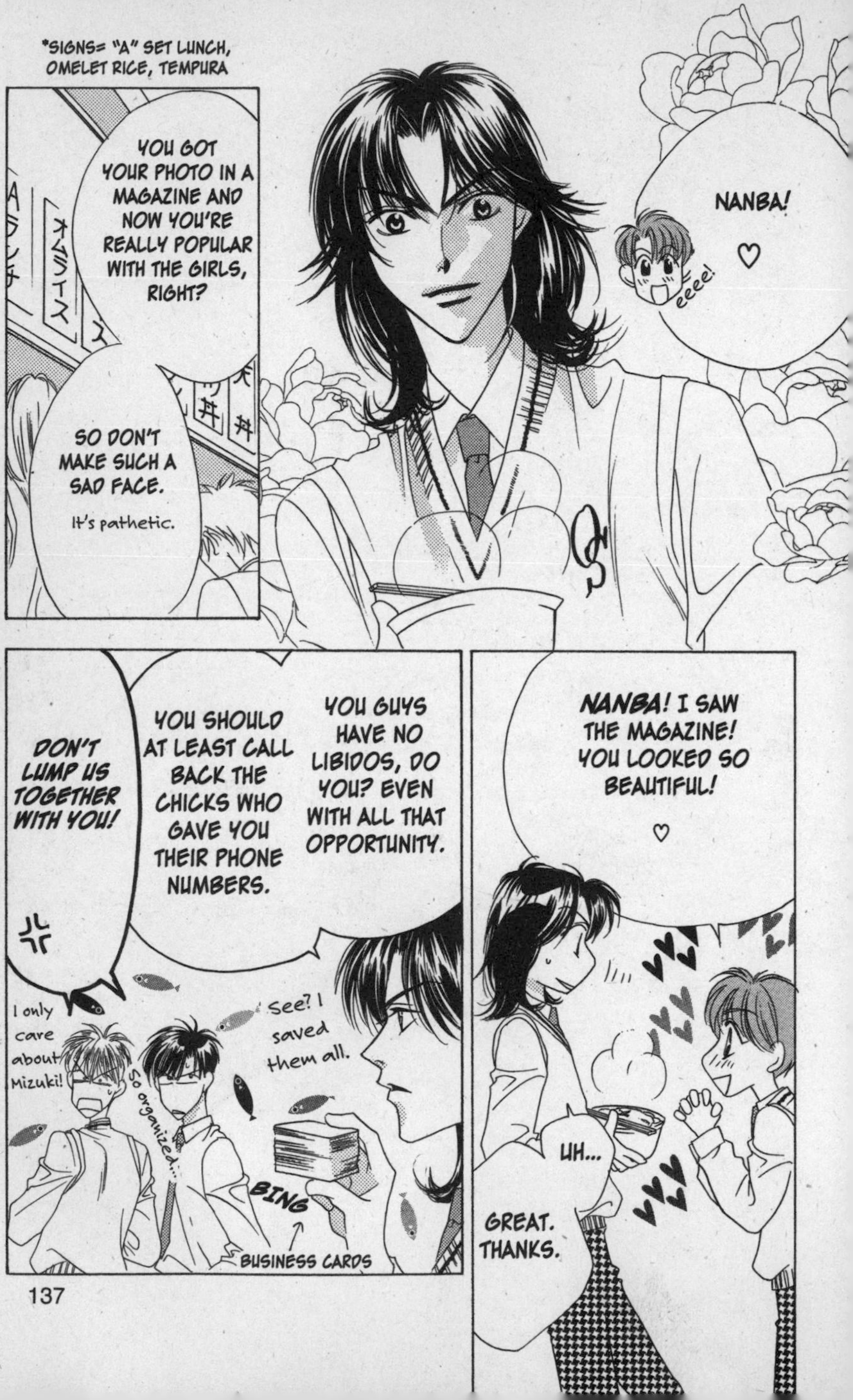
NANBA! ♥
eeee!
YOU GOT YOUR PHOTO IN A MAGAZINE AND NOW YOU'RE REALLY POPULAR WITH THE GIRLS, RIGHT?
SO DON'T MAKE SUCH A SAD FACE.
It's pathetic.
NANBA! I SAW THE MAGAZINE! YOU LOOKED SO BEAUTIFUL! ♥
UH...
GREAT. THANKS.
YOU GUYS HAVE NO LIBIDOS, DO YOU? EVEN WITH ALL THAT OPPORTUNITY.
YOU SHOULD AT LEAST CALL BACK THE CHICKS WHO GAVE YOU THEIR PHONE NUMBERS.
DON'T LUMP US TOGETHER WITH YOU!
See? I saved them all.
BING
BUSINESS CARDS
So organized...
I only care about Mizuki!

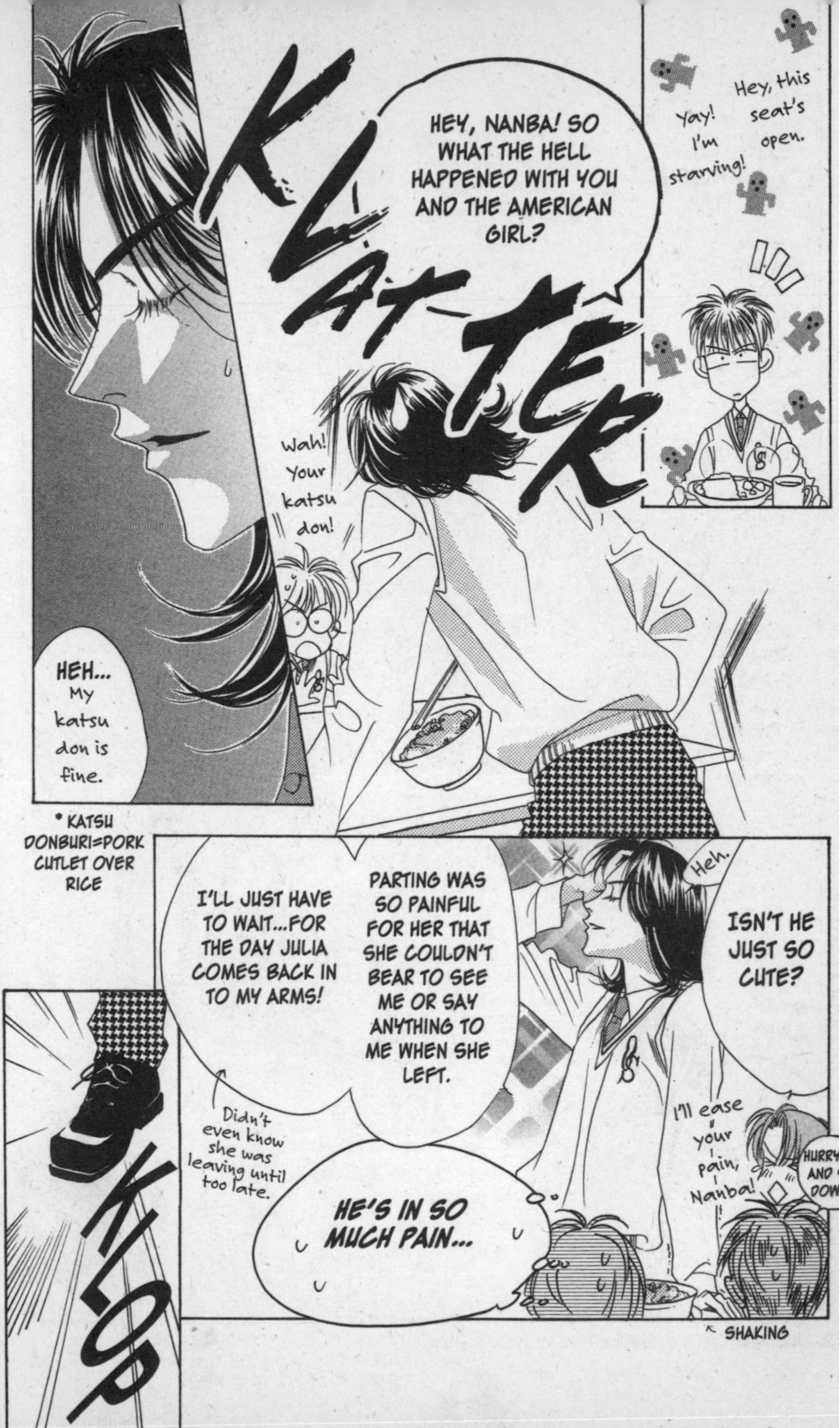
Hey, this seat's open.
Yay! I'm starving!
!!!
KLATTER
HEY, NANBA! SO WHAT THE HELL HAPPENED WITH YOU AND THE AMERICAN GIRL?
Wah! Your katsu don!
HEH... My katsu don is fine.
* KATSU DONBURI=PORK CUTLET OVER RICE
Heh.
ISN'T HE JUST SO CUTE?
PARTING WAS SO PAINFUL FOR HER THAT SHE COULDN'T BEAR TO SEE ME OR SAY ANYTHING TO ME WHEN SHE LEFT.
I'LL JUST HAVE TO WAIT...FOR THE DAY JULIA COMES BACK IN TO MY ARMS!
Didn't even know she was leaving until too late.
HE'S IN SO MUCH PAIN...
I'll ease your pain, Nanba!
HURRY UP AND SIT DOWN.
SHAKING
KLOP

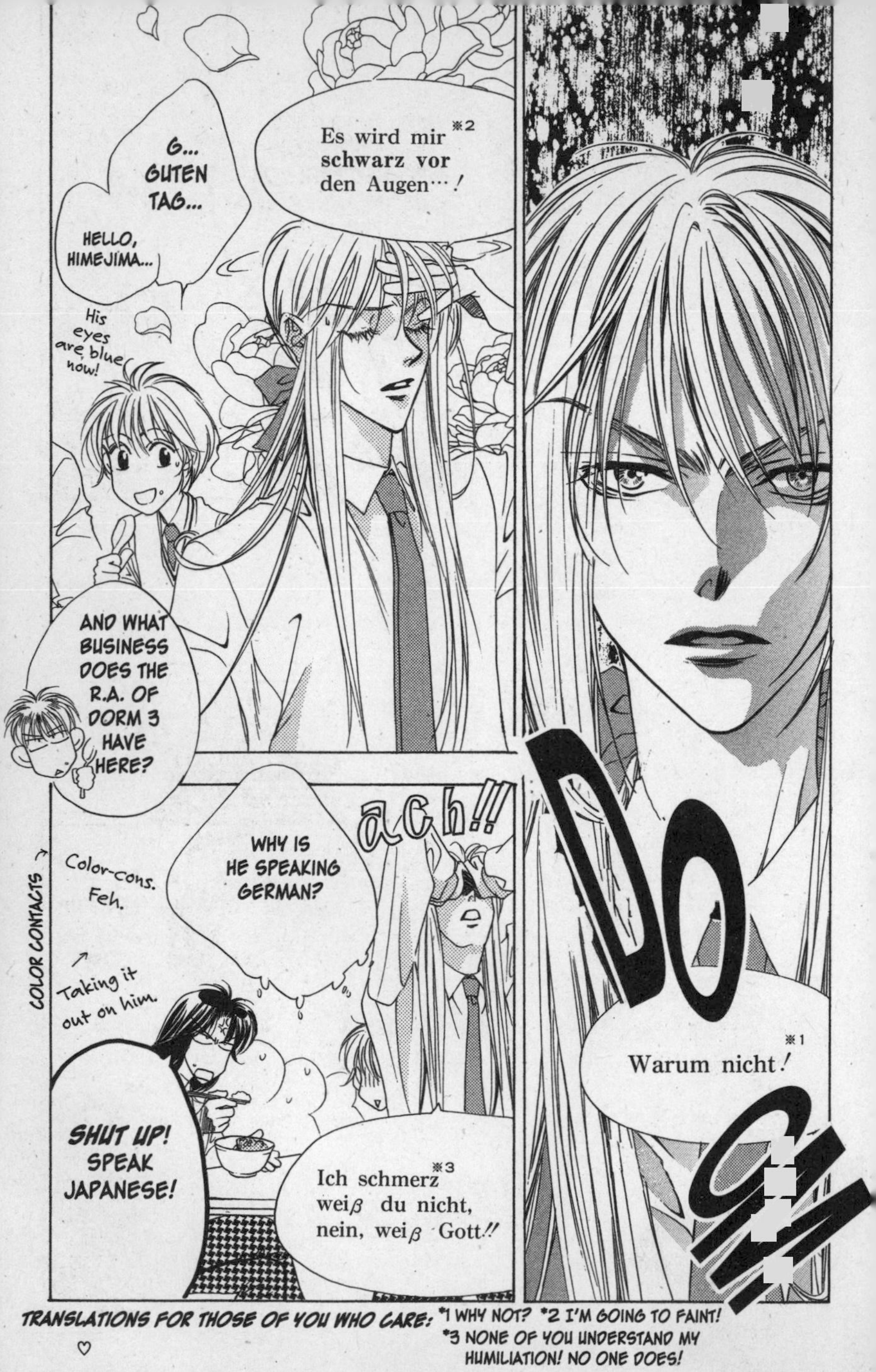
DOOM
Warum nicht!*1
Es wird mir schwarz vor den Augen…!*2
G... GUTEN TAG...
HELLO, HIMEJIMA...
His eyes are blue now!
AND WHAT BUSINESS DOES THE R.A. OF DORM 3 HAVE HERE?
ach!!
WHY IS HE SPEAKING GERMAN?
Color-cons. Feh.
COLOR CONTACTS
Taking it out on him.
Ich schmerz*3 weiβ du nicht, nein, weiβ Gott!!
SHUT UP! SPEAK JAPANESE!

TRANSLATIONS FOR THOSE OF YOU WHO CARE: ♡ *1 WHY NOT? *2 I'M GOING TO FAINT! *3 NONE OF YOU UNDERSTAND MY HUMILIATION! NO ONE DOES!

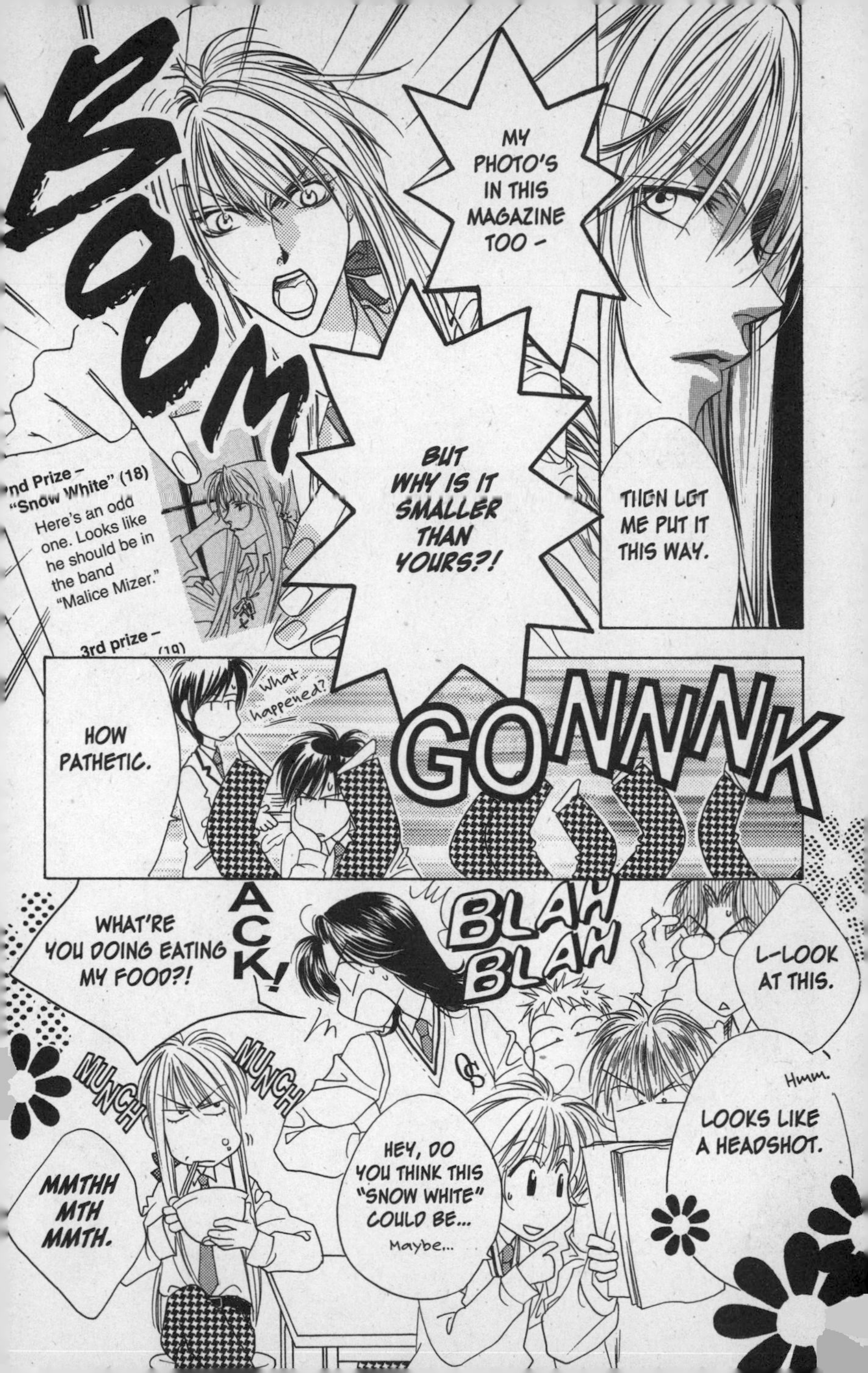
MY PHOTO'S IN THIS MAGAZINE TOO –
THEN LET ME PUT IT THIS WAY.
BOOM
nd Prize – "Snow White" (18)
Here's an odd one. Looks like he should be in the band "Malice Mizer."
3rd prize – (19)
BUT WHY IS IT SMALLER THAN YOURS?!
GONNNK
What happened?
HOW PATHETIC.
L-LOOK AT THIS.
BLAH BLAH
ACK!
WHAT'RE YOU DOING EATING MY FOOD?!
Hmm.
LOOKS LIKE A HEADSHOT.
HEY, DO YOU THINK THIS "SNOW WHITE" COULD BE...
Maybe...
MUNCH MUNCH
MMTHH MTH MMTH.

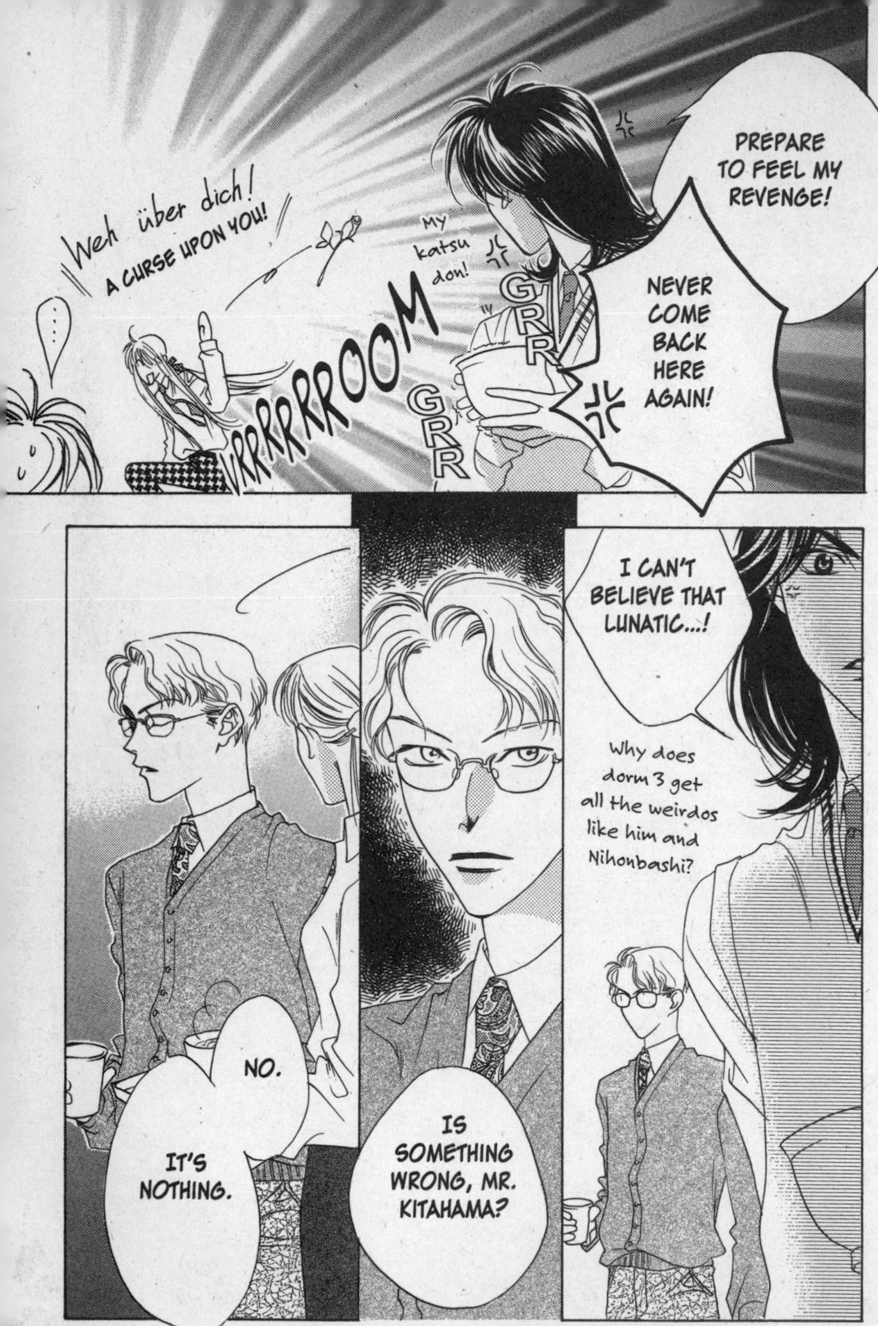
PREPARE TO FEEL MY REVENGE!
NEVER COME BACK HERE AGAIN!
GRR
GRR
My katsu don!
VRRRRRROOM
Weh über dich!
A CURSE UPON YOU!
I CAN'T BELIEVE THAT LUNATIC...!
Why does dorm 3 get all the weirdos like him and Nihonbashi?
IS SOMETHING WRONG, MR. KITAHAMA?
NO.
IT'S NOTHING.

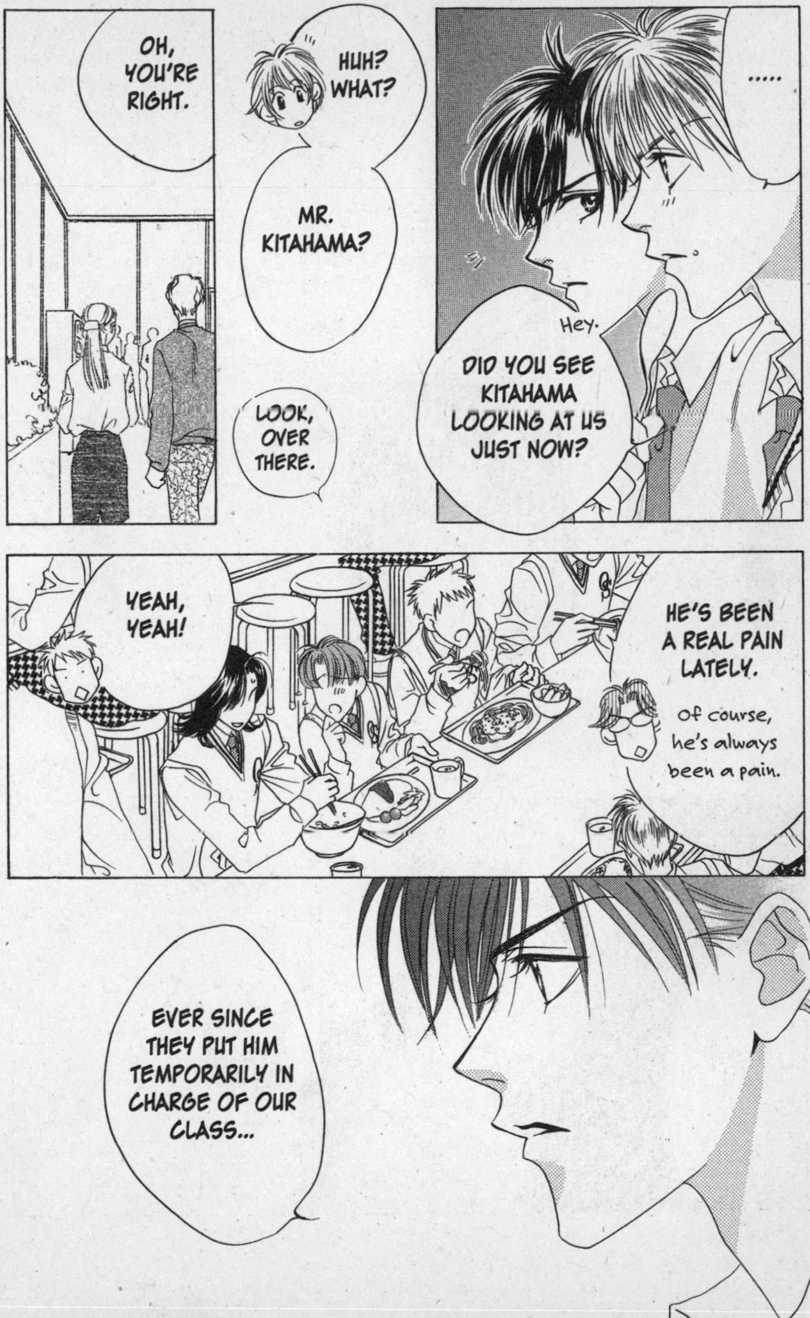
.....
Hey.
DID YOU SEE KITAHAMA LOOKING AT US JUST NOW?
HUH? WHAT?
MR. KITAHAMA?
LOOK, OVER THERE.
OH, YOU'RE RIGHT.
HE'S BEEN A REAL PAIN LATELY.
Of course, he's always been a pain.
YEAH, YEAH!
EVER SINCE THEY PUT HIM TEMPORARILY IN CHARGE OF OUR CLASS...

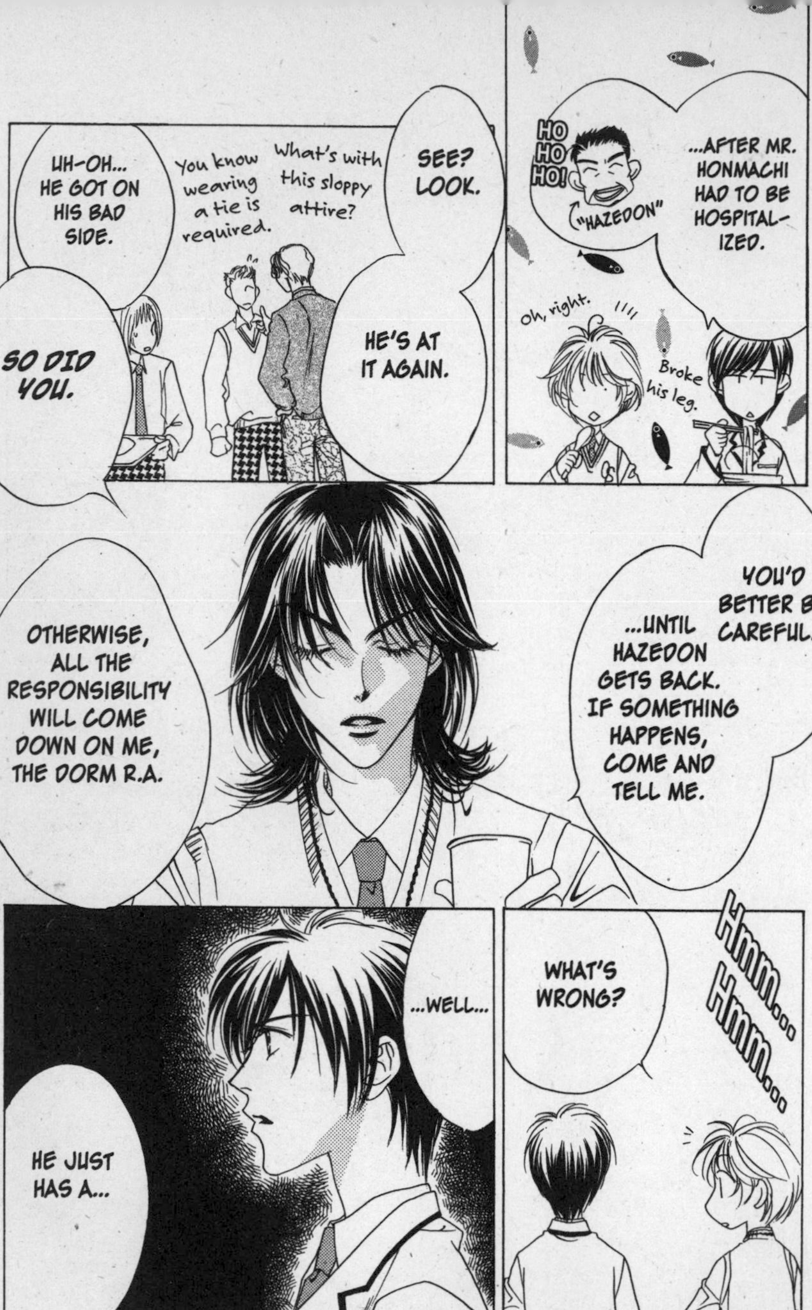
...AFTER MR. HONMACHI HAD TO BE HOSPITALIZED.
HO HO HO!
"HAZEDON"
Broke his leg.
Oh, right.
SEE? LOOK.
What's with this sloppy attire?
You know wearing a tie is required.
UH-OH... HE GOT ON HIS BAD SIDE.
HE'S AT IT AGAIN.
SO DID YOU.
YOU'D BETTER BE CAREFUL...
...UNTIL HAZEDON GETS BACK. IF SOMETHING HAPPENS, COME AND TELL ME.
OTHERWISE, ALL THE RESPONSIBILITY WILL COME DOWN ON ME, THE DORM R.A.
Hmm... Hmm...
WHAT'S WRONG?
...WELL...
HE JUST HAS A...

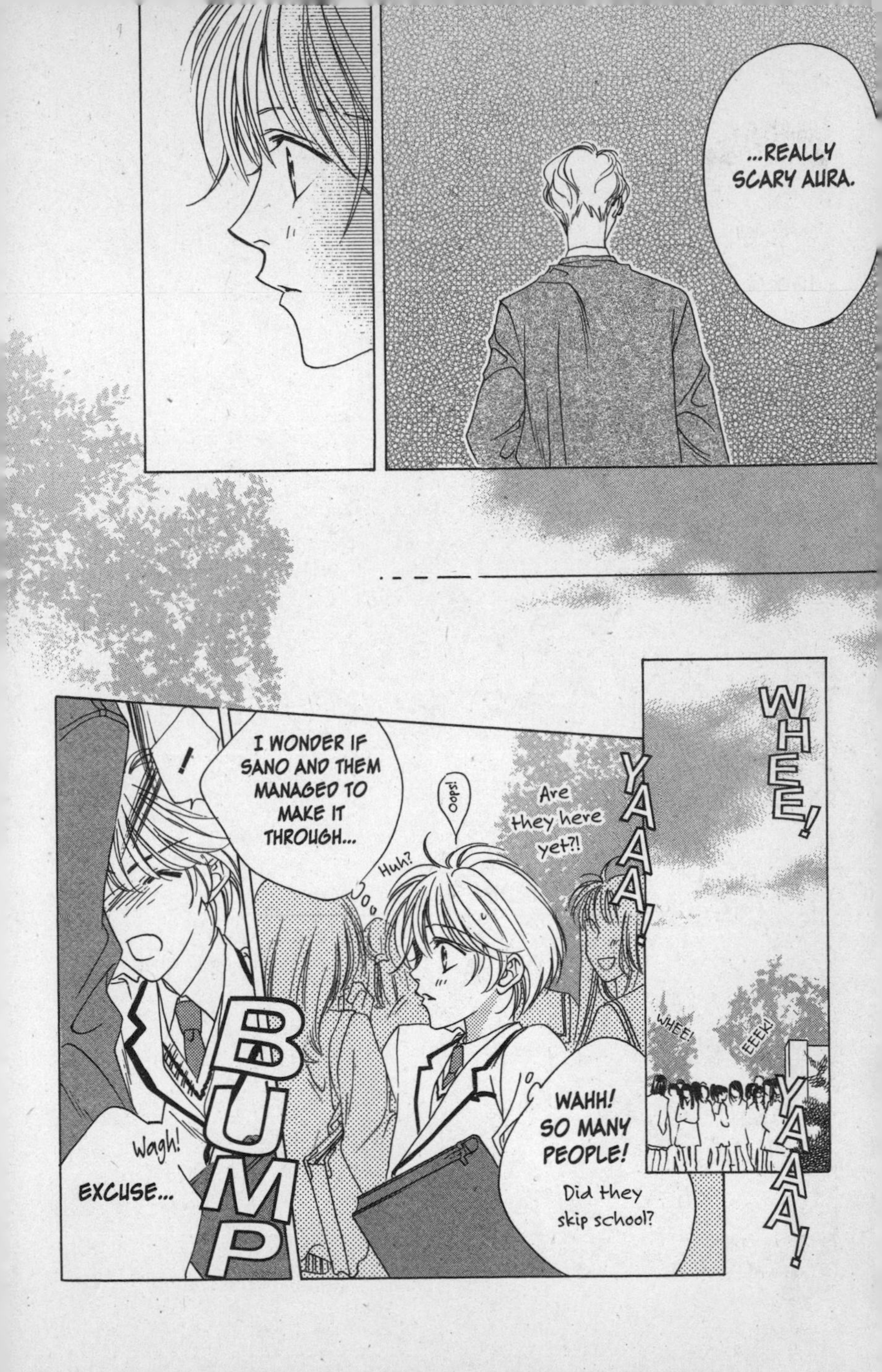
...REALLY SCARY AURA.
WHEE!
EEEK!
WHEE!
YAAA!
YAAA!
Are they here yet?!
Oops!
I WONDER IF SANO AND THEM MANAGED TO MAKE IT THROUGH...
Huh?
!
WAHH! SO MANY PEOPLE!
Did they skip school?
BUMP
Wagh!
EXCUSE...

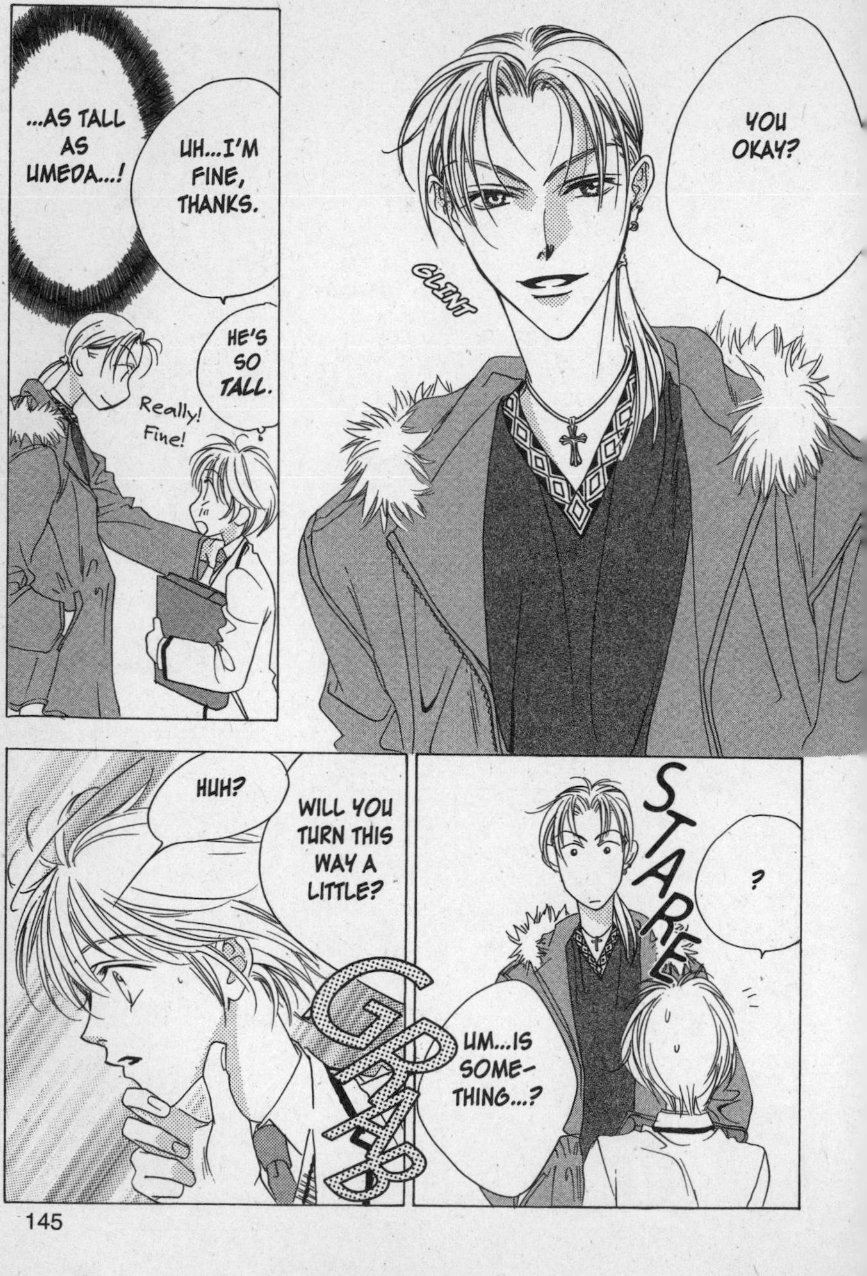
YOU OKAY?
GLINT
UH...I'M FINE, THANKS.
...AS TALL AS UMEDA...!
HE'S SO TALL.
Really! Fine!
STARE
?
UM...IS SOME-THING...?
HUH?
WILL YOU TURN THIS WAY A LITTLE?
GRAB

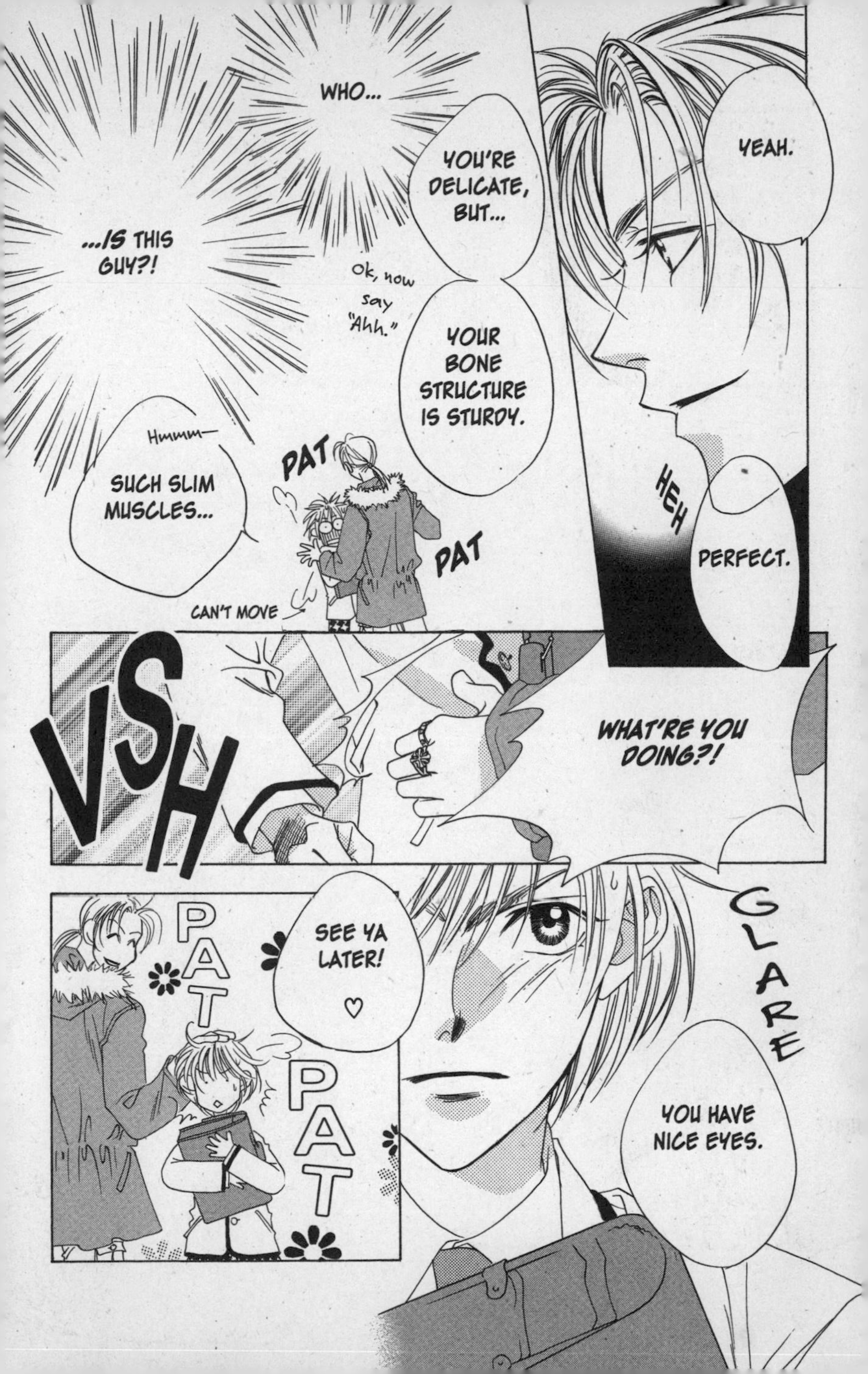

YEAH.
HEH
PERFECT.
YOU'RE DELICATE, BUT...
WHO...
...IS THIS GUY?!
Ok, now say "Ahh."
YOUR BONE STRUCTURE IS STURDY.
Hmmm—
SUCH SLIM MUSCLES...
PAT
PAT
CAN'T MOVE
WHAT'RE YOU DOING?!
VSH
GLARE
YOU HAVE NICE EYES.
SEE YA LATER! ♡
PAT PAT

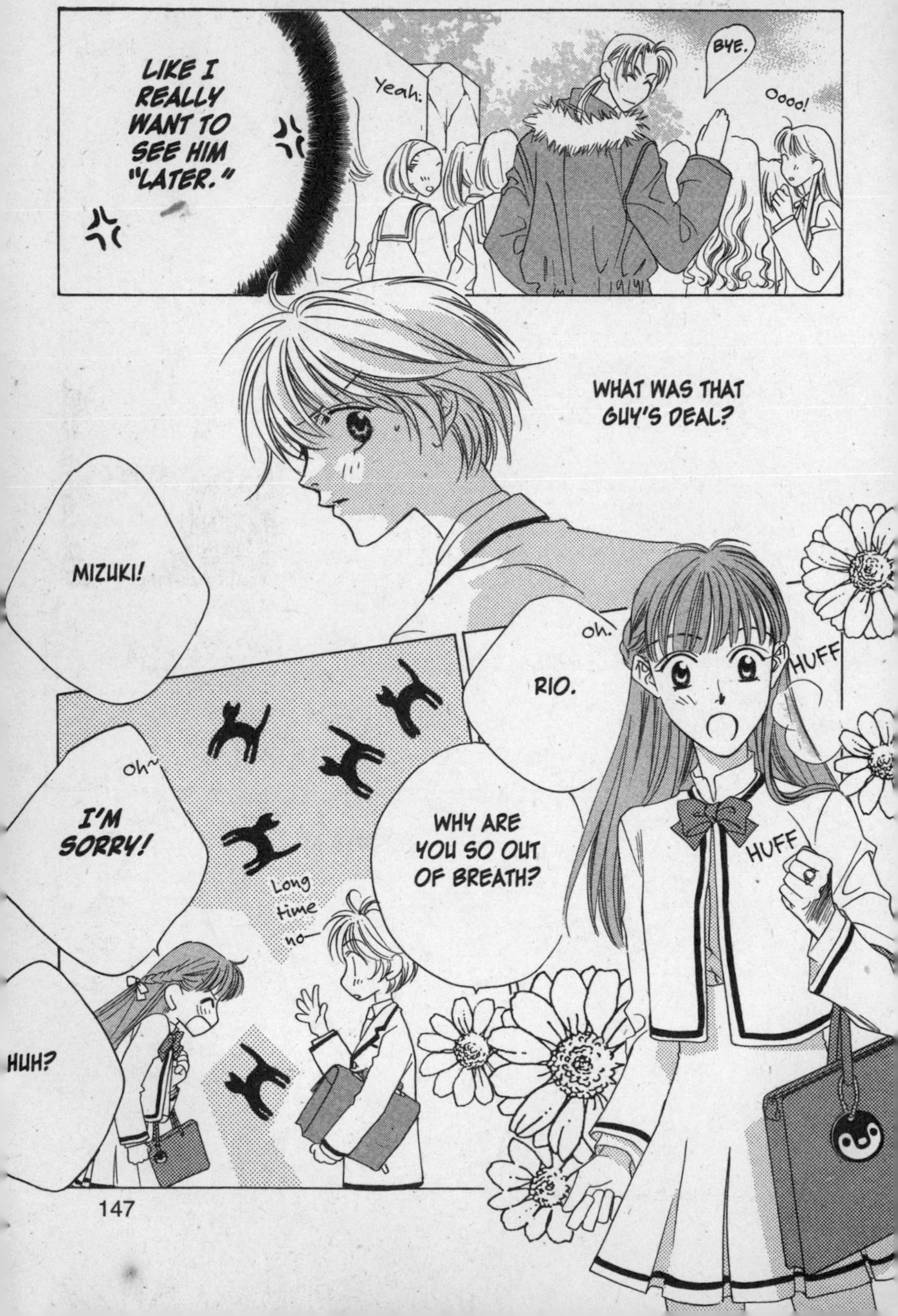
BYE.
Oooo!
Yeah.
LIKE I REALLY WANT TO SEE HIM "LATER."
WHAT WAS THAT GUY'S DEAL?
MIZUKI!
oh.
RIO.
HUFF
HUFF
WHY ARE YOU SO OUT OF BREATH?
Long time no—
oh~
I'M SORRY!
HUH?

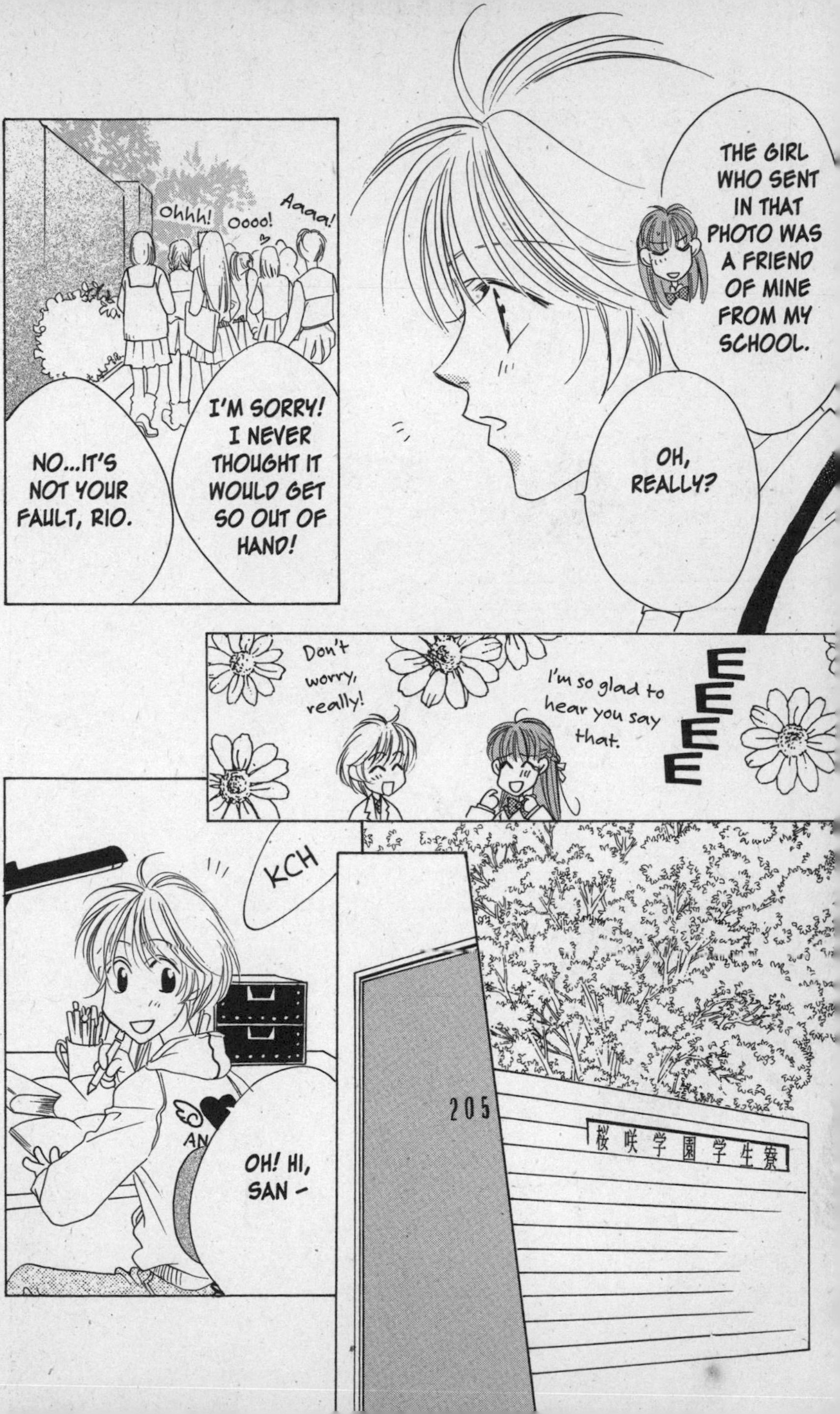
THE GIRL WHO SENT IN THAT PHOTO WAS A FRIEND OF MINE FROM MY SCHOOL.
OH, REALLY?
Aaaa!
Oooo!
Ohhh!
I'M SORRY! I NEVER THOUGHT IT WOULD GET SO OUT OF HAND!
NO...IT'S NOT YOUR FAULT, RIO.
EEEEE
I'm so glad to hear you say that.
Don't worry, really!
205
桜咲学園学生寮
KCH
AN
OH! HI, SAN -

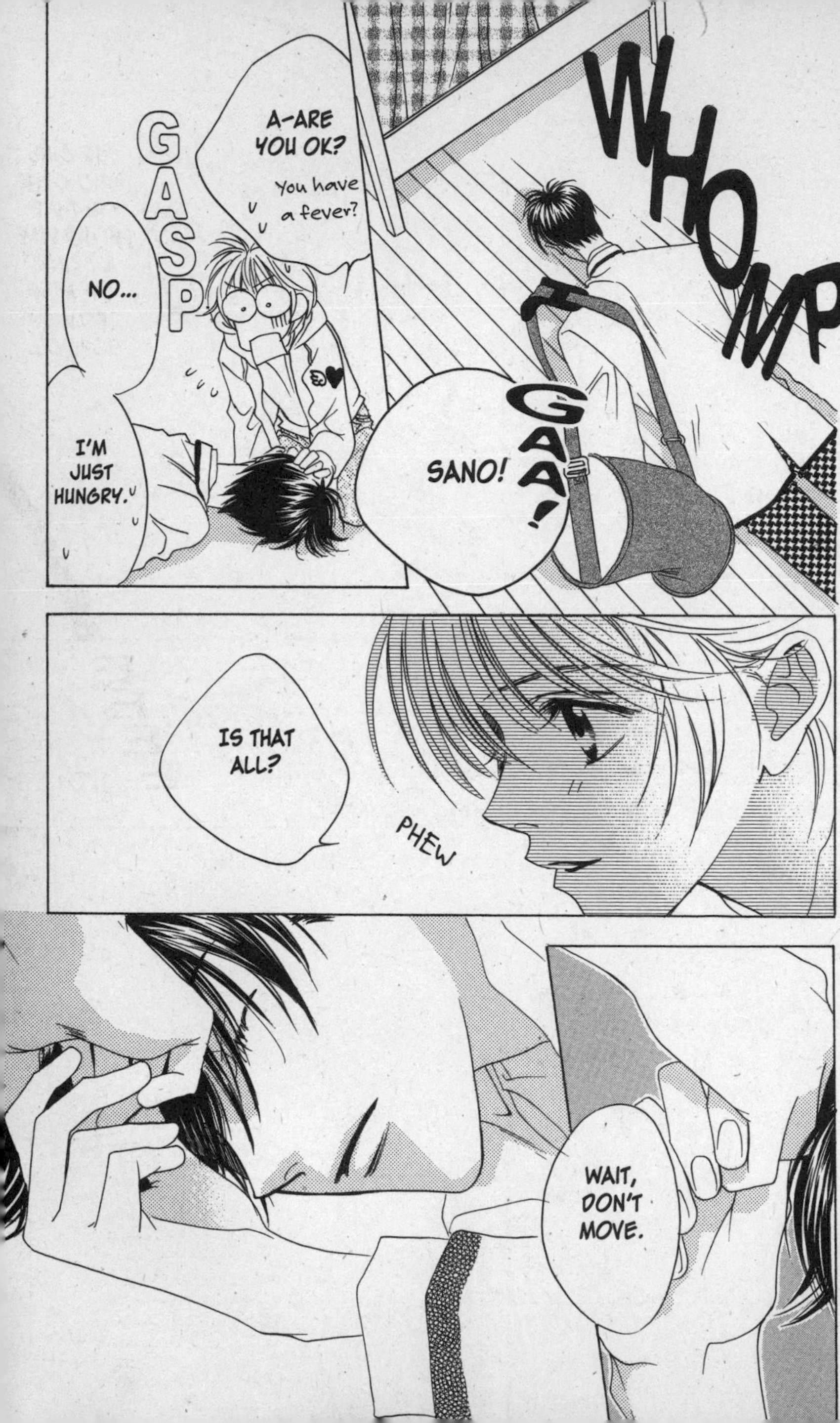
WHOMP
GAA!
SANO!
A-ARE YOU OK?
You have a fever?
GASP
NO...
I'M JUST HUNGRY.
PHEW
IS THAT ALL?
WAIT, DON'T MOVE.

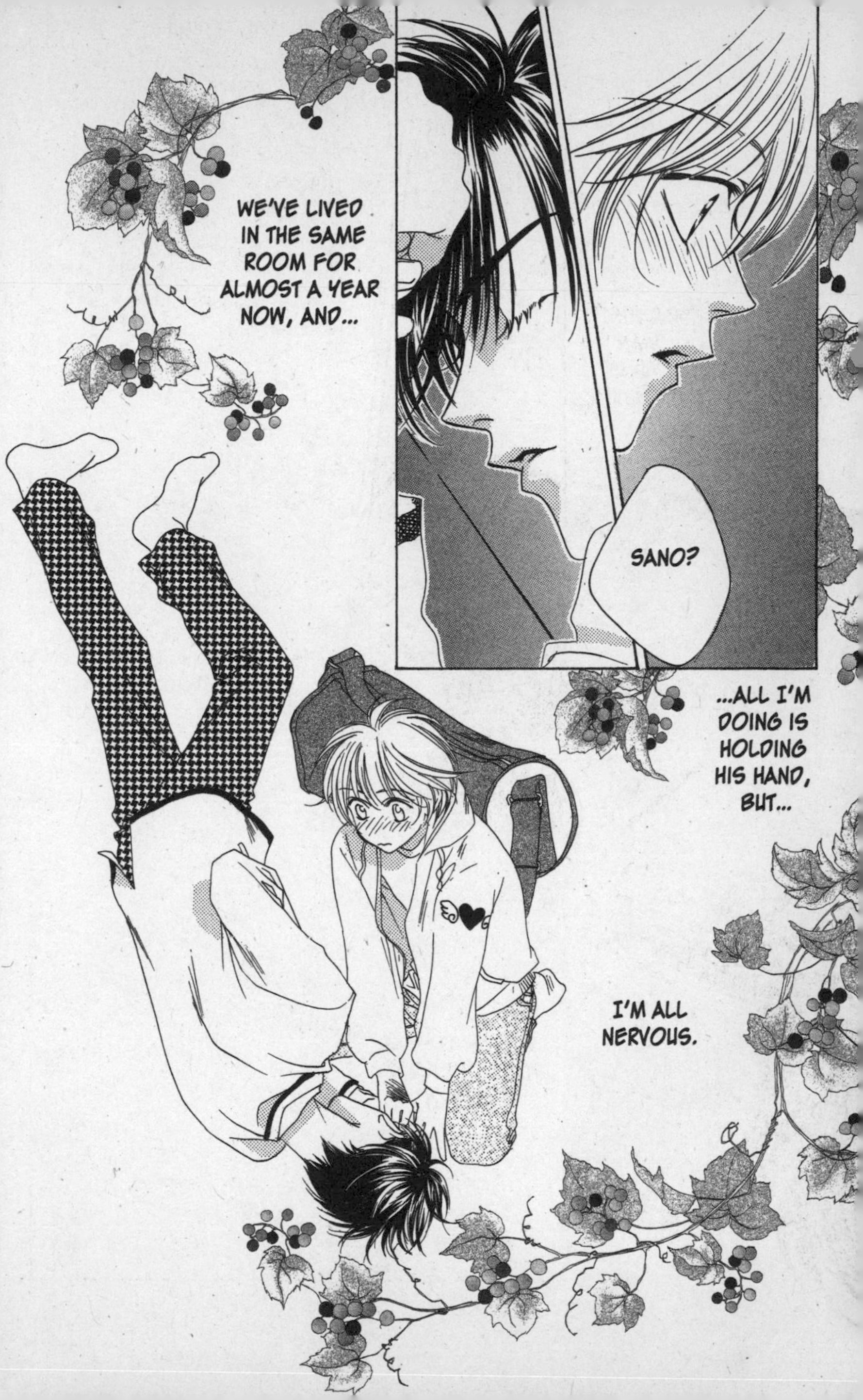
SANO?
WE'VE LIVED IN THE SAME ROOM FOR ALMOST A YEAR NOW, AND...
...ALL I'M DOING IS HOLDING HIS HAND, BUT...
I'M ALL NERVOUS.

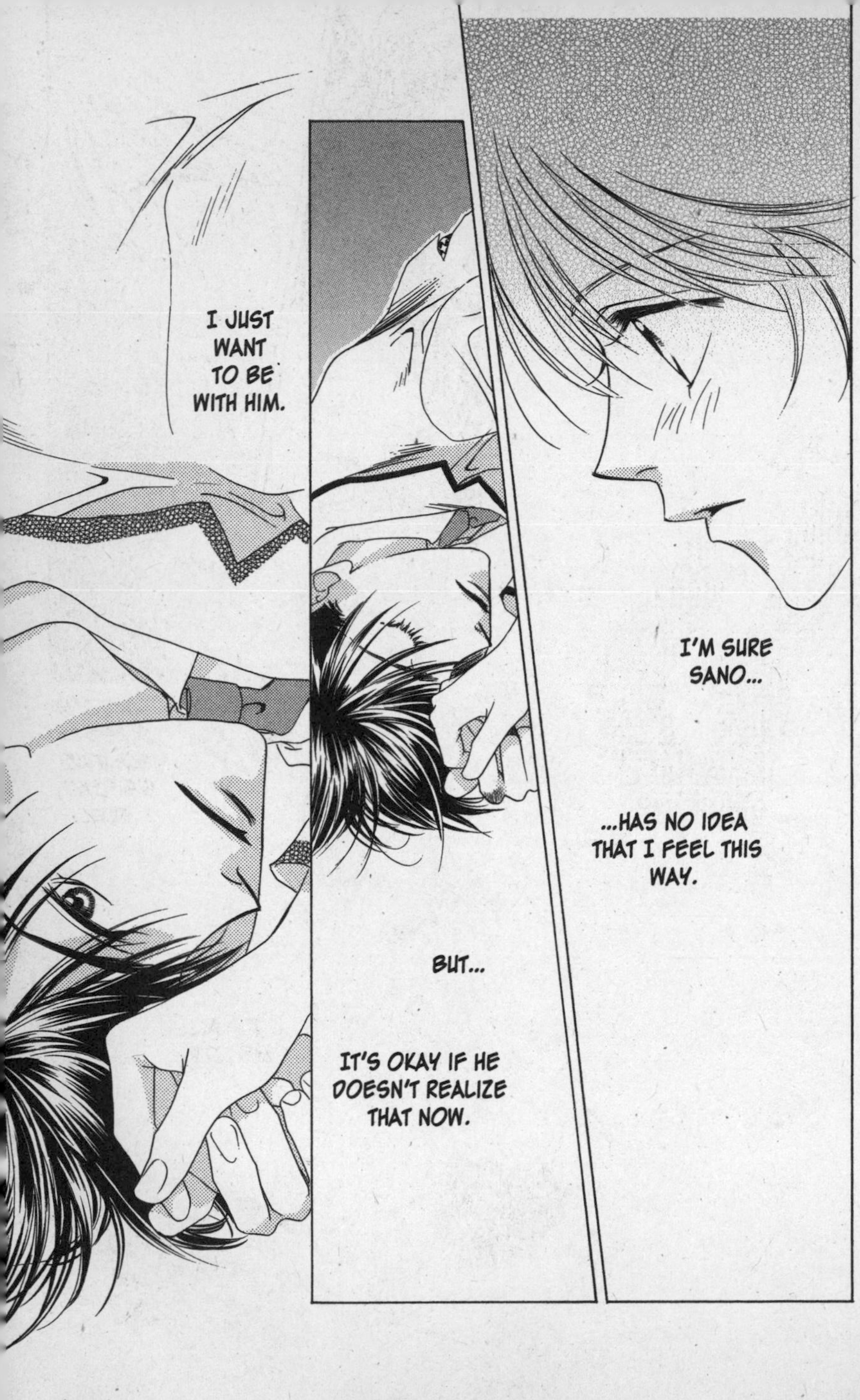
I'M SURE SANO...
...HAS NO IDEA THAT I FEEL THIS WAY.
BUT...
IT'S OKAY IF HE DOESN'T REALIZE THAT NOW.
I JUST WANT TO BE WITH HIM.

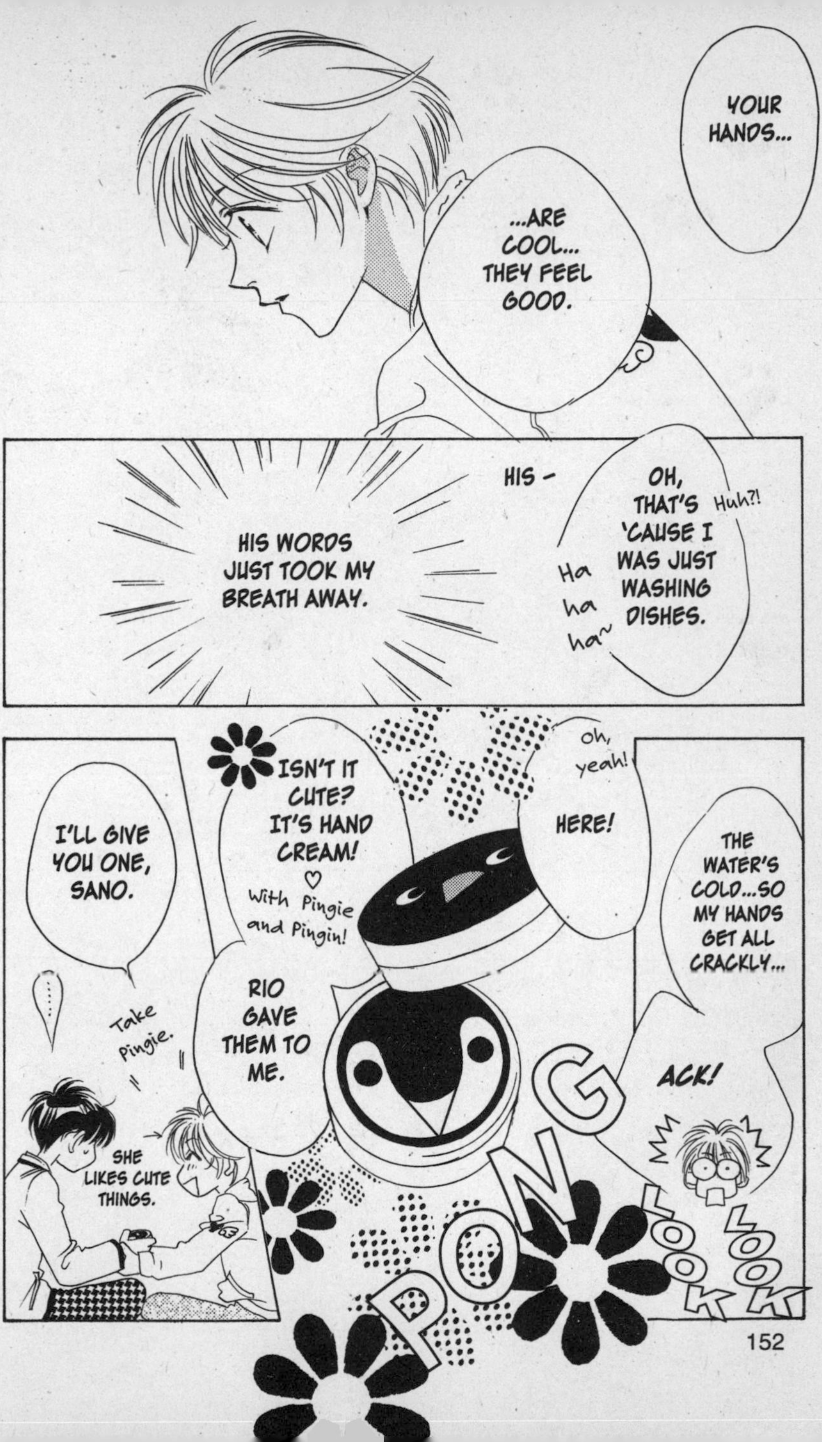
YOUR HANDS...
...ARE COOL... THEY FEEL GOOD.
OH, THAT'S 'CAUSE I WAS JUST WASHING DISHES.
Huh?!
Ha ha ha~
HIS -
HIS WORDS JUST TOOK MY BREATH AWAY.
THE WATER'S COLD...SO MY HANDS GET ALL CRACKLY...
ACK!
LOOK LOOK
Oh, yeah!
HERE!
ISN'T IT CUTE? IT'S HAND CREAM! ♡
With Pingie and Pingin!
PONG
RIO GAVE THEM TO ME.
I'LL GIVE YOU ONE, SANO.
Take Pingie.
SHE LIKES CUTE THINGS.

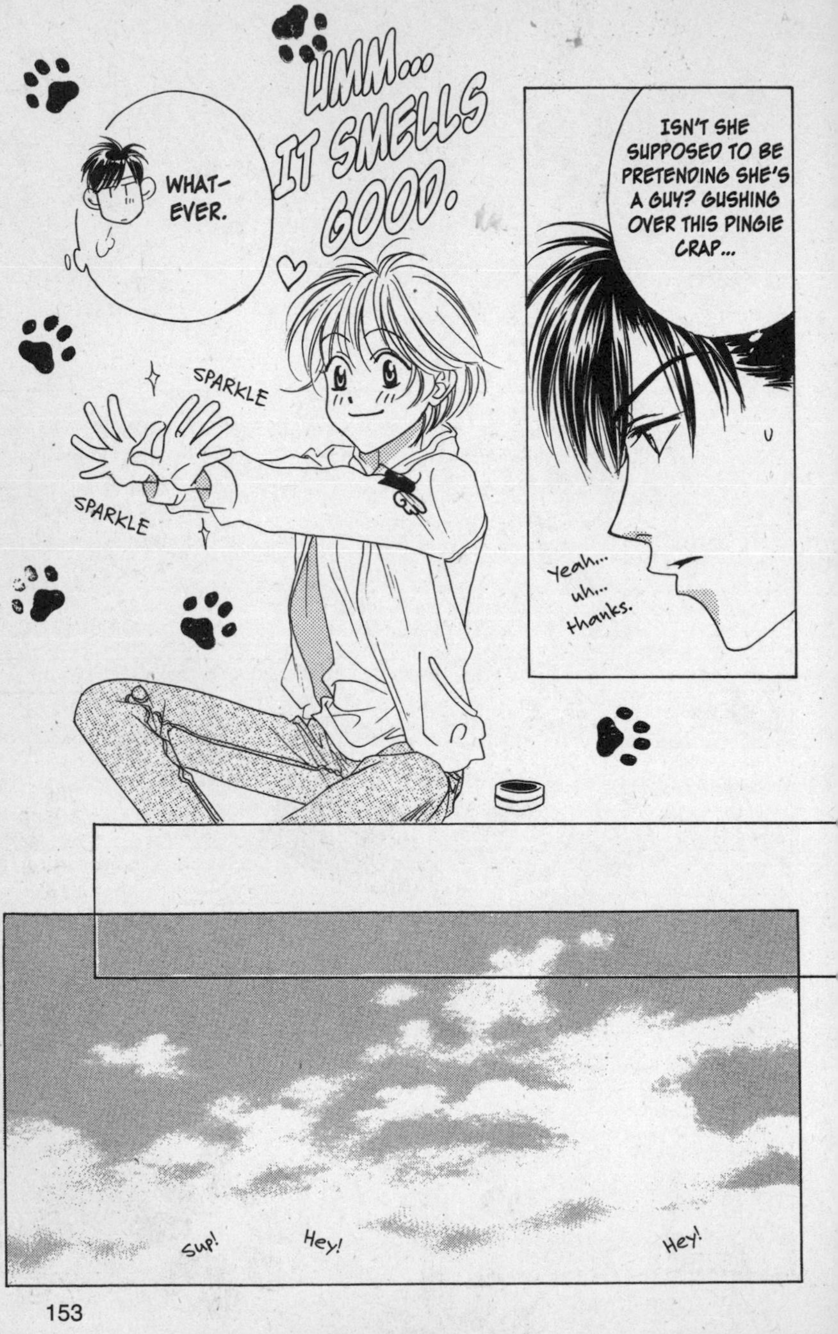
ISN'T SHE SUPPOSED TO BE PRETENDING SHE'S A GUY? GUSHING OVER THIS PINGIE CRAP...
Yeah... uh... thanks.
UMM... IT SMELLS GOOD.
SPARKLE
SPARKLE
WHAT-EVER.
Hey!
Hey!
Sup!

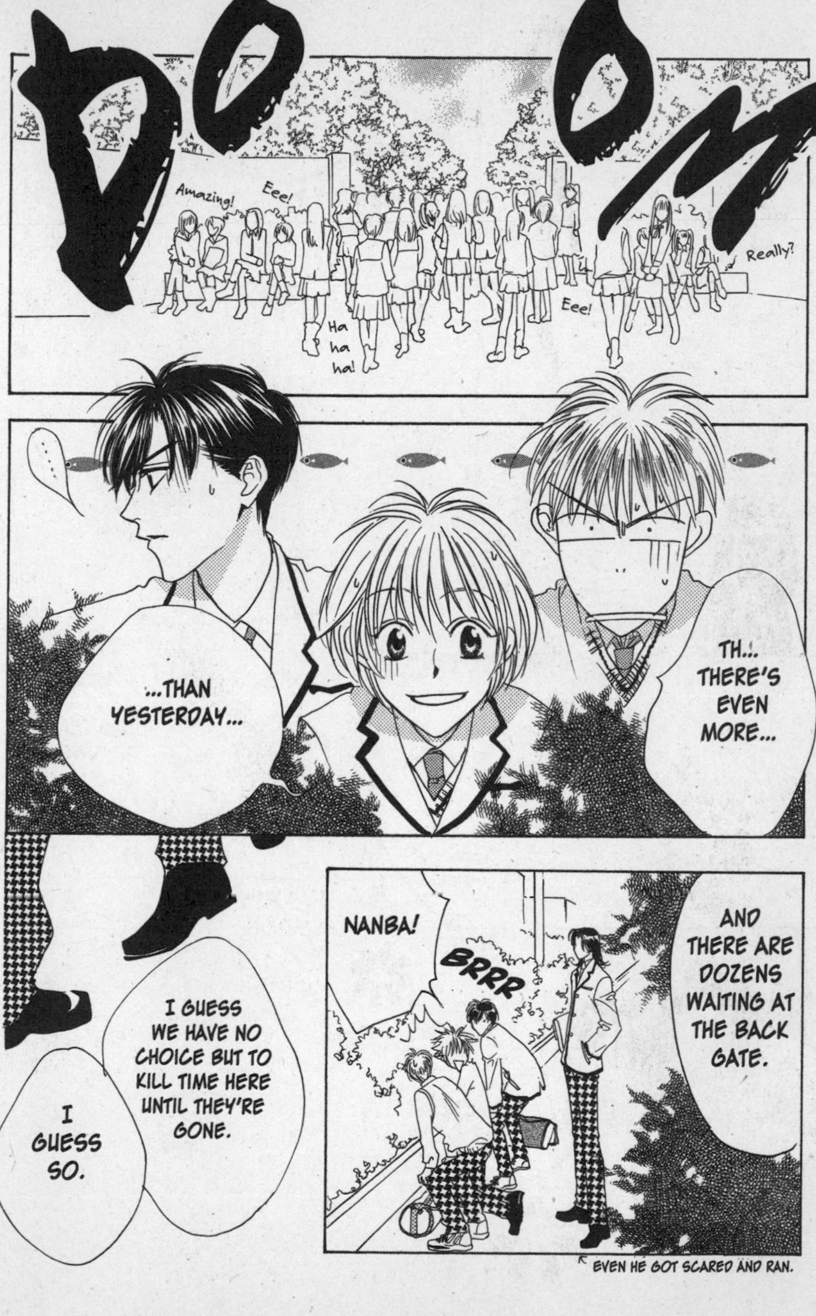
DOOM
Really?
Eee!
Ha ha ha!
Eee!
Amazing!
TH... THERE'S EVEN MORE...
...THAN YESTERDAY...
...
AND THERE ARE DOZENS WAITING AT THE BACK GATE.
BRRR
NANBA!
EVEN HE GOT SCARED AND RAN.
I GUESS WE HAVE NO CHOICE BUT TO KILL TIME HERE UNTIL THEY'RE GONE.
I GUESS SO.

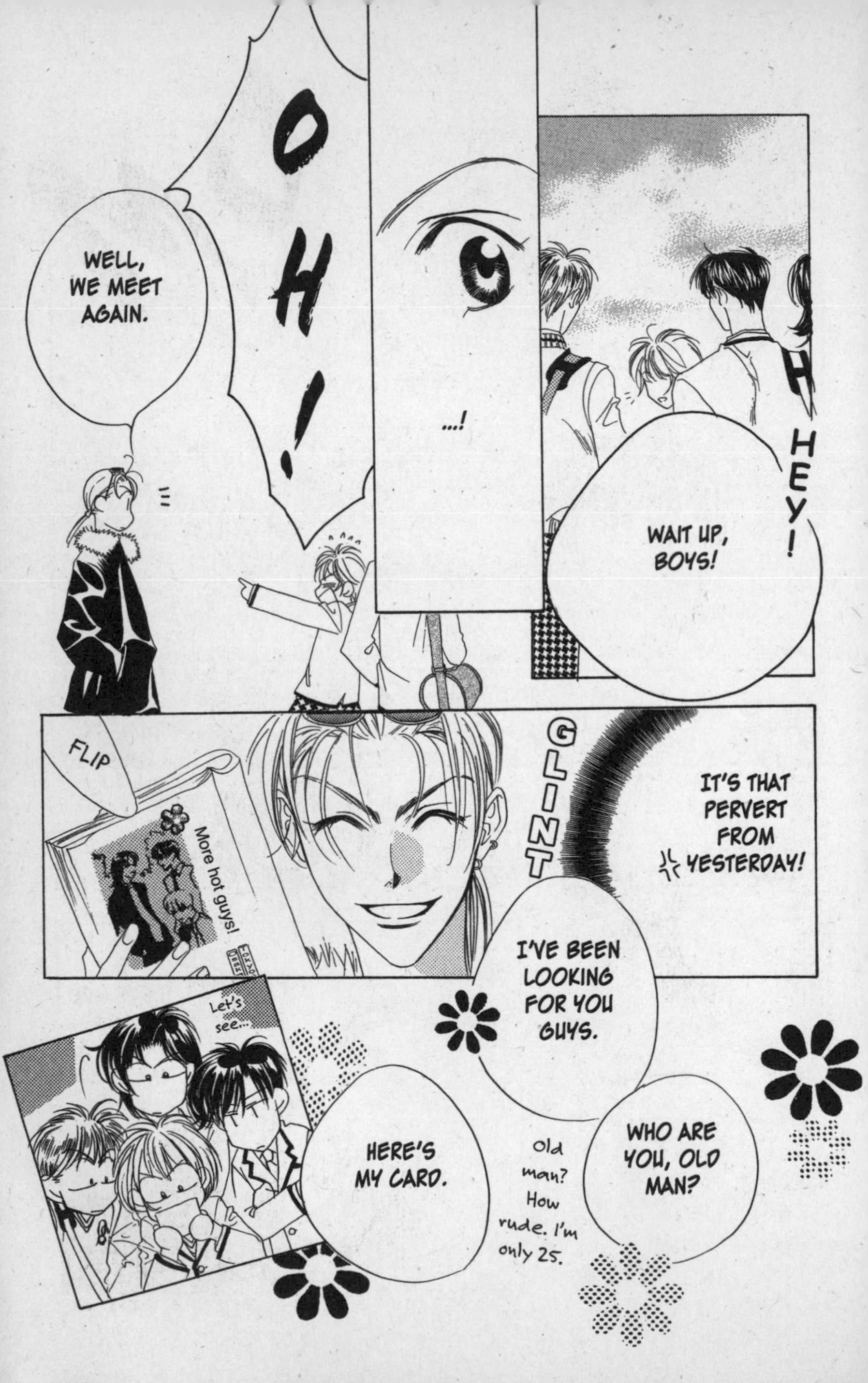
HEY!
WAIT UP, BOYS!
...!
OH!
WELL, WE MEET AGAIN.
GLINT
IT'S THAT PERVERT FROM YESTERDAY!
FLIP
More hot guys!
I'VE BEEN LOOKING FOR YOU GUYS.
WHO ARE YOU, OLD MAN?
Old man? How rude. I'm only 25.
HERE'S MY CARD.
Let's see...

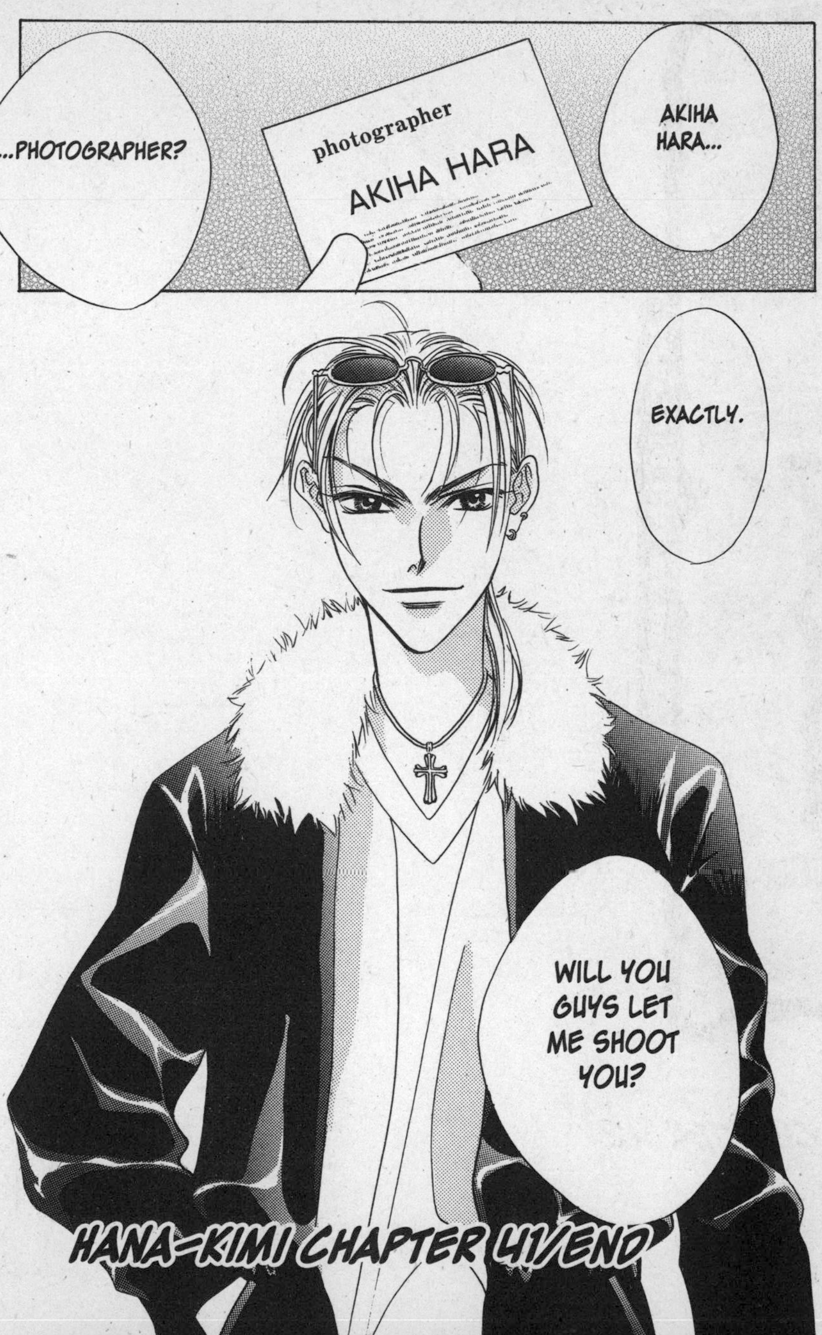
AKIHA HARA...
photographer
AKIHA HARA
...PHOTOGRAPHER?
EXACTLY.
WILL YOU GUYS LET ME SHOOT YOU?
HANA-KIMI CHAPTER 41/END

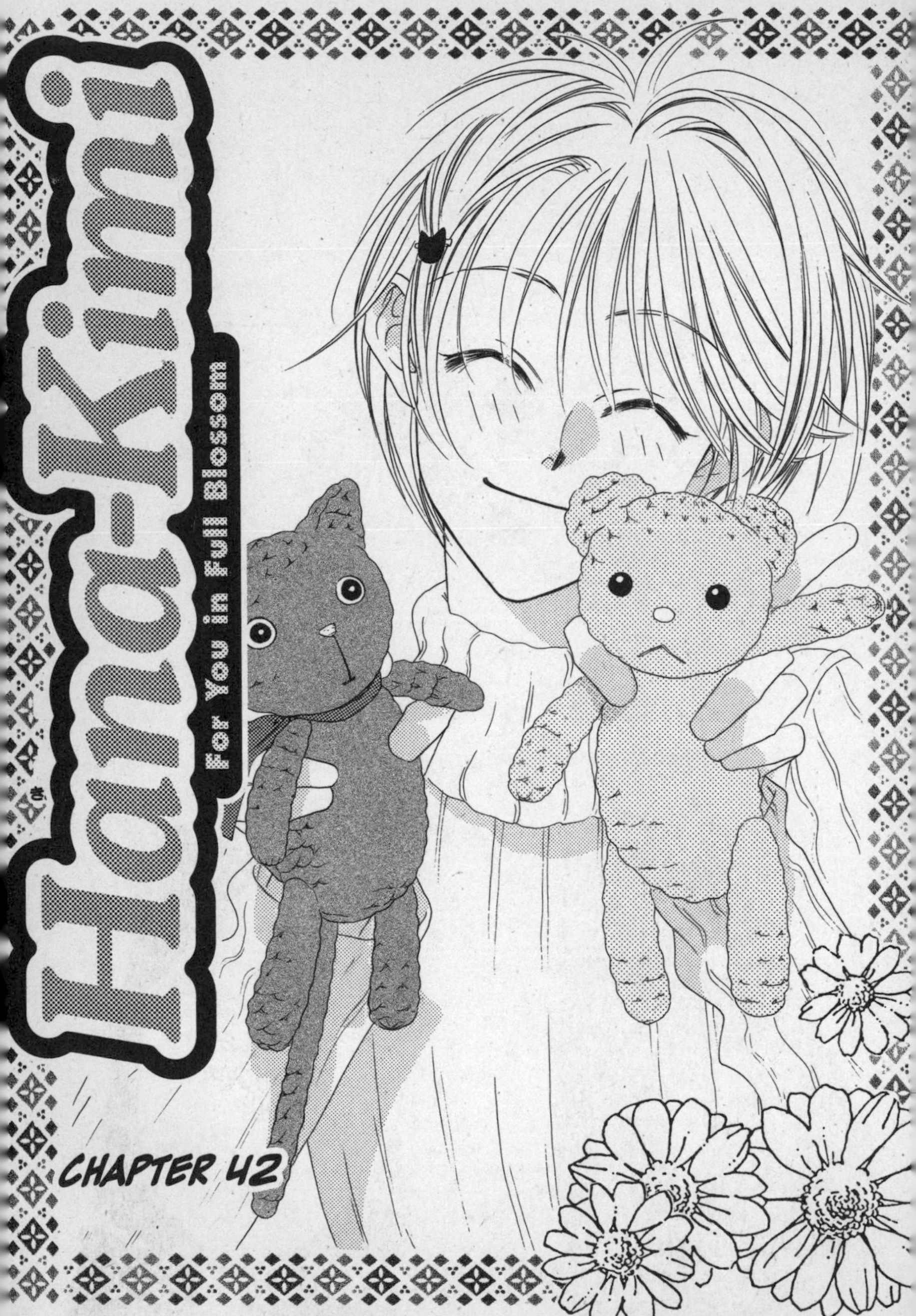
Hana-Kimi
For You in Full Blossom
CHAPTER 42

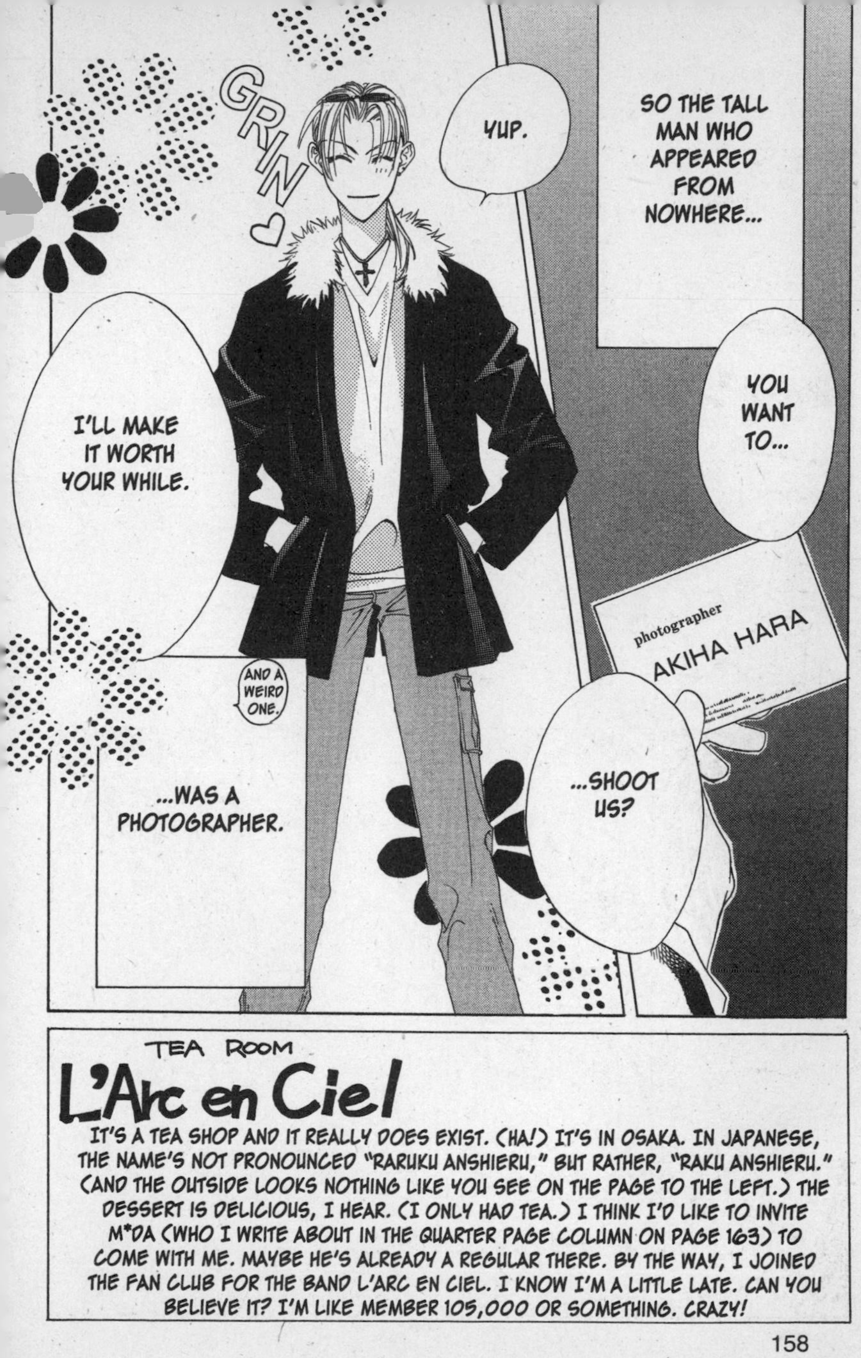
SO THE TALL MAN WHO APPEARED FROM NOWHERE...
...WAS A PHOTOGRAPHER.
AND A WEIRD ONE.
YOU WANT TO...
photographer
AKIHA HARA
...SHOOT US?
YUP.
GRIN
I'LL MAKE IT WORTH YOUR WHILE.

TEA ROOM

L'Arc en Ciel

IT'S A TEA SHOP AND IT REALLY DOES EXIST. (HA!) IT'S IN OSAKA. IN JAPANESE, THE NAME'S NOT PRONOUNCED "RARUKU ANSHIERU," BUT RATHER, "RAKU ANSHIERU." (AND THE OUTSIDE LOOKS NOTHING LIKE YOU SEE ON THE PAGE TO THE LEFT.) THE DESSERT IS DELICIOUS, I HEAR. (I ONLY HAD TEA.) I THINK I'D LIKE TO INVITE M*DA (WHO I WRITE ABOUT IN THE QUARTER PAGE COLUMN ON PAGE 163) TO COME WITH ME. MAYBE HE'S ALREADY A REGULAR THERE. BY THE WAY, I JOINED THE FAN CLUB FOR THE BAND L'ARC EN CIEL. I KNOW I'M A LITTLE LATE. CAN YOU BELIEVE IT? I'M LIKE MEMBER 105,000 OR SOMETHING. CRAZY!

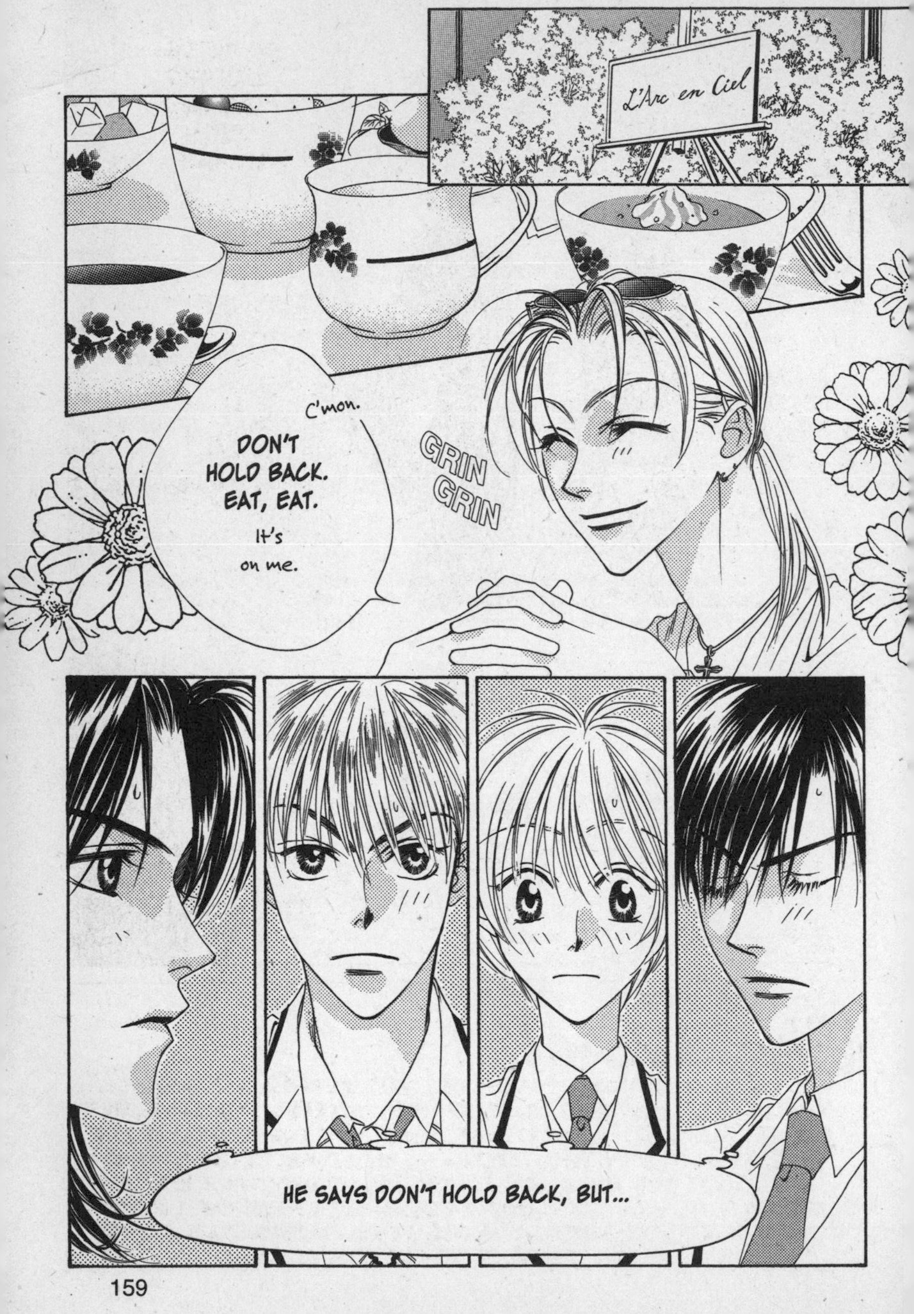
L'Arc en Ciel
C'mon.
DON'T HOLD BACK. EAT, EAT.
It's on me.
GRIN GRIN
HE SAYS DON'T HOLD BACK, BUT...

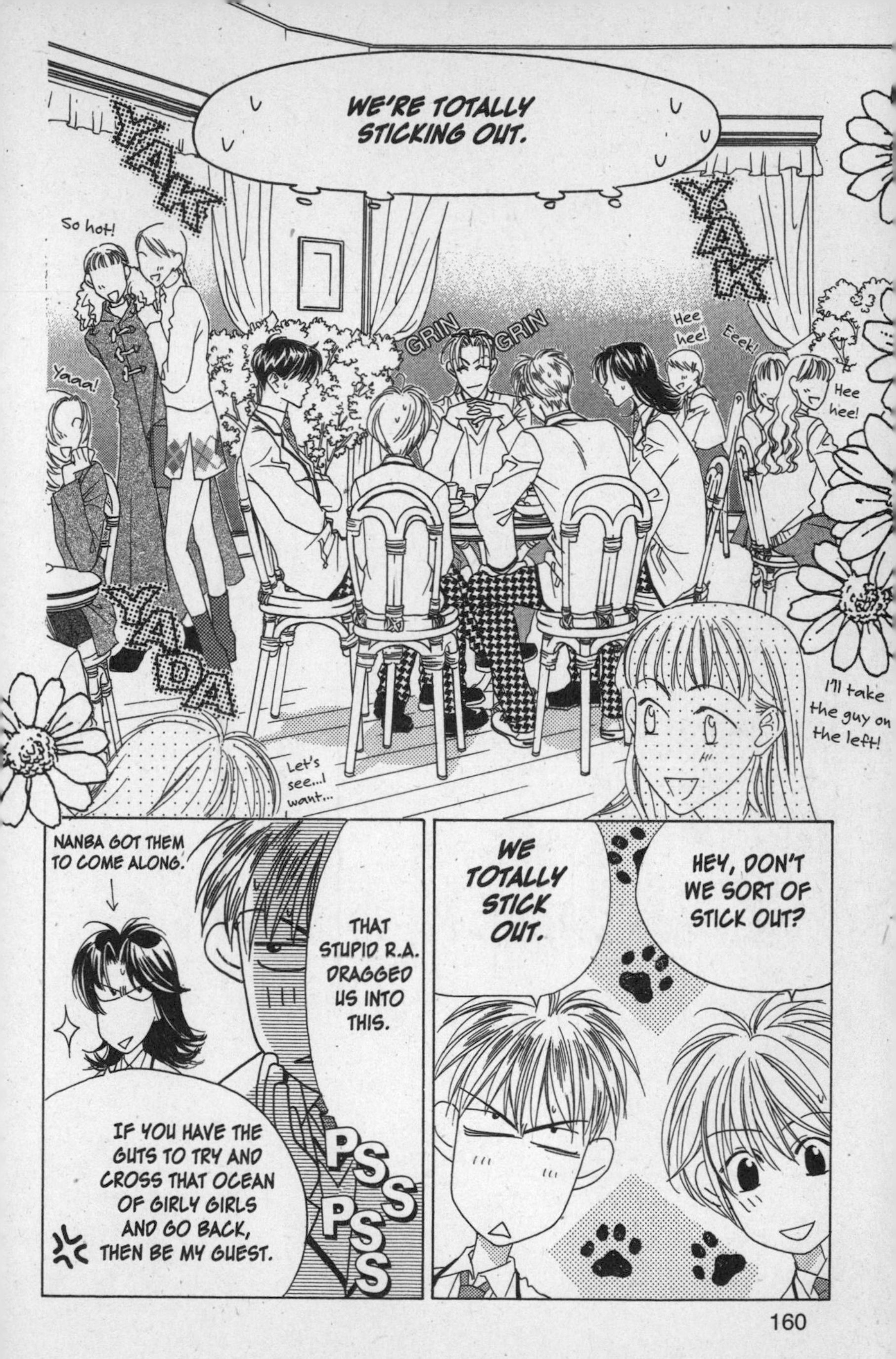
WE'RE TOTALLY STICKING OUT.
YAK YAK
Hee hee!
Eeek!
Hee hee!
GRIN GRIN
YAK
So hot!
Yaaa!
YADA
I'll take the guy on the left!
Let's see...I want...
HEY, DON'T WE SORT OF STICK OUT?
WE TOTALLY STICK OUT.
THAT STUPID R.A. DRAGGED US INTO THIS.
NANBA GOT THEM TO COME ALONG.
PSS PSS
IF YOU HAVE THE GUTS TO TRY AND CROSS THAT OCEAN OF GIRLY GIRLS AND GO BACK, THEN BE MY GUEST.

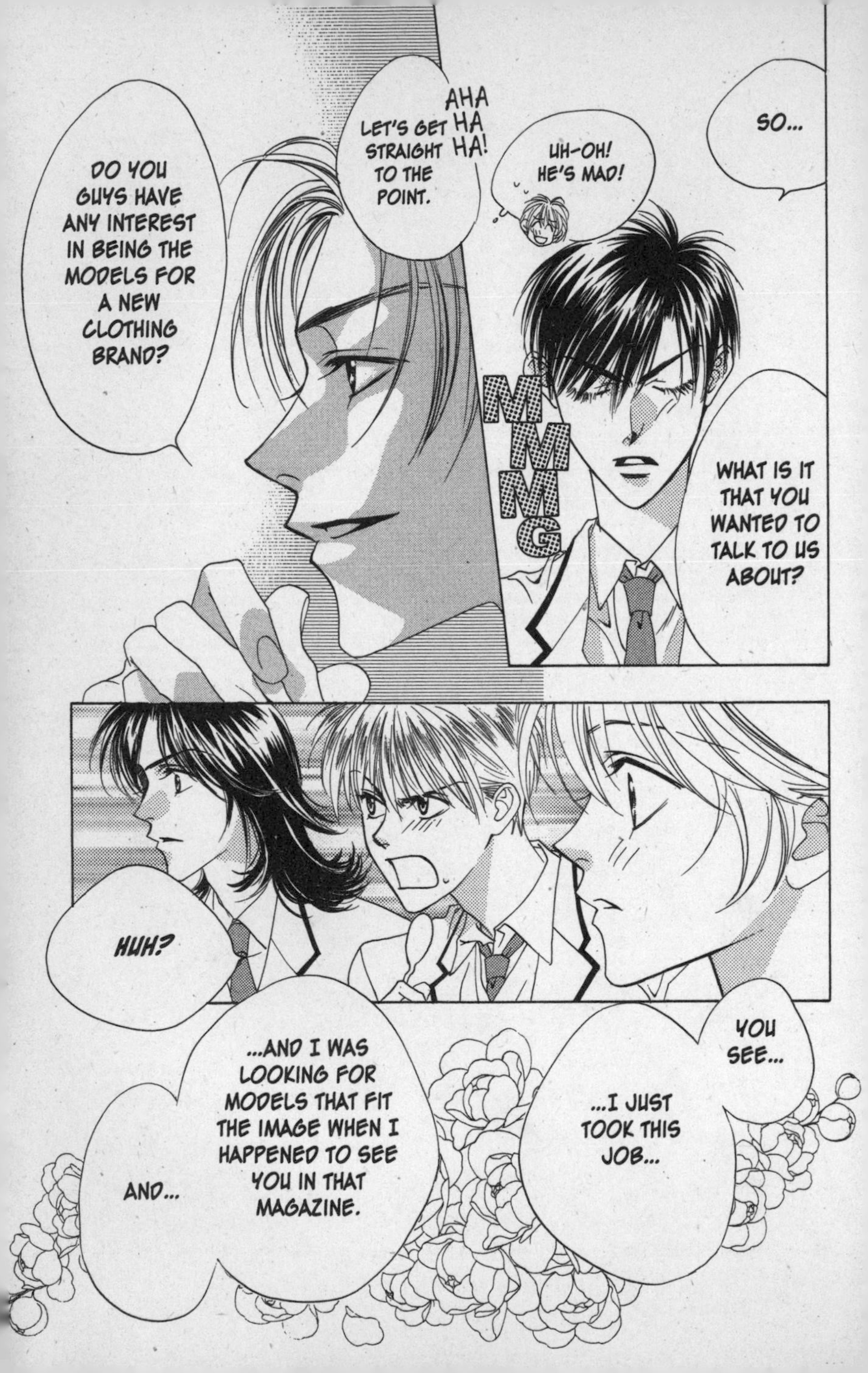
SO...
WHAT IS IT THAT YOU WANTED TO TALK TO US ABOUT?
MMMMG
UH-OH! HE'S MAD!
AHA HA HA!
LET'S GET STRAIGHT TO THE POINT.
DO YOU GUYS HAVE ANY INTEREST IN BEING THE MODELS FOR A NEW CLOTHING BRAND?
HUH?
YOU SEE...
...I JUST TOOK THIS JOB...
...AND I WAS LOOKING FOR MODELS THAT FIT THE IMAGE WHEN I HAPPENED TO SEE YOU IN THAT MAGAZINE.
AND...

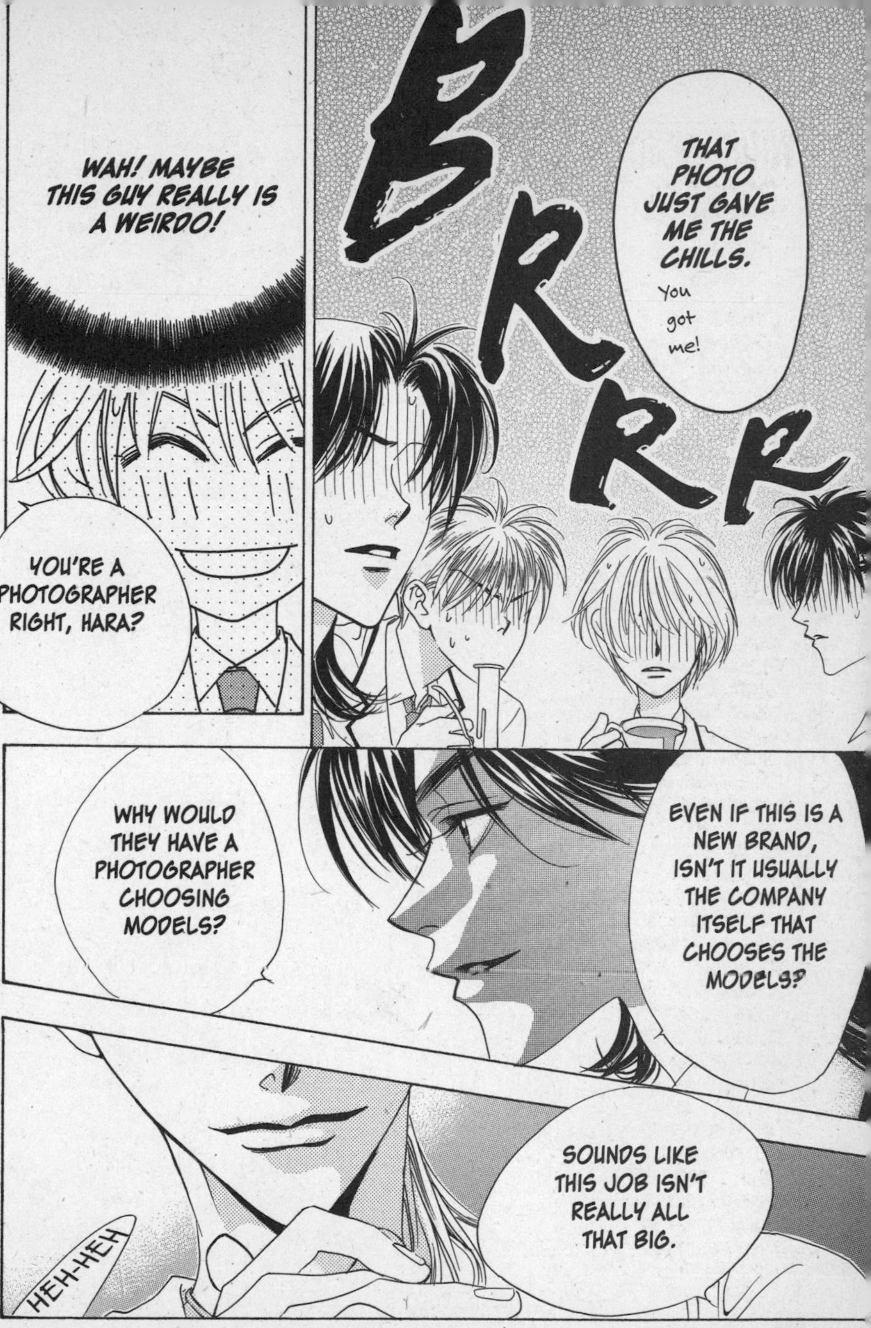
BRRR
THAT PHOTO JUST GAVE ME THE CHILLS.
You got me!
WAH! MAYBE THIS GUY REALLY IS A WEIRDO!
YOU'RE A PHOTOGRAPHER RIGHT, HARA?
EVEN IF THIS IS A NEW BRAND, ISN'T IT USUALLY THE COMPANY ITSELF THAT CHOOSES THE MODELS?
WHY WOULD THEY HAVE A PHOTOGRAPHER CHOOSING MODELS?
SOUNDS LIKE THIS JOB ISN'T REALLY ALL THAT BIG.
HEH-HEH

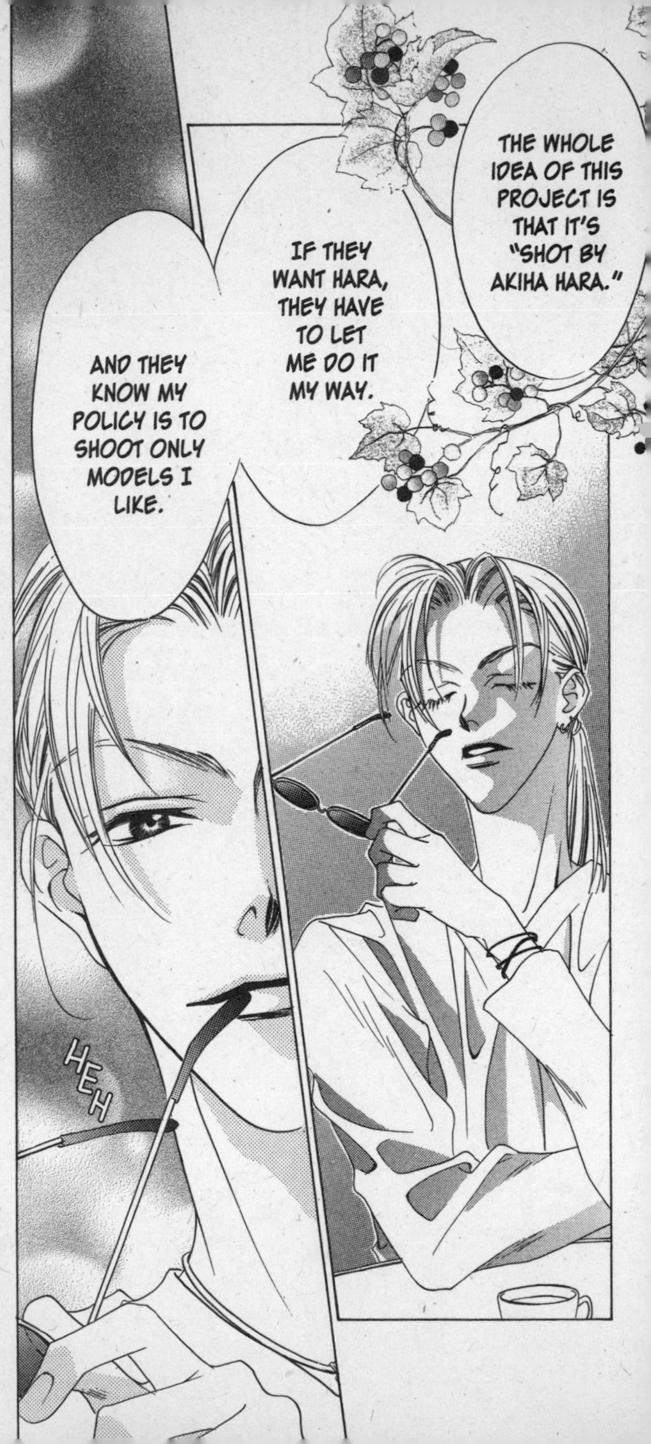
THE WHOLE IDEA OF THIS PROJECT IS THAT IT'S "SHOT BY AKIHA HARA."
IF THEY WANT HARA, THEY HAVE TO LET ME DO IT MY WAY.
AND THEY KNOW MY POLICY IS TO SHOOT ONLY MODELS I LIKE.
HEH

WHISPERED SECRETS

THE SWEET TOOTH

THERE'S NO MODEL FOR THE LOOK OF THE CHARACTER AKIHA, BUT I DID BASE HIS PERSONALITY ON SOMEONE REAL: MY FRIEND M*DA WHO I'VE KNOWN SINCE HIGH SCHOOL. HE LOOKS JUST LIKE THE CHARACTER DANSHIKA FROM KYOKO HIKAWA'S "ONNA NO KO WA YOYU," AND HE SINGS LIKE UTSUNOMIYA FROM THE BAND TM NETWORK. HE'S A TOTAL SWEET TOOTH. ONE DAY WHEN HE TOOK ME TO THIS ICE CREAM PARLOR HE ALWAYS GOES TO, HE ORDERED A HUGE SUNDAE ON A LONG PLATE, LAYERED WITH ICE CREAM, NUTS AND CHOCOLATE. AND UNDERNEATH IT ALL WAS MAPLE SYRUP. THEN HE EVEN ORDERED A DRINK: HOT CHOCOLATE. WHAT AM I GONNA DO WITH THIS GUY?

MY FRIENDS THINK HE LOOKS LIKE HAKUEI (A MUSICIAN).

BRAVO M*DA!

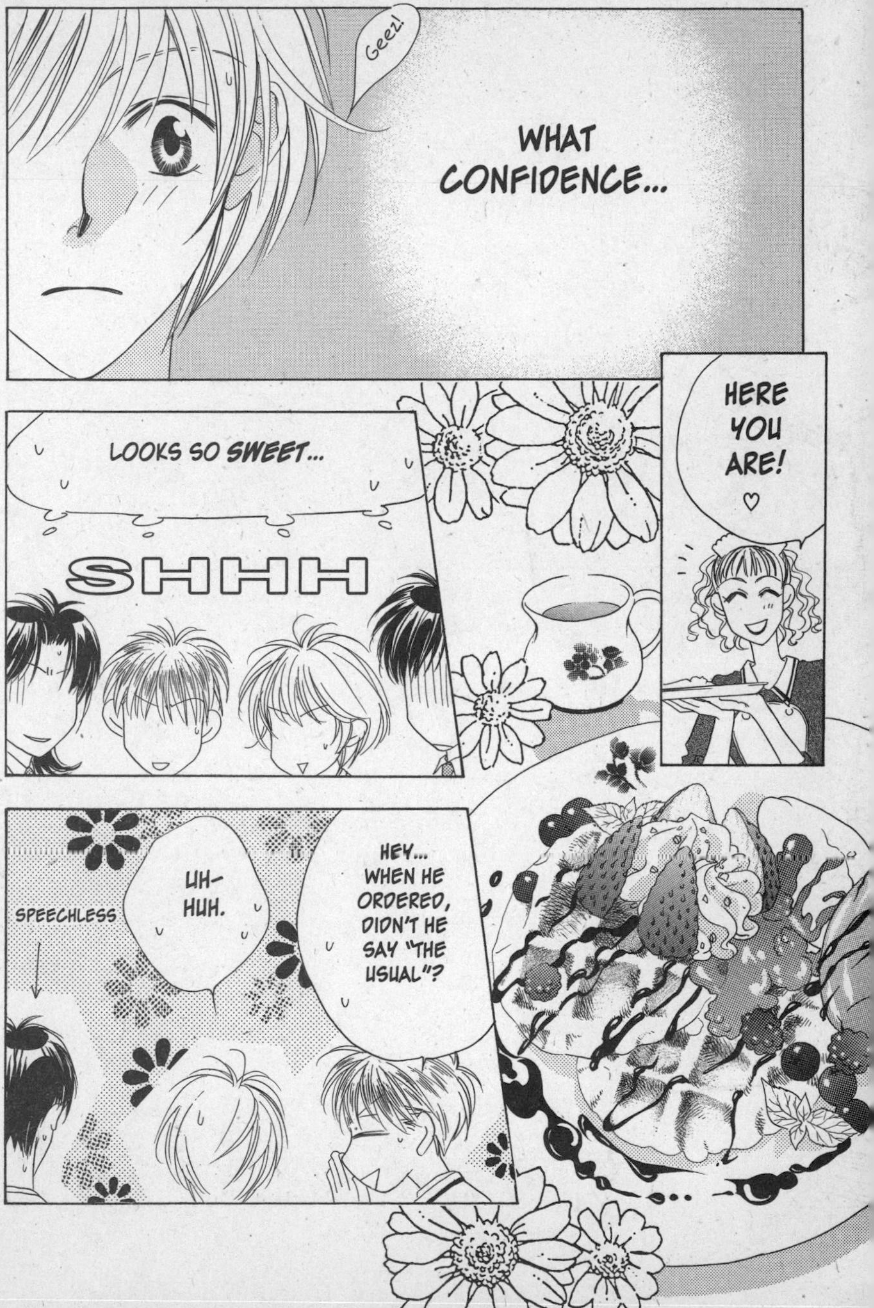
Geez!
WHAT CONFIDENCE...
HERE YOU ARE! ♡
LOOKS SO SWEET...
SHHH
HEY... WHEN HE ORDERED, DIDN'T HE SAY "THE USUAL"?
UH-HUH.
SPEECHLESS

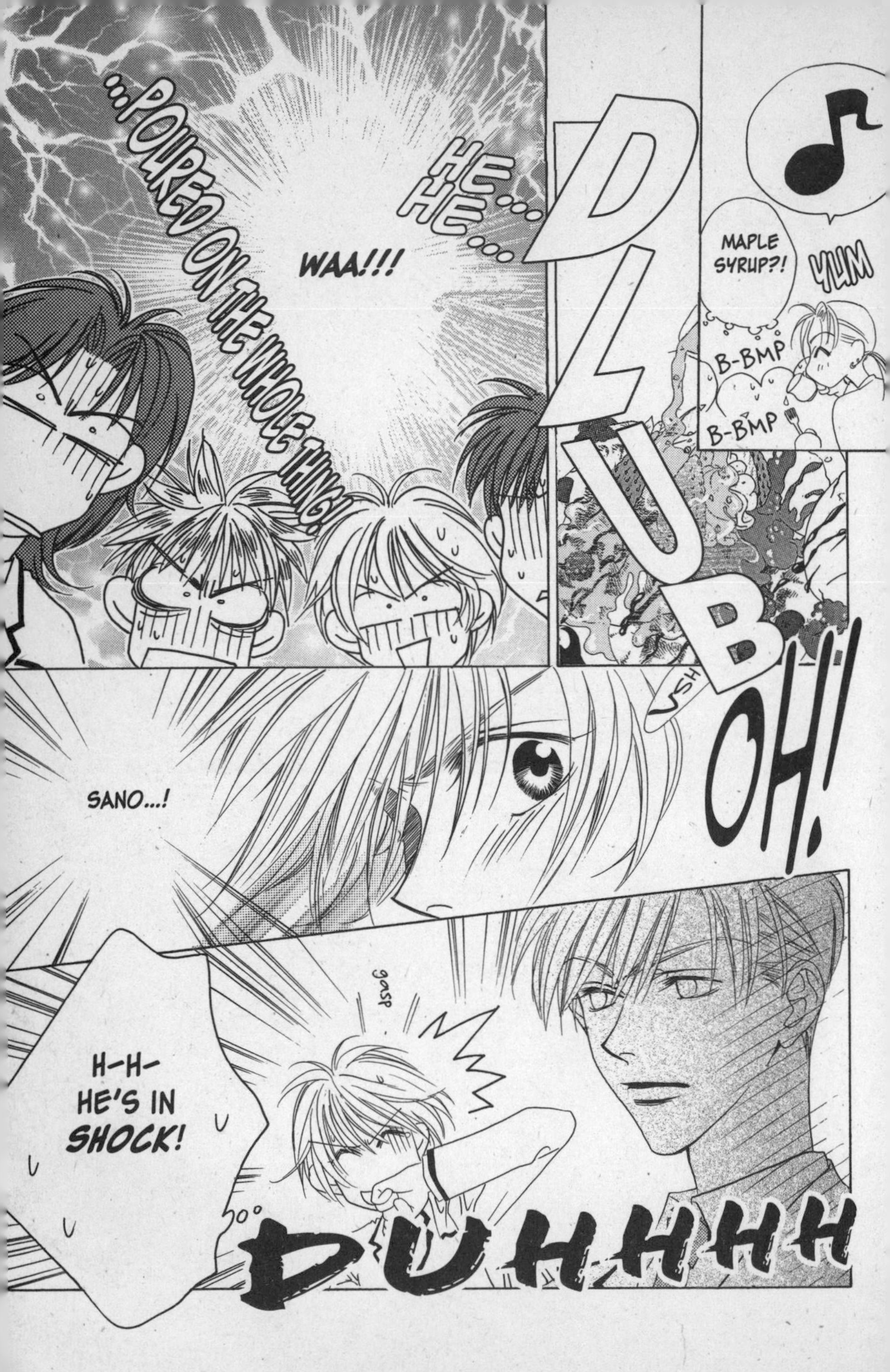

MAPLE SYRUP?!
YUM
B-BMP
B-BMP
DLUB
SH
HE HE... HE...
WAA!!!
...POURED ON THE WHOLE THING!!
OH!
SANO...!
gasp
H-H-HE'S IN SHOCK!
DUHHHH

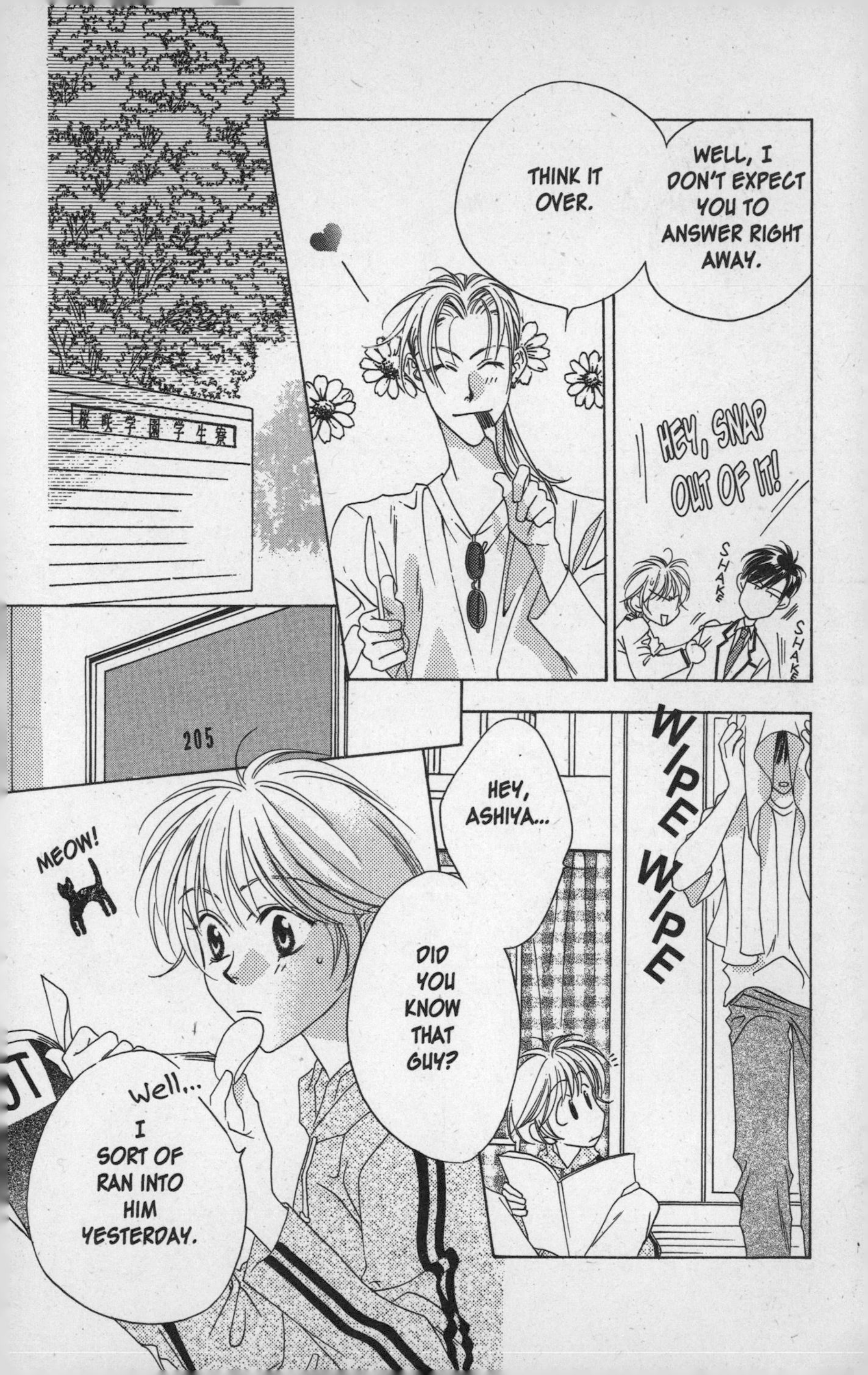
WELL, I DON'T EXPECT YOU TO ANSWER RIGHT AWAY.
THINK IT OVER.
HEY, SNAP OUT OF IT!
SHAKE
SHAKE
桜咲学園学生寮
WIPE WIPE
HEY, ASHIYA...
DID YOU KNOW THAT GUY?
205
MEOW!
Well... I SORT OF RAN INTO HIM YESTERDAY.

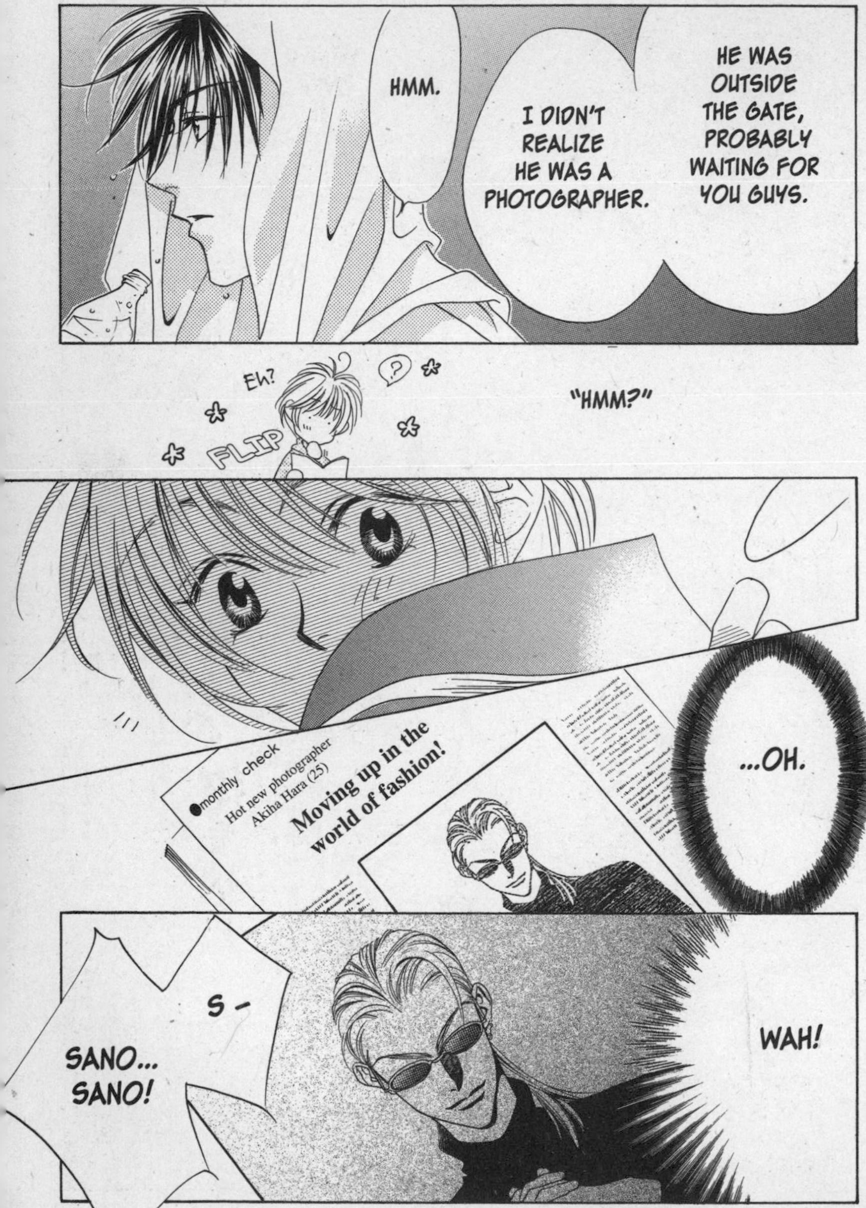
HE WAS OUTSIDE THE GATE, PROBABLY WAITING FOR YOU GUYS.
I DIDN'T REALIZE HE WAS A PHOTOGRAPHER.
HMM.
"HMM?"
Eh?
FLIP
...OH.
●monthly check
Hot new photographer Akiha Hara (25)
Moving up in the world of fashion!
WAH!
S-
SANO... SANO!

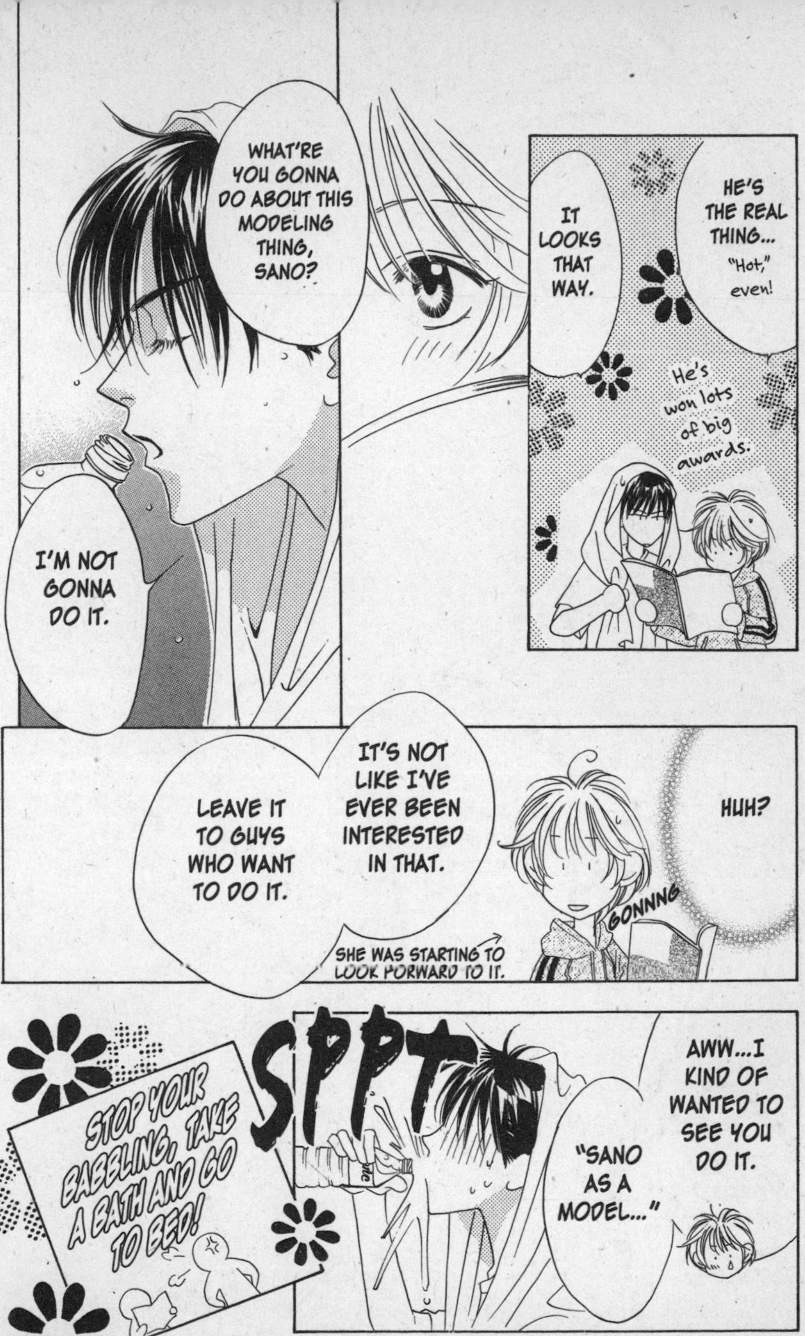
HE'S THE REAL THING... "Hot," even!
IT LOOKS THAT WAY.
He's won lots of big awards.
WHAT'RE YOU GONNA DO ABOUT THIS MODELING THING, SANO?
I'M NOT GONNA DO IT.
HUH?
IT'S NOT LIKE I'VE EVER BEEN INTERESTED IN THAT.
LEAVE IT TO GUYS WHO WANT TO DO IT.
GONNNG
SHE WAS STARTING TO LOOK FORWARD TO IT.
AWW...I KIND OF WANTED TO SEE YOU DO IT.
"SANO AS A MODEL..."
SPPT
STOP YOUR BABBLING, TAKE A BATH AND GO TO BED!

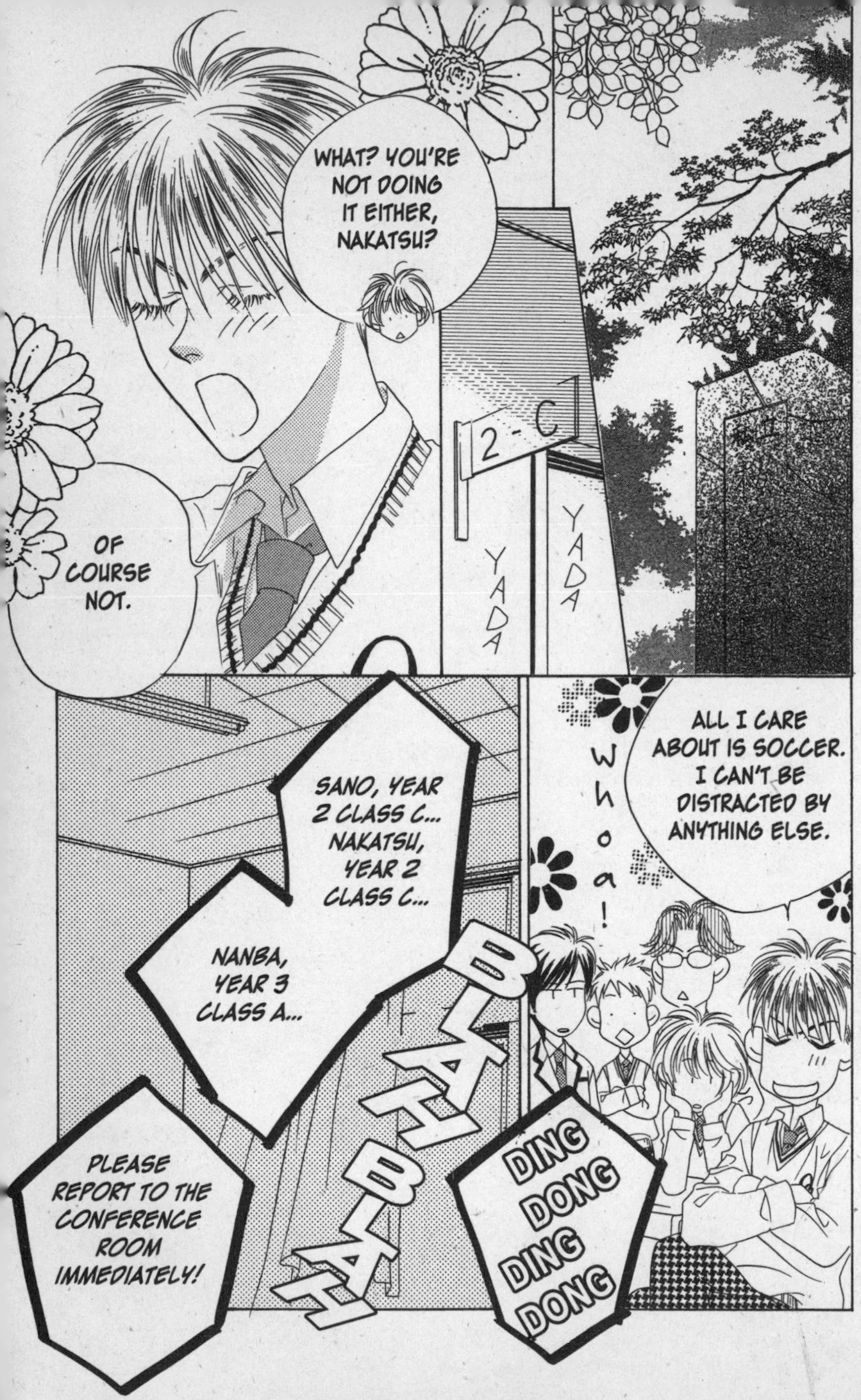
WHAT? YOU'RE NOT DOING IT EITHER, NAKATSU?
YADA YADA
OF COURSE NOT.
ALL I CARE ABOUT IS SOCCER. I CAN'T BE DISTRACTED BY ANYTHING ELSE.
Whoa!
DING DONG DING DONG
SANO, YEAR 2 CLASS C... NAKATSU, YEAR 2 CLASS C...
NANBA, YEAR 3 CLASS A...
BLAH BLAH
PLEASE REPORT TO THE CONFERENCE ROOM IMMEDIATELY!

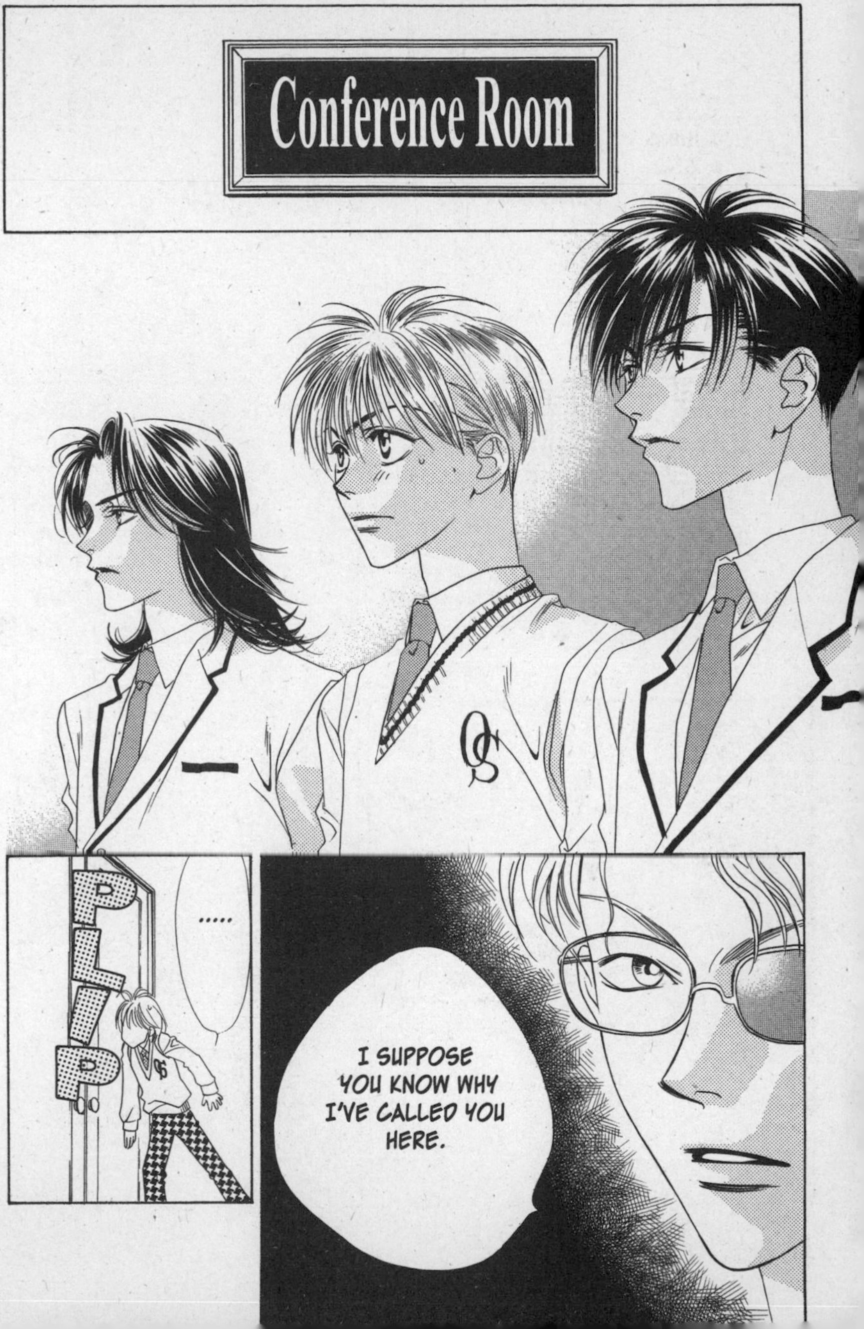
Conference Room
I SUPPOSE YOU KNOW WHY I'VE CALLED YOU HERE.
PLIP
......

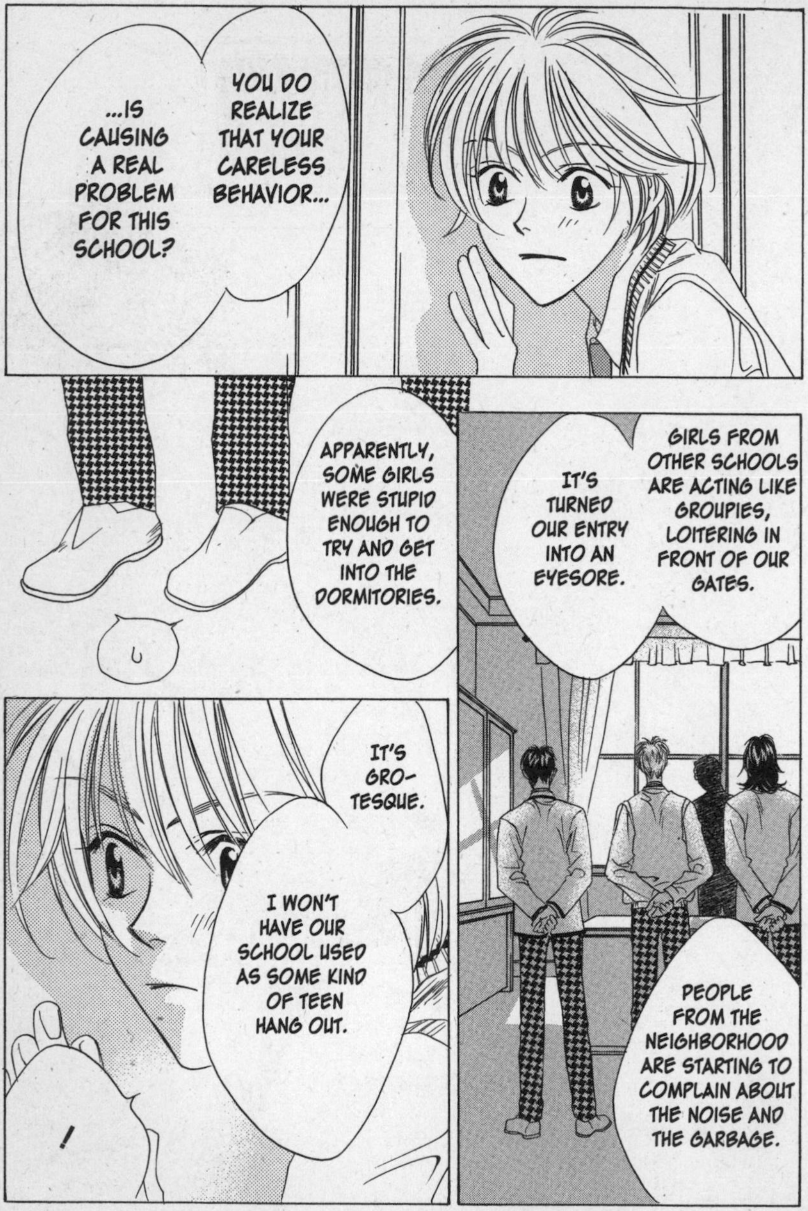
YOU DO REALIZE THAT YOUR CARELESS BEHAVIOR...
...IS CAUSING A REAL PROBLEM FOR THIS SCHOOL?
GIRLS FROM OTHER SCHOOLS ARE ACTING LIKE GROUPIES, LOITERING IN FRONT OF OUR GATES.
IT'S TURNED OUR ENTRY INTO AN EYESORE.
PEOPLE FROM THE NEIGHBORHOOD ARE STARTING TO COMPLAIN ABOUT THE NOISE AND THE GARBAGE.
APPARENTLY, SOME GIRLS WERE STUPID ENOUGH TO TRY AND GET INTO THE DORMITORIES.
IT'S GRO- TESQUE.
I WON'T HAVE OUR SCHOOL USED AS SOME KIND OF TEEN HANG OUT.
!

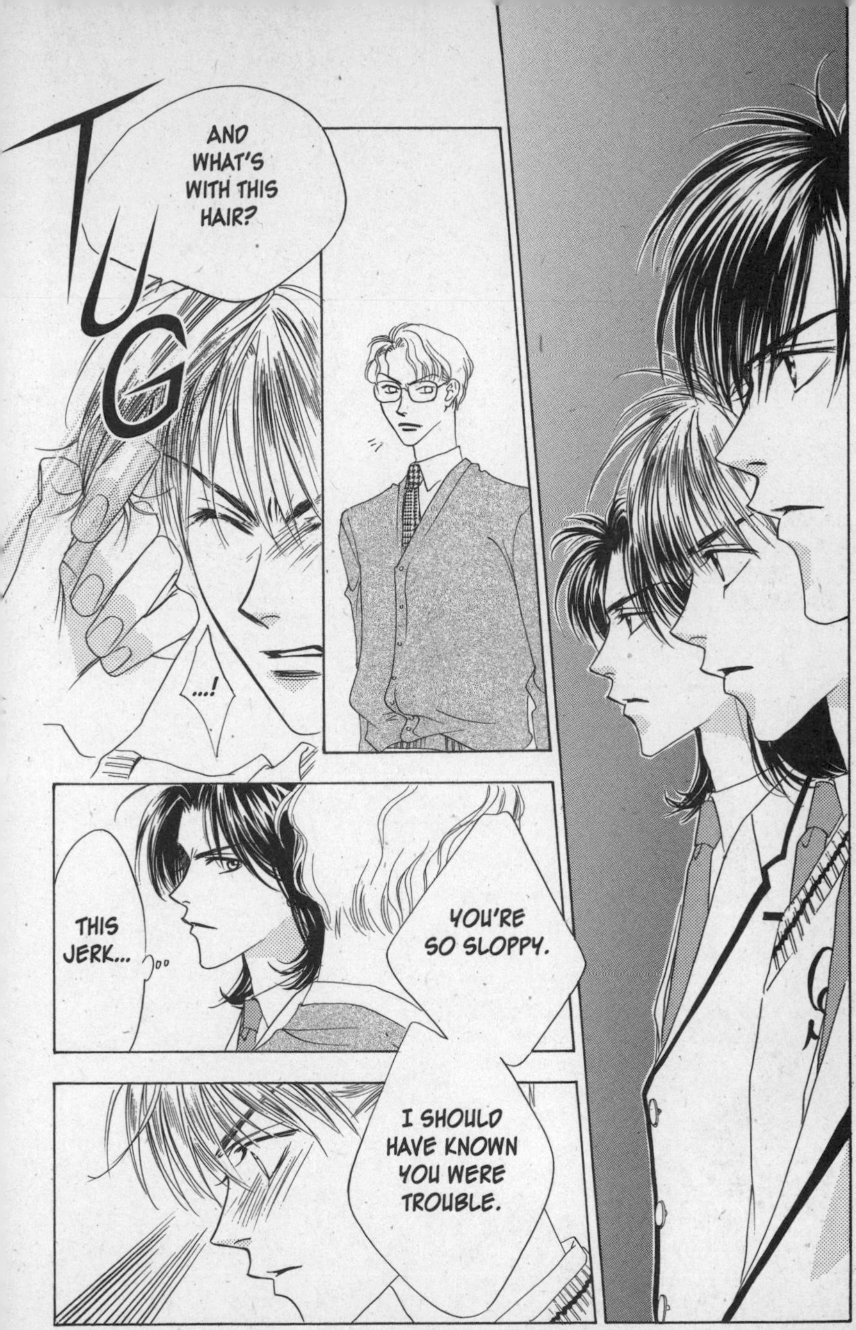
AND WHAT'S WITH THIS HAIR?
TUG
...!
YOU'RE SO SLOPPY.
THIS JERK...
I SHOULD HAVE KNOWN YOU WERE TROUBLE.

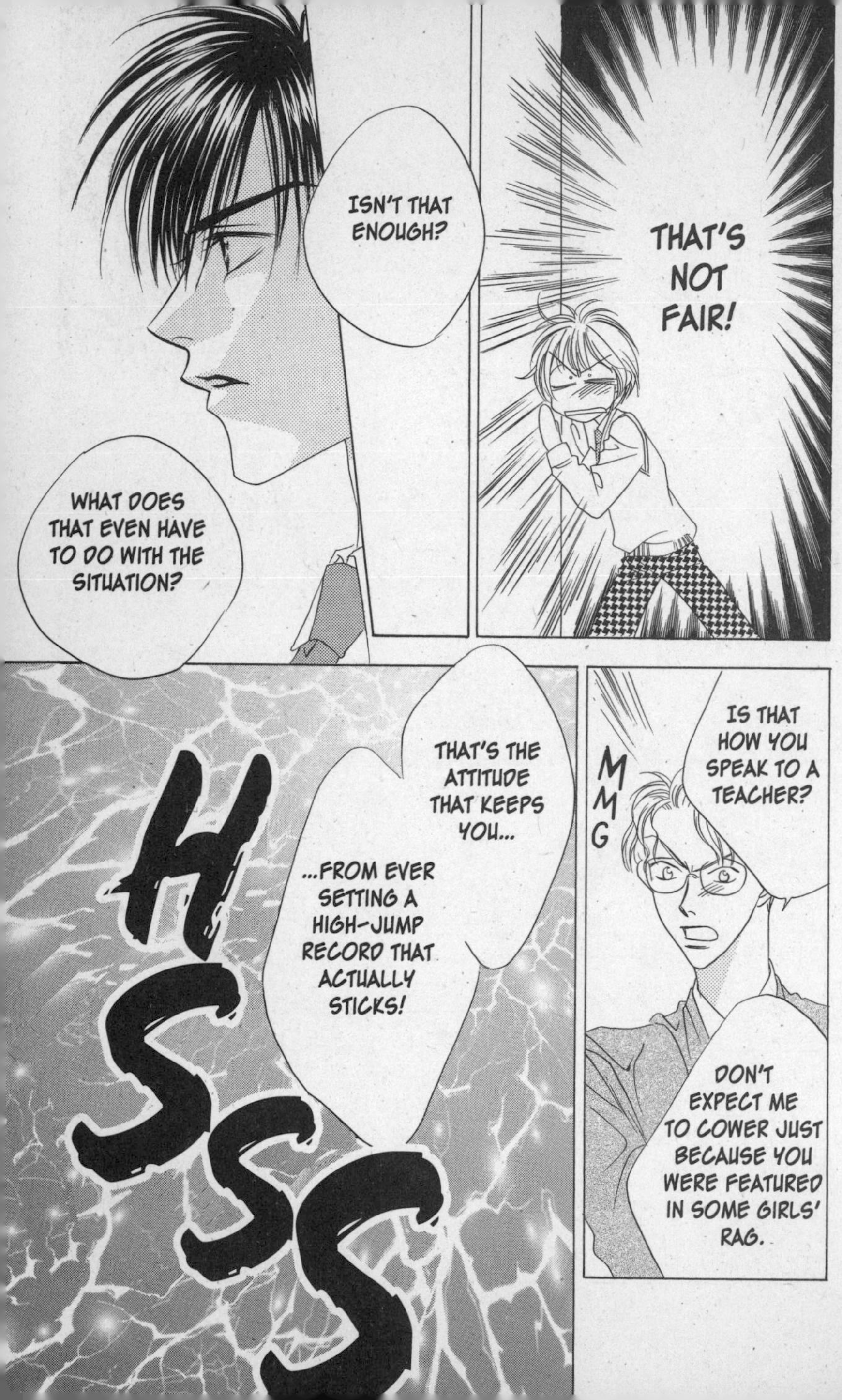
THAT'S NOT FAIR!
ISN'T THAT ENOUGH?
WHAT DOES THAT EVEN HAVE TO DO WITH THE SITUATION?
MMG
IS THAT HOW YOU SPEAK TO A TEACHER?
DON'T EXPECT ME TO COWER JUST BECAUSE YOU WERE FEATURED IN SOME GIRLS' RAG.
HSSS
THAT'S THE ATTITUDE THAT KEEPS YOU...
...FROM EVER SETTING A HIGH-JUMP RECORD THAT ACTUALLY STICKS!

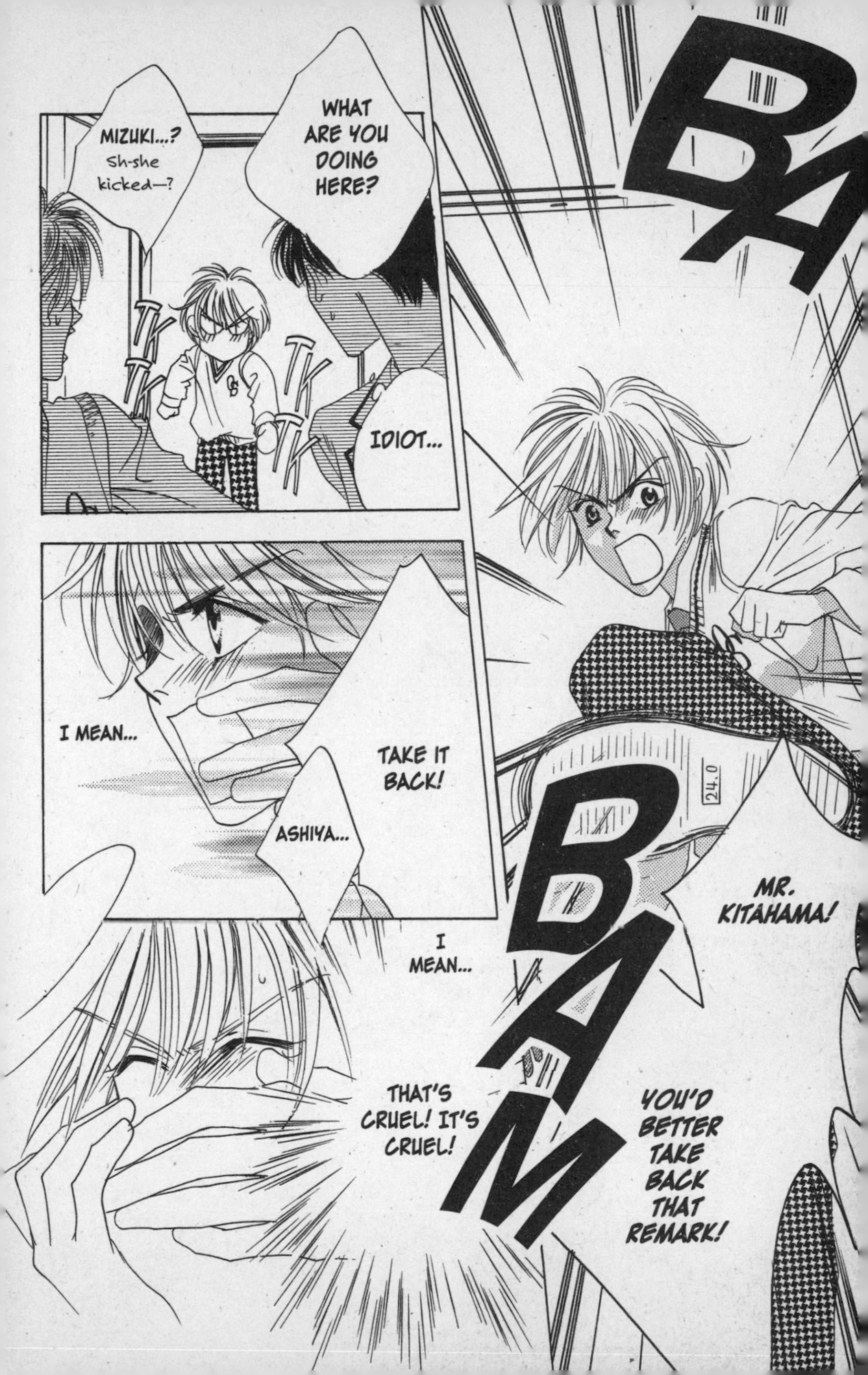
BA
BAM
MR. KITAHAMA!
YOU'D BETTER TAKE BACK THAT REMARK!
WHAT ARE YOU DOING HERE?
MIZUKI...? Sh-she kicked—?
IDIOT...
TAKE IT BACK!
ASHIYA...
I MEAN...
I MEAN...
THAT'S CRUEL! IT'S CRUEL!

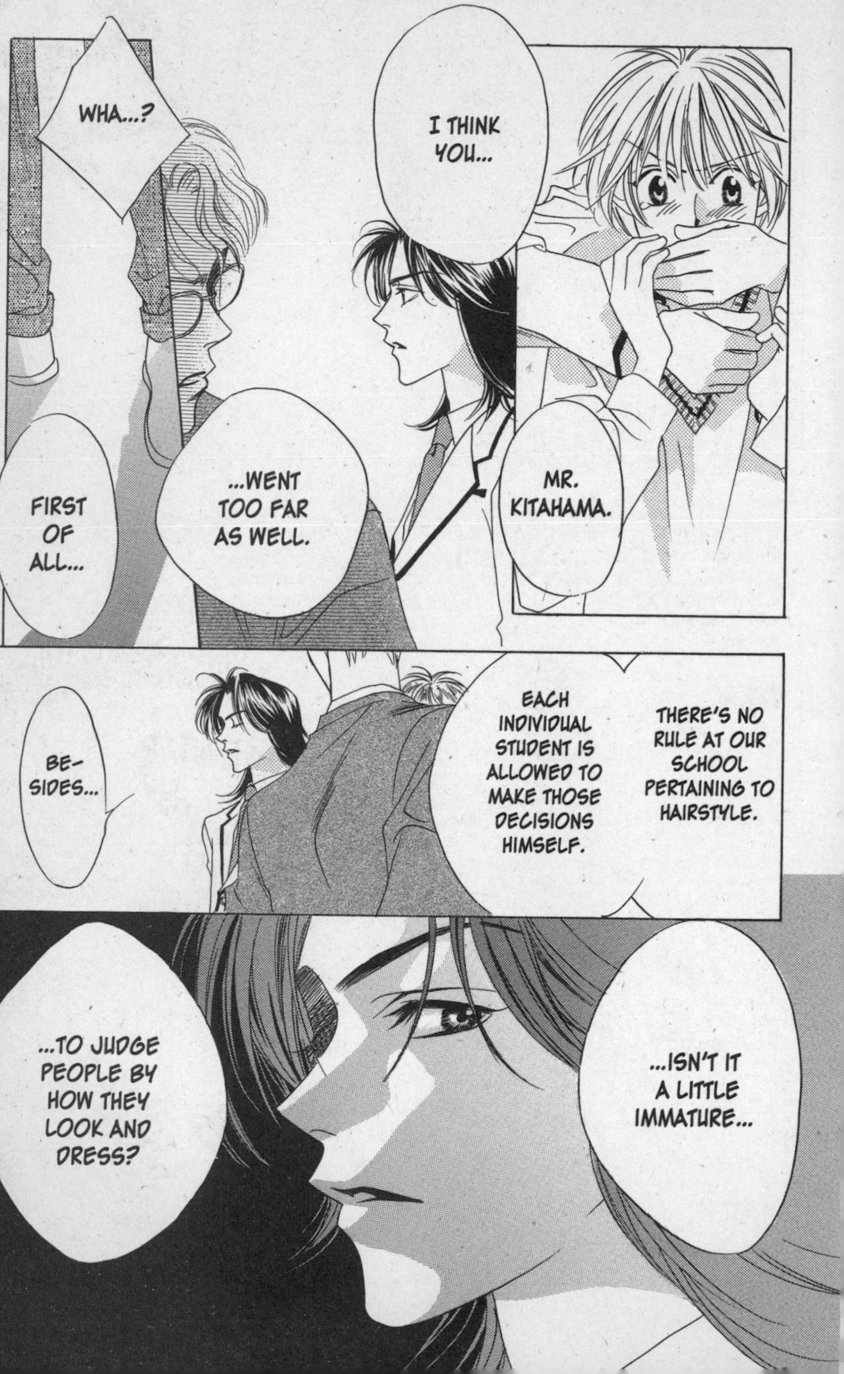
MR. KITAHAMA.
I THINK YOU...
...WENT TOO FAR AS WELL.
WHA...?
FIRST OF ALL...
THERE'S NO RULE AT OUR SCHOOL PERTAINING TO HAIRSTYLE.
EACH INDIVIDUAL STUDENT IS ALLOWED TO MAKE THOSE DECISIONS HIMSELF.
BE-SIDES...
...ISN'T IT A LITTLE IMMATURE...
...TO JUDGE PEOPLE BY HOW THEY LOOK AND DRESS?

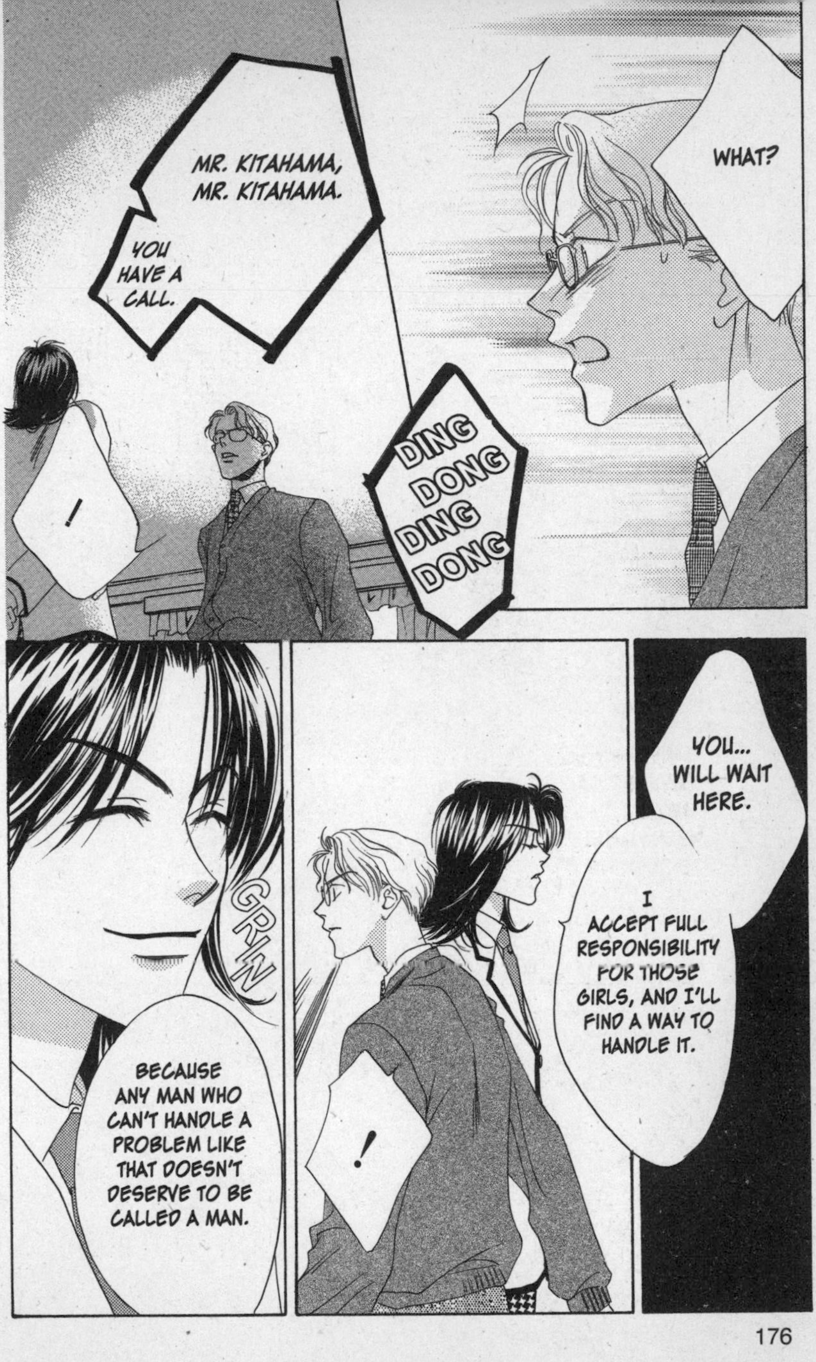
WHAT?
DING DONG DING DONG
MR. KITAHAMA, MR. KITAHAMA.
YOU HAVE A CALL.
!
YOU... WILL WAIT HERE.
I ACCEPT FULL RESPONSIBILITY FOR THOSE GIRLS, AND I'LL FIND A WAY TO HANDLE IT.
!
GRIN
BECAUSE ANY MAN WHO CAN'T HANDLE A PROBLEM LIKE THAT DOESN'T DESERVE TO BE CALLED A MAN.

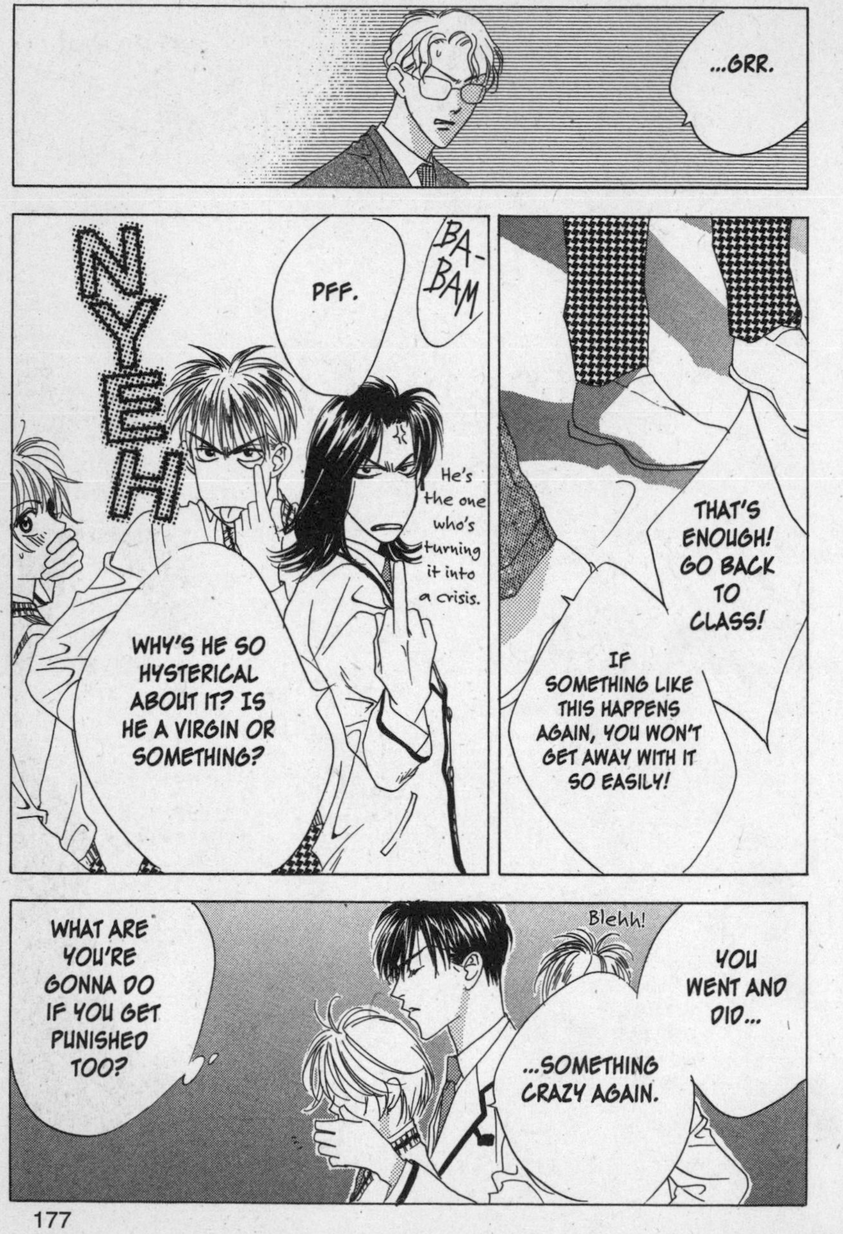
...GRR.
THAT'S ENOUGH! GO BACK TO CLASS!
IF SOMETHING LIKE THIS HAPPENS AGAIN, YOU WON'T GET AWAY WITH IT SO EASILY!
BA-BAM
PFF.
He's the one who's turning it into a crisis.
NYEH
WHY'S HE SO HYSTERICAL ABOUT IT? IS HE A VIRGIN OR SOMETHING?
Blehh!
YOU WENT AND DID...
...SOMETHING CRAZY AGAIN.
WHAT ARE YOU'RE GONNA DO IF YOU GET PUNISHED TOO?

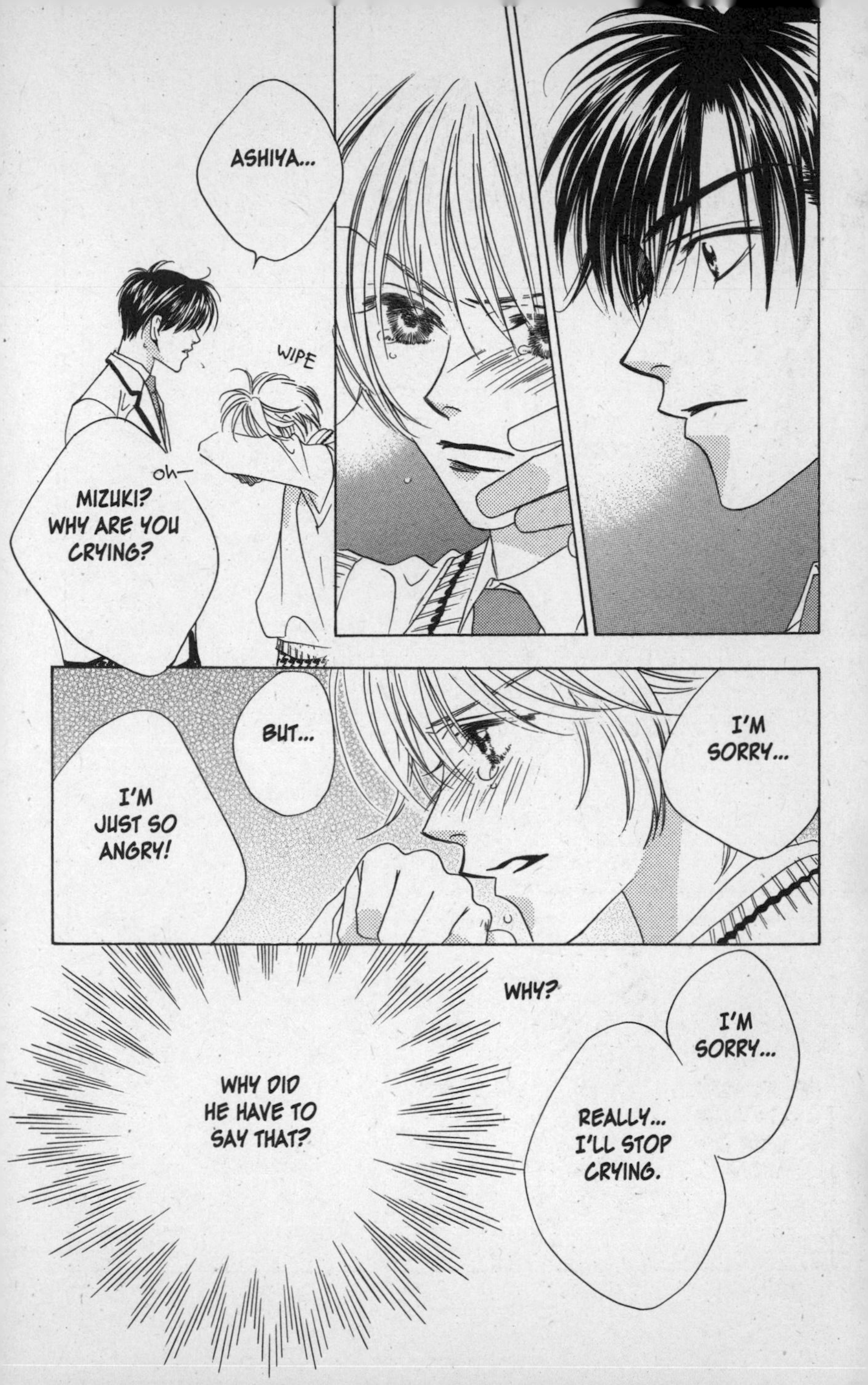
ASHIYA...
WIPE
oh—
MIZUKI? WHY ARE YOU CRYING?
I'M SORRY...
BUT...
I'M JUST SO ANGRY!
WHY?
I'M SORRY...
REALLY... I'LL STOP CRYING.
WHY DID HE HAVE TO SAY THAT?

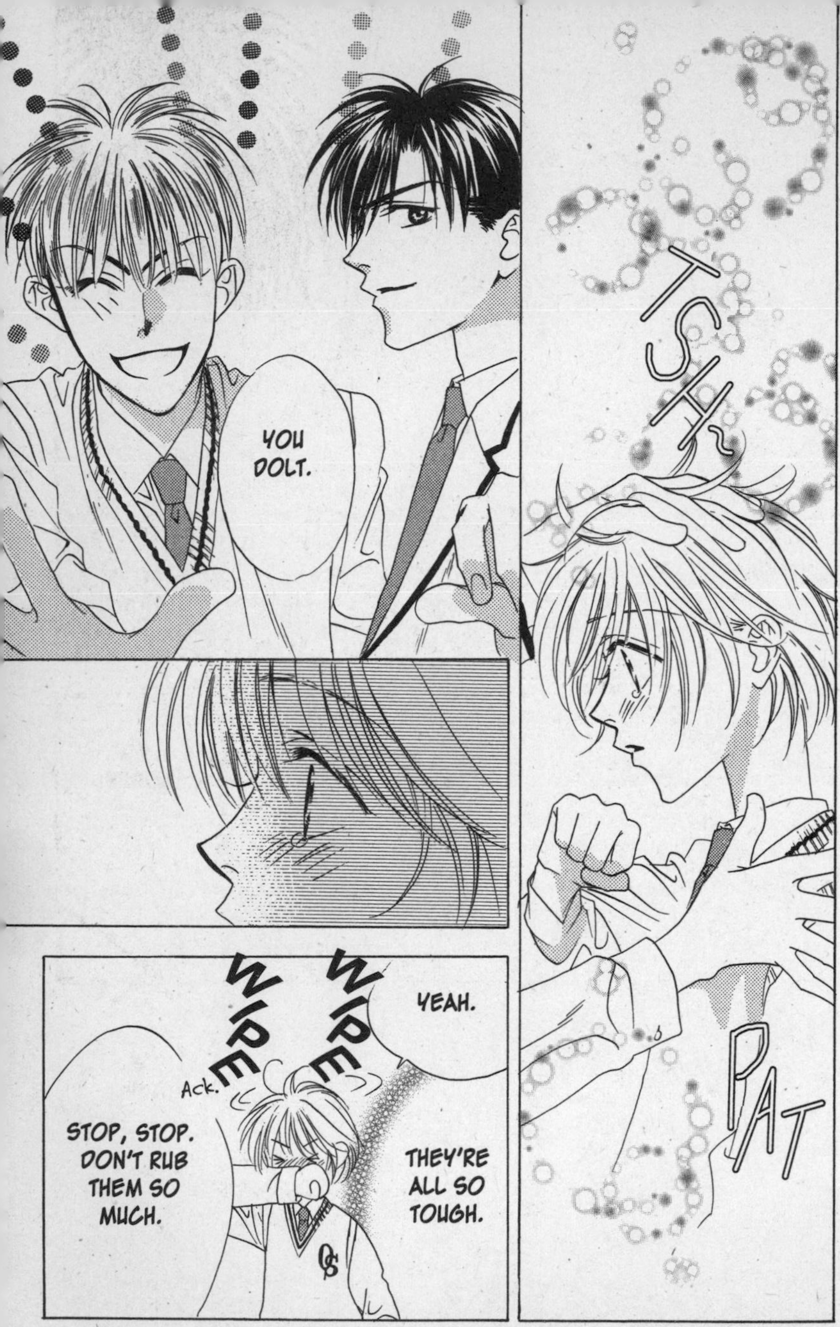
TSH~
PAT
YOU DOLT.
YEAH.
WIPE
WIPE
Ack.
THEY'RE ALL SO TOUGH.
STOP, STOP. DON'T RUB THEM SO MUCH.

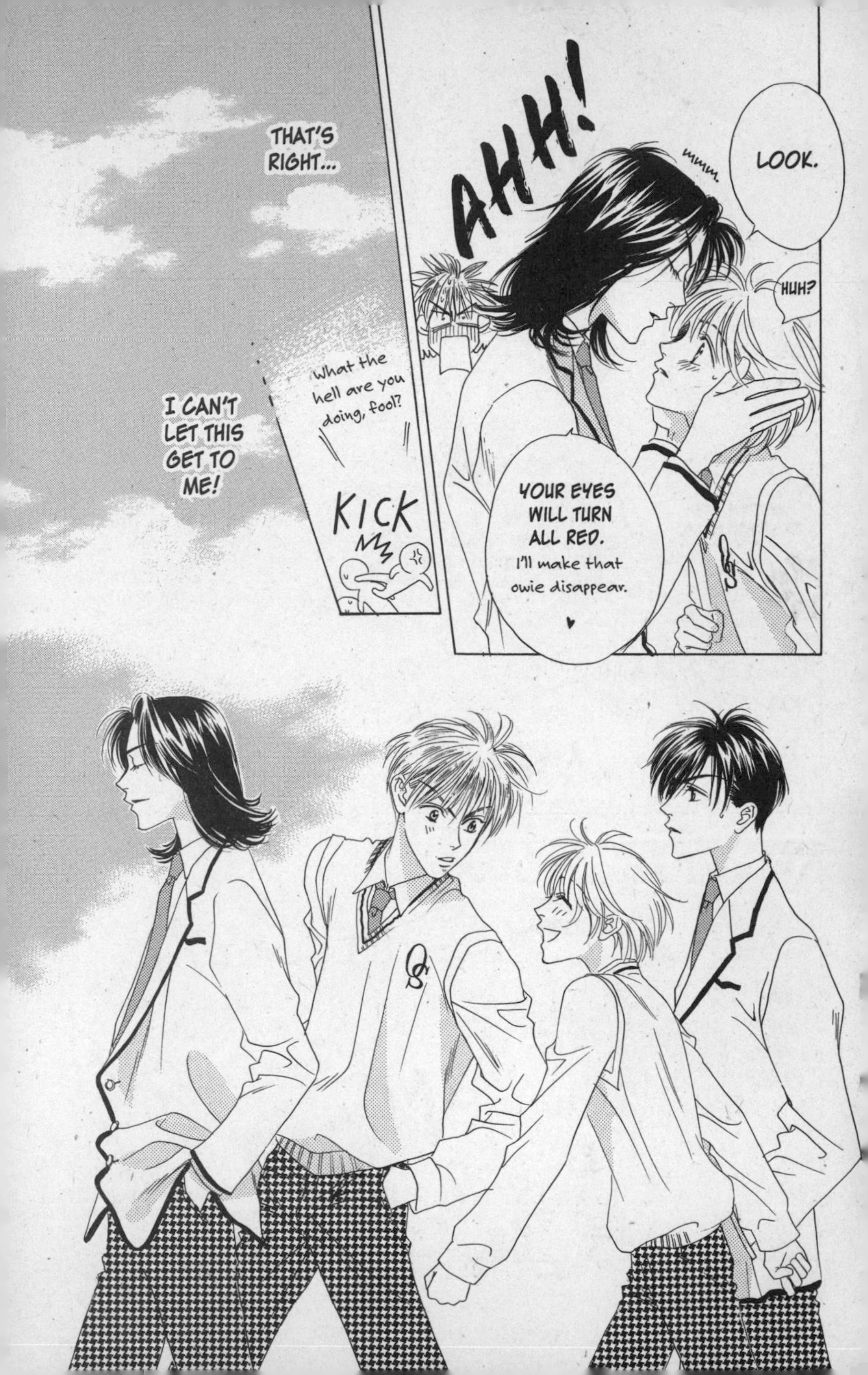
LOOK.
mmm.
HUH?
AHH!
YOUR EYES WILL TURN ALL RED.
I'll make that owie disappear.
What the hell are you doing, fool?
KICK
THAT'S RIGHT...
I CAN'T LET THIS GET TO ME!

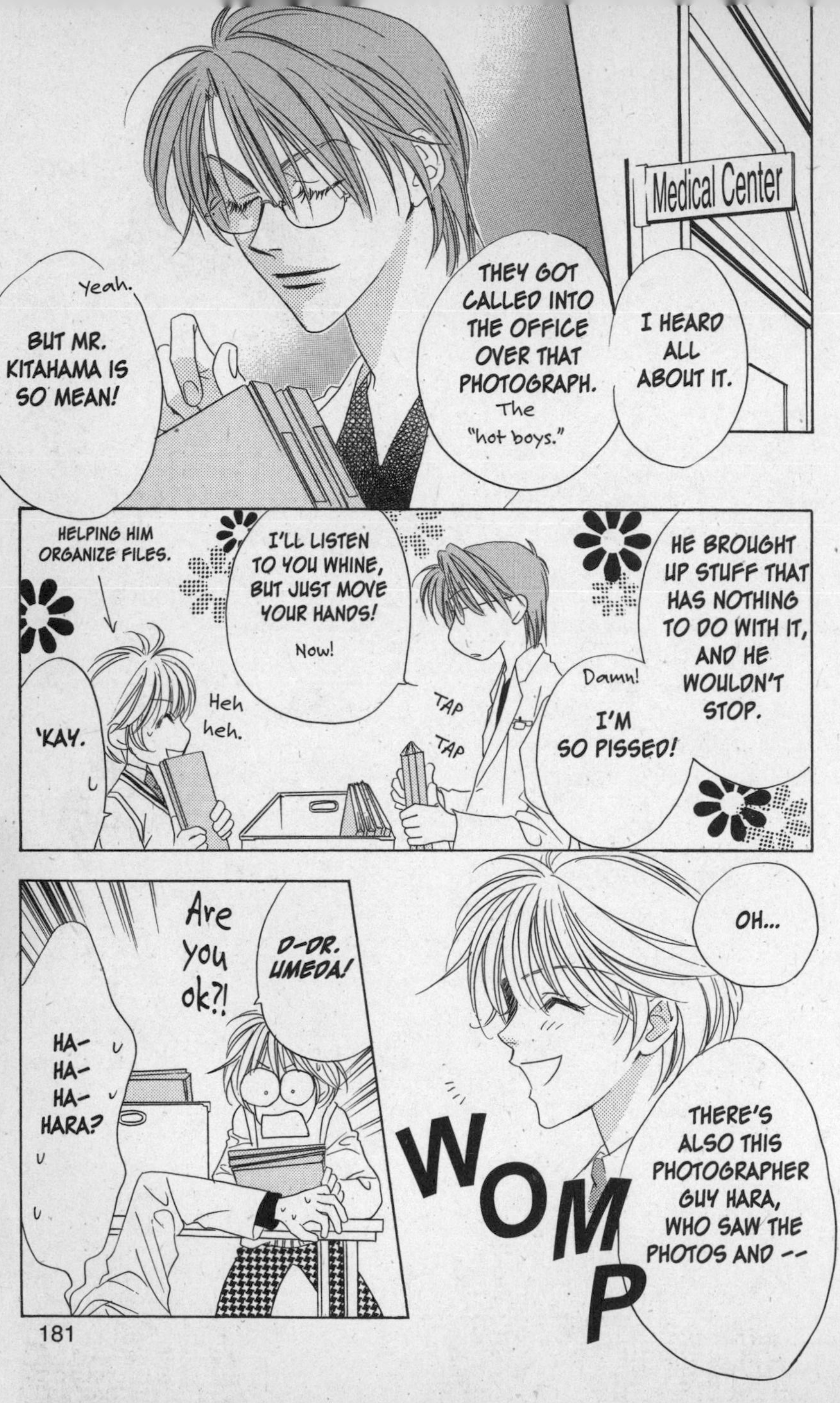
Medical Center
I HEARD ALL ABOUT IT.
THEY GOT CALLED INTO THE OFFICE OVER THAT PHOTOGRAPH.
The "hot boys."
Yeah.
BUT MR. KITAHAMA IS SO MEAN!
HE BROUGHT UP STUFF THAT HAS NOTHING TO DO WITH IT, AND HE WOULDN'T STOP.
Damn!
I'M SO PISSED!
TAP
TAP
I'LL LISTEN TO YOU WHINE, BUT JUST MOVE YOUR HANDS!
Now!
HELPING HIM ORGANIZE FILES.
Heh heh.
'KAY.
OH...
THERE'S ALSO THIS PHOTOGRAPHER GUY HARA, WHO SAW THE PHOTOS AND --
WOMP
D-DR. UMEDA!
Are you ok?!
HA-HA-HA-HARA?

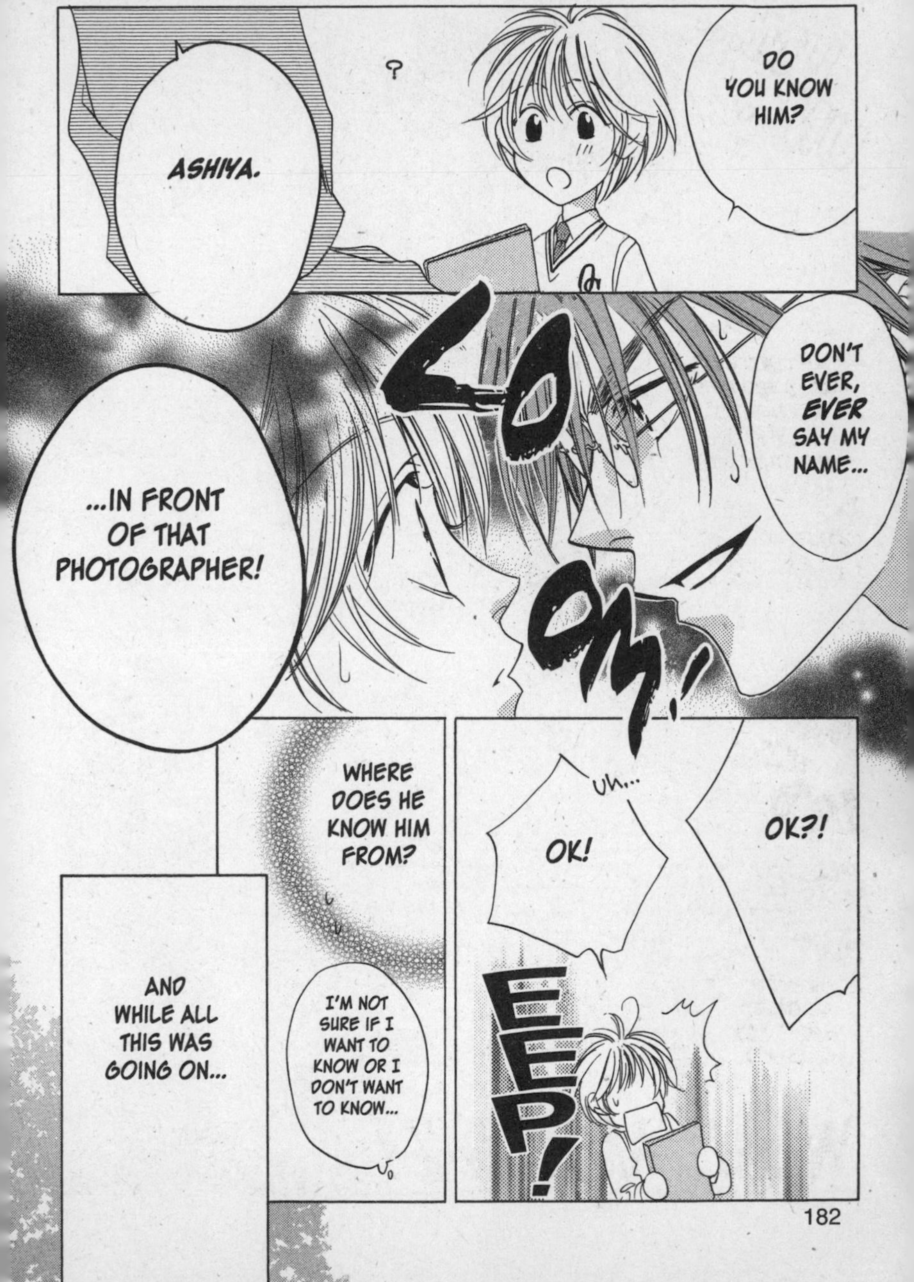
DO YOU KNOW HIM?
?
ASHIYA.
DON'T EVER, EVER SAY MY NAME...
...IN FRONT OF THAT PHOTOGRAPHER!
LOOM!
OK?!
Uh...
OK!
EEP!
WHERE DOES HE KNOW HIM FROM?
I'M NOT SURE IF I WANT TO KNOW OR I DON'T WANT TO KNOW...
AND WHILE ALL THIS WAS GOING ON...

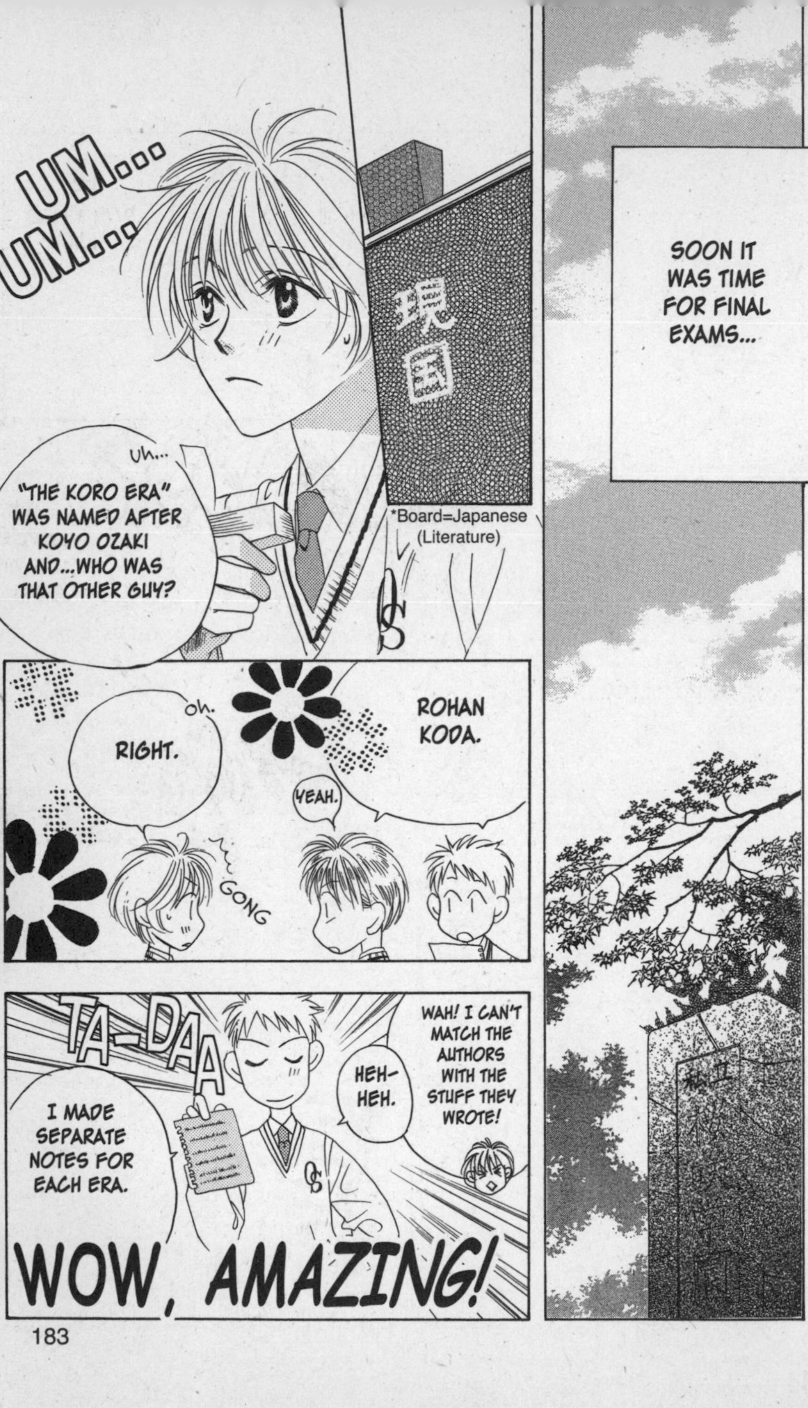
SOON IT WAS TIME FOR FINAL EXAMS...
UM... UM...
Uh...
"THE KORO ERA" WAS NAMED AFTER KOYO OZAKI AND...WHO WAS THAT OTHER GUY?
現国
*Board=Japanese (Literature)
ROHAN KODA.
YEAH.
Oh.
RIGHT.
GONG
WAH! I CAN'T MATCH THE AUTHORS WITH THE STUFF THEY WROTE!
HEH-HEH.
TA-DAA
I MADE SEPARATE NOTES FOR EACH ERA.
WOW, AMAZING!

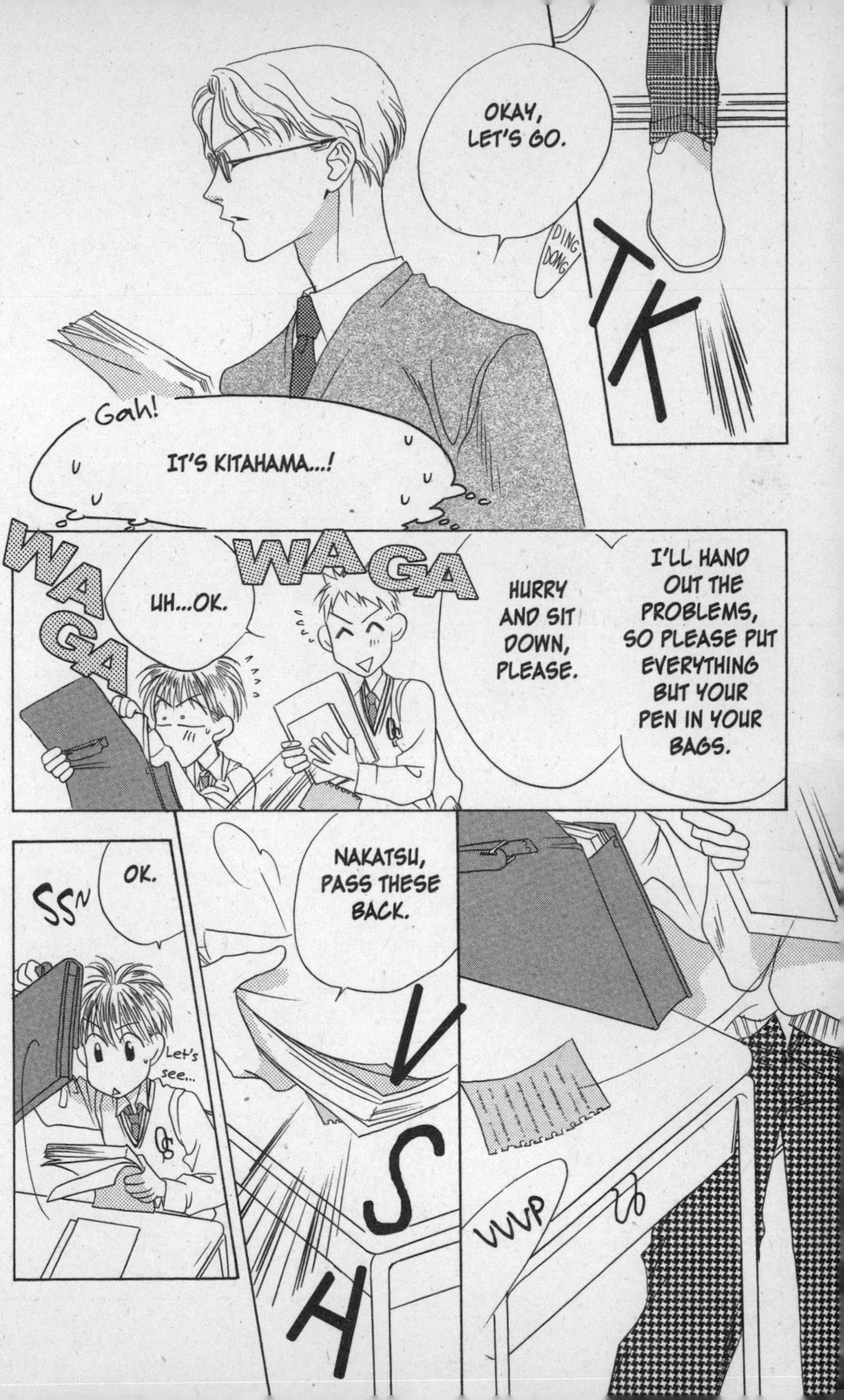
OKAY, LET'S GO.
DING DONG
TK
Gah!
IT'S KITAHAMA...!
I'LL HAND OUT THE PROBLEMS, SO PLEASE PUT EVERYTHING BUT YOUR PEN IN YOUR BAGS.
HURRY AND SIT DOWN, PLEASE.
WAGA
UH...OK.
WAGA
NAKATSU, PASS THESE BACK.
VVVP
SHH
OK.
SSN
Let's see...

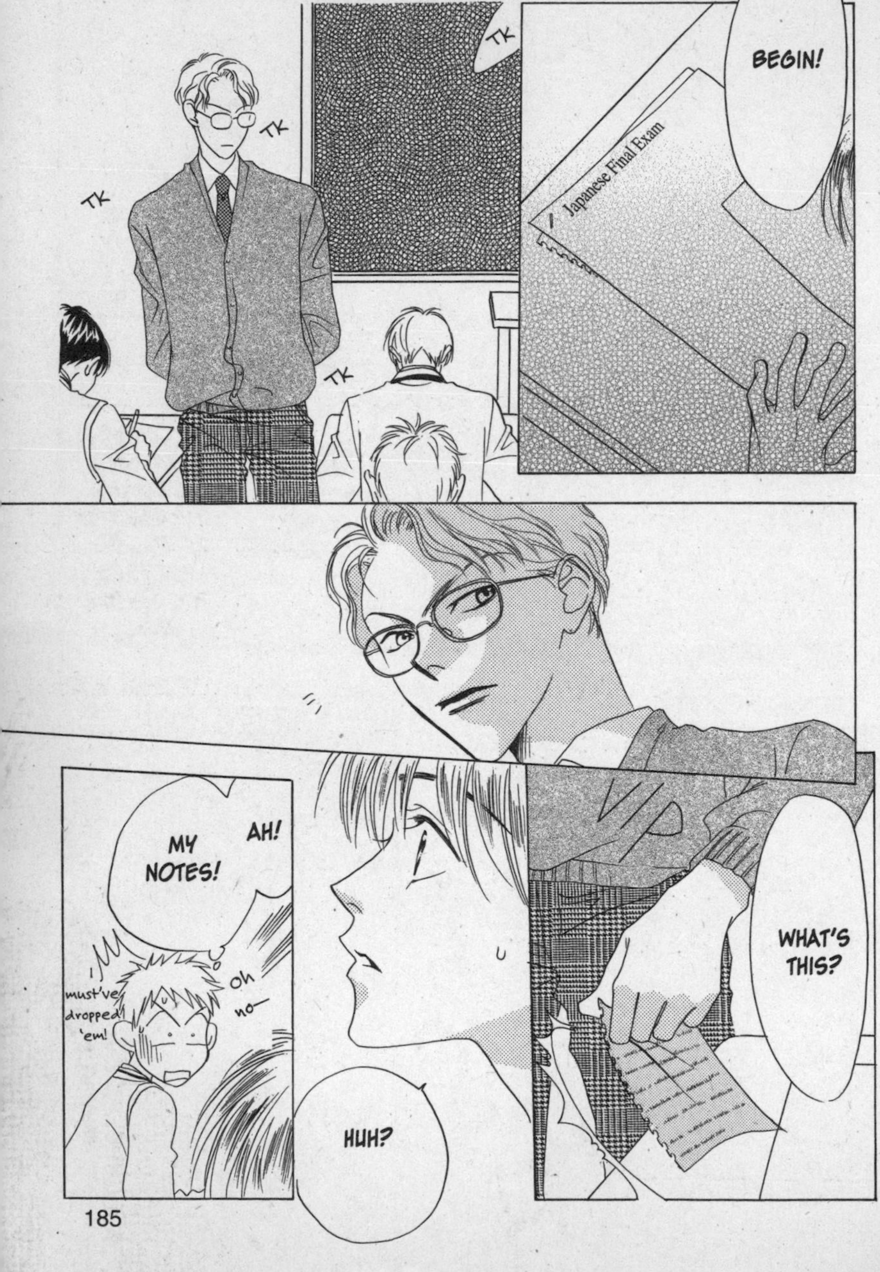
BEGIN!
Japanese Final Exam
TK
TK
TK
TK
WHAT'S THIS?
HUH?
AH!
MY NOTES!
Oh no—
I must've dropped 'em!

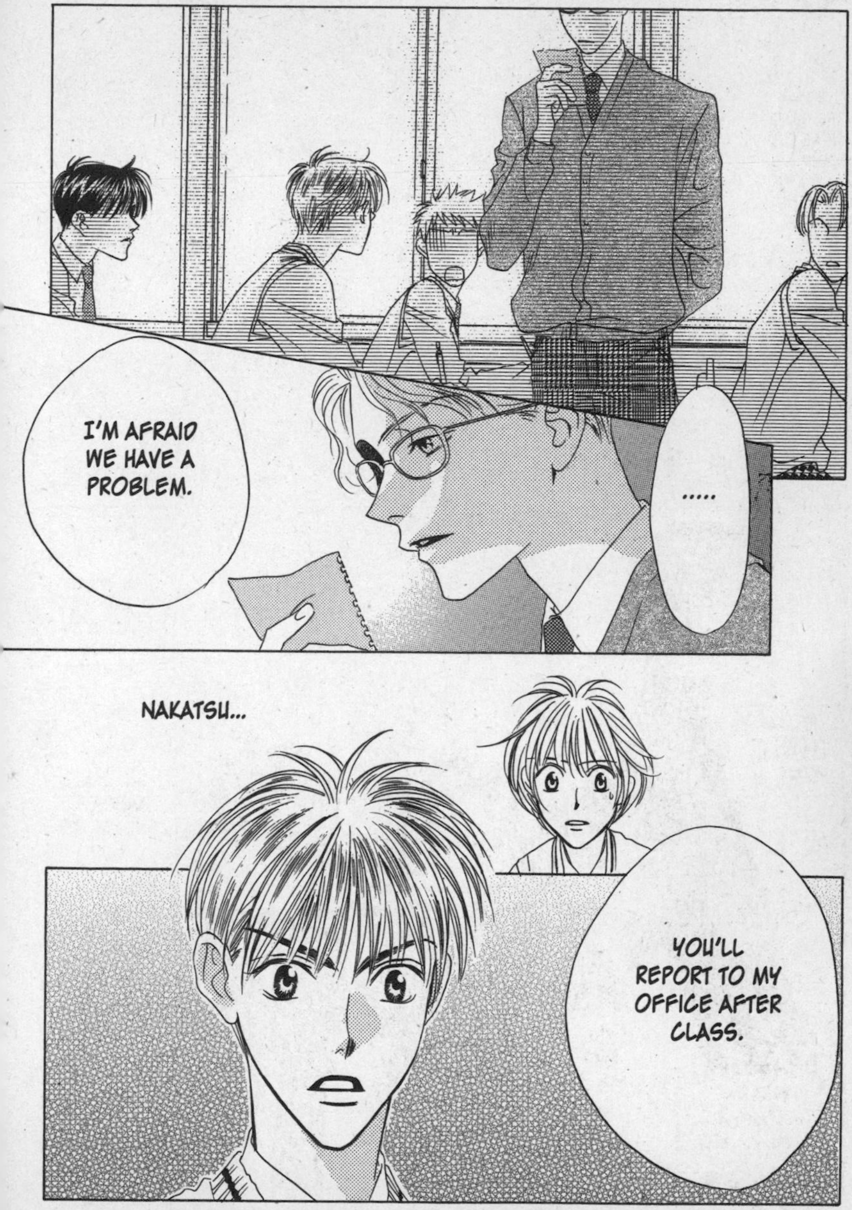
I'M AFRAID WE HAVE A PROBLEM.
.....
NAKATSU...
YOU'LL REPORT TO MY OFFICE AFTER CLASS.

HANA-KIMI CHAPTER 42/END

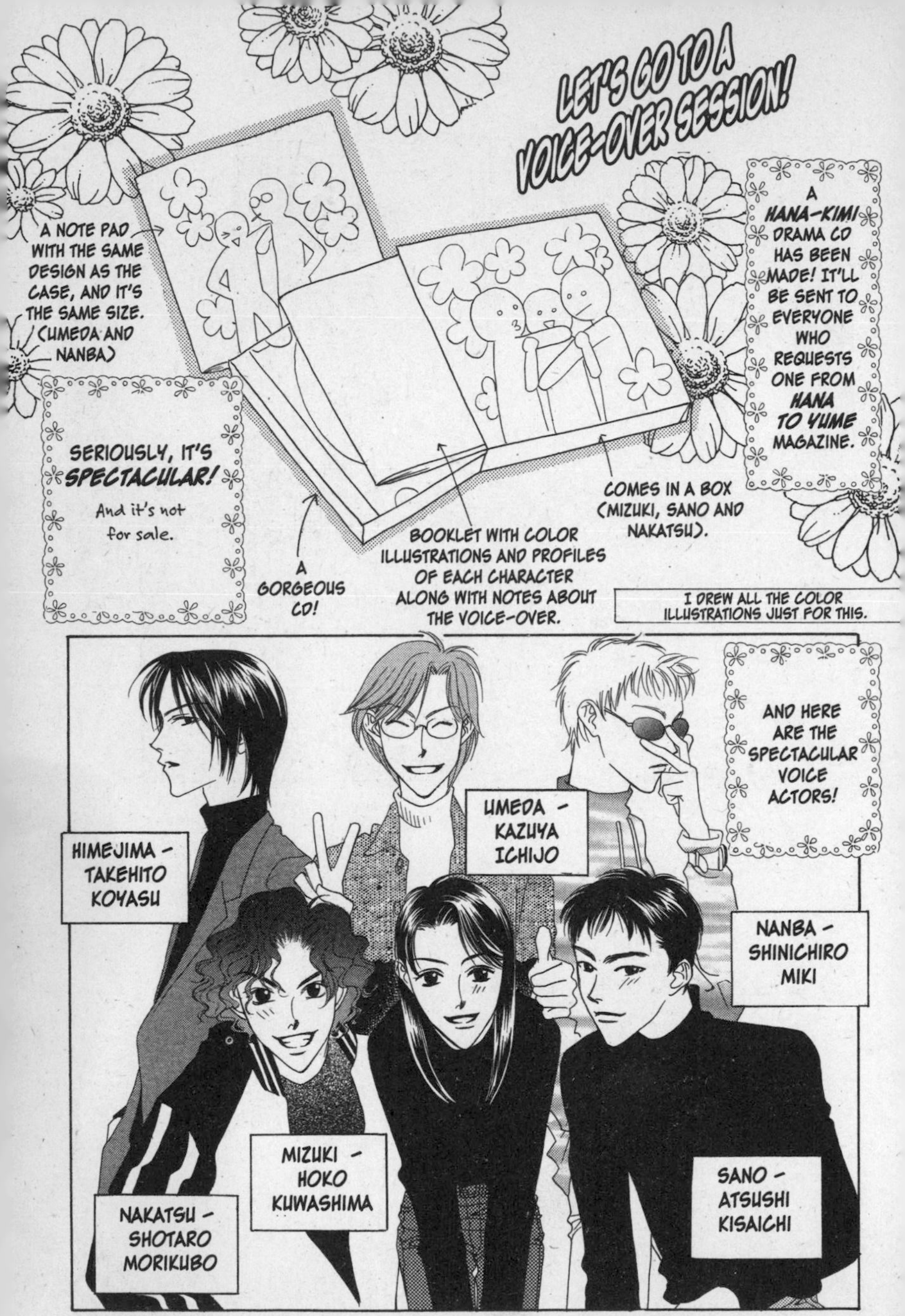
LET'S GO TO A VOICE-OVER SESSION!
A HANA-KIMI DRAMA CD HAS BEEN MADE! IT'LL BE SENT TO EVERYONE WHO REQUESTS ONE FROM HANA TO YUME MAGAZINE.
COMES IN A BOX (MIZUKI, SANO AND NAKATSU).
I DREW ALL THE COLOR ILLUSTRATIONS JUST FOR THIS.
BOOKLET WITH COLOR ILLUSTRATIONS AND PROFILES OF EACH CHARACTER ALONG WITH NOTES ABOUT THE VOICE-OVER.
A GORGEOUS CD!
A NOTE PAD WITH THE SAME DESIGN AS THE CASE, AND IT'S THE SAME SIZE. (UMEDA AND NANBA)
SERIOUSLY, IT'S SPECTACULAR!
And it's not for sale.
AND HERE ARE THE SPECTACULAR VOICE ACTORS!
NANBA - SHINICHIRO MIKI
UMEDA - KAZUYA ICHIJO
HIMEJIMA - TAKEHITO KOYASU
SANO - ATSUSHI KISAICHI
MIZUKI - HOKO KUWASHIMA
NAKATSU - SHOTARO MORIKUBO

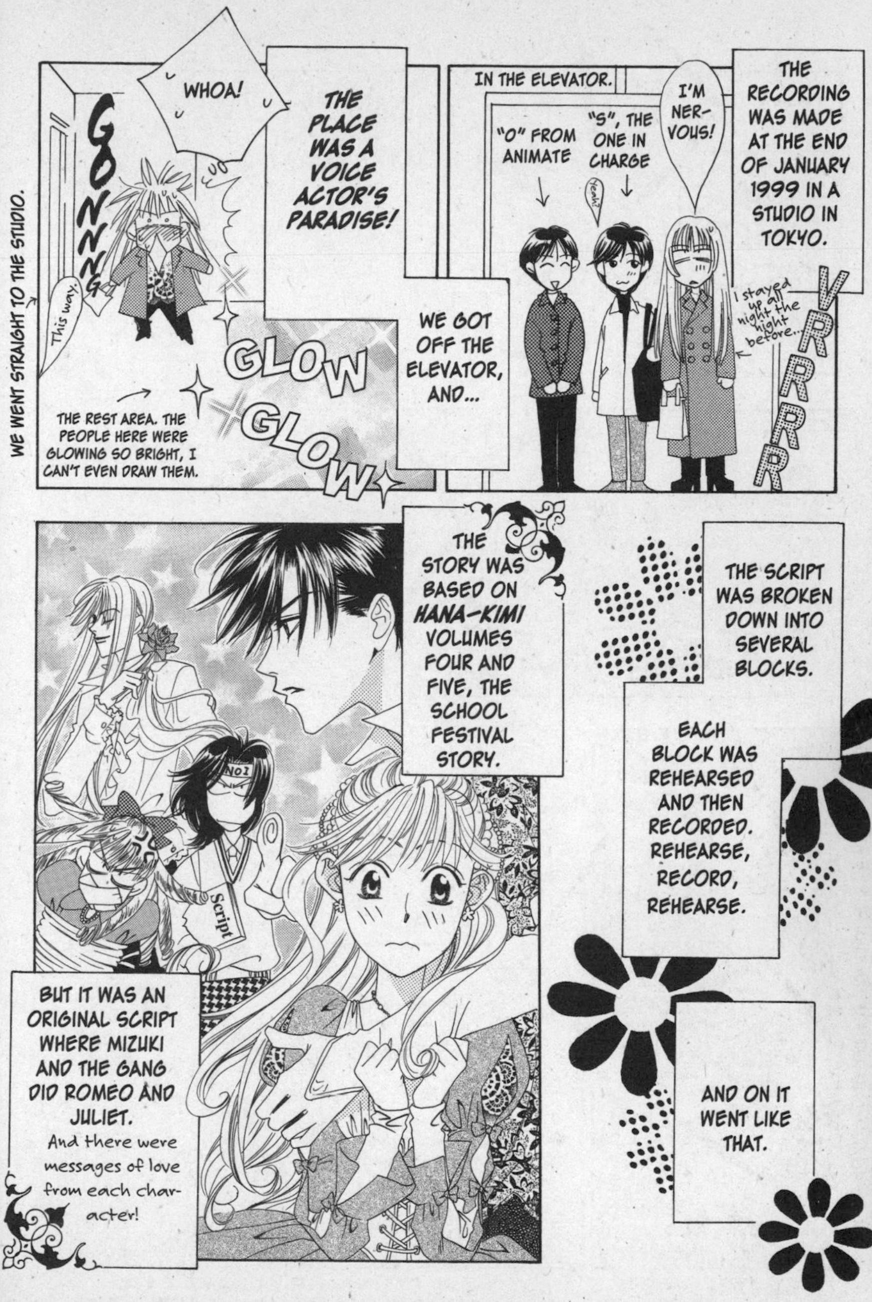
THE RECORDING WAS MADE AT THE END OF JANUARY 1999 IN A STUDIO IN TOKYO.
I'M NER-VOUS!
VRRRRR
I stayed up all night the night before...
IN THE ELEVATOR.
"S", THE ONE IN CHARGE
Yeah!
"O" FROM ANIMATE
THE PLACE WAS A VOICE ACTOR'S PARADISE!
WE GOT OFF THE ELEVATOR, AND...
WHOA!
GONNNG
GLOW
GLOW
This way.
THE REST AREA. THE PEOPLE HERE WERE GLOWING SO BRIGHT, I CAN'T EVEN DRAW THEM.
WE WENT STRAIGHT TO THE STUDIO.
THE SCRIPT WAS BROKEN DOWN INTO SEVERAL BLOCKS.
THE STORY WAS BASED ON HANA-KIMI VOLUMES FOUR AND FIVE, THE SCHOOL FESTIVAL STORY.
EACH BLOCK WAS REHEARSED AND THEN RECORDED. REHEARSE, RECORD, REHEARSE.
AND ON IT WENT LIKE THAT.
NO1
Script
BUT IT WAS AN ORIGINAL SCRIPT WHERE MIZUKI AND THE GANG DID ROMEO AND JULIET.
And there were messages of love from each character!

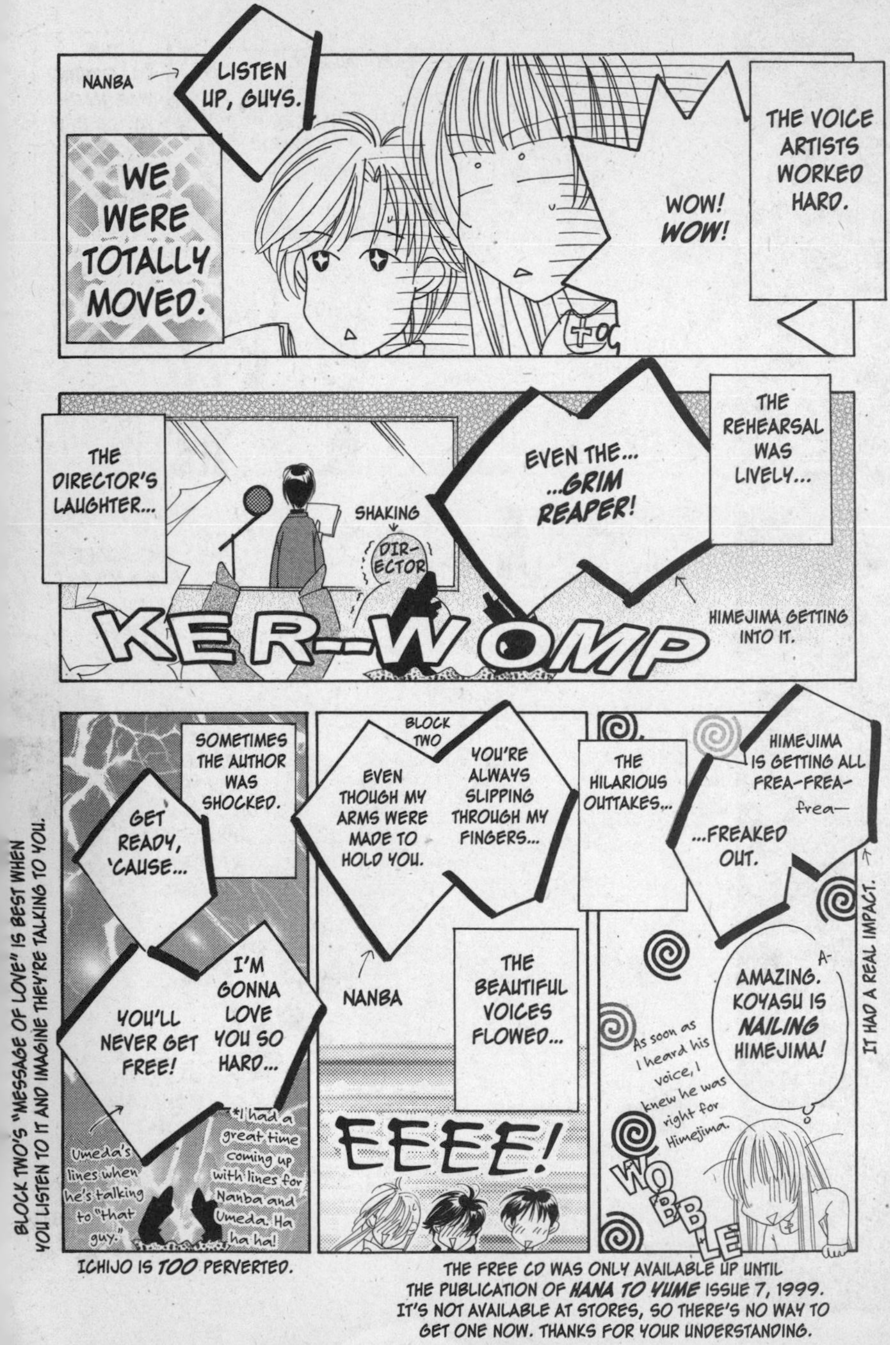
THE VOICE ARTISTS WORKED HARD.
WOW! WOW!
LISTEN UP, GUYS.
NANBA
WE WERE TOTALLY MOVED.
THE REHEARSAL WAS LIVELY...
EVEN THE... ...GRIM REAPER!
HIMEJIMA GETTING INTO IT.
SHAKING
DIR-ECTOR
THE DIRECTOR'S LAUGHTER...
KER--WOMP
IT HAD A REAL IMPACT.
HIMEJIMA IS GETTING ALL FREA-FREA-
frea—
...FREAKED OUT.
THE HILARIOUS OUTTAKES...
A- AMAZING. KOYASU IS NAILING HIMEJIMA!
As soon as I heard his voice, I knew he was right for Himejima.
WOBBLE
BLOCK TWO
YOU'RE ALWAYS SLIPPING THROUGH MY FINGERS...
EVEN THOUGH MY ARMS WERE MADE TO HOLD YOU.
NANBA
THE BEAUTIFUL VOICES FLOWED...
EEEE!
SOMETIMES THE AUTHOR WAS SHOCKED.
GET READY, 'CAUSE...
I'M GONNA LOVE YOU SO HARD...
YOU'LL NEVER GET FREE!
*I had a great time coming up with lines for Nanba and Umeda. Ha ha ha!
Umeda's lines when he's talking to "that guy."
BLOCK TWO'S "MESSAGE OF LOVE" IS BEST WHEN YOU LISTEN TO IT AND IMAGINE THEY'RE TALKING TO YOU.

ICHIJO IS *TOO* PERVERTED.

THE FREE CD WAS ONLY AVAILABLE UP UNTIL THE PUBLICATION OF *HANA TO YUME* ISSUE 7, 1999. IT'S NOT AVAILABLE AT STORES, SO THERE'S NO WAY TO GET ONE NOW. THANKS FOR YOUR UNDERSTANDING.

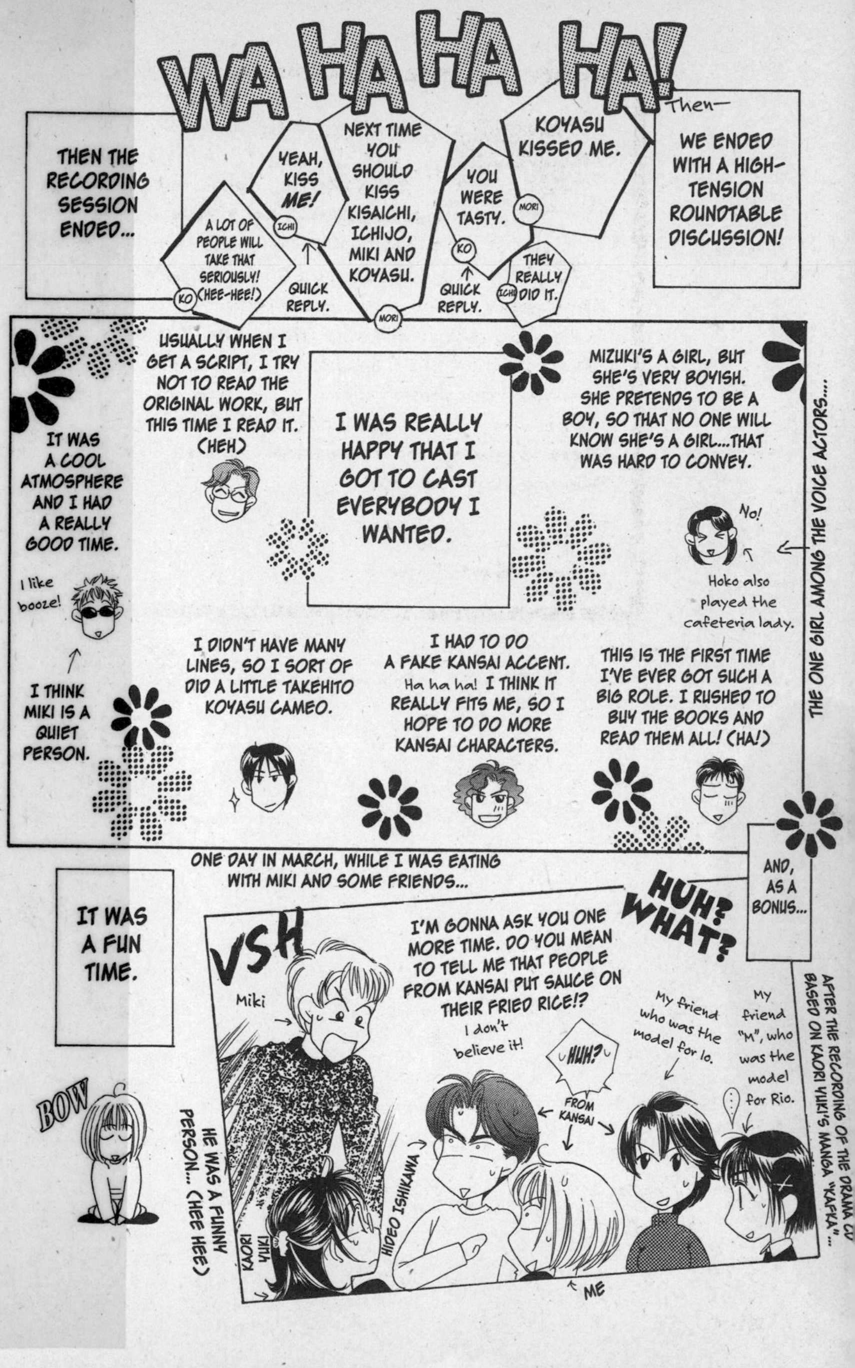
WA HA HA HA!
Then—
WE ENDED WITH A HIGH-TENSION ROUNDTABLE DISCUSSION!
MORI: KOYASU KISSED ME.
ICHI: THEY REALLY DID IT.
KO: YOU WERE TASTY.
QUICK REPLY.
MORI: NEXT TIME YOU SHOULD KISS KISAICHI, ICHIJO, MIKI AND KOYASU.
ICHI: YEAH, KISS ME!
QUICK REPLY.
KO: A LOT OF PEOPLE WILL TAKE THAT SERIOUSLY! (HEE-HEE!)
THEN THE RECORDING SESSION ENDED...
THE ONE GIRL AMONG THE VOICE ACTORS...
MIZUKI'S A GIRL, BUT SHE'S VERY BOYISH. SHE PRETENDS TO BE A BOY, SO THAT NO ONE WILL KNOW SHE'S A GIRL...THAT WAS HARD TO CONVEY.
No!
Hoko also played the cafeteria lady.
I WAS REALLY HAPPY THAT I GOT TO CAST EVERYBODY I WANTED.
USUALLY WHEN I GET A SCRIPT, I TRY NOT TO READ THE ORIGINAL WORK, BUT THIS TIME I READ IT. (HEH)
IT WAS A COOL ATMOSPHERE AND I HAD A REALLY GOOD TIME.
I like booze!
I THINK MIKI IS A QUIET PERSON.
THIS IS THE FIRST TIME I'VE EVER GOT SUCH A BIG ROLE. I RUSHED TO BUY THE BOOKS AND READ THEM ALL! (HA!)
I HAD TO DO A FAKE KANSAI ACCENT. Ha ha ha! I THINK IT REALLY FITS ME, SO I HOPE TO DO MORE KANSAI CHARACTERS.
I DIDN'T HAVE MANY LINES, SO I SORT OF DID A LITTLE TAKEHITO KOYASU CAMEO.
AND, AS A BONUS...
AFTER THE RECORDING OF THE DRAMA CD BASED ON KAORI YUKI'S MANGA "KAFKA"...
ONE DAY IN MARCH, WHILE I WAS EATING WITH MIKI AND SOME FRIENDS...
HUH? WHAT?
I'M GONNA ASK YOU ONE MORE TIME. DO YOU MEAN TO TELL ME THAT PEOPLE FROM KANSAI PUT SAUCE ON THEIR FRIED RICE!?
I don't believe it!
My friend "M", who was the model for Rio.
My friend who was the model for Io.
HUH?
FROM KANSAI
ME
HIDEO ISHIKAWA
KAORI YUKI
Miki
VSH
HE WAS A FUNNY PERSON... (HEE HEE)
IT WAS A FUN TIME.
BOW

ABOUT THE AUTHOR

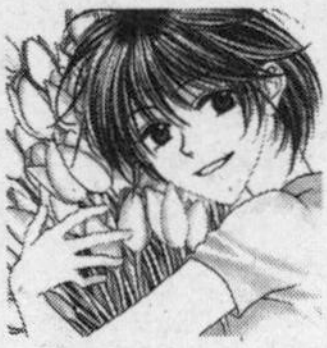

Hisaya Nakajo's manga series **Hanazakari no Kimitachi he** ("For You in Full Blossom," casually known as **Hana-Kimi**) has been a hit since it first appeared in 1997 in the shôjo manga magazine **Hana to Yume** ("Flowers and Dreams"). In Japan, two **Hana-Kimi** art books and several "drama CDs" have been released. Her other manga series include **Missing Piece** (2 volumes) and **Yumemiru Happa** ("The Dreaming Leaf," 1 volume).

Hisaya Nakajo's website:
www.wild-vanilla.com

IN THE NEXT VOLU

Nakatsu...a cheater?! As th snowballs, Nakatsu finds himself forced to choose between his integrity and the most important thing in his life! But he's not the only one suffering as the power-mad Kitahama begins to rule the school with an iron fist. Who can save the students of Osaka High now? Then, suave photographer Akiha Hara invites our heroes to his studio for a photo shoot. But the world of high fashion will transform them more than they expect...!

はいっ オッケー おわりッ
えっ
エビちゃんッ それじゃ まるっきり 女の子メイクだって
ゲ…ッ
え?

COMING DECEMBER 2005!